# Architectural Patterns

Uncover essential patterns in the most indispensable realm of enterprise architecture

**Pethuru Raj**
**Anupama Raman**
**Harihara Subramanian**

BIRMINGHAM - MUMBAI

# Architectural Patterns



First published: December 2017

Production reference: 1211217

Published by Packt Publishing Ltd.
Livery Place
35 Livery Street
Birmingham
B3 2PB, UK.

ISBN 978-1-78728-749-5

www.packtpub.com

# Credits

**Authors**
Pethuru Raj
Anupama Raman
Harihara Subramanian

**Copy Editor**
Safis Editing

**Reviewer**
Dr. Kayarvizhy N

**Project Coordinator**
Vaidehi Sawant

**Commissioning Editor**
Aaron Lazar

**Proofreader**
Safis Editing

**Acquisition Editor**
Chaitanya Nair

**Indexer**
Francy Puthiry

**Content Development Editor**
Rohit Kumar Singh

**Graphics**
Jason Monteiro

**Technical Editor**
Ketan Kamble

**Production Coordinator**
Shantanu Zagade

# About the Authors

**Pethuru Raj** holds the PhD degree in computer science and works as the chief architect and vice-president of the Site Reliability Engineering (SRE) division of Reliance Jio Infocomm. Ltd (RJIL), Bangalore. He previously worked as a cloud infrastructure architect in the IBM Global Cloud Center of Excellence (CoE), IBM India, and as a TOGAF-certified Enterprise Architecture (EA) consultant in the Wipro Consulting Services (WCS) division, Bangalore. He also had a fruitful stint as a lead architect in the Corporate Research (CR) division of Robert Bosch, Bangalore. He has more than 17 years of IT industry experience and 8 years of research experience. He has authored eight books thus far and co-authored the *Learning Docker* book by Packt.

**Anupama Raman** recently joined Flipkart as a senior manager. Prior to this, she worked as an architect in the IBM Business Analytics Business Unit (smarter cities product lines) in the IBM Software labs. She has worked extensively on all IBM business analytics product lines, which include products and technologies on predictive and prescriptive analytics. She is very passionate about storage area networking, data centers, and cloud technologies. Anupama is EMC certified as a cloud infrastructure and services management professional, data center architect, storage and management professional, networking design and management professional, and EMC Technology Foundation professional.

**Harihara Subramanian** works for SABRE Corporation as a principal software architect. He has been evolving and practicing software development and various software architecture concepts since 1999. He is an energetic and highly focused technology leader with a proven track record in software development, software architecture principles, and implementations. He has been an active contributor to various online and offline forums in different technologies and focuses on technology consulting, software development, SOA, and more.

# About the Reviewer

**Dr. Kayarvizhy N** is currently working as an associate professor in the computer science department of BMS College of Engineering, Bangalore. She has over 12 years of experience in academia. She obtained her bachelor's and master's of technology degrees in computer science from Pondicherry University. She was awarded her doctoral degree from Anna University in 2014 for her work in object-oriented metrics. She has published over 17 papers in various journals and conferences and is actively guiding research scholars in several emerging areas. She has also helped set up the IoT curriculum and lab in her department and is pursuing a project sponsored by the Government of Karnataka through the VGST grant program.

# www.PacktPub.com

For support files and downloads related to your book, please visit www.PacktPub.com. Did you know that Packt offers eBook versions of every book published, with PDF and ePub files available? You can upgrade to the eBook version at www.PacktPub.com and as a print book customer, you are entitled to a discount on the eBook copy. Get in touch with us at service@packtpub.com for more details. At www.PacktPub.com, you can also read a collection of free technical articles, sign up for a range of free newsletters and receive exclusive discounts and offers on Packt books and eBooks.

https://www.packtpub.com/mapt

Get the most in-demand software skills with Mapt. Mapt gives you full access to all Packt books and video courses, as well as industry-leading tools to help you plan your personal development and advance your career.

## Why subscribe?

- Fully searchable across every book published by Packt
- Copy and paste, print, and bookmark content
- On demand and accessible via a web browser

# Customer Feedback

Thanks for purchasing this Packt book. At Packt, quality is at the heart of our editorial process. To help us improve, please leave us an honest review on this book's Amazon page at `https://www.amazon.com/dp/1787287491`.

If you'd like to join our team of regular reviewers, you can e-mail us at `customerreviews@packtpub.com`. We award our regular reviewers with free eBooks and videos in exchange for their valuable feedback. Help us be relentless in improving our products!

# Table of Contents

# Preface

Heterogeneity, along with the multiplicity factor, leads to heightened complexity for any system development and operation. The enigmatic yet exemplary software engineering (SE) space is being stuffed and sandwiched with innumerable and heterogeneous technologies and tools. Their intended and insightful use seems a bit challenging, but their contributions are mesmerizing and meteoric indeed if utilized properly.

Interestingly, every kind of asset and artifact in our personal, professional, and social environments is being embedded and emboldened by pioneering software libraries. With continuous software penetration and participation in everything we touch, feel, and use, we are to have a bevy of sophisticated and smarter applications in plenty. Precisely speaking, we are heading toward the promised software-defined world. However, the developmental and operational complexities of next-generation software applications are literally threatening. That is, leveraging the various delectable advancements in the software engineering domain actually turns out to be a difficult affair. Therefore, there is a clarion call for unearthing easy to understand and use approaches to moderate software engineering complexity.

Accentuating, assimilating, and articulating architecturally sound principles for high-quality software implementation and delivery has been pronounced by technology experts, exponents, and evangelists as a workable way out of this dilemma. Elegantly employing architectural patterns, along with design, deployment, integration, and other specialized patterns, is the way forward for producing and running next-generation software solutions. An arsenal of software patterns (architecture, design, deployment, integration, and so on.) come in handy for the risk-free and rewarding production of highly reliable, scalable, available, performant, adaptive, and secure software systems. This book has been produced with the sole and simple aim of enumerating and expressing prominent and dominant software patterns for its readers. The various chapters and their unique contributions are briefly explained here.

# What this book covers

`Chapter 1`, *Demystifying Software Architecture Patterns*, illustrates the context for the book and describes the need for software patterns. The various architectural patterns are listed and explained in detail in order to convey the what, why, where, and how of architectural patterns.

`Chapter 2`, *Client/Server Multi-Tier Architectural Patterns*, covers the client-server architecture pattern, which is one of the oldest patterns in the enterprise architecture space. There are several variants available in this architectural space, such as two-tier client-server architecture patterns, three-tier patterns, and *n*-tier patterns. With the evolution of several new types of architecture for enterprises, client-server architecture has taken a back seat in enterprise architecture. The second part of this chapter covers web application patterns. The key types of web application patterns covered in this chapter are MVC, MVP, and MVVM. Several examples of each type of pattern are also provided in this chapter.

`Chapter 3`, *Object-Oriented Software Engineering Patterns*, covers object-oriented (OO) software engineering patterns. This chapter serves to give you a refresher on the fundamentals of OO design principles and best practices. We believe that OO programming patterns are the basis of the modern software design paradigm and help you get a better understanding of other patterns. This chapter covers various prominent creational, structural, and behavioral OO patterns, along with concurrency architectural patterns such as half-sync/half-async, and leader/followers as well.

`Chapter 4`, *Enterprise Integration Patterns*, describes the various enterprise integration patterns. In the modern world, there are a plethora of commercial applications. Some of them are commercial off-the-shelf applications, while others are legacy applications that are custom built as per the requirements of the organization. Since there are so many silos of applications within an enterprise, it becomes necessary to integrate them to ensure they work seamlessly. This chapter covers the key patterns that are available for enterprise integration. The key types of enterprise integration patterns that are covered in this chapter are messaging patterns, mobile integration patterns, and API management patterns.

`Chapter 5`, *Domain-Driven Design (DDD) Principles and Patterns*, illustrates **domain-driven design** (**DDD**) principles and patterns. This chapter helps you learn about DDD principles, practices, and a few critical patterns, and how they support technology and business excellence brought together to create sophisticated software. We focus on the domain, ubiquitous language communication, bounded contexts, aggregates, and more DDD aspects. This chapter covers a few critical and prominent DDD patterns to help you learn about strategic, tactical, legacy integration, distributed contexts, and also learn about two emerging patterns, domain events and event sourcing.

`Chapter 6`, *Enterprise Architecture Platforms and Tools*, presents the unique capabilities of enterprise architecture platforms and tools. Enterprise architecture helps to map all software-related processes in an enterprise into a framework in such a way that all the objectives of the enterprise are fulfilled. This chapter discusses two prominent enterprise architecture frameworks that are widely used in the IT industry landscape: TOGAF and Zachman's framework. Some prominent architecture platforms and tools, such as Enterprise Architect, Dragon, and Abacus, are also discussed in this chapter.

`Chapter 7`, *Service-Oriented Architecture (SOA)*, demystifies the popular **service-oriented architecture** (**SOA**) patterns that produce service-oriented applications. This chapter provides details on the principles, best practices, and characteristics of SOA. You will also learn about the most common SOA patterns that deal with web service security, inter-service communication, messaging, service versioning, and service refactoring. This chapter has a table that helps you understand various patterns and their associated SOA principles.

`Chapter 8`, *Event-Driven Architectural Patterns*, covers emerging and evolving event-driven architecture patterns. Modern organizations are agile in nature and want to adopt architectural styles that permit them to work in an agile manner. Event-driven architectural patterns were developed mainly to meet this need. This chapter provides exhaustive coverage of popular event-driven patterns. Recent trends in the event-driven architecture space are also discussed in this chapter.

`Chapter 9`, *Microservices Architecture Patterns*, explains the various **microservices architecture** (**MSA**). With containerization spreading its wings wider, the roles and responsibilities of microservices in producing enterprise-scale, elastic, extensible, and dynamic applications is bound to increase. The various architecture and design patterns are explained, along with use cases.

`Chapter 10`, *Patterns for Containerized and Highly Reliable Applications*, talks about the distinct contributions of various design patterns for producing containerized and highly reliable applications. The convergence of containers and microservices, along with the arrival of various container and cluster management and orchestration platforms, guarantees the realization of highly resilient microservices that in turn lead to reliable applications.

`Chapter 11`, *Software-Defined Clouds - Architecture and Design Patterns*, provides information about cloud application architecture and its various design patterns. As we all know, all kinds of legacy and monolithic applications are being modernized and migrated to cloud environments. This chapter prescribes the ways and means of smartly leveraging the patterns for swift and sagacious cloud adoption.

`Chapter 12`, *Big Data Architecture and Design Patterns*, provides you with a head start with big data architecture patterns and big data design patterns. The patterns are grouped by layers, such as the data ingestion layer, data storage layer, and data access layer, to help you learn about unified architecture involving data sources, data messaging, data analysis, and consumption. A few of the prominent patterns covered in this chapter are data lakes, lambda architecture, short summaries for workload patterns, polyglots, and connectors. This chapter also covers a few of the fundamentals of big data.

# What you need for this book

There are no specific requirements before you start with this book. You will find all the required information as you go through the chapters.

# Who this book is for

This book will empower and enrich IT architects (such as enterprise architects, software product architects, and solution and system architects), technical consultants, evangelists, and experts.

# Conventions

In this book, you will find a number of text styles that distinguish between different kinds of information. Here are some examples of these styles and an explanation of their meaning.

Code words in text, database table names, folder names, filenames, file extensions, pathnames, dummy URLs, user input, and Twitter handles are shown as follows: "We can include other contexts through the use of the `include` directive."

A block of code is set as follows:

```
package main
import "fmt"
// this is a comment
func main() {
    fmt.Println("Hello World")
}
```

When we wish to draw your attention to a particular part of a code block, the relevant lines or items are set in bold:

```
package main
import "fmt"
// this is a comment
func main() {
    fmt.Println("Hello World")
}
```

Any command-line input or output is written as follows:

```
docker run --rm -ti -v $(pwd):/go/src/myapp google/golang go build myapp
```

New terms and important words are shown in bold.

Warnings or important notes appear like this.

Tips and tricks appear like this.

# Reader feedback

Feedback from our readers is always welcome. Let us know what you think about this book-what you liked or disliked. Reader feedback is important for us as it helps us develop titles that you will really get the most out of. To send us general feedback, simply e-mail `feedback@packtpub.com`, and mention the book's title in the subject of your message. If there is a topic that you have expertise in and you are interested in either writing or contributing to a book, see our author guide at `www.packtpub.com/authors`.

# Downloading the color images of this book

We also provide you with a PDF file that has color images of the screenshots/diagrams used in this book. The color images will help you better understand the changes in the output. You can download this file from `https://www.packtpub.com/sites/default/files/downloads/ArchitecturalPatterns_ColorImages.pdf`.

# Errata

Although we have taken every care to ensure the accuracy of our content, mistakes do happen. If you find a mistake in one of our books-maybe a mistake in the text or the code-we would be grateful if you could report this to us. By doing so, you can save other readers from frustration and help us improve subsequent versions of this book. If you find any errata, please report them by visiting `http://www.packtpub.com/submit-errata`, selecting your book, clicking on the **Errata Submission Form** link, and entering the details of your errata. Once your errata are verified, your submission will be accepted and the errata will be uploaded to our website or added to any list of existing errata under the Errata section of that title. To view the previously submitted errata, go to `https://www.packtpub.com/books/content/support` and enter the name of the book in the search field. The required information will appear under the **Errata** section.

# Piracy

Piracy of copyrighted material on the Internet is an ongoing problem across all media. At Packt, we take the protection of our copyright and licenses very seriously. If you come across any illegal copies of our works in any form on the Internet, please provide us with the location address or website name immediately so that we can pursue a remedy. Please contact us at `copyright@packtpub.com` with a link to the suspected pirated material. We appreciate your help in protecting our authors and our ability to bring you valuable content.

# Questions

If you have a problem with any aspect of this book, you can contact us at `questions@packtpub.com`, and we will do our best to address the problem.

# 1
# Demystifying Software Architecture Patterns

It is going to be the software-defined, digitization-enabled, cloud-hosted, context-aware, service-oriented, event-driven, and people-centric era. It is a well-known and widely accepted truth that reactive and cognitive software plays a very vital role in shaping up the projected and pronounced era of knowledge-filled and insight-driven services and applications. That is, we need highly responsive, reliable, scalable, adaptive, and secure software suites and libraries to fulfill the identified goals for the forthcoming era of knowledge. There are competent **information and communication technologies** (ICTs), tools, techniques, and tips emerging and evolving fast to artistically enable the realization of such kinds of advanced and astute software modules.

The quickly-enlarging domain of patterns has been there for several decades. The complexity of software engineering is also increasing in an uninhibited fashion. Software experts, evangelists, and exponents have articulated and accentuated the deft and decisive leverage of software patterns in order to mitigate the rising complexity of software engineering. Therefore, software patterns are widely being recognized as one prime and paramount method for building resilient and versatile software packages and programs. Professionals and professors have been steady in unearthing newer patterns. As a result, a bevy of path-breaking and promising architectural, design, deployment, delivery, and integration patterns are quickly emerging and evolving to speed up and streamline the increasingly complicated processes of designing, developing, debugging, deploying, and delivering robust and rewarding software applications.

This chapter aims to explain the prominent software patterns, particularly the following widely deliberated and detailed architecture patterns:

- **Object-oriented architecture** (OOA)
- **Component-based assembly** (CBD) architecture
- Domain-driven design architecture
- Client/server architecture
- Multi-tier distributed computing architecture
- Layered/tiered architecture
- **Event-driven architecture** (EDA)
- **Service-oriented architecture** (SOA)
- **Microservices architecture** (MSA)
- **Space-based architecture** (SBA)
- Special-purpose architectures

# Envisioning the software-defined world

There are newer requirements such as smarter homes, hotels, hospitals, and so on, and the crucial role and responsibility of **information and communication technologies** (ICT) fulfilling the varying business and people needs are growing steadily. There are a variety of noteworthy trends and transitions happening in the enigmatic ICT space these days. The prominent ones include the following:

- IT industrialization through cloud computing
- IT compartmentalization through virtualization and containerization
- IT consumerization through handhelds, wearables, mobiles, nomadic devices, and so on
- The extreme and deeper connectivity amongst all kinds of physical, electrical, mechanical, and electronic systems through the leverage of the **Internet of Things** (IoT) technologies, **cyber-physical systems** (CPSs), and so on
- Cognitive IT to empower our everyday systems to be cognitive of their actions and reactions

With everything getting connected with one another, the amount of data getting generated, collected, cleansed, and crunched goes up exponentially. There are integrated platforms for big, fast, streaming, and IoT data analytics to extricate useful information and actionable insights out of data heaps. The database paradigm is going through a slew of changes and challenges.

The middleware domain is upping the ante as there are heterogeneous and multiple systems and services to be integrated and made to work together. I can go on and on. In short, both the IT and business landscapes are changing day by day. Also, businesses expect their IT service providers to be innovative, disruptive, and transformative in order to achieve more with less. As the IT budgets are being pruned by businesses across the world, the IT domain has to pick the latest advancements in order to be right and relevant to their stakeholders.

As usual, the field of software engineering is also progressing steadily with a dazzling array of noteworthy progressions. There are agile programming models for enabling the business agility. In the recent past, there have been DevOps methods germinating for guaranteeing IT agility. There are newer software infrastructure and platform solutions coming up fast in order to meet various requirements from different stakeholders. Professionals and professors are working overtime to ensure process excellence and infrastructure optimization. Strategically sound architectural paradigms and styles are being assimilated. Further on, the automation level will pick up and reach greater heights with the adoption of **artificial intelligence** (**AI**) methods.

As we all know, the most powerful domain of software engineering has been accomplishing grandiose things for the business acceleration, augmentation, and automation. With the arrival and articulation of the IoT and CPS paradigms, the software field is steadily and sagaciously veering towards the much-expected people empowerment. Accordingly, there is a greater demand for software applications and services to intelligently empower not only business operations and offerings, but also to contribute to everyday decisions, deals, and deeds of individuals, innovators, and institutions. The currently available programming models, frameworks, and tools are helping us out in producing applications that fulfill functional requirements. Hereafter, the crucial challenge ahead for software professionals and practitioners is to bring forth software libraries and suites that comply with all kinds of **non-functional requirements** (**NFRs**) / **Quality of Service** (**QoS**) attributes. That is, we ought to construct applications that innately ensure various abilities, such as reliability, scalability, availability, modifiability, sustainability, security, and so on. Software patterns come in handy here. Precisely speaking, the penetration, participation, and pervasiveness of software patterns are consistently on the increase.

# Software patterns

As we all know, patterns are a kind of simplified and smarter solution for a repetitive concern and recurring challenge in any field of importance. In the field of software engineering, there are primarily many designs, integration, and architecture patterns. These patterns come in handy in speedily surmounting some of the routine and fresh issues being encountered by software architects, developers, and integrators in their everyday assignments and engagements. Design patterns are very popular and are used for expertly designing enterprise-class software systems whereas architectural patterns are used for skilfully deciding the optimized and organized architecture for a system under development. The changes and complexities are substantially taken care of through the deft leverage of various architectural patterns. The architectural patterns enable taking a series of decisions regarding the choice of technologies and tools. The various system components, their distinct capabilities, and how they connect and collaborate with one another are the key ingredients in architecting and designing next-generation software systems. The architectural patterns render their yeoman services here. With system architectures increasingly becoming complicated, the role and responsibility of architectural patterns are consistently on the increase. Similarly, as we tend towards the distributed and decentralized era, the integration patterns are very significant as they bring a lot of praiseworthy simplifications and delegations.

With the flourishing of the DevOps concept, there are additional patterns emerging in IT agility. Patterns also assiduously accelerate the process of building newer and powerful software packages. Besides the development-centric patterns, there are deployment and delivery-specific patterns also. In the ensuing DevOps and NoOps days, the deployment patterns are going to be highly beneficial in automating the time-consuming and tedious tasks. Similarly, there are delivery-enablement patterns. Patterns are fast-evolving and stabilizing tellingly with more usage and continuous refinements. Patterns are capable of overcoming the initial hiccups for newer technologies, too. Patterns will be a key ingredient for IT to survive and shine in the market-driven, knowledge-driven and cut-throat competitive environment. Precisely speaking, patterns are a crucial enabler in building sophisticated software by minimizing the workload of software developers. The risks being associated with constructing enterprise-scale, high-quality, and microservices-based applications are being substantially moderated by meticulously using the proven software patterns.

## Why software patterns?

There is a bevy of noteworthy transformations happening in the IT space, especially in software engineering. The complexity of recent software solutions is continuously going up due to the continued evolution of the business expectations. With complex software, not only does the software development activity become very difficult, but also the software maintenance and enhancement tasks become tedious and time-consuming. Software patterns come as a soothing factor for software architects, developers, and operators.

Software systems are becoming extremely complicated and sophisticated in order to meet up the newer demands of the business. The field of software architecture helps to smoothen and straighten the path towards producing well-defined and designed software suites. Software architecture is primarily tuned for moderating the rising software complexities and changes. Hence, there are purported efforts to bring forth software architecture patterns to arrive at easy-to-implement and sustainable software architectures. This section begins with some basics about architecture and goes on to elaborate on some of the widely used software architectural patterns.

Architecture is essential for systems that are increasingly becoming complex due to the continuous addition of fresh modules. Architectures generally are decided by three crucial aspects: the participating components, the distinct capabilities of each of those components, and, finally, the connectivity between those components. Establishing software architectures is not an easy job. A variety of factors need to be taken into consideration while deciding the architecture. A number of architectural decisions need to be meticulously considered in order to strengthen the final architecture. Not only functional requirements but also non-functional requirements too need to be inscribed in the architecture. Typically, the architecture pattern is for designing a generic architecture for a system, such as a software solution.

## The prime ingredients of a software pattern

Several different formats are used in the literature for describing patterns, and no single format has achieved widespread acceptance. The following elements described will be found in most patterns, even if different headings are used to describe them. In the Opengroup.org site, the following terminologies are used:

- **Name**: A meaningful and memorable way to refer to the pattern, typically a single word or short phrase.
- **Problem**: This is a concise description of the problem at hand. It has to throw some light on the intended goals and objectives to be reached within the context.

- **Context**: The context typically illustrates the preconditions under which the pattern can be applied. That is, it is a description of the initial state before the pattern is applied.
- **Forces**: This is for describing the relevant forces and constraints and how they interact/conflict with each other. It inscribes the intended goals and objectives. The description should clarify the intricacies of the problem and make explicit the kinds of trade-offs that must be considered. The notion of *forces* more or less equates to the *QoS attributes* (availability, scalability, security, sustainability, composability, maneuverability, resiliency, reliability, reusability, and so on) that architects seek to obtain and optimize besides the concerns they seek to address in designing architectures.
- **Solution**: This is all about clearly explaining how to achieve the intended goals and objectives. The description should identify both the solution's static structure and its dynamic behavior.
- **Resulting context**: This indicates the post-conditions after the pattern is applied. Implementing the solution normally requires trade-offs among competing forces. This element describes which forces have been resolved and how, and which remain unresolved. It may also indicate other patterns that may be applicable in the new context.
- **Examples**: This is about incorporating a few sample applications of the pattern for illustrating each of the elements (a specific problem, the context, the set of forces, how the pattern gets applied, and the resulting context).
- **Rationale**: It is necessary to give a convincing explanation/justification of the pattern as a whole or of the individual components within it. The rationale has to indicate how the pattern actually works and how it resolves the forces to achieve the desired goals and objectives.
- **Related patterns**: There are other similar patterns and hence the relationships between this pattern and others have to be clearly articulated. These may be predecessor patterns, whose resulting contexts correspond to the initial context of this one. Or, these may be successor patterns, whose initial contexts correspond to the resulting context of this one. There may also be alternative patterns, which describe a different solution to the same problem, but under different forces. Finally these may be co-dependent patterns, which may/must be applied along with this pattern.
- **Known uses**: This has to detail the known applications of the pattern within existing systems. This is for verifying that the pattern does indeed describe a proven solution to a recurring problem. The known uses can also serve as value-added examples.

Patterns may also begin with an *abstract* providing an overview of the pattern and indicating the types of problems it addresses. The abstract may also identify the target audience and what assumptions are made of the reader.

# The types of software patterns

Several newer types of patterns are emerging in order to cater to different demands. This section throws some light on these.

An **architecture pattern** expresses a fundamental structural organization or schema for complex systems. It provides a set of predefined subsystems, specifies their unique responsibilities, and includes the decision-enabling rules and guidelines for organizing the relationships between them. The architecture pattern for a software system illustrates the macro-level structure for the whole software solution. An architectural pattern is a set of principles and a coarse-grained pattern that provides an abstract framework for a family of systems. An architectural pattern improves partitioning and promotes design reuse by providing solutions to frequently recurring problems. Precisely speaking, an architectural pattern comprises a set of principles that shape an application.

A **design pattern** provides a scheme for refining the subsystems or components of a system, or the relationships between them. It describes a commonly recurring structure of communicating components that solves a general design problem within a particular context. The design pattern for a software system prescribes the ways and means of building the software components. The design pattern articulates how the various components within the system collaborate with one another in order to fulfil the desired functionality.

There are other patterns, too. The dawn of the big data era mandates for distributed computing. The monolithic and massive nature of enterprise-scale applications demands microservices-centric applications. Here, application services need to be found and integrated in order to give an integrated result and view. Thus, there are integration-enabled patterns. Similarly, there are patterns for simplifying software deployment and delivery. Other complex actions are being addressed through the smart leverage of simple as well as composite patterns. In the next section, we will discuss the various dimensions of IT with the intention of conveying the tremendous impacts of software patterns for next-generation IT.

# Software architecture patterns

This section is allocated for describing the prominent and dominant software architecture patterns.

There are several weaknesses associated with monolithic applications:

- **Scalability**: Monolithic applications are designed to run on a single and powerful system within a process. Increasing the application's speed or capacity requires fork lifting onto newer and faster hardware, which takes significant planning and consideration.
- **Reliability and availability**: Any kind of faults or bugs within a monolithic application can take the entire application offline. Additionally, updating the application typically requires downtime in order to restart services.
- **Agility**: Monolithic code bases become increasingly complex as features are being continuously added, and release cycles are usually measured in periods of 6-12 months or more.

As already mentioned, legacy applications are monolithic in nature and massive in size. Refactoring and remedying them to be web, cloud, and service-enabled is bound to consume a lot of time, money, and talent. As enterprises are consistently pruning the IT budget and still expecting more with less from IT teams, the time for leveraging various architectural patterns individually or collectively to prepare and put modernized applications has arrived. The following sections detail the various promising and potential architecture patterns.

# Object-oriented architecture (OOA)

Objects are the fundamental and foundational building blocks for all kinds of software applications. The structure and behavior of any software application can be represented through the use of multiple and interoperable objects. Objects elegantly encapsulate the various properties and the tasks in an optimized and organized manner. Objects connect, communicate, and collaborate through well-defined interfaces. Therefore, the object-oriented architectural style has become the dominant one for producing object-oriented software applications. Ultimately, a software system is viewed as a dynamic collection of cooperating objects, instead of a set of routines or procedural instructions.

We know that there are proven object-oriented programming methods and enabling languages, such as C++, Java, and so on. The properties of inheritance, polymorphism, encapsulation, and composition being provided by OOA come in handy in producing highly modular (highly cohesive and loosely coupled), usable and reusable software applications.

The object-oriented style is suitable if we want to encapsulate logic and data together in reusable components. Also, the complex business logic that requires abstraction and dynamic behavior can effectively use this OOA.

# Component-based assembly (CBD) architecture

Monolithic and massive applications can be partitioned into multiple interactive and smaller components. When components are found, bound, and composed, we get the full-fledged software applications. Components emerge as the building-block for designing and developing enterprise-scale applications. Thus, the aspects of decomposition of complicated applications and the composition of components to arrive at competent applications receive a lot of traction. Components expose well-defined interfaces for other components to find and communicate. This setup provides a higher level of abstraction than the object-oriented design principles. CBA does not focus on issues such as communication protocols and shared states. Components are reusable, replaceable, substitutable, extensible, independent, and so on. Design patterns such as the **dependency injection** (**DI**) pattern or the service locator pattern can be used to manage dependencies between components and promote loose coupling and reuse. Such patterns are often used to build composite applications that combine and reuse components across multiple applications.

**Aspect-oriented programming** (**AOP**) aspects are another popular application building block. By deft maneuvering of this unit of development, different applications can be built and deployed. The AOP style aims to increase modularity by allowing the separation of cross-cutting concerns. AOP includes programming methods and tools that support the modularization of concerns at the level of the source code. Aspect-oriented programming entails breaking down program logic into distinct parts (*concerns*, the cohesive areas of functionality). All programming paradigms intrinsically support some level of grouping and encapsulation of concerns into independent entities by providing abstractions (for example, functions, procedures, modules, classes, methods, and so on). These abstractions can be used for implementing, abstracting, and composing various concerns. Some concerns anyway cut across multiple abstractions in a program and defy these forms of implementation. These concerns are called *cross-cutting concerns* or horizontal concerns.

Logging exemplifies a cross-cutting concern because a logging strategy necessarily affects every logged part of the system. Logging thereby *cross-cuts* all logged classes and methods. In short, aspects are being represented as cross-cutting concerns and they are injected on a need basis. Through the separation of concerns, the source code complexity comes down sharply and the coding efficiency is bound to escalate.

**Agent-oriented software engineering** (**AOSE**) is a programming paradigm where the construction of the software is centered on the concept of software agents. In contrast to the proven object-oriented programming, which has objects (providing methods with variable parameters) at its core, agent-oriented programming has externally specified agents with interfaces and messaging capabilities at its core. They can be thought of as abstractions of objects. Exchanged messages are interpreted by receiving *agents*, in a way specific to its class of agents.

A software agent is a persistent, goal-oriented computer program that reacts to its environment and runs without continuous direct supervision to perform some function for an end user or another program. A software agent is the computer analog of an autonomous robot. There are a set of specific applications and industry verticals that require the unique services of software agents. Thus, we have software objects, components, aspects, and agents as the popular software construct for building a bevy of differently abled applications.

# Domain-driven design (DDD) architecture

Domain-driven design is an object-oriented approach to designing software based on the business domain, its elements and behaviors, and the relationships between them. It aims to enable software systems that are a correct realization of the underlying business domain by defining a domain model expressed in the language of business domain experts. The domain model can be viewed as a framework from which solutions can then be readied and rationalized.

Architects have to have a good understanding of the business domain to model. The development team has too often worked with business domain experts to model the domain in a precise and perfect manner. In this, the team agrees to only use a single language that is focused on the business domain, by excluding any technical jargon. As the core of the software is the domain model, which is a direct projection of this shared language, it allows the team to quickly find gaps in the software by analyzing the language around it. The DDD process holds the goal not only of implementing the language being used, but also improving and refining the language of the domain. This, in turn, benefits the software being built.

DDD is good if we have a complex domain and we wish to improve communication and understanding within the development team. DDD can also be an ideal approach if we have large and complex enterprise data scenarios that are difficult to manage using the existing techniques.

# Client/server architecture

This pattern segregates the system into two main applications, where the client makes requests to the server. In many cases, the server is a database with application logic represented as stored procedures. This pattern helps to design distributed systems that involve a client system and a server system and a connecting network. The simplest form of client/server architecture involves a server application that is accessed directly by multiple clients. This is referred to as a two-tier architecture application. Web and application servers play the server role in order to receive client requests, process them, and send the responses back to the clients. The following figure is the pictorial representation of the client/server pattern:

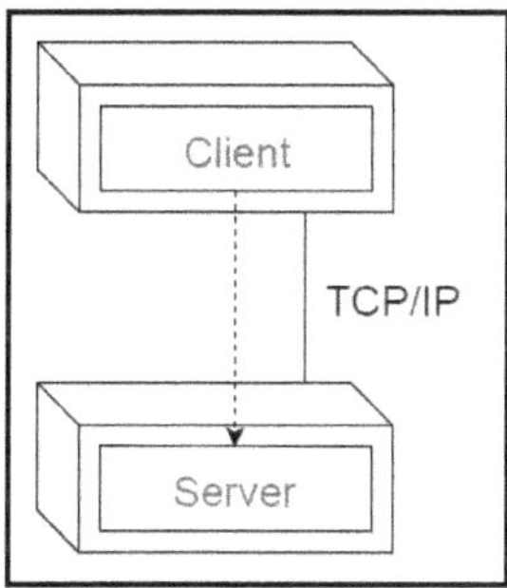


The **peer-to-peer** (**P2P**) applications pattern allows the client and server to swap their roles in order to distribute and synchronize files and information across multiple clients. Every participating system can play the client as well as the server role. They are just peers working towards the fulfillment of business functionality. It extends the client/server style through multiple responses to requests, shared data, resource discovery, and resilience to the removal of peers.

The main benefits of the client/server architecture pattern are:

- **Higher security**: All data gets stored on the server, which generally offers a greater control of security than client machines.
- **Centralized data access**: Because data is stored only on the server, access and updates to the data are far easier to administer than in other architectural styles.
- **Ease of maintenance**: The server system can be a single machine or a cluster of multiple machines. The server application and the database can be made to run on a single machine or replicated across multiple machines to ensure easy scalability and high availability. The multiple machines eventually form a cluster through appropriate networking. Lately, the enterprise-grade server application is made up of multiple subsystems and each subsystem/microservice can be run on the separate server machine in the cluster. Another trend is each subsystem and its instances are also being hosted and run on multiple machines. This sort of single or multiple server machines being leveraged for executing server applications and databases ensures that a client remains unaware and unaffected by a server repair, upgrade, or relocation.

However, the traditional two-tier client/server architecture pattern has numerous disadvantages. Firstly, the tendency of keeping both application and data in a server can negatively impact system extensibility and scalability. The server can be a single point of failure. The reliability is the main worry here. To address these issues, the client-server architecture has evolved into the more general three-tier (or N-tier) architecture. This multi-tier architecture not only surmounts the issues just mentioned, but also brings forth a set of new benefits.

# Multi-tier distributed computing architecture

The two-tier architecture is neither flexible nor extensible. Hence, multi-tier distributed computing architecture has attracted a lot of attention. The application components can be deployed in multiple machines (these can be co-located and geographically distributed). Application components can be integrated through messages or **remote procedure calls (RPCs)**, **remote method invocations (RMIs)**, **common object request broker architecture (CORBA)**, **enterprise Java beans (EJBs)**, and so on. The distributed deployment of application services ensures high availability, scalability, manageability, and so on. Web, cloud, mobile, and other customer-facing applications are deployed using this architecture.

Thus, based on the business requirements and the application complexity, IT teams can choose the simple two-tier client/server architecture or the advanced N-tier distributed architecture to deploy their applications. These patterns are for simplifying the deployment and delivery of software applications to their subscribers and users.

# Layered/tiered architecture

This pattern is an improvement over the client/server architecture pattern. This is the most commonly used architectural pattern. Typically, an enterprise software application comprises three or more layers: presentation / user interface layer, business logic layer, and data persistence layer. Additional layers for enabling integration with third-party applications/services can be readily inscribed in this layered architecture. There are primarily database management systems at the backend, the middle tier involves an application and web server, and the presentation layer is primarily user interface applications (thick clients) or web browsers (thin clients). With the fast proliferation of mobile devices, mobile browsers are also being attached to the presentation layer. Such tiered segregation comes in handy in managing and maintaining each layer accordingly. The power of plug-in and play gets realized with this approach. Additional layers can be fit in as needed. There are **model view controller** (**MVC**) pattern-compliant frameworks hugely simplifying enterprise-grade and web-scale applications. MVC is a web application architecture pattern. The main advantage of the layered architecture is the *separation of concerns*. That is, each layer can focus solely on its role and responsibility. The layered and tiered pattern makes the application:

- Maintainable
- Testable
- Easy to assign specific and separate *roles*
- Easy to update and enhance layers separately

This architecture pattern is good for developing web-scale, production-grade, and cloud-hosted applications quickly and in a risk-free fashion. The current and legacy-tiered applications can be easily modified at each layer with newer technologies and tools. This pattern remarkably moderates and minimizes the development, operational, and management complexities of software applications. The partitioning of different components participating in the system can be replaced and substituted by other right components. When there are business and technology changes, this layered architecture comes in handy in embedding newer things in order to meet varying business requirements.

As illustrated in the following figure, there can be multiple layers fulfilling various needs. Some layers can be termed as open in order to be bypassed during some specific requests. In the figure, the services layer is marked as open. That is, requests are allowed to bypass this opened layer and go directly to the layer under it. The business layer is now allowed to go directly to the persistence layer. Thus, the layered approach is highly open and flexible.

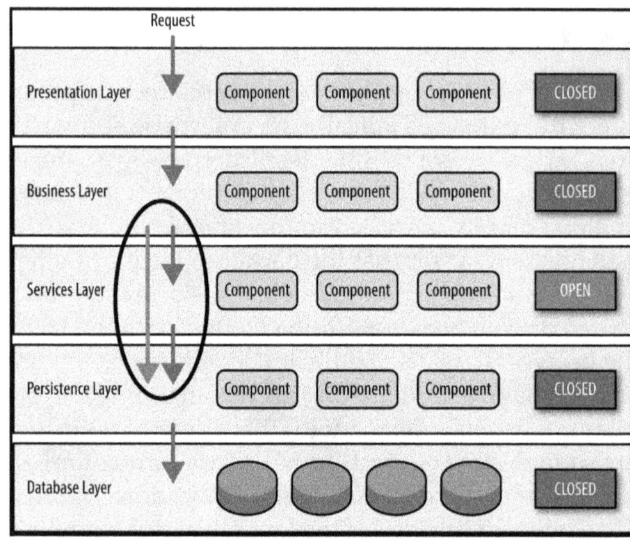


In short, the layered or tiered approach is bound to moderate the rising complexity of software applications. Also, bypassing certain layers, the flexibility is being incorporated easily. Additional layers can be embedded as needed in order to bring highly synchronized applications.

# Event-driven architecture (EDA)

Generally, server applications respond to clients requests. That is, the *request and reply* method is the main one for interactions between clients and servers as per the famous client-server architectural style. This is kind of pulling information from servers. The communication is also synchronous. In this case, both clients and servers have to be available online in order to initiate and accomplish the tasks. Further on, when service requests are being processed and performed by server machines, the requesting services/clients have to wait to receive the intended response from servers. That means clients cannot do any other work while waiting to receive servers' responses.

The world is eventually becoming event-driven. That is, applications have to be sensitive and responsive proactively, pre-emptively, and precisely. Whenever there is an event happening, applications have to receive the event information and plunge into the necessary activities immediately. The *request and reply* notion paves the way for the *fire and forgets* tenet. The communication becomes asynchronous. There is no need for the participating applications to be available online all the time.

An event is a noteworthy thing that happens inside or outside of any business. An event may signify a problem, an opportunity, a deviation, state change, or a threshold break-in. Every event occurrence has an event header and an event body. The event header contains elements describing the event occurrence details, such as specification ID, event type, name, creator, timestamp, and so on. The event body concisely yet unambiguously describes what happened. The event body has to have all the right and relevant information so that any interested party can use that information to take necessary action in time. If the event is not fully described, then the interested party has to go back to the source system to extract the value-adding information.

EDA is typically based on an asynchronous message-driven communication model to propagate information throughout an enterprise. It supports a more natural alignment with an organization's operational model by describing business activities as series of events. EDA does not bind functionally disparate systems and teams into the same centralized management model. EDA ultimately leads to highly decoupled systems. The common issues being introduced by system dependencies are getting eliminated through the adoption of the proven and potential EDA.

We have seen various forms of events used in different areas. There are business and technical events. Systems update their status and condition emitting events to be captured and subjected to a variety of investigations in order to precisely understand the prevailing situations. The submission of web forms and clicking on some hypertexts generate events to be captured. Incremental database synchronization mechanisms, RFID readings, email messages, **short message service** (**SMS**), instant messaging, and so on are events not to be taken lightly. There can be coarse-grained and fine-grained events. Typically, a coarse-grained event is composed of multiple fine-grained events. That is, a coarse-grained event gets abstracted into business concepts and activities. For example, a new customer registration has occurred on the external website, an order has completed the checkout process, a loan application is approved in underwriting, a market trade transaction is completed, a fulfillment request is submitted to a supplier, and so on. On the other hand, fine-grained events such as infrastructure faults, application exceptions, system capacity changes, and change deployments are still important. But their scope is local and limited.

There are event processing engines, **message-oriented middleware** (**MoM**) solutions such as message queues and brokers to collect and stock event data and messages. Millions of events can be collected, parsed, and delivered through multiple topics through these MoM solutions. As event sources/producers publish notifications, event receivers can choose to listen to or filter out specific events and make proactive decisions in real-time on what to do next.

EDA style is built on the fundamental aspects of event notifications to facilitate immediate information dissemination and reactive business process execution. In an EDA environment, information can be propagated to all the services and applications in real-time. The EDA pattern enables highly reactive enterprise applications. Real-time analytics is the new normal with the surging popularity of the EDA pattern.

Anuradha Wickramarachchi in his blog writes that this is the most common distributed asynchronous architecture. This architecture is capable of producing highly scalable systems. The architecture consists of single-purpose event processing components that listen to events and process them asynchronously. There are two main topologies in the event-driven architecture:

- **Mediator topology**: The mediator topology has a single event queue and a mediator which directs each of the events to relevant event processors. Usually, events are fed into the event processors passing through an event channel to filter or pre-process events. The implementation of the event queue could be in the form of a simple message queue or through a message passing interface leveraging a large distributed system, which intrinsically involves complex messaging protocols. The following diagram demonstrates the architectural implementation of the mediator topology:

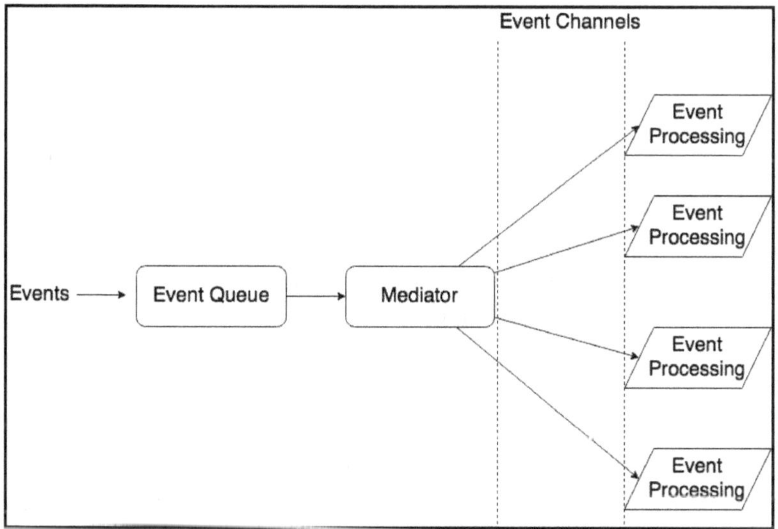


* **Broker topology**: This topology involves no event queue. Event processors are responsible for obtaining events, processing and publishing another event indicating the end. As the name of the topology implies, event processors act as brokers to chain events. Once an event is processed by a processor, another event is published so that another processor can proceed.

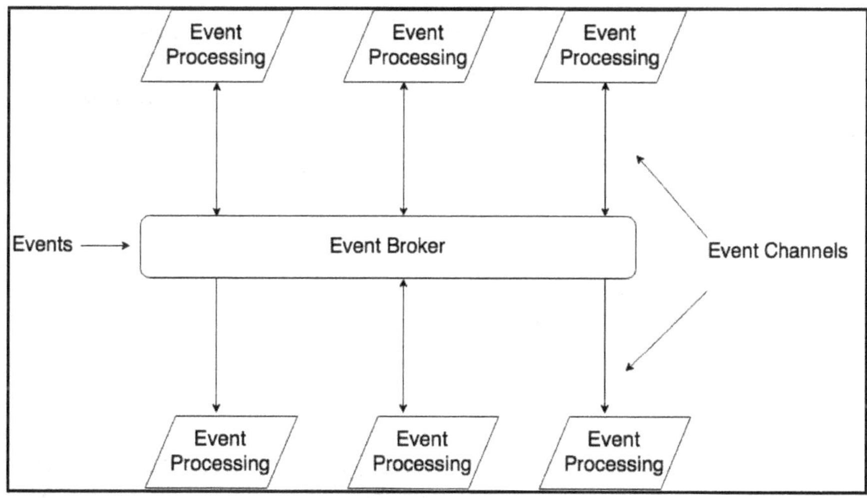

As the diagram indicates, some event processors just process and leave no trace and some tend to publish new events. The steps of certain tasks are chained in the manner of callbacks. That is, when one task ends, the callback is triggered, and all the tasks remain asynchronous in nature.

The prominent examples include programming a web page with JavaScript. This application involves writing the small modules that react to events like mouse clicks or keystrokes. The browser itself orchestrates all of the inputs and makes sure that only the right code sees the right events. This is very different from the layered architecture where all data will typically pass through all layers.

## The major issues with EDA

The EDA pattern lacks the atomicity of transactions since there is no execution sequence of the events. This is because event processors are being implemented to be highly distributed, decoupled, and asynchronous. The results are also expected to be provided at a future time mostly through callbacks. Testing of the systems with event-driven architecture is not easy due to the asynchronous nature of the processing. Finally, since the tasks are asynchronous and non-blocking, the executions happen in parallel, guaranteeing higher performance. This setup outweighs the cost of queueing mechanisms.

Business enterprises are being bombarded with a large number of simple as well as complex events every day, and the enterprise and cloud IT teams have to have the appropriate event capture and processing engines in place to take corrective actions and to give a pertinent answer in real-time. The well-known examples include all kinds of real-time and real-world IT systems, such as trade settlement systems, flight reservation systems, real-time vehicle location data for transportation and logistics companies, streaming stock data for financial services companies, and so on. Companies empower these systems to comfortably handle large volumes of complex data in real time.

# Service-oriented architecture (SOA)

We have been fiddling with object-oriented, component-based, aspect-oriented, and agent-based software development processes. However, with the arrival of service paradigms, software packages and libraries are being developed as a collection of services. That is, software systems and their subsystems are increasingly expressed and exposed as services. Services are capable of running independently of the underlying technology. Also, services can be implemented using any programming and script languages.

Services are self-defined, autonomous, and interoperable, publicly discoverable, assessable, accessible, reusable, and compostable. Services interact with one another through messaging. There are service providers/developers and consumers/clients. There are service discovery services that innately leverage both private and public service registries and repositories. Client services can find their serving services dynamically through service discovery services.

Every service has two parts: the interface and the implementation. The interface is the single point of contact for requesting services. Interfaces give the required separation between services. All kinds of deficiencies and differences of service implementation get hidden by the service interface. To make the service interface easy to use by other services, it is a good idea to use a schema definition that defines the structure of the messages. When a service is used by multiple other services, formalizing the service with a contract is paramount. A contract bounds the service with schemas, a clear message exchange pattern, and policies. Policies define the QoS attributes, such as scalability, sustainability, security and so on. SOA differs from the client/server architecture in the sense that services are universally available and stateless, while client/server architecture requires tight coupling among the participants.

Precisely speaking, SOA enables application functionality to be provided as a set of services, and the creation of personal as well as professional applications that make use of software services.

# Service-inspired integration (SOI)

Services can integrate disparate and distributed applications and data sources. The **Enterprise service bus** (**ESB**) is the service middleware enabling service-based integration of multiple assets and resources. The ESB facilitates service interconnectivity, routing, remediation, enrichment, governance, and so on. The ESB is the integration middleware for any service environment, where the message is the basic unit of interaction between services. An ESB is lightweight compared with previous middleware solutions, such as the EAI hub. The ESB is lightweight because it obviates the need of using custom-made connectors, drivers, and adapters for integrating processes/applications, data sources, and UIs.

Let us consider a sample scenario. Application A is only capable of exporting files to a particular directory and application B would like to get some information out of an exported file in a SOAP message over HTTP. The ESB can implement a *message flow* that is triggered by a SOAP request message from application B and read the requested information of the exported file of application A with a file adapter.

The ESB gathers the requested information and transforms it into a SOAP message corresponding to an agreed upon XML schema. Then the ESB sends the SOAP message back to application B over HTTP.

The *message flow* is an important ingredient of any ESB solution. A message flow is a definition that describes where the message originates from, how it arrives at the ESB, and then how it lands at the target service/application. Matching is another prominent functionality provided by the ESB. This function prescribes which message flow must be executed when a message arrives in the ESB.

There are other key functionalities, routing, translation, and transformation of the message format. The *routing* is all about routing messages from one service to another service. Routing is often used by a message flow module to describe what service will be called for a particular incoming message. The second core functionality is the protocol *translation*. There are many application and message transmission protocols. An ESB can translate the requester protocol into the provider-compatible protocol. Suppose the requester supports the HTTP protocol and the provider/receiver supports the FTP protocol. Then, this functionality of ESB translates the HTTP protocol to the FTP protocol to enable different and distributed applications to find, bind, and interact. The following figure is the macro-level SOA:

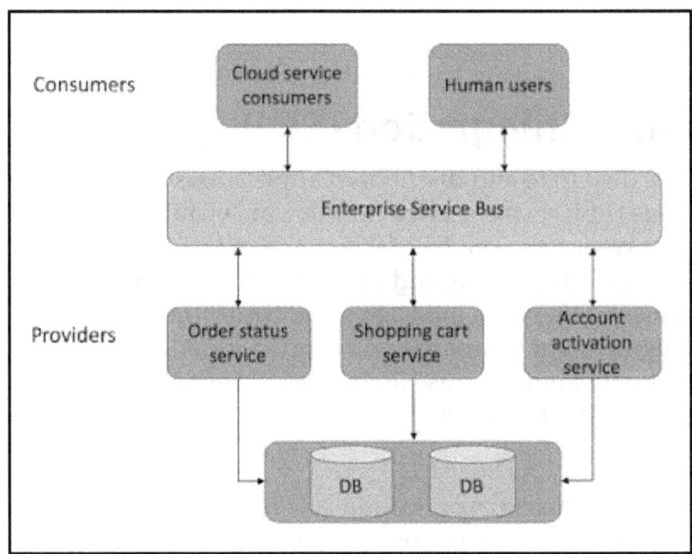

The last core function of the ESB is the message/data format transformation. When a requestor sends a message in SOAP format, the provider can be called by the ESB with an EDIFACT message format. The technology behind such message-format transformations can be the proven **XML stylesheet language transformation** (**XSLT**).

SOA is essentially a dynamic collection of services which communicate with each other. The communication can involve either simple data passing or it could involve two or more services coordinating some activity. SOA is based on a conventional request-response mechanism. A service consumer invokes a service provider through the network and has to wait until the completion of the operation on the provider's side. Replies are sent back to the consumer in a synchronous way.

In conclusion, heterogeneous applications are deployed in an enterprise and cloud IT environments to automate business operations, offerings, and outputs. Legacy applications are service-enabled by attaching one or more interfaces. By putting the ESB in the center, service-enabled applications are easily getting integrated to connect, communicate, collaborate, corroborate and correlate to produce the desired results. In short, SOA is for service-enablement and service-based integration of monolithic and massive applications. The complexity of enterprise process/application integration gets moderated through the smart leverage of the service paradigm. The ESB is the most optimal middleware solution for enabling disparate and distributed applications to talk with one another in a risk-free fashion.

# Event-driven service-oriented architecture

Today, most of the SOA efforts are keen on implementing synchronous request-response interaction patterns to connect different and distributed processes. This approach works well for highly centralized environments and creates a kind of loose coupling for distributed software components at the IT infrastructure level. However, SOA leads to the tight coupling of application functions due to the synchronous communication. This being said, increasingly enterprise environments are tending towards being dynamic and real-time in their interactions, decision-enablement, and actuation. The SOA patterns may find it difficult in ensuring the overwhelmingly pronounced requirements of next-generation enterprise IT.

SOA is a good option if the requirement is just to send requests and receive responses synchronously. But SOA is not good enough to handle real-time events asynchronously. That is why the new pattern of event-driven SOA, which intrinsically combines the proven SOA's request-response and the EDA's event publish-subscribe paradigms, is acquiring a lot of attention and attraction these days. That is, in order to fulfil the newly incorporated requirements, there is a need for such a composite pattern. This is being touted as the new-generation SOA (alternatively touted as SOA 2.0). It is based on the asynchronous message-driven communication model to propagate information across all sorts of enterprise-grade applications throughout an enterprise. Services are activated by differently sourced events and the resulting event messages pass through the right services to accomplish the predestined business operation. Precisely speaking, the participating and contributing services are fully decoupled and joined through event messages. All kinds of dependencies get simply eliminated in this new model.

Applications are being designed, developed, and deployed in such a way to be extremely yet elegantly sensitive and responsive. With enterprise applications and big data mandating the distributed computing model, undoubtedly the event-driven SOA pattern is the way forward. The goals of dynamism, autonomy, and real-time interactions can be achieved through this new pattern. This new event-driven SOA pattern allows system architects and designers to process both event messages and service requests (RPC/RMI). This enables a closer affinity and association between business needs and the respective IT solutions. This invariably results in business agility, adaptivity, autonomy, and affordability.

The following diagram illustrates the traditional request-and-response SOA style. The SOA pattern generally prescribes the synchronous and pull-based approach:

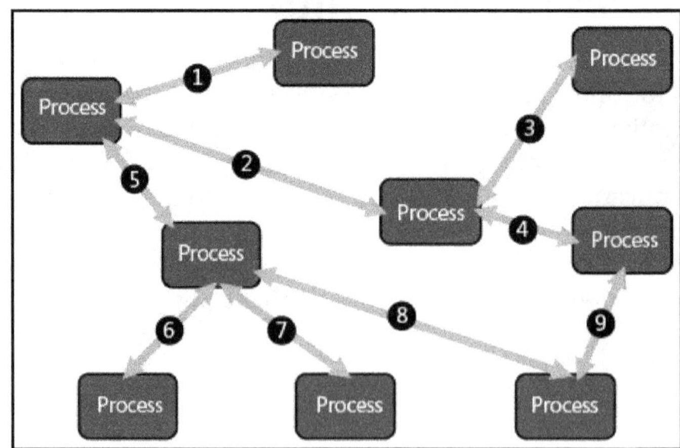

The following diagram depicts the message-oriented, event-driven, asynchronous, and non-blocking process architecture:

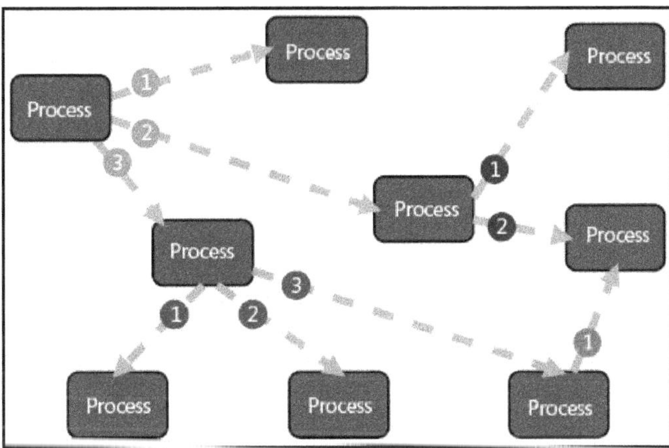


# The EDA fundamental principles

In an asynchronous push-based messaging pattern, the EDA model builds on the pub/sub model to push a variety of real-time notifications and alerts out to the subscribed listeners in a *fire-and-forget* fashion. This neither blocks nor waits for a synchronous response. Also, this is a unidirectional and asynchronous pattern.

- **Autonomous messages**: Events are communicated in the form of autonomous/self-defined messages. That is, each message contains just enough details to represent a unit of work and this provides the decision-enablement capability for notification receivers. Event messages should not require any additional context. Also, they should not require any kind of dependencies on the in-memory session state of the connected applications. The event message is simply intended to communicate the business state transitions of each application, domain, or workgroup within an enterprise.
- **Decoupled and distributed systems**: As mentioned, the EDA pattern logically decouples connected systems. SOA guarantees loose and light coupling. That is, participating applications need not be available online all the time to accomplish the business tasks. The middleware (ESB) does take care in unobtrusively delivering the messages to the target application. The issue here is that the sender system has to know the relevant details of the target application towards service invocation to process completion.

- In the synchronous SOA case, connected and dependent systems are often required to meet the various non-functional requirements/quality of service (QoS) attributes, such as scalability, availability, performance, and so on. But in the case of asynchronous EDA, the transaction load of one system does not need to influence or depend on the service levels of downstream systems. This decoupling-enabled autonomy allows application architects to be a bit carefree in designing their respective physical architectures and capacity planning. Decoupled systems can be deployed independently and are horizontally scalable, as there are no dependencies among the participating modules.
- **Receiver-driven flow control**: The EDA pattern shifts much of the responsibility of control-flow away from the event source (or sender system) and distributes/delegates it to event receivers. The EDA-centric connected systems have more autonomy in deciding whether to propagate the events further or not. The knowledge used to support these decisions is distributed into discrete steps or stages throughout the architecture and is encapsulated where the ownerships reside. The following diagram is the grandiose mix of both the SOA and EDA patterns:

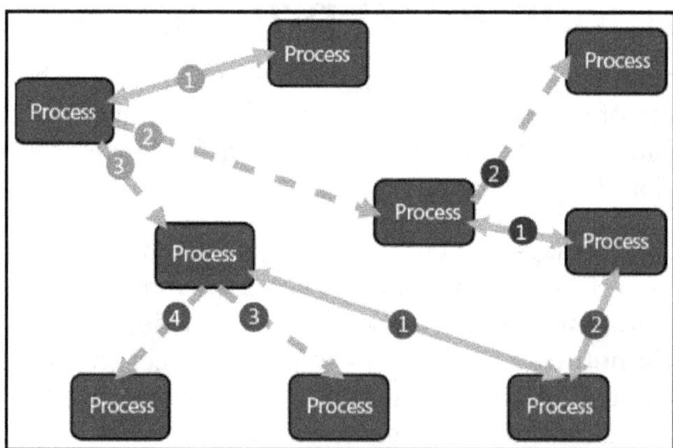

# The ED-SOA composite pattern benefits

A monolithic application puts all of its functionality into a single process. For scaling, it is mandatory to replicate the whole application. However, the partitioning of an application into a collection of dynamic application services facilitates the choice and the replication of one or more application components/services for scaling. Thus, the technique of divide and conquer is still doing a great job for the increasingly complicated world of software engineering. This section illustrates the other benefits of SOA and EDA patterns combined.

- **Effective data integration**: In the synchronous request-driven architecture, the focus is on reusing remotely held functions and implementing process-oriented integration. That means the data integration, which is the important aspect of integrated environments, is innately not supported in the SOA environments. But in the case of EDA, the data integration is intrinsically accomplished as the event data/message is the base unit of communication and collaboration.
- **Timeliness and trustworthiness**: Events are propagated across all the participating applications in real-time for real-time data capture, processing, decision making, and actuation. The timely exchange of event data/messages enables operational systems to have the most accurate and recent view of the business state/situation. The decisions being arrived based on the precise and perfect data are going to be correct and informed.
- **Improved scalability and sustainability**: It is a fact that asynchronous systems tend to be more scalable when compared with synchronous systems. Individual processes block less and have less dependency on remote/distributed processes. Furthermore, the intermediaries (message queues and brokers) can be made more stateless, thus reducing the overall complexity of distributed systems. Less dependency ultimately results in them being highly scalable, reliable/dependable, resilient, responsive, and manageable. Any kind of replacement, substitution, and advancements can be easily performed in decoupled systems.

Thus, the beneficial combination of SOA and EDA patterns are capable of producing real-time, adaptive, and extensible enterprises. This hybrid pattern is all set to result in innumerable innovations, disruptions, and transformations.

# Microservices architecture (MSA)

We have discussed the unique contributions of the SOA pattern towards establishing and sustaining service-enabled environments and enterprises. The service-oriented architectural pattern has evolved over decades to express and expose any legacy, monolithic, and massive application as a dynamic collection of interdependent services. Services are blessed with interfaces and implementations. Interfaces are the contacting and contracting mechanism for any service-enabled application. There are standards, languages, models, frameworks, platforms, patterns, and a bevy of toolkits to shepherd the service paradigm towards its logical conclusion. Though SOA has done a lot of things for the IT enterprise, there are some issues, drawbacks, and limitations.

The popular SOA style majorly relies on a shared data model with multiple hierarchies. The sharing of databases in SOA tends to create a kind of tight data coupling between services and other system components. This tight coupling comes in the way of bringing forth desired changes in the database. That is, if a few RESTful services are tightly coupled with a backend database and if there is any change mandated and enacted on the database schema, then there is a need for a retesting of services to verify and validate how the services work on the altered schema. This dependency is a bit troublesome for the increasingly automated and dynamic world.

The other challenge is that the services in the SOA style are typically coarse-grained and hence the aspect of reusability is quite a tough affair. Most of the application components of legacy applications are fitted with service-oriented interfaces for enabling discovery, integration, and interactions. At the infrastructure level, there is no dependency problem because these service-enabled application components can literally run anywhere. There is no restriction for co-location. SOA uses a kind of tiered organizational architecture that contains a centralized messaging middleware for service invocation, intermediation, and coordination. But the prickling issue here is that application components need to know the corresponding details of one another in order to initiate and bring the required collaboration, corroboration, and correlation to closure. There are other challenges being associated with the highly matured and stabilized SOA paradigm.

Let us move over to the MSA pattern, which is growing by leaps and bounds. Microservices architecture is the new architectural pattern for defining, designing, developing, deploying, and delivering distributed and enterprise-grade software applications. This fast-emerging and evolving pattern is being positioned as the one for easily and quickly achieving the non-functional requirements such as scalability, availability, and reliability for any software application.

The MSA pattern is for producing fine-grained, loosely coupled, horizontally scalable, independently deployable, interoperable, publicly discoverable, network-accessible, easily manageable, and composable services, which is not only the optimized unit of software construction, but also allows enabling quicker software deployment and delivery. In the past, software companies assembled large teams of engineers to build applications which, over a period of time, became monolithic and unwieldy. Legacy applications are close, bulky, tough to maintain, inflexible, and not modern. We need applications that are adaptive, dynamic, open, easy to modify and enhance, and so on. Having understood the distinct contributions of the MSA pattern, today corporates across the globe are keenly strategizing and planning to embrace this new pattern with clarity and confidence. As a result, enterprise-class cloud, mobile, and embedded applications are being built using the powerful and pioneering MSA pattern.

The growing ecosystem of tools, engines, platforms, and other software infrastructure solutions speeds up the process of producing microservices-centric applications. With the tools-assisted orchestration, microservices are being deftly orchestrated to bring forth versatile applications for business automation, acceleration, and augmentation.

Microservices are built upon a concept known as a bounded context, which leads to a self-contained association between a single service and its data. There is no technology or vendor lock-in as far as the MSA-inspired applications are concerned. Every microservice is being empowered with its own data source, which can be a filesystem, SQL, NoSQL, NewSQL, in-memory cache, and so on. There are API gateway solutions to streamline the end-to-end lifecycle management of microservices. Microservices rely solely on inter-service communication. Each microservice calls another microservice as required to complete its function. Furthermore, called microservices may call other services as needed in a process known as service chaining. Microservices use a non-coordinating API layer over the services composing an application. As Docker containers are emerging as the most appropriate runtime for microservices, the MSA pattern is seeing a lot of traction these days.

Each microservice is being designed as an atomic and self-sufficient piece of software. Implementing an application will often require composing multiple calls to these single responsibility and distributed endpoints. Although synchronous request-response calls are required when the requester expects an immediate response, the integration patterns based on eventing and asynchronous messaging provide maximum scalability and resiliency. The microservices approach is well-aligned to a typical big data deployment.

We can gain the required modularity, extensive parallelism, and cost-effective scaling by deploying services across many commodity hardware servers. Microservices modularity facilitates independent updates/deployments and helps to avoid single points of failure, which can help prevent large-scale outages.

# Event-driven microservices patterns

As mentioned, the microservice architectural style is an approach for developing an application as a suite of discrete yet self-sufficient services built around specific business capabilities. Microservices-centric applications are being enabled to be event-driven. There are a few interesting architectural patterns quickly emerging and evolving. In this section, we will look at the event stream pattern.

Like polyglot and decentralized persistence, the decentralized polyglot messaging method should be a key to achieving the intended success in microservices architectures. This allows different groups of services to be developed in their own cadence. Furthermore, it minimizes the need for highly coordinated and risky big-bang releases. The microservices approach gives more flexibility to developers for choosing the optimal messaging middleware solution. Every use case will have its own specific needs mandating different messaging technologies such as Apache Kafka, RabbitMQ, or even event-driven NoSQL data grids, such as Apache Geode / Pivotal GemFire.

In the MSA approach, a common architecture pattern is event sourcing using an append-only event stream such as Kafka or MapR Streams, which implements Kafka. With MapR Streams, events are grouped into logical collections of events called topics. Topics are partitioned for parallel processing. We can think of a partitioned topic as a queue. Events are delivered in the order they are received. Unlike a queue, events are persisted, even after they are delivered they remain on the partition, available to other consumers. Older messages are automatically deleted based on the stream's time-to-live setting; if the setting is zero, then they will never be deleted. Messages are not deleted from topics when read, and topics can have multiple different consumers. This allows processing of the same messages by different consumers for different purposes.

Pipelining is also possible where a consumer enriches an event and publishes it to another topic:

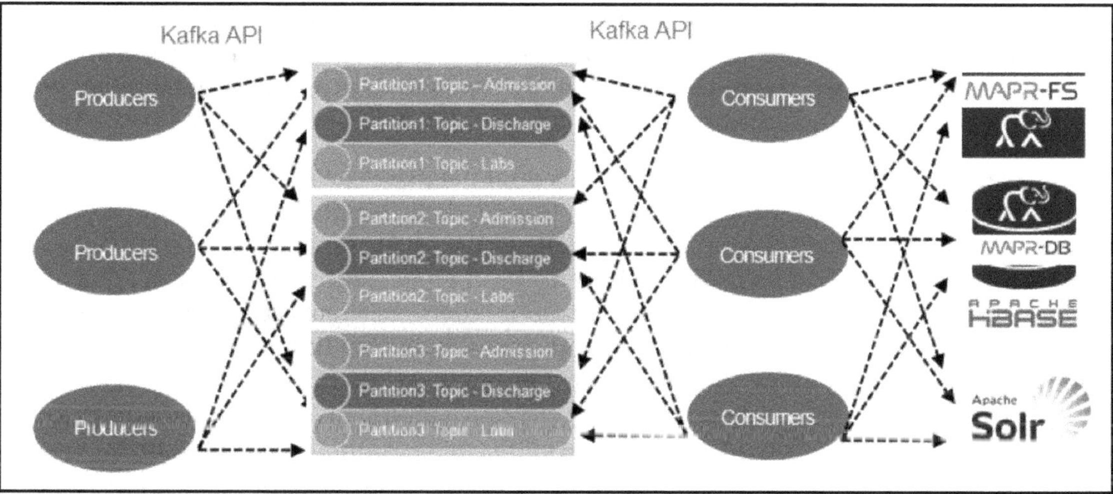


With the faster proliferation, penetration, and participation of the microservices architecture, there will be fresh patterns to address its growing and prevailing issues and limitations. Furthermore, existing patterns can be seamlessly combined to come out with bigger and better patterns for enabling the realization of microservices-centric applications. We have detailed the architecture and design patterns in `Chapter 9`, *Microservices Architecture Patterns*.

# Space-based architecture (SBA)

Typically, enterprise applications are being blessed with a backend database management system. These enterprise-scale applications function well as long as the database is able to keep up with the load. But when usage peaks and the database can't keep up with the constant challenge of writing a log of the transactions, the application is bound to fail. In any high-volume application with an extremely large concurrent user load, the database will usually be the final limiting factor in how many transactions we can process concurrently. While various caching technologies and database scaling products help to address these issues, it is still a pipe dream that scaling out a normal application for extreme loads is a very difficult proposition.

The space-based architecture is designed with the aim of empowering software systems to work even under the heavy load of users. This is being achieved by splitting up both the processing and the storage between multiple servers. The data is spread out across many nodes. The space-based architecture pattern is widely used to address and solve scalability and concurrency issues. Customer-facing applications are quite unpredictable and this specialized architecture is competent and cognitive enough to support a large number of users.

High scalability is achieved by removing the central database constraint and using replicated in-memory data grids instead. Application data is kept in-memory and replicated among all the active processing units. Processing units can be dynamically started up and shut down as the user load increases and decreases, thereby addressing variable scalability. Because there is no central database, the database bottleneck is removed, providing near-infinite scalability within the application. Most applications that fit into this pattern are standard websites that receive a request from a browser and perform some sort of action. A bidding auction site is a good example of this. The site continually receives bids from internet users through a browser request. The application would receive a bid for a particular item, record that bid with a timestamp, update the latest bid information for the item, and send the information back to the browser.

Precisely speaking, the SBA style is primarily for ensuring the goals of higher concurrency. Next-generation applications have to be scalable, available, and dependable. The SBA pattern is a great enabler.

# Combining architecture patterns

As we all know, it is becoming a software-defined world. Everything is being stuffed with software to exhibit adaptive behavior. Thus, the buzzwords such as software-defined networking, storage, compute, security, and environment are acquiring significance these days. Also, the concept of software-defined everything is becoming prominent and paramount. The role and responsibility of software, therefore, is increasing. Along with the faster proliferation, penetration, and participation, the software product is also becoming a complicated task. Software experts and exponents are recommending the combination of multiple architecture patterns that we have discussed previously in order to soften and speed up the realization of next-generation software solutions and services. We have described how SOA and EDA team up to put a stimulating foundation for producing dynamic and adaptive applications. Similarly, other architectural patterns can be synchronized in order to bring forth composite patterns in order to produce competent and versatile applications.

# Special-purpose architectures

A context-aware event-driven service-oriented architecture (ALFONSO GARCÍA DE PRADO and his team).

Context awareness has become a fundamental requirement for realizing people-centric IT applications. People leave their homes expecting the lights, which they left on, to be turned off automatically. The mobile phone can warn people if there is traffic congestion on the way to the office. Windscreen wipers automatically turn on if it is raining. If there is any possibility of a fire at home, hotel, or hospital, then sensors have to integrate with one another to do data fusion in time to facilitate any fire, flame, and fall detection. Our current IT services and systems are not typically context-aware. Every common, casual, and cheap item has to be self-, surroundings, and situation-aware in order to be unique in their decisions, deals, and deeds. Software packages, libraries, and suites have to be event-driven in order to be sensitive and responsive. They have to be designed and deployed in such a way that they are receptive to any kind of noteworthy events and to answer accordingly. We have discussed service-oriented and event-driven architectures. They need to be blended with the new-generation technologies, such as the IoT, in order to be right and relevant for the increasingly connected world.

The connected things, sensors, actuators, robots, drones, beacons, machines, equipment, instruments, wares, utensils, and other devices are to empower software services to be context-aware. There are IoT data analytics platforms, the growing array of different and distributed event sources, the faster maturity and stability of event processors, streaming analytics engines, scores of connectors, drivers and adapters, knowledge visualization dashboards, and other enabling frameworks, patterns, processes, practices, and products aimed towards producing context-aware applications across industry verticals.

The authors have devised with a high-level context-aware event-driven service-oriented architecture:

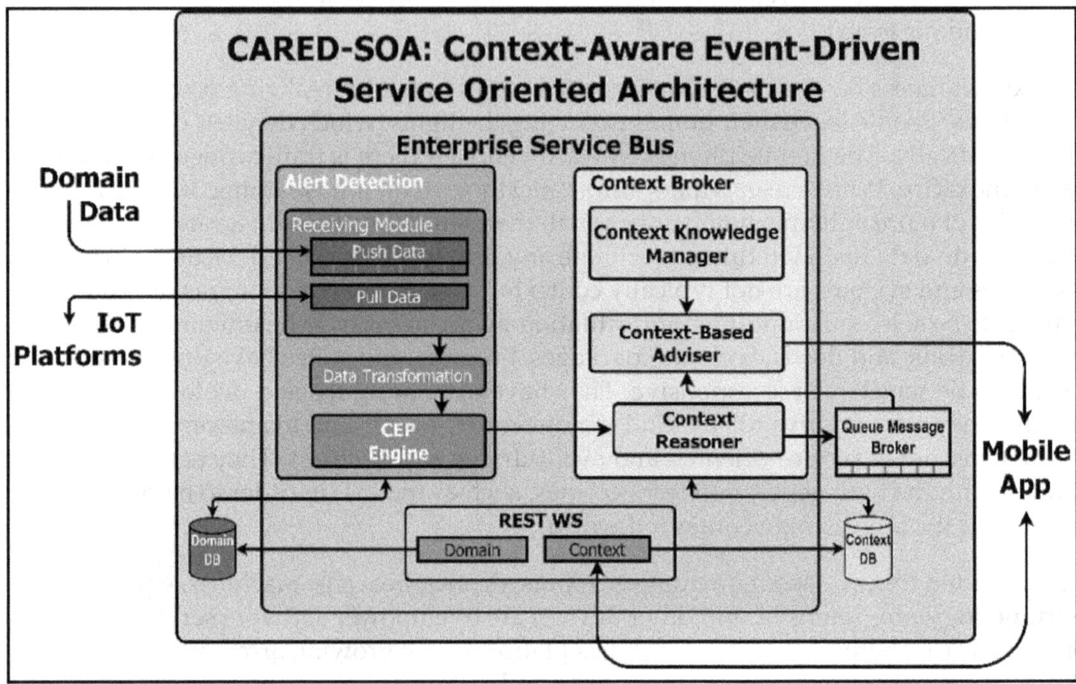


With the dawning of the game-changing IoT era, application and data architectures are set to be synchronized to create versatile architectures for various use cases.

# Real-time context-aware prediction architecture

With the setting up of IoT environments across our personal, professional, and social environments to fulfill the dreams of connected and smarter environments, the amount of multi-structured data getting generated, collected, cleansed, and crunched is growing exponentially. With the arrival of a dazzling array of specific and generic, disappearing, disposable yet indispensable, slim and sleek, handy and trendy, embedded yet networked devices, the projected big data era has set in. This has opened up fresh possibilities and opportunities for businesses as well as IT service/solution providers.

With our manufacturing floors, retail stores, warehouses, airports, railway stations, and bus bays, multi-specialty clinics, shopping complexes, malls and hypermarkets, auditoriums and stadiums, entertainment centers and cinema theaters, food joints, and so on, slowly yet steadily tending towards being smarter through the application of pioneering edge technologies, the long-awaited context-aware computing is becoming a reality. That is, software applications have to be context-aware to be adaptive, accommodating, and adjustable.

Considering the trends and transitions happening in the IT space, a few researchers (David Corral-Plaza and his team) have envisioned a holistic **event-driven service-oriented architecture** (**ED-SOA**) and it has the following important factors:

- Data producers should gather data from several sources (databases, IoT sensors, social networks, and so on) and send them to the data collector.
- The data collector follows the necessary transformations so that the information received can be used in the following phases of their solution. It is an intermediate layer that performs a process of homogenization since information will most probably be received in different formats and structures in most scenarios.
- Data processing should provide the **complex event processing** (**CEP**), context-awareness, and prediction module.

- Data consumers, which can be databases, end users, or additional endpoints, pave the way for the collaborative architecture. Such data consumers communicate with the previous module through a REST interface:

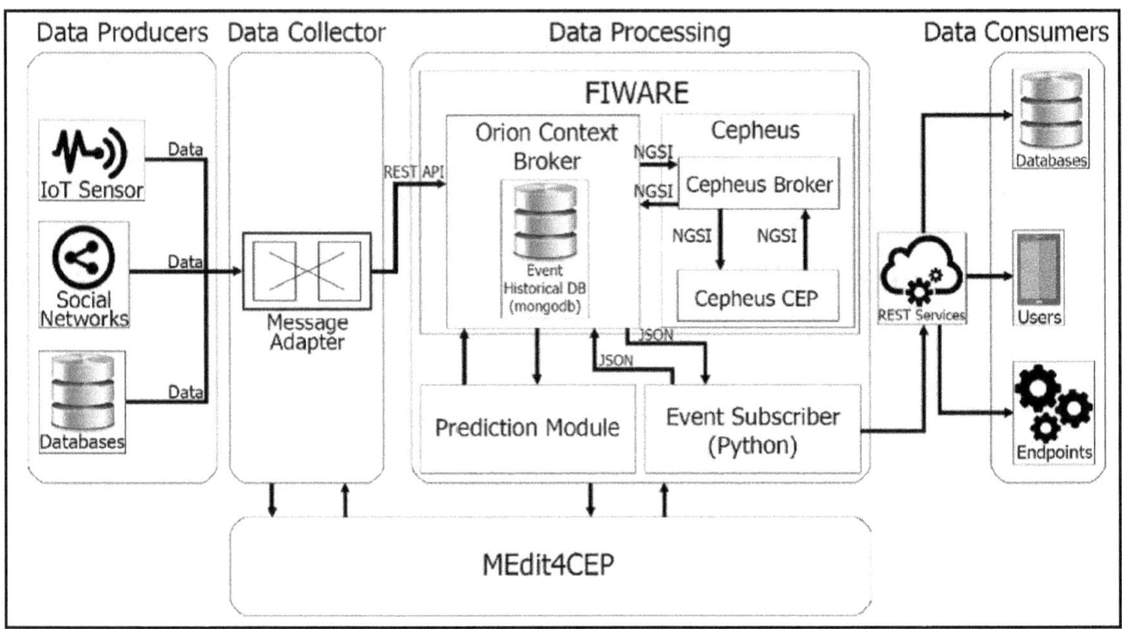


We are heading towards the world of real-time applications and enterprises. Real-time data capture, processing, knowledge discovery and dissemination, decision making, and actuation turn out to be the new normal. IT systems are being enabled to be real-time. The preceding architecture spells out the ways and means of achieving real-time predictions.

# Summary

We have detailed the prominent and dominant software architecture patterns and how they are distinctly foundational and fundamental for producing and running any kind of enterprise-class and production-grade software applications. To accommodate the evolution and revolutions and to surmount the complications due to constant changes happening in the business and technology spaces, the smart leverage of a variety of software patterns is being recommended as the way forward. Increasingly, to design and develop sophisticated and smarter applications, various architectural patterns are being meticulously chosen and cognitively clubbed together to produce composite patterns.

Besides this, there are several application and domain-specific architectures being formed, verified, and validated by worldwide researchers and presented as research contributions. Thus, the domain of architectural patterns is consistently on the growth in order to support and sustain the software engineering field. The forthcoming chapters will go deep and dig further to bring forth a lot of useful and usable details on design patterns for existing and fresh technologies. We have covered the emerging and evolving technologies such as Docker-enabled containerization, **microservices architecture** (**MSA**), big data analytics, reactive programming, **high-performance computing** (HPC), and so on.

# Additional reading materials

To learn more, you can refer to the following reading resources:

- .NET microservices architecture for containerized .NET applications: `https://docs.microsoft.com/en-us/dotnet/standard/microservices-architecture/`
- SOA patterns: `http://www.soapatterns.org/`
- Using events in highly distributed architectures: `https://msdn.microsoft.com/en-us/library/dd129913.aspx`
- All about microservices and the design patterns: `http://microservices.io/index.html`
- Event-driven architecture pattern: `https://towardsdatascience.com/event-driven-architecture-pattern-b54fc50276cd`
- Common software architectural patterns in a nutshell: `https://towardsdatascience.com/10-common-software-architectural-patterns-in-a-nutshell-a0b47a1e9013`

# 2
# Client/Server Multi-Tier Architectural Patterns

This chapter provides a bird's eye view of client-server architectural patterns. It starts with the need for the evolution of two-tier client-server patterns and highlights how the limitations of two-tier client-server patterns led to the evolution of three-tier and consequently *n*-tier client-server patterns. The different variants of client-server patterns like the master-slave pattern, peer-to-peer patterns, and so on are also explained in-depth with relevant use cases. The second part of the chapter focuses on web application frameworks. The requirements of web applications are different from that of client-server applications, the key differentiating factor being the dynamic updates to the UI based on the changes in the underlying data. All the popular patterns used in web application design are covered in this part of the chapter.

The major topics covered in this chapter are as follows:

- Two-tier, three-tier, and *n*-tier client-server patterns
- The master-slave pattern
- The peer-to-peer pattern
- The distributed client-server pattern
- The model-view-controller pattern
- The model-view-presenter pattern
- The model-view-model pattern
- The front controller pattern
- Some common design patterns used for web application development

The client-server pattern is one of the oldest architectural patterns. In simple terms, how do we describe a client and a server? It is described as follows:

- **Client**: This is the component that is a requestor of a service and sends requests for various types of services to the server
- **Server**: This is the component that is a service provider and continuously provides services to the client as per the requests placed by it

Clients and servers typically comprise of distributed systems, which communicate over a network.

The following diagram is a simple graphic depicting the client-server architecture:

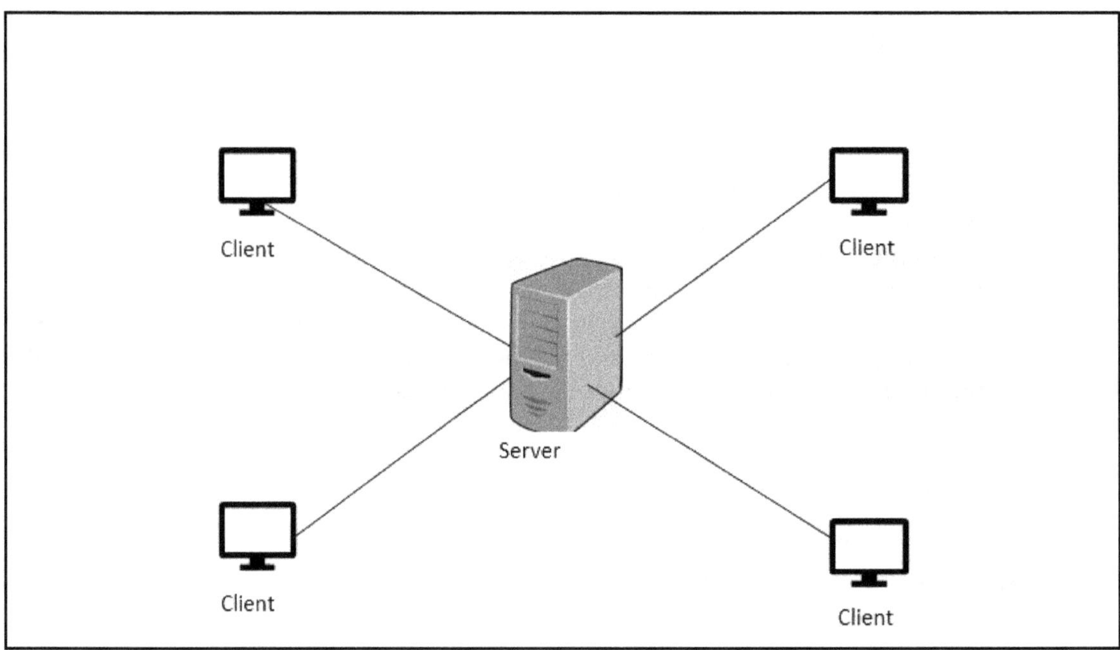

There is no upper bound on the number of clients that can be serviced by a single server. It is also not mandatory that the client and server should reside in separate systems. Both client and server can reside in the same system based on the hardware configuration of the system and the type of functionality or service provided by the server. The communication between client and server happens by exchange of messages using a request-response pattern. The client basically sends a request for a service and server returns a response. This request-response pattern of communication which happens between a client and a server is a very good example of inter-process communication. For this communication to happen efficiently, it is necessary to have a well-defined communication protocol which lays down the rules of communication such as the format of request messages, response messages, error handling, and so on. All communication protocols that are used for client-server communication work in the application layer of the protocol stack. To further streamline the process of client-server communication, the server sometimes implements specific **application programming interfaces** (**APIs**) which could be used by the client to access any specific service from the server. This client-server pattern depicted in the graphic has two tiers: the client tier and the server tier, and hence it is also called the **two-tier client-server pattern**.

The term "service" used in the context of client-server architecture refers to the abstraction of a resource. The resource could be of any type, and the server is named based on the resource that is provided by the server (service). For example, if the server provides web pages, it is called a **web server** and if the server provides files, it is called a **file server**, and so on. A server can receive requests from *n* number of clients at a specific point in time. But any server will have its own limitations about its processing capabilities. So, many times, it becomes necessary for a server to prioritize the incoming requests and service them as per their priority. The scheduling system present in the server helps the server with the assignment of priorities. The common applications of client-server patterns for different use cases are as follows.

**Email server** and **email client**: An email server provides emails as per the request received from the email client. Some commonly used enterprise email solutions are Microsoft Exchange from Microsoft, Lotus notes from IBM, Gmail from Google, and so on. Working on an email system is described as follows.

A mail server which is also known as an email server is the server that processes and delivers emails over the network, which is typically internet. A mail server is also equipped to receive emails from client computers and deliver them to other mail servers that are present in the network. An email client is a system in which the emails are read. It could be a desktop, laptop or a smartphone which can support emails.

The working of an email system is depicted in the following diagram:

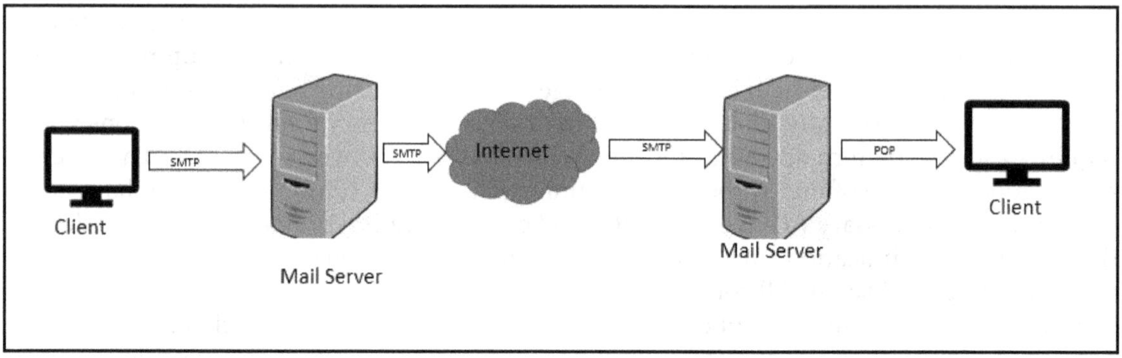

When an email is sent from a client, the email software which is present in the client system will connect to a server which is present in the network called the **simple mail transfer protocol** (**SMTP**) server. SMTP refers to a protocol which is used to deliver emails from clients to servers and from one server to another.

When emails are downloaded using the email software present on your client machine, the email software will connect to another server, which performs a function called a **post office protocol version3** (**POP3**) server. POP3 server uses a POP3 protocol. This protocol works like a mail delivery system used in a post office and hence the name. A detailed discussion of these protocols is beyond the scope of this chapter.

# Domain name service (DNS) server and DNS client

DNS is one of the most important services that is present on the internet. An internet has thousands of devices that are a part of it and each of these devices is referred to as a host. Each host could be a printer, router, computer, or any other device. Each host has a unique IP address associated with it. Apart from the IP address, each host also has a unique hostname associated with it. For example, if the hostname is `LP471` and it is present in a domain `technest.com`, then the **fully qualified domain name** (**FQDN**) of the host is `LP471.technest.com`. The FQDN is used to identify the host uniquely within the DNS namespace. The DNS namespace contains some commonly used name suffixes; they are as follows:

- `.com`: Commercial organizations
- `.edu`: Educational institutions

- `.gov`: Government organizations
- `.org`: Non-profit bodies like IEEE
- `.net`: Networking organizations

Apart from these commonly used name suffixes, there are several others, too.

# The workings of a DNS

A DNS works using the concept of distributed databases based on the client-server model. DNS clients are entities that require a name resolution (mapping of host names to IP addresses). DNS servers maintain the data that is required for name resolution. The high-level schematic of a DNS client-server architecture is given in the following diagram:

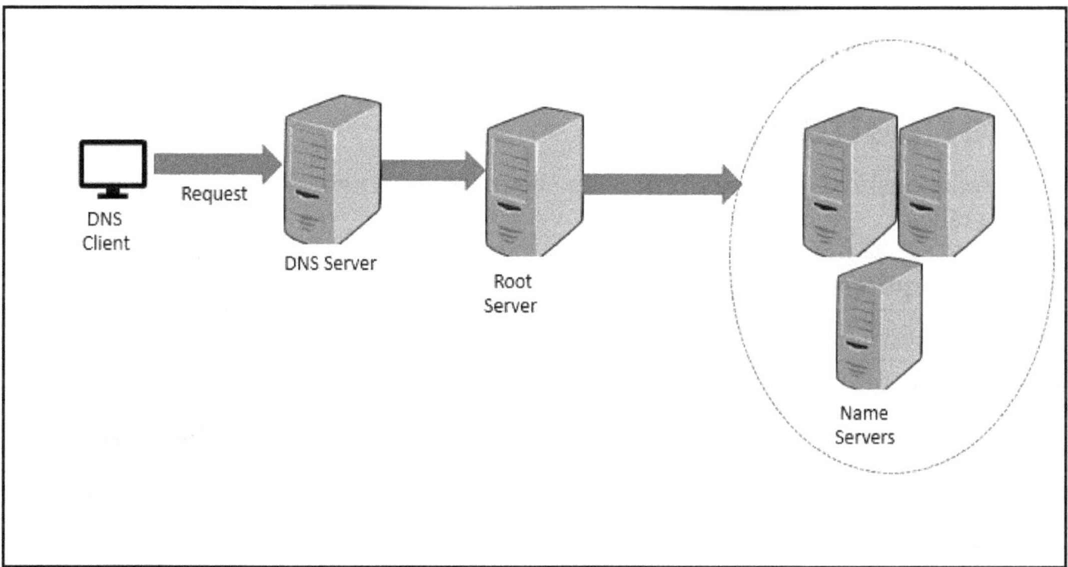


Suppose the URL `www.xyzworks.com` is typed into the browser of the DNS client. The browser gets connected to a DNS server to get the equivalent IP address. The DNS server performs this task by first connecting to one of the root DNS servers. The root servers will store the IP addresses of all DNS servers that handle top-level domains such as `.edu`, `.com`, and so on. In this example, the root server after getting the IP address of the top-level domain `.com`, sends it a query asking for the IP address of `www.xyzworks.com`. The DNS server that handles the `.com` domain will respond with the IP addresses of the name servers that handle the `www.xyzworks.com` domain.

The name server then sends the query to the `www.xyzworks.com` DNS server. This DNS server responds with the entire IP address to the name server, which in turn sends it back to the DNS client which had initiated the DNS request. The DNS client machine can then use the IP address to access the required web page.

The salient aspects of this client-server architecture are as follows:

- **Redundancy**: There are multiple DNS servers at each level so that even if one fails, the other server can take its role.
- **Caching**: Once a DNS request is resolved, the DNS server caches the IP address received by it. For example, where the IP address of the `.com` domain server is cached by the DNS server so that any subsequent requests for a `.com` domain can be handled by it without initiating repetitive DNS query mechanisms.

# Functional requirements in two-tier client-server patterns

The key functional requirements in two-tier client-server patterns are classified in the following table:

| Functional requirement | Description |
|---|---|
| Presentation services | Provides user interface and dialog control |
| Presentation logic | User interaction and validation of inputs |
| Business logic | Set of business rules that specify how data can be stored, created, and changed |
| Distribution service | Management of communication |
| Database logic | Data operations and manage integrity of data |
| Database services | Management of various attributes of a database transaction |
| File services | Operations on files and sharing of files |

# Distribution of functional requirements in a client-server pattern

Clients are broadly classified into the following two major categories:

- **Fat client**: Most of the functional services are performed by the client component. One classic example of a fat client is a file server.
- **Thin client**: If it is a thin client, it relies on the server component for most of its computational capability.

The choice of the client is made based on the type of client-server pattern, which is planned and implemented in a system. For example, if the pattern involves a lot of functionality to be done on the client side, then the choice of client is typically fat client, and vice versa. The functional requirements that are discussed in this section will give a better idea regarding the choice of client and server systems for implementing specific client-server patterns.

There are various ways in which functional requirements can be implemented in a client-server pattern. The following are some of the prominent ways of implementing client-server patterns:

- The remote data access client-server pattern
- The remote presentation client-server pattern
- The split logic data client-server architecture pattern

## The remote data access client-server pattern

In the remote data access client-server pattern, the application resides on the client component, whereas the data management is done by the server component. The server that performs data management is typically referred to as **database management server** (**DBMS**) or data server. Most of the **relational database management system** (**RDBMS**) products available in the market are implemented using this pattern. These RDBMS products typically provide a layer or component of software at the client side, which handles communication with the data server. This component of the software is called **data manipulation language** (**DML**). Client systems support the presentation and business logic and interact with the data server using DML. These patterns typically involve the usage of fat clients as a significant amount of processing is done by the client systems as well.

The implementation of functional requirements in a remote data access client-server architecture is depicted in the following diagram:

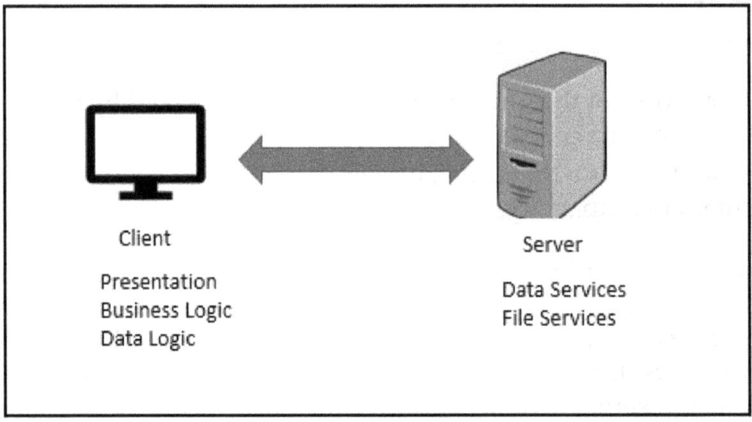


## The remote presentation client-server pattern

In the remote presentation client-server pattern, the **graphical user interface** (**GUI**) frontend is mapped to an existing application's text-based screen. This process is called Remote mapping or Front ending. The typical mode of operation of this pattern involves the use of intelligent workstations, which are equipped with the capability to intercept the text screen streams of data that are sent from a server system, and display them in a windowed system using a GUI. However, in these systems, most of the processing and computation happens on the server end only. One ideal example of this implementation is IBM's 3270 (mainframe) application. In this application, data from the application is sent to 3270's screen program on the mainframe to be displayed. The data is then sent to the client workstation in the form of a 3270-data stream. The client workstation receives the data, interprets it, and converts it to a graphical form to be displayed in a window. If the user enters any data through the client workstation in the GUI window, the front ware application that runs in the client workstation converts the data into a 3270-compatible format and sends it back to the server for the next course of action. The split of functions in a remote **presentation** client-server pattern is depicted in the following diagram:

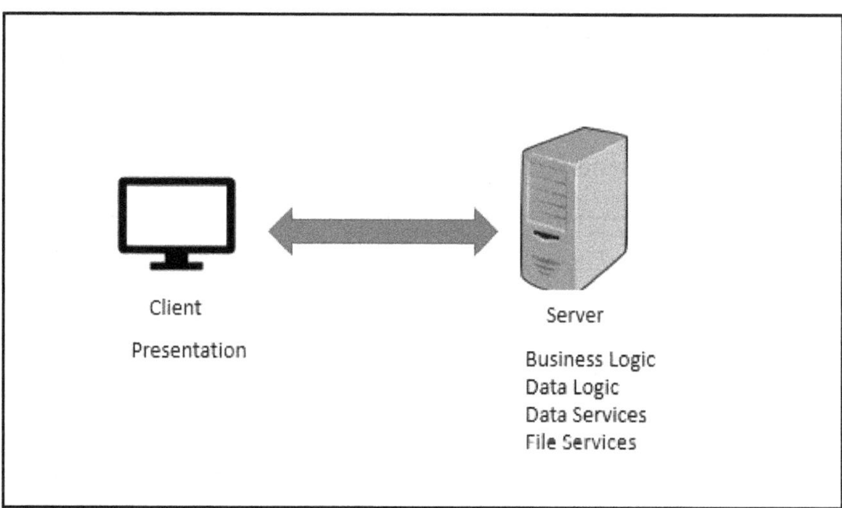


## The split logic data client-server architecture pattern

In the split logic data client-server architecture pattern, the application functionality is split into two parts: one will be implemented on the client side and the other one will be implemented on the server side. This pattern is very complex when compared to the other two patterns because both client and server need separately compiled application programs for their functioning. Before implementing this pattern, it is very important for developers to identify the functions to be implemented on the client and the server side and list out the type of communication dialogs that must happen between the application programs running on the client and the server side.

# The three-tier pattern / multi-tier pattern client-server

The following diagram represents a client-server interaction:

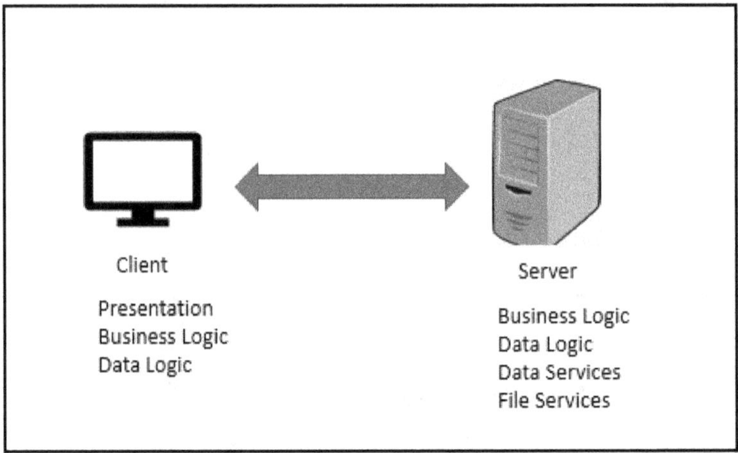


We will discuss some of the variants of client-server patterns in this section. Some of the prominent variants of client-server patterns are as follows:

- The master-slave pattern
- The peer-to-peer pattern

Let's discuss them in detail.

## The master-slave pattern

The master-slave pattern is applied for designing a system if the system involves similar or identical computations that need to be performed repeatedly with separate set of inputs and context. The master-slave pattern offers support for fault tolerance and parallel computation.

The master-slave pattern is depicted in the following diagram:

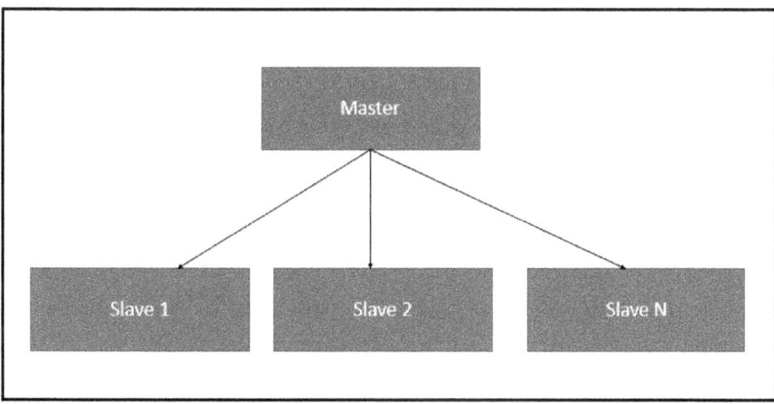


The master component distributes the work among all the slave components and calculates the final result by summing up the results that are returned by each slave. The master-slave pattern is used for architecting embedded systems and used in the design of systems that perform massive parallel computations. The following is a sequence diagram of the master-slave pattern:

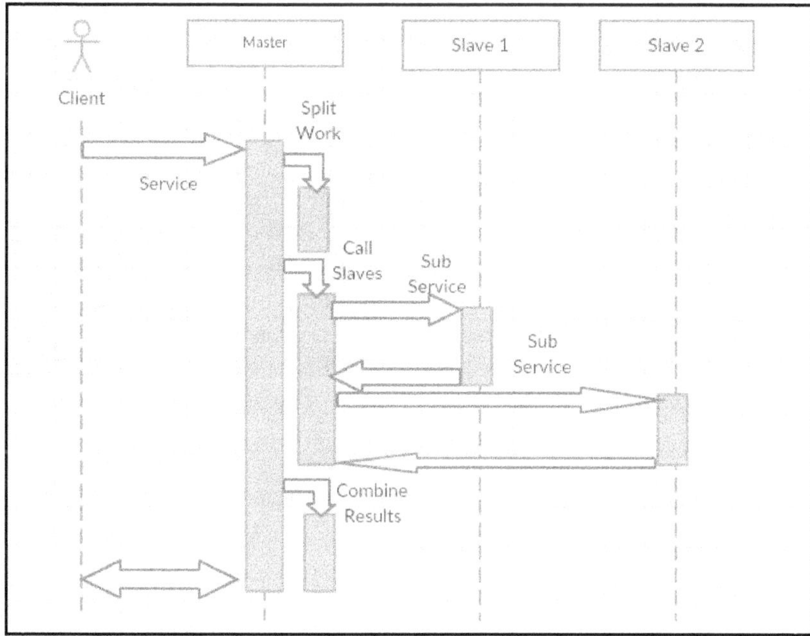

## Issues in the master-slave pattern

The master-slave pattern works based on the divide and conquer principle. In the working of this pattern, the coordination concept is separated from the actual work as all the slaves work in parallel. Hence, the slaves have not shared state and they work in isolation. Another issue in the master slave pattern is its latency. This could cause an issue in systems where the response time is very critical, for example, real-time systems. Moreover, this pattern can be applied to a specific problem only if it is decomposable.

One of the ways of implementing the master-slave pattern is through a single master thread, which creates multiple slave threads. Each of the slave threads performs a variant of the required computation and returns the result to the master. Once the computation is complete, the master thread accumulates the results and terminates the slave threads.

**Client-queue-client patterns**
This is also called passive queue architecture. This is a variant of the client-server architecture in which all components, including servers, are treated only as client systems. This is because servers were treated as passive queues by the clients which are present in the system and are used by the clients for transferring messages to other clients present in the network. This architecture could be treated as one of the early evolutions of peer-to-peer architecture, which is discussed in the next section and is obsolete today.

# Peer-to-peer patterns

Peer-to-peer architectural patterns belong to the category of symmetric client-server patterns. Symmetric in this context refers to the fact that there is no need for a strict division in terms of client, server, and so on in the network of systems. In a peer-to-peer pattern, a single system acts as both client and server. Each system, also called a peer, sends requests to other peers in the network and at the same time receives and services requests from other peers, which are part of the network. This is a great difference when compared to a traditional client server network where a client must only send a request and wait for the server to process.

In general, this pattern is typically used to implement a decentralized network of systems using distributed resources that are expected to perform specific function. The distributed resources could be either processing power, data, or bandwidth which may be used for any distributed computing task like Sharing of content, communication, and so on. The generic architecture of a peer-to-peer pattern is depicted in the following diagrams (however, some variations are possible, which we will discuss later):

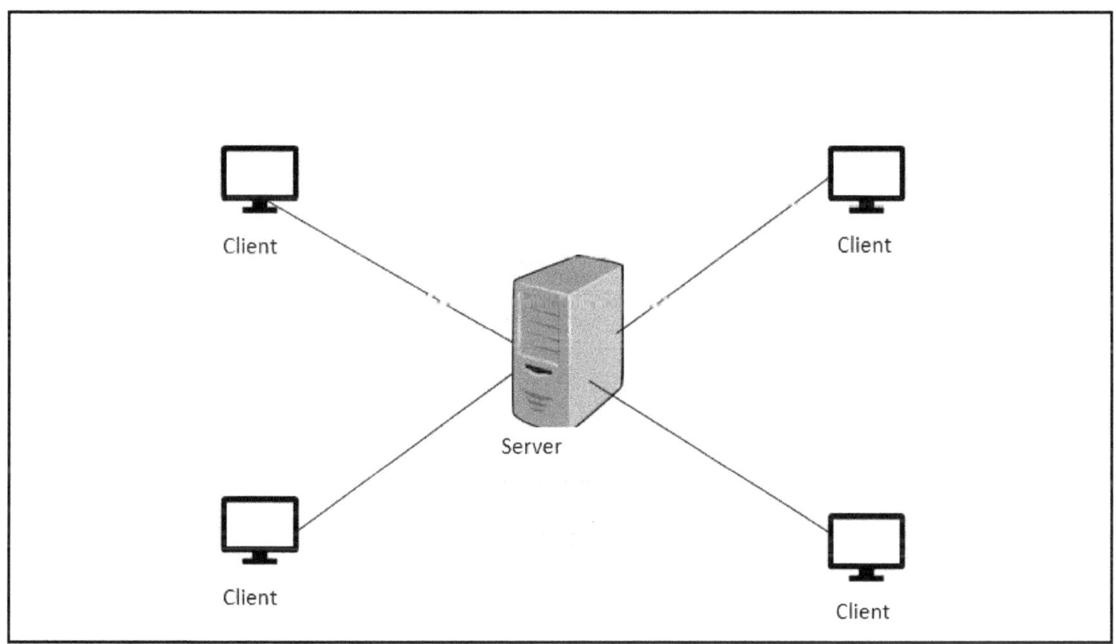

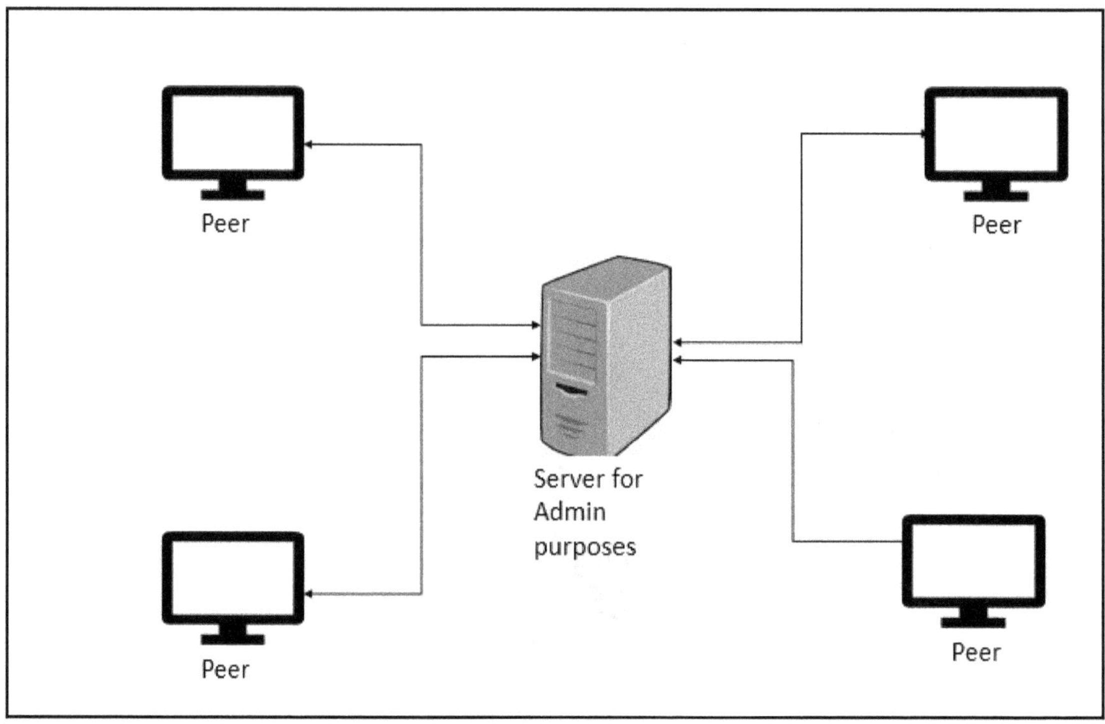


Peer-to-peer patterns are basically implemented in two ways:

- A pure peer-to-peer pattern
- A hybrid peer-to-peer pattern

In a pure peer-to-peer pattern, all the systems that are part of the network are peers and they act as both client and server. There is no dependency on a centralized server for managing the various operations. The main advantage of this architecture is its fault tolerance. Another advantage is the simplicity and ease of implementation as this architecture moves away from the concept of centralization. The downside of the architecture is that the network bandwidth gets overused due to flooding of requests from all the peers that are part of the network. Gnutella, a popular file sharing protocol, is implemented using the pure peer-to-peer pattern. The preceding diagram is an example of a pure peer-to-peer pattern.

In the hybrid peer-to-peer pattern, there exists a central server to perform certain administrative tasks that are required for the smooth functioning of P2P services. This can be better explained with the help of a simple example. Napster, a file sharing protocol is designed based on hybrid peer-to-peer pattern. In Napster, there is a server whose main functionality is to help peer systems which are part of the network search for files. Transfer of files between the systems are then initiated based on the search results which are returned by the server. In other words, only the catalogue of files is maintained in the server whereas the actual files which are present in the catalogue are scattered across all the peer systems which are part of the network. This pattern is less fault tolerant when compared to the pure peer-to-peer pattern because of the dependency on centralized server component. However, the main benefit of this pattern is that there is no unnecessary consumption of network resources and this architecture is highly scalable. The hybrid peer-to-peer pattern is depicted in the following diagram:

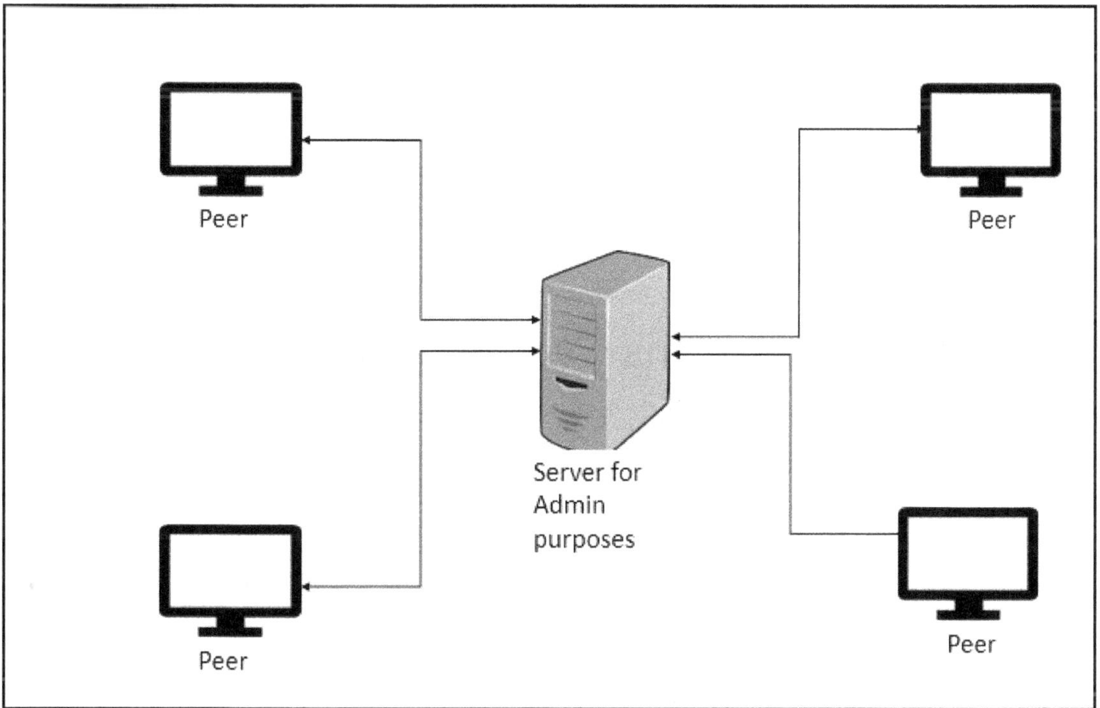

Though peer-to-peer patterns are very effective for applications like file sharing, they also provide options for a lot of security threats and malicious code to enter the network and get propagated to other peer systems which are part of the network. Hence, the TCP ports which are used by peer-to-peer application should be constantly monitored and kept under the surveillance of **intrusion detection systems / intrusion prevention systems**.

# Advantages of two-tier client-server patterns

Some of the key advantages of client server systems are as follows:

- **Security**: Data is stored centrally in the server. This offers greater control over the server and offers higher level of security than protecting the data that will be spread across a large number of client machines, which may involve offering special security mechanisms for each client machine.
- **Centralized access to data**: As most of the data is stored centrally in the server, it is much easier to do updates on the data. This is one of the simplest architectural styles.
- **Ease of maintenance**: In this architectural pattern, the client is unaware of details of the server and hence server maintenance activities like repair, upgrade, and so on do not affect the functioning of the client.

# Design considerations - when to use a two-tier client-server pattern?

Having read so much about the two-tier client-server pattern, the next question which arises in our mind is when to use two-tier client server pattern for a specific architectural design. The following points could be used as a guideline to decide that:

- If the application under consideration is server based and will support numerous client, then the two-tier client server pattern is a good choice.
- Some of the applications that work well with a two-tier client server pattern are web applications that are accessed through a web browser or for business process applications that are likely to be used throughout the organization.

- If you are looking at centralizing data operations like storage, backup, and other related administration tasks, even then a two-tier client server pattern is an ideal choice.

# Limitations of two-tier client-server patterns

The following are some of the main limitations of client-server patterns:

- **Limited extensibility, scalability, and reliability**: In most of the implementations, application data and business logic reside on the same central server. This aspect impacts the system extensibility, scalability, and reliability.
- **Excessive network bandwidth usage:** communication between and the client and the server consumes excessive bandwidth. Request and response data often need to be converted to a common format as they might have a different format of representation on the client side and the server side. This aspect also contributes to additional traffic.

To overcome these limitations of the two-tier client server pattern, three-tier/multi-tier client-server architecture was developed. Most of the applications of the present day, which are developed using the client-server architecture, are based on the three-tire/multi-tier architectural model, which is discussed in the next section.

Because of the slight difference in their architecture, three-tier and multi-tiered architectures are handled as separate topics in this chapter, though they may be referred to interchangeably in many other forums.

# Three-tier client-server architecture

The three tiers that are present in this architecture are as follows:

- The presentation tier
- The application or business logic tier
- Data tier

The diagram depicting the three-tier client-server architecture is as follows:

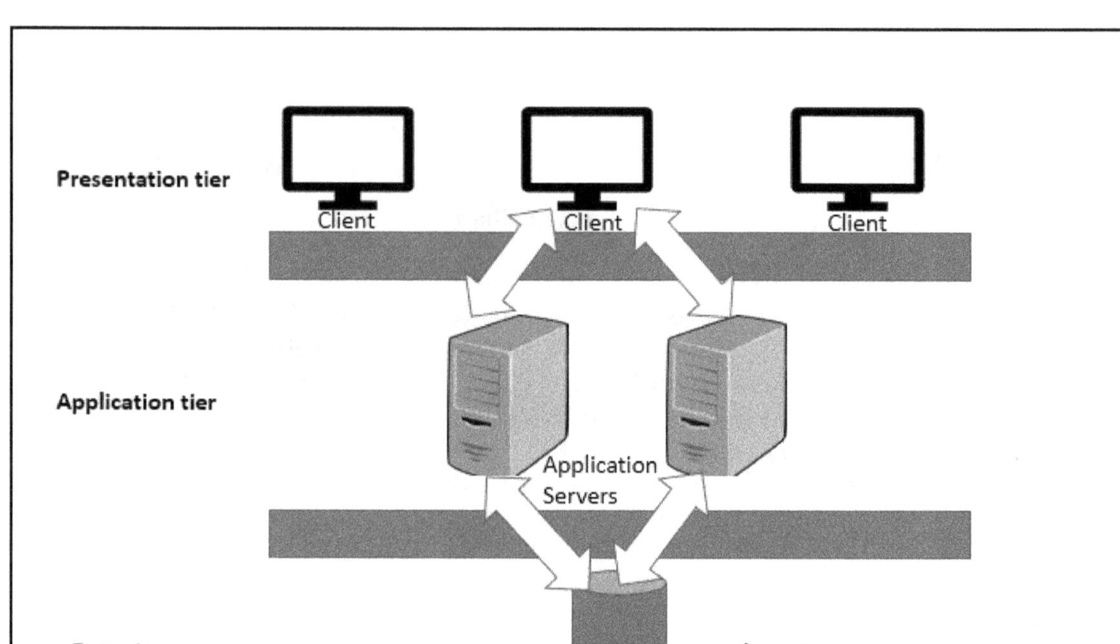


In a three-tier architecture, the different layers are developed and maintained as different modules, sometimes on different platforms as well. The following are the functions of each layer:

- **Presentation tier**: This is the first and topmost layer which is present in the application. This tier provides presentation services, that is presentation, of content to the end user through GUI. This tier can be accessed through any type of client device like desktop, laptop, tablet, mobile, thin client, and so on. For the content to the displayed to the user, the relevant web pages should be fetched by the web browser or other presentation component which is running in the client device. To present the content, it is essential for this tier to interact with the other tiers that are present preceding it.
- **Application tier**: This is the middle tier of this architecture. This is the tier in which the business logic of the application runs. Business logic is the set of rules that are required for running the application as per the guidelines laid down by the organization. The components of this tier typically run on one or more application servers.

- **Data tier**: This is the lowest tier of this architecture and is mainly concerned with the storage and retrieval of application data. The application data is typically stored in a database server, file server, or any other device or media that supports data access logic and provides the necessary steps to ensure that only the data is exposed without providing any access to the data storage and retrieval mechanisms. This is done by the data tier by providing an API to the application tier. The provision of this API ensures complete transparency to the data operations which are done in this tier without affecting the application tier. For example, updates or upgrades to the systems in this tier do not affect the application tier of this architecture.

Benefits of the three-tier architecture are as follows:

- **Scalability** and **flexibility**: The major advantage of this architecture is its scalability and flexibility. Each tier of this architecture is a modular component, that is, any kind of operations like changes or upgrades done to one tier does not affect or cause downtime to the other tiers. Less functionality performed by the client and no high-end configuration is required for client systems which are present in the presentation tier.
- **Increased security**: Splitting of tasks among the various tiers provides increased security to each tier.

Though three-tier architectural patterns offer several benefits, there are still limits on the scalability of the architecture when it comes to networks like internet which require massive scalability.

# Design considerations for using three-tier architecture

The following are some of the scenarios in which the three-tier architecture is a good choice:

- If you are developing an application with limited functionality/configuration for client systems. In this case, other components of the architecture like business logic and data logic can be distributed to other tiers.
- If you are in the process of developing an application to be deployed within an intranet where all the servers are located within a specific private network.
- If you are developing an internet application where there are no security constraints for deploying the business logic on the public networks of web or application servers.

A variant of the three-tier architectural pattern which offers massive scalability is the *n*-tier architectural pattern. In an *n*-tier architectural pattern, the total number of tiers is *n*, where *n* has a value greater than three in order to differentiate it from the three-tier architectural pattern. In *n*-tier architecture, the application tier (which is the middle tier) is split into many tiers. The distribution of application code and functions among the various tiers varies from one architectural design to another. The diagram of the *n*-tier architectural pattern is depicted as follows:

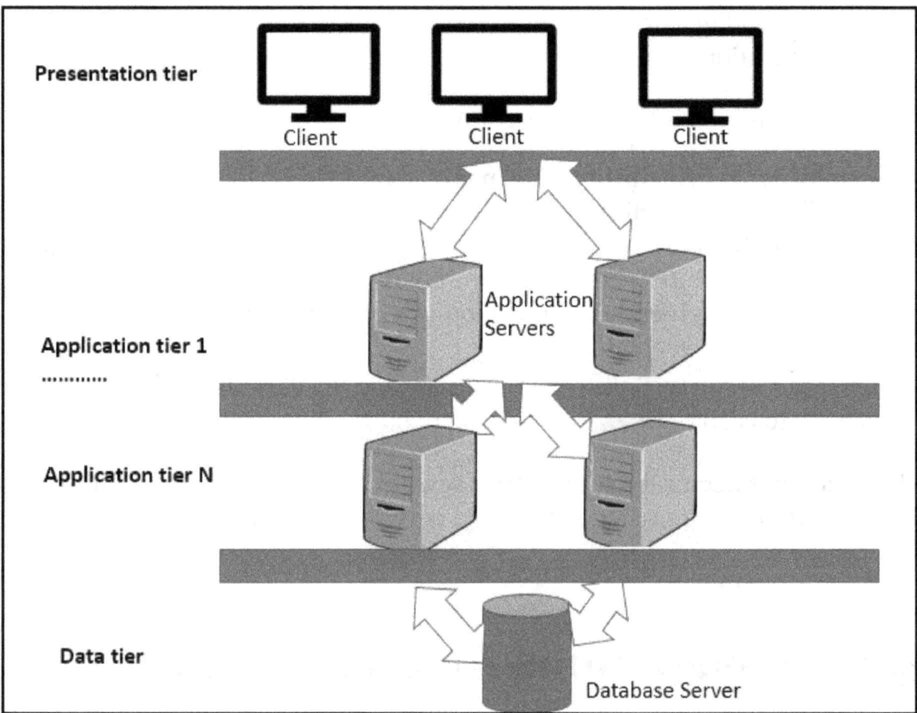

# Design considerations for *n*-tier architecture

The following are some of the scenarios in which *n*-tier architecture is a good choice:

- If you are architecting a system in which it is possible to split the application logic into smaller components that could be spread across several servers. This could lead to the design of multiple tiers in the application tier.
- If the system under consideration requires faster network communications, high reliability, and great performance, then *n*-tier has the capability to provide that as this architectural pattern is designed to reduce the overhead which is caused by network traffic.

# An example of *n*-tier architecture (shopping cart web application)

We can illustrate the working of an *n*-tier architecture with the help of an example of a shopping cart web application which is present in all e-commerce sites. The shopping cart web application is used by the e-commerce site user to complete the purchase of items through the e-commerce site.

Hence, the application should have several features which enable the user to do activities like the following:

- Adding selected items to the cart
- Changing the quantities of items in the cart
- Making payments

The client tier, which is present in the shopping cart application, interacts with the end user through a GUI. The client tier also interacts with the application that runs in the application servers present in multiple tiers. Since the shopping cart is a web application, the client tier contains the web browser. The presentation tier present in the shopping cart application displays information related to the services like browsing merchandise, buying them, adding them to the shopping cart, and so on. The presentation tier communicates with other tiers by sending results to the client tier and all other tiers which are present in the network.

The presentation tier also makes calls to database stored procedures and web services. All these activities are done with the objective of providing a quick response time to the end user. The presentation tier plays a vital role by acting as a glue which binds the entire shopping cart application together by allowing the functions present in different tiers to communicate with each other and display the outputs to the end user through the web browser.

In this *n*-tier architecture, the business logic which is required for processing activities like calculation of shipping cost and so on are pulled from the application tier to the presentation tier. The application tier also acts as the integration layer and allows the applications to communicate seamlessly with both the data tier and the presentation tier. The last tier which is the data tier is used to maintain data. This layer typically contains database servers. This layer maintains data independent from the application server and the business logic. This approach provides enhanced scalability and performance to the data tier.

# The distributed client-server architecture

The *n*-tier client-server architecture used for the shopping cart web application, which is discussed in the earlier section, is an ideal example of a distributed client-server architecture. Distributed architectures typically have some kind of backend host components (such as Mainframe, Database server, and so on), an intelligent client in the frontend, and multiple agents in the middle, which takes care of all activities pertaining to transactions like transaction processing, security, handling messages, and so on, and a network for communication.

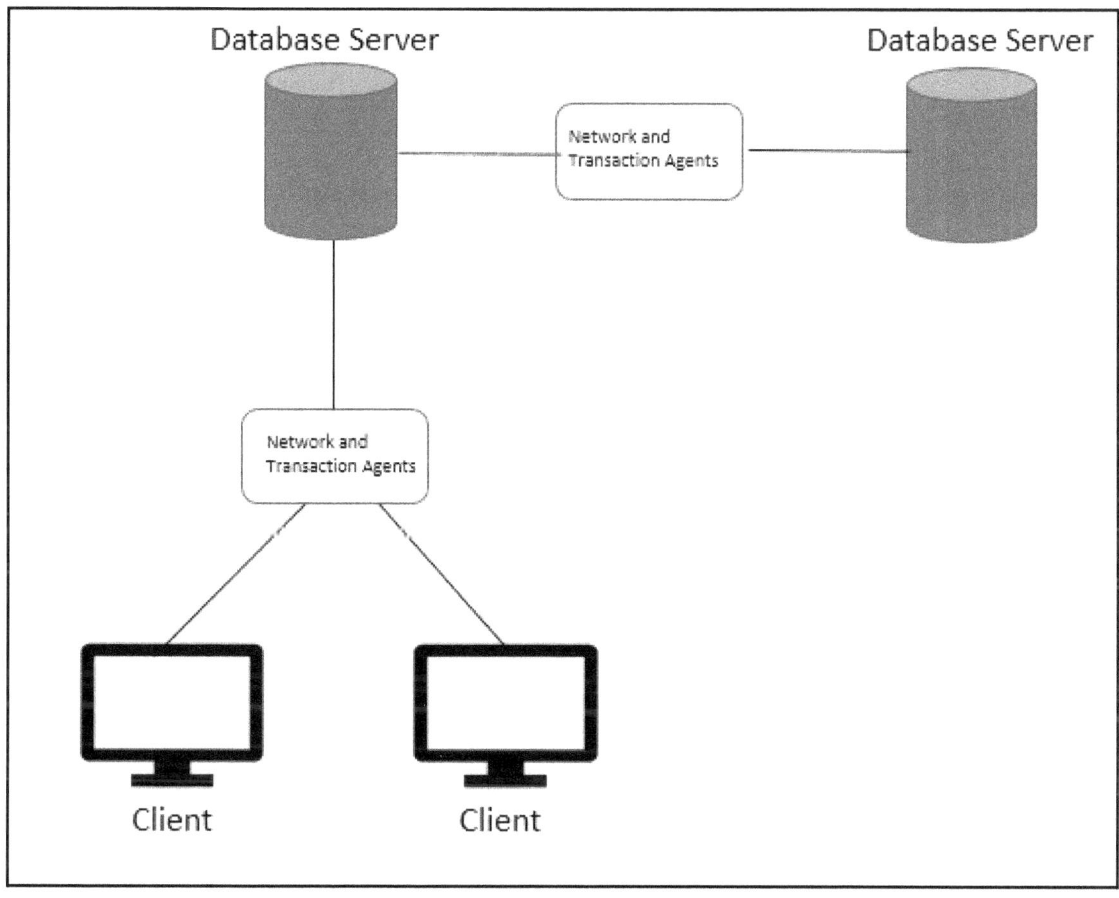


Some of the key concepts associated with distributed architectures are as follows:

- **Transaction processing**: Transaction processing is the automated processing of transactions in order to update a shared database. A transaction processing application in general will have many users who are concurrently interacting with the system in order to process business transactions on a shared database.
- **Transaction processing monitor** (**TP monitor**): The main task of the TP monitor is to manage the flow of transactions through a client server system efficiently. The TP monitor also works to ensure that simultaneous transactions which are happening on a shared database do not cause any inconsistency to the data which is present in the database.

TP monitors also provide the following functions:

- They help in setting up back and forth connections between client and server components
- They provide services that help in transaction-tracking, load balancing, and the capability to restart servers and the queues present in them automatically

# Motivation for development of web application patterns

Most of the web applications are highly interactive in nature. This means that when there is a change to the data, it should be reflected in the UI instantaneously without any further delay. To add on to this scenario, different users of the application may demand outputs in various formats like excel sheets, bar charts, pie charts, dashboards, and so on, as depicted in the following diagram:

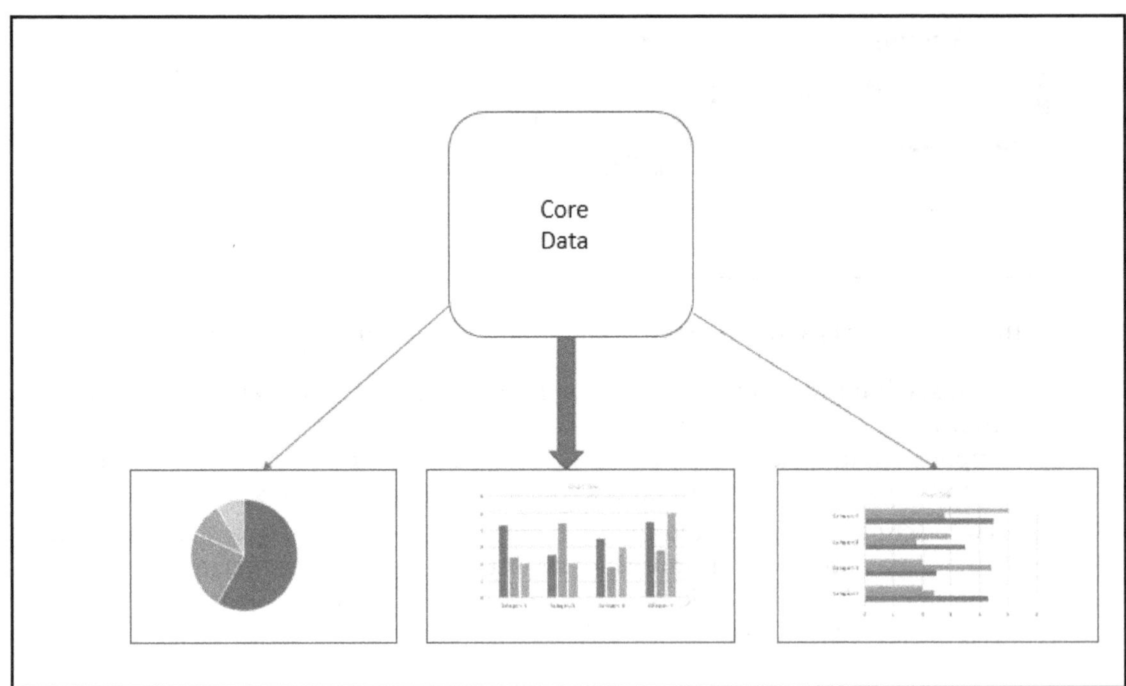

When there is a change in the functionality of a specific application, the user interface of the application should also be able to reflect the changes with the addition of new options like menus, dropdowns, and so on. This emphasizes the fact that user interfaces of web applications are always subjected to series of change requests. These **user interfaces** (**UIs**) change requests can happen in various circumstances, as follows:

- A request from the end user/customer for a change in the UI feature for various reasons like ease of use, adaptability, and so on
- Porting of a system from one platform to another
- Upgrades of system to new versions
- Changes to database design

From this, we can infer that user interfaces are always a target for changes. Different users of an application place different types of conflicting requirements on the user interface in order to make their operations easy. For example, an executive who uses a form-based interface for data entry may need more ease of use in the form based interface, whereas an administrator who is in charge of reporting may require more feature addition to the reporting interface. All this warrants a user interface where the design is flexible enough to accommodate all types of UI paradigms. It is impossible to build a system with this kind of flexibility if the UI is tightly tied to the functional core of the application. In such a scenario, it becomes necessary to develop and maintain several types of software applications, one for each type of user interface. The following are the main aspects that need to be kept in mind for the design of design patterns for web applications:

- It should be possible to represent the same information in different formats in different windows, for example, in one window as a pie chart, in another window as an excel sheet, and so on
- It should be possible to change the UI easily even at runtime
- It should be possible to provide various look and feel standards and changes to the user interface should not imply changes to the application code

All these factors are the motivation for the design of the **model view controller** (**MVC**) pattern, which is predominantly used for the design and development of mobile and web applications. The following are the main components of the MVC architectural pattern:

- **Model**: The function of the model component of MVC is to encapsulate core data and functionality. The model component has the capability to function independently, irrespective of output representations and input behavior. In design terms, the model essentially represents a set of classes which are used to depict the business logic.
- **View**: The function of the view component is to display information to the end user. The view component gets the data to be displayed from the model. A model can have any number of views depending on the requirements of the application. In design terms, the view essentially depicts the UI components such as HTML, jQuery, and so on.
- **Controller**: Each view is associated with a controller. Controllers get inputs, usually in the form of events from the user. The events could be received in the form of mouse clicks, keystrokes from the keyboard, and so on. These event are converted to service requests and are passed on to the model or the view. The controller is the only component through which the user interacts with the system.

The separation of model, view, and controller components provide flexibility by allowing multiple views of the same model. In case the user changes, the model data using the controller component of one view, all other views which use the same data should be updated immediately to reflect the new changes. This is taken care of by the model by notifying all the views whenever its data changes. The view in turn takes the updated data from the model and updates all relevant views. All these sequences of actions necessitate the presence of a change propagation mechanism in the MVC model. This change in the propagation mechanism is explained in the next section.

# Workings of the MVC pattern

The model component exports procedures for application-specific processing. These procedures are called by the controller components in response to inputs received from the user. The model component also provides functions that can be used by the view component to access its data.

View components are used for presenting information to the end user. There may be different views for providing information in different ways as per the requirements of users. Each view is associated with an update procedure that is activated by the change propagation mechanism. The change propagation mechanism works by maintaining a registry of all the dependent components that are present within the model. All the related views and controllers that will be impacted by changes to these components also register their need so that they are kept informed of all the changes. Any change in model state in turn triggers the change-propagation mechanism. With the help of the update procedure, the view component retrieves the most updated data values from the model and displays them on the user interface screens.

The controller component accepts user input in the form of events. The format in which this event data is delivered to the controller is dependent on the user interface platform. But in general, each controller executes an event-handling procedure that is associated with an event. The overall working of the MVC pattern is depicted in the graphic which is given here:

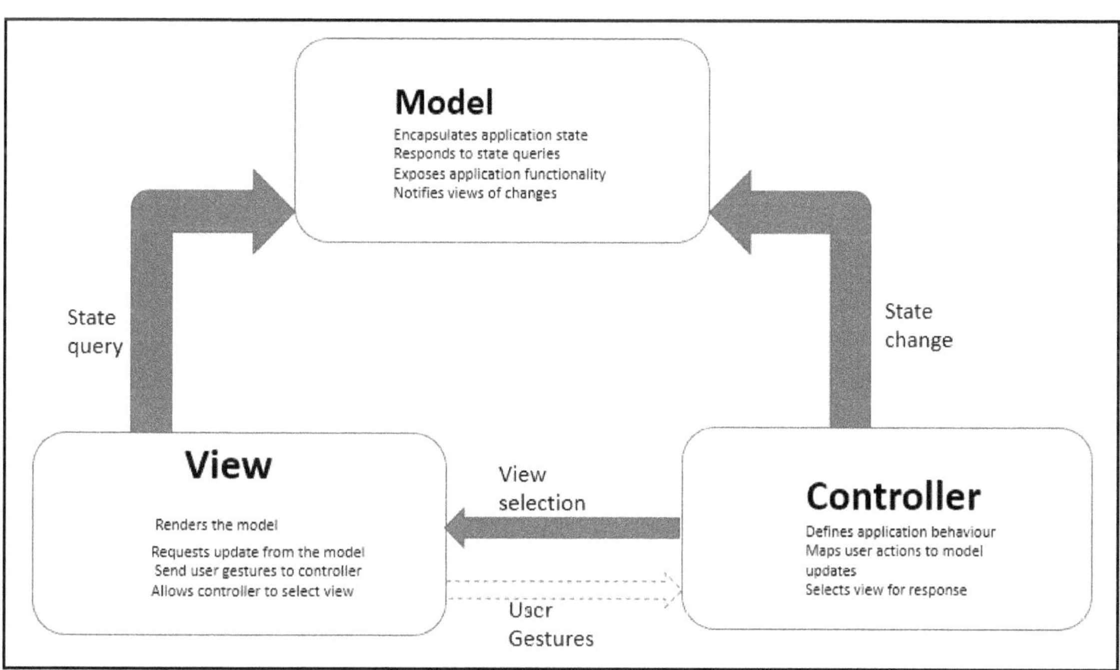


In the next section, we will discuss a popular programming framework which is developed using the MVC pattern.

# The ASP.Net framework

In ASP.Net, the patterns for the view component and the controller component are well-defined. Only the pattern for the model component is left to be designed by the developer as per the specific application requirements.

**View**: The files that handle the responsibilities associated with the view component are ASPX and ASCX. In this design, the view object typically inherits from the controller object.

**Controller**: The responsibilities of the controller component are split among two components. The generation and passing of events is done by the framework and, to be more specific, is done by the Page and Control classes. The event handling is taken care of by the code-behind class.

**Model**: ASP.NET does not necessarily require a model. It is left to the choice of the developer whether to create a model class, or to forgo it. In case a model is not used, the event handlers in the controller can be used to perform any calculations and also ensure data persistence.

# The model view presenter (MVP) pattern

The MVP pattern is a variant of MVC pattern and is mainly used for the development of user interfaces for web applications. It was mainly designed to make it easier to perform automated unit testing. The graphic given here depicts the architecture of the MVP pattern:

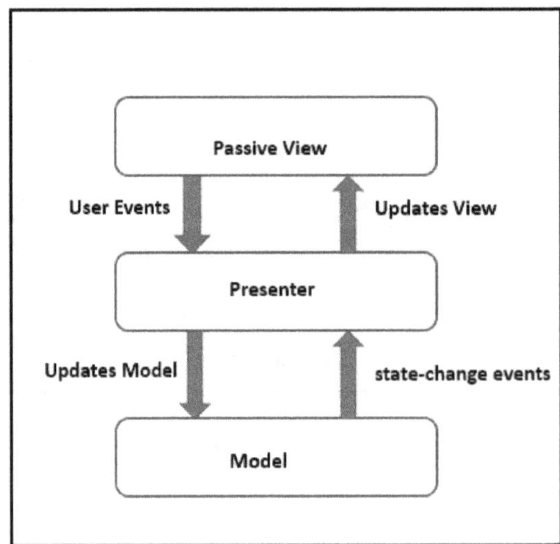

The various components of the MVP pattern are as follows:

- **Model**: This component specifies the data to be displayed/sent from or to the user interface.
- **View**: The presentation logic lies in the Presenter component. It acts on both the model and the view components. It is responsible for fetching data from the model, applying appropriate logic, and sending it back for display in the view. When compared to the view and controller components in the MVC model, the view and presenter components present in the MVP pattern are fully decoupled from each other and they communicate by means of an interface.
- **Presenter**: The view component just acts as a passive interface. It displays data from the model and sends user inputs and commands to the presenter component. These user inputs and commands will be used to perform operations on the data.

The following are some of the key considerations about the MVP pattern:

- The end user interacts only with the View
- One View component is mapped only to one Presenter component
- View references Presenter component but it has no reference to Model component
- The pattern facilitates two way communication between the View component and the Presenter component

Some of the common applications that use this pattern are ASP.Net forms and Windows forms.

# The model-view-viewmodel (MVVM) pattern

MVVM is a popular pattern used for developing reusable and easily testable web applications. MVVM is a modern variant of MVC and the core objective is to have true separation between the Model and the View components. The main components of the pattern are the following:

- Model
- View
- ViewModel

The layered architecture of the pattern is depicted in the following diagram:

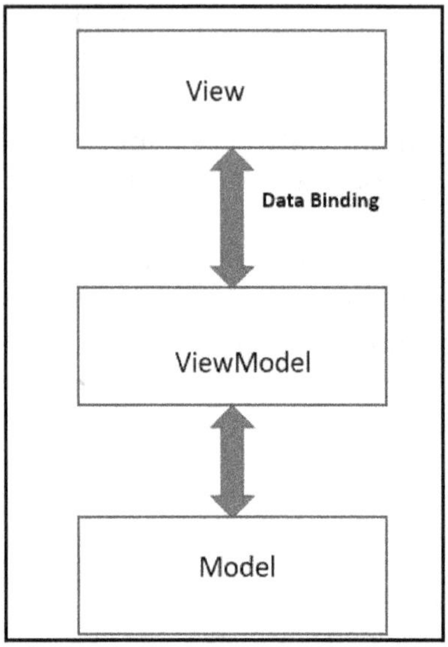

The various components of the MVVM pattern are as follows:

**Model**: This component represents business logic and data. This means that the business logic that specifies how the data should be manipulated is present in the Model component.

**View**: This component represents the UI components and will essentially contain UI elements such as CSS, HTML, and so on. It is only responsible for representing the data and does not perform any manipulations on data. However, unlike MVM, the View in MVVM is an active component and contains behaviors, events, and data-bindings that require information about the underlying model and viewModel components.

**ViewModel**: The ViewModel is a very important component of the architecture as it helps in presentation separation, that is, it helps to keep the view separate from the model and, at the same time, acts as a controller that supports interaction and coordination between the View and the model components. The ViewModel component also contains commands and methods that help maintain the state of the view and help to manipulate the Model as per the actions, which are performed on the view. The ViewModel component also helps to trigger events in the view component itself.

## Key advantages of the MVVM pattern

The following are the key advantages of using the MVVM pattern for design:

- **Maintainability**: In this pattern, the clear separation of the different pieces of code makes it easier to maintain the code and also ensures quick releases using the code.
- **Testability**: In this pattern, the different pieces of code are very granular and are a key away from the core functional logic. This makes unit testing very easy.
- **Extensibility**: The granular pieces of code facilitate the reuse of code and also allows quick modification of code snippets.

## Design considerations for using the MVVM pattern

The MVVM pattern is a right choice for design web applications that require the following aspects:

- Thorough unit testing of various components
- Development of applications using the concept of reusable code and development of applications which can generate reusable snippets of code
- Flexibility to change the user interface without changing the code base

In the next section, we will discuss a sample framework that is built using the MVVM pattern.

## Prism

Prism is a framework that is built using the MVVM pattern. It helps in the design and development of flexible and easy to maintain **Windows presentation foundation** (**WPF**) desktop applications. It also helps to build rich internet applications using the Microsoft Silverlight Browser plugin. The following are the key features of the Prism framework:

- It uses architectural pattern that supports important design concepts such as separation of concerns and loosely coupled components.
- Prism helps in the design of code snippets/components that can be easily integrated to form an application. Applications of this type which are formed by integrating components are called composite applications.

The following are some of the important features of Prism:

- Support for the MVVM pattern, which in turn provides a bindable base class.
- It has a flexible ViewModelLocator, which allows the View and ViewModel component to be hooked up in a loosely coupled way. It provides full support for the development of modular applications as it has several loosely coupled class libraries. These libraries can be brought together at runtime in the form of an application for the end user. The code base still remains decoupled.
- Supports a rich set of navigation features that supports features like forward navigation, backward navigation, and so on. The navigation stack of prism allows ViewModels to be part of the navigation process directly.
- Prism supports the concept of Pub/Sub events. These refer to a mechanism of loosely coupled events where the publisher and subscriber components can communicate with the help of events. It is not necessary that the publisher or subscriber components should have explicit references or the same lifetimes.

# Design patterns for web application development

Apart from the MVC, MVP, and MVVM architectural patterns, which were discussed in the previous sections, there are several design patterns that are used for the design of applications along with these patterns. In this section, we will discuss some of the commonly used design patterns for web application design. These patterns and their functionalities are described in the following table:

| **Pattern name** | **Functionality** |
|---|---|
| **Interpreter design pattern** | This pattern is widely used in the development of menus for applications like editors and Integrated Development Environments (IDEs). This pattern works by interpreting instructions that are written in the form of a language grammar or as notations. This pattern involves the implementation of an expression interface, which is used to interpret a given context. |

| | |
|---|---|
| **Mediator design pattern** | The key feature of this pattern is that it allows objects to interact with each other without knowing their structure. This is made possible by defining an object by encapsulating how they interact with other objects. This feature also helps in easy maintainability and the reuse of code. This pattern is also widely used for developing menus for applications like editor and IDE. |
| **Memento design pattern** | The key feature of this pattern is that it helps to capture the present state of an object and store it as is so that it can be used again at a later point in time when needed without actually breaking the rules associated with object encapsulation. |
| **Observer design pattern** | This pattern is used in scenarios where there exists a one to many relationship between objects. In such scenarios, if an object is modified, it becomes necessary to notify its dependent objects about the changes. That is the main motivation for the use of observer design pattern. This pattern allows a single object called subject to notify its state changes to all other observer objects that are dependent on it. |
| **State design pattern** | This pattern is used in scenarios where there exists a one to many relationship between objects. In such scenarios, if an object is modified, it becomes necessary to notify its dependent objects about the changes. This pattern is primarily used in situations where it is necessary to alter the behaviour of an object when there is a change in its internal state. This pattern works by creating an object to represent various states and an associated context object whose behaviour changes as per the state changes of the created object. |
| **Strategy design pattern** | This pattern provides flexibility to a client to choose any specific algorithm from a group of algorithms at runtime. It also provides a simple way for the client to access the algorithm. This pattern works by removing an algorithm from its host class and placing it in a separate class. This will help in the prevention of code-related issues that will arise if the algorithm is present in the host class. |
| **Template method design pattern** | This pattern provides the feature to define basic steps of algorithm execution while allowing specific execution steps to be changed. This is very similar to the Strategy design pattern; the only difference is that it allows modification of certain algorithm steps instead of the entire algorithm. |

| | |
|---|---|
| **Visitor design pattern** | This pattern provides flexibility to create and perform new operations on a set of objects without altering the structure of the object and its associated classes. This pattern allows the loose coupling of components and hence new operations can be done on them without altering the existing object structure. |
| **Bridge pattern** | This pattern provides the flexibility to separate an abstraction from its implementation. This allows both of them to be modified independently. The separation of abstraction from implementation is done by means of an interface that provides a bridge between the abstraction class and implementer class. This separation also makes the implementer class functionality independent of the abstraction class functionality. |
| **Composite pattern** | This pattern provides the flexibility to treat a group of objects and a single object in the same manner. The composite pattern arranges objects in the form of a tree structure to represent part as well as whole hierarchies. |
| **Factory method design pattern** | This pattern provides the flexibility to create an object without exposing its creation logic. In this pattern, an interface is used for creating an object. The subclass decides which class needs to be instantiated. The creation of an object is done only as and when it is required. |
| **Builder design pattern** | This pattern allows us to build a complex object by using a step by step approach. A specialized interface called the Builder interface specifies the steps that are required to build the final object. This Builder interface is independent of the objects creation process. A class known as Director controls the object creation process. Another speciality of this pattern is that it specifies a way to separate an object from its construction. The same construction method can be used to create multiple representations of the same object. |
| **Adapter pattern** | This pattern is used when it is required to provide a bridge between two incompatible interfaces. This pattern provides a single class called adapter that facilitates communication between two independent or incompatible interfaces.<br>**For example:** A card reader acts as an adapter for the memory card present in the laptop. This is done by plugging in the memory card into the card reader. The card reader is then plugged into the laptop so that the memory card can be read through the laptop. |

# The front controller pattern

Another architectural pattern that is popular in web application development is the front controller pattern. This pattern ensures that there is only one point of entry for all incoming requests. A single piece of code called the controller handles all the incoming requests and then delegates the processing of each request to other application objects, which are present in the system. This core feature of the pattern helps the web application developers by providing necessary flexibility using the reuse of code. The architecture of the front controller pattern is depicted in the following graphic:

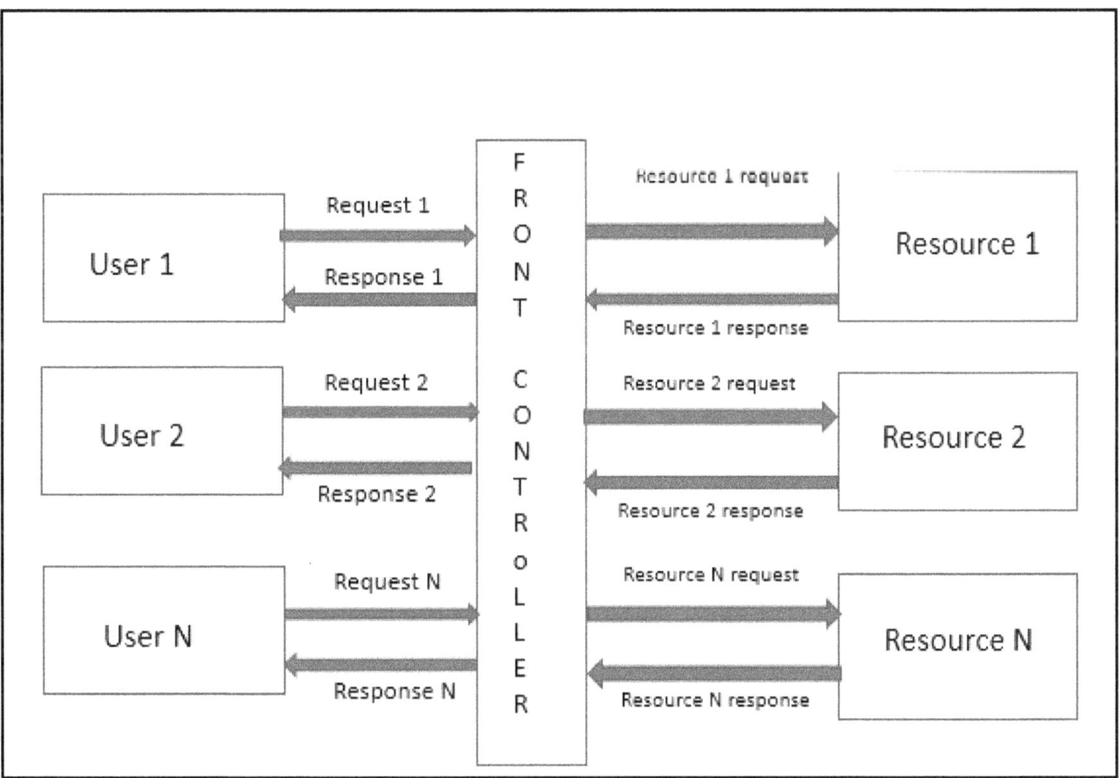


The following are the different components of this pattern:

- **Front controller**: This component handles all types of incoming requests for the application

- **Dispatcher**: This component is used to dispatch a request to a specific handler for further processing
- **Views**: These correspond to the objects for which the requests are made

In the next section, we will discuss a popular framework that is developed using the front controller pattern.

# Spring framework

Spring, a very popular framework for web application development, follows two architectural patterns for its design: the front controller pattern and the MVC pattern. The architecture is depicted in the following graphic:

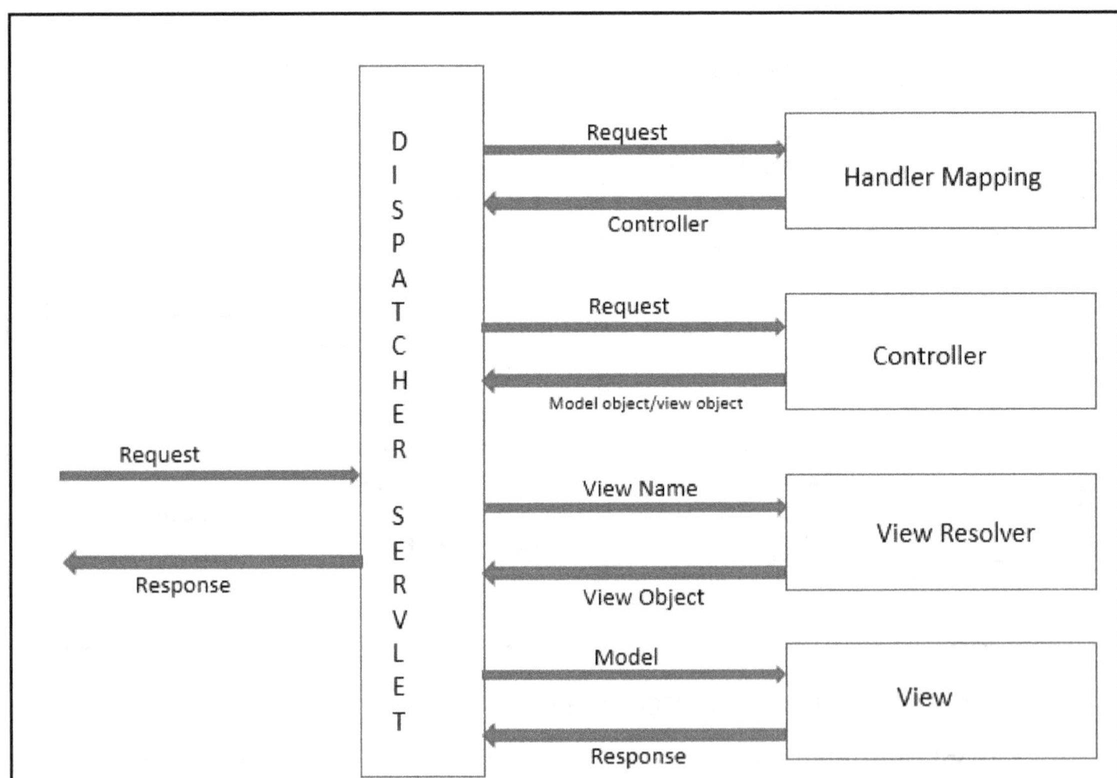

The Dispatcher Servlet component is the single servlet that functions as the front controller and handles all incoming requests. The Dispatcher Servlet then calls Handler Mapping in order to find an object that could service the request. The request is then given to the controller object so that the Dispatcher becomes free to perform functions associated with the fulfilment of business logic as per the user's request. The controller object returns an encapsulated object that contains the model object and view object. This is represented by the ModelandView class. If the ModelandView contains the logical name of the view, the Dispatcher Servlet calls the View Resolver to get details of the actual view object from its logical name. The Dispatcher Servlet then gives the model object to the view object so that it can be displayed to the end user.

# Summary

In this chapter, we started the discussion with a two-tier client-server pattern. This is one of the earliest and oldest client-server patterns. With the growth of the information technology industry, this two-tier client server pattern was not sufficient to meet the infrastructure requirements. This led to the evolution of the three-tier client-server pattern followed by *n*-tier client-server pattern. Some other variants of the client-server pattern like the master-slave pattern, peer-to-peer pattern, and so on were also discussed in this chapter. The applications and the design considerations for each type of pattern was also discussed in this chapter.

Web application development, which caught steam later could not use client-server architecture because of its inherent limitations. This led to the evolution of some patterns that were custom-made for the development of web applications. These patterns needed the basic flexibility to be able to change the UI without altering the code base. The second half of this chapter dealt mainly with these patterns. The main patterns that were discussed in this part were MVC, MVP, MVVM, and the front controller.

Some of the common design patterns that are used along with these patterns were also discussed in this chapter.

Additional reference for this chapter: `http://www.dotnettricks.com/learn/designpatterns/adapter-design-pattern-dotnet`

# 3
# Object-Oriented Software Engineering Patterns

Object-oriented (OO) concepts in software engineering are not new, and let's start this chapter with a brief introduction before we dive into OO design patterns. While you are reading this chapter, look around you; whatever you see is an object: the book, bookshelves, reading lamp, table, chair, and so on. Everything around you can be imagined as an object, and all of them share two primary characteristics, as follows:

- State
- Behavior

A reading lamp has *off and on* as states, and *turn on and turn off* as behaviors. Objects may also have many states and many behaviors, sometimes even other objects as well.

**Object-oriented design** (**OOD**) intends to provide modularity, abstraction (information hiding), code reuse, and pluggable (plug and play) and easy code debug.

Grady Booch defined OOD in his book titled *Object Oriented Analysis and Design with Application* as follows:

> *"OOD is a method of design encompassing the process of object-oriented decomposition and a notation for depicting both logical and physical as well as static and dynamic models of the system under design."*

This chapter covers the following elements of OOD:

- Essential and non-essential elements of OOD
- Primary characteristics of OOD
- Core principles of OOD
- Most common design patterns of OOD
- Cross-reference of OO design patterns

# Key elements of OOD

There are four key elements of OOD. They are as follows:

- **Abstraction**: Hiding the complexity and low-level implementation details of internals.
  For instance, you see electrical switch buttons that can toggle on and off, but how it is achieving on and off is not shown to outside world, and in fact, it is not necessary for the common users.
- **Encapsulation**: Bundling of the data with the methods that operate on that data, preventing accidental or unauthorized access to the data.
  For example, switching off function should turn only the targeted element off, say a reading lamp, and it should not affect any other electrical functions that are part of the same electrical system.
- **Modularization**: The process of decomposing and making it as modules to reduce the complexity of the overall program/function.
  For example, switch off and on is a common functionality of an electrical system. Switching a reading lamp on and off may be a separate module and decoupled from other complex functions such as switching off washing machine and AC.
- **Hierarchy**: It is ordering of abstraction and hierarchy of an interrelated system with other subsystems. Those subsystems might own other subsystems as well, so hierarchy helps reach the smallest possible level of components in a given system.

# Additional elements of OOD

There are three additional elements of OOD. They are as follows:

- **Typing**: Characterization of a set of items. A Class (in object-oriented programming) is a distinct type. It has two subtypes. They are as follows:
    - Strong Typing
    - Weak Typing
- **Concurrency**: Operating system allows Performing multiple tasks or process simultaneously.
- **Persistence**: Class or object occupies space and exists for a particular time.

# Design principles

This chapter and the following sections cover object-oriented design principles, its characteristics, and the design patterns in detail. Each pattern section covers its need, design considerations, and best practices so that readers get the idea of patterns and its applications.

Let's start with a core principle usually referred to as an acronym "SOLID," in detail.

# Single responsibility principle (SRP) – SOLID

In object-oriented programming style, the *single responsibility* enforces that each class should represent one and only one responsibility and so if it needs to undergo changes, that should be for only one reason, that is, a class should have one and only one reason to change.

When we design a class or refactor a class and if it needs more than one reason to change, split the functionality into as many parts as there are classes and so, each class represents only one responsibility.

Responsibility in this context is any changes to the function/business rules that causes the class to change; any changes to the connected database schema, user interfaces, report format, or any other system should not force that class also to change:

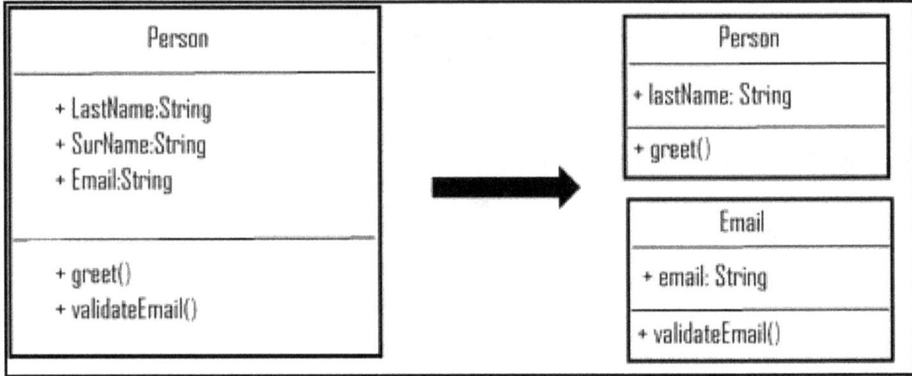


The preceding class diagram depicts a **Person** class having two responsibilities: one responsibility is to greet the user with their last name or surname, and another responsibility is to validate the email. If we need to apply SRP on the **Person** class, we can separate it into two; **Person** has a method greet, and **Email** has email validation.

The SRP applies not only at the class level, but also on methods, packages, and the modules.

# Open and close principle – SOLID

The open and close principle of OO programming suggests that the OO software entities such as classes, methods or functions, and modules, should be open for extensions, but closed for any modifications.

Imagine a class that you never need to change, and any new functionality gets added only by adding new methods or subclasses, or by reusing the existing code, and so we can prevent any new defects to the existing code or functionality.

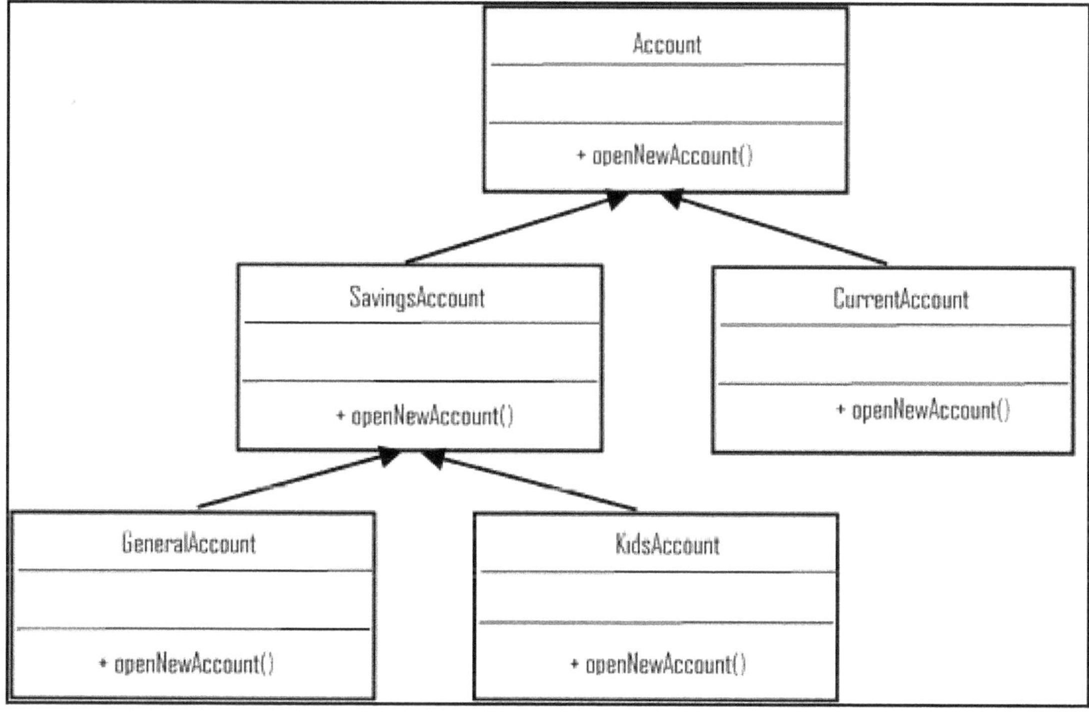


The preceding class diagram shows the application of the open and close principle on the **Account** class and its subclasses. The account can be any type, savings or current. A **SavingsAccount** may categorize as **GeneralAccount**, **KidsAccount**, and so on, so we can enforce that Account and other subclasses are available for Enhancements but closed for modifications.

The open and close principle brings benefits of no changes to the code, no introduction of any new defects but perhaps a disadvantage that the existing defects never get addressed as well.

# Liskov substitution principle (LSP) – SOLID

This principle states that any of the child classes should not break the parent class's type definitions or, in other words, derived classes should be substitutable for their base classes.

Let's first understand the violation of substitution principle, and then we see how we can resolve the same by taking our earlier example of account classes as LSP is a prime enabler of OCP:

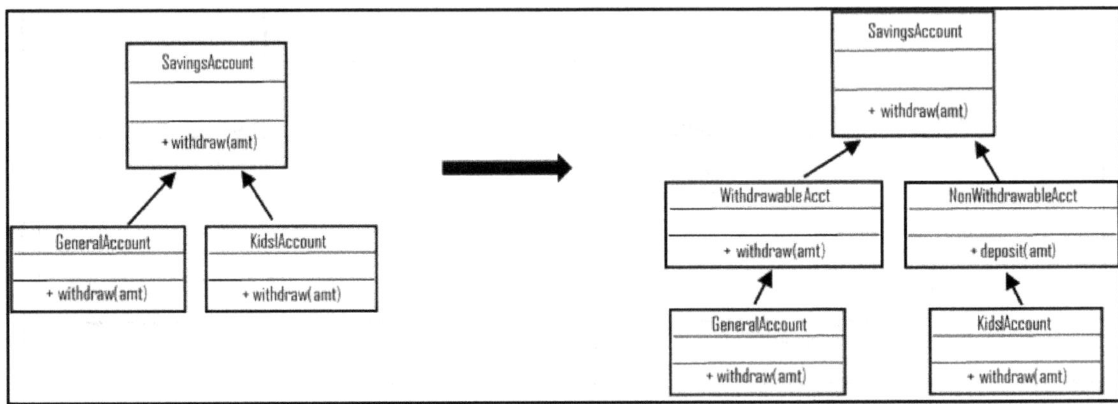


Let's assume that withdrawal from kids account is not allowed, unlike general account. As you see in the preceding class diagram, a *withdraw* method in the kids account class is a breach of LSP, so by introducing other withdrawable and non-withdrawable classes inherited from **SavingsAccount** class to handle non-withdrawable behavior, we can get rid of the breach and the subclass does not change the base class behavior:

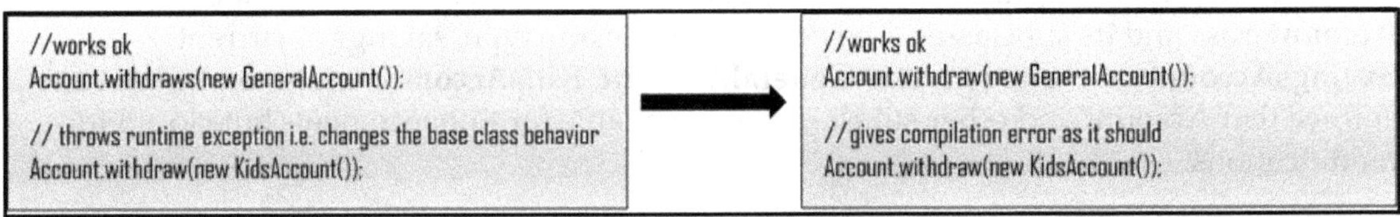


So, the behavior of **SavingsAccount** is preserved while inheriting it for **KidsAccount**. The preceding code snippet proves the same.

# Interface segregation principle (ISP) – SOLID

Imagine that you are implementing an interface of a class pets, and the compiler complains about the non-inclusion of bark method in your **Cat** class; strange, isn't it?

ISP suggests a*ny interface of a class should not force the clients to include any unrequired methods by that client*; in our example, **Cat** does not need to implement bark method, and it is exclusive to **Dog** class:

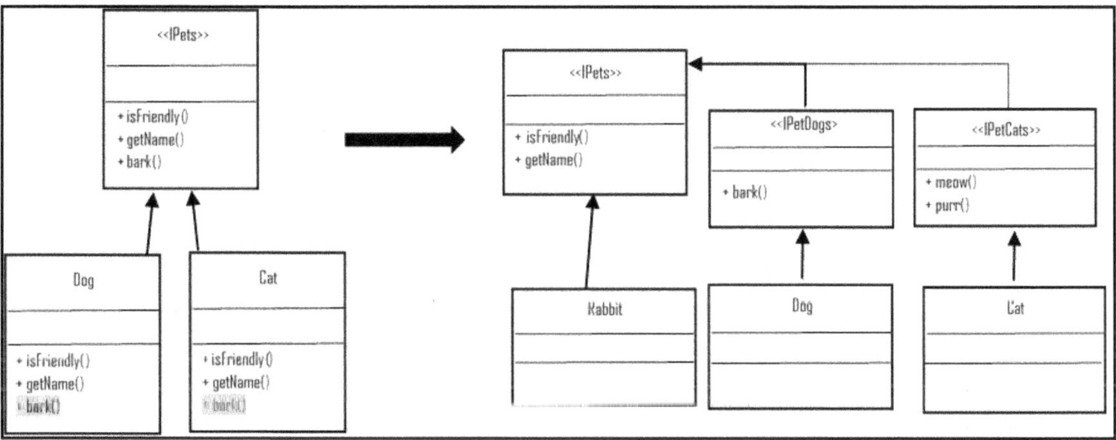


The preceding diagram depicts ISP violation and how to get rid of the same by splitting the **<<IPets>>** interface to represent the **Cat** and **Dog** interface explicitly.

# Dependency inversion principle (DIP) – SOLID

The DIP enforces two points, as listed:

- Any higher-level modules should not depend on lower-level modules, and both should depend on abstract modules
- Abstraction of modules should not depend on its implementation or details, but the implementation should depend on abstraction

Please refer to the earlier *Interface segregation principle (ISP) – SOLID* section, and the example classes (Figure 3.5) Pets classes and its abstract classes. **Dog** and **Cat** depend on abstractions (interface), and any changes to any of the underlying implementation do not impact any other implementations.

# Other common design principles

Other common principles are as follows; however, detailing of each principle is not in the scope of this chapter, and we request you to refer to other materials if you need to read more information about those principles:

- Encapsulate
- Always encapsulate the code that you think may change sooner or later
- Composition over inheritance
- In some cases, you may need the class behavior to change during runtime, and those cases favor composition over inheritance
- Program for interface (not for the implementation)
- Bring flexibility to the code and can work with any new implementation
- **General responsibility assignment software patterns** (**GRASP**)
- Guides in assigning responsibilities to collaborate objects
- **Don't repeat yourself** (**DRY**)
- Avoid duplicate codes by proper abstraction of the common codes into one place
- **Single layer abstraction principle** (**SLAP**)
- Every line in a method should be on the same level of abstraction

# OO design patterns

Object-oriented design patterns solve many common software design problems, as follows, that architects come across every day:

- Finding appropriate objects
- Determining object granularity
- Specifying object interfaces
- Specifying object implementations
- Programming to an interface, not an implementation
- Putting the reuse mechanism to work

We will touch upon some of the common problems and how design patterns solve the mentioned glitches in this section and cover OO design patterns in detail.

We can categorize the patterns into three types: creational, structural, and behavioral. Refer to the table at the end of this chapter, which depicts the patterns and its categories as a simple reference before we move ahead with the details.

# Creational design patterns

The creational patterns intend to advocate a better way of creating objects or classes, and its primary focuses are as follows:

- Abstracting the class instantiation process
- Defining ways to create, compose, and represent objects and hide the implementation details from the involving system
- Emphasizing avoiding hard code of a fixed set of behaviors and defining a smaller set of core behaviors instead, which can compose into any number of (complex) sets

Creational design patterns have two basic characteristics: one is that they encapsulate knowledge about which concrete class the system use, and the second is that they hide how the instances of these classes are created and put together.

The class creational pattern uses inheritance for instantiation, whereas object creations delegates it to another object.

The following section deals with each pattern, its general structure, and sample implementation diagram in most of the cases.

## Factory method (virtual constructor)

This pattern suggests to let the subclasses instantiate the needed classes. The factory method defines an interface, but the instantiation is done by subclasses:

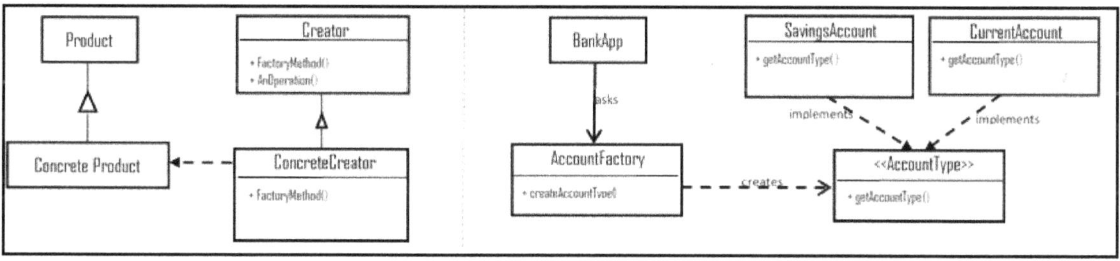

The preceding structure depicts a factory method, and an application uses a factory to create subtypes with an interface.

The benefits of using this are as listed:

- **Loose coupling**: Separates application from the classes and subclasses
- **Customization hooks**: The factory method gives subclasses a hook for providing an extended version of an object

The impact of using this is that it creates parallel class hierarchies (mirroring each other's structures), so we need to structure in the best possible ways using intelligent children pattern or Defer identification of state variables pattern.

## Abstract factory (kit)

Abstract factory pattern is intended to provide an interface if we want to create families of related or dependent objects, but without explicitly specifying their concrete classes:

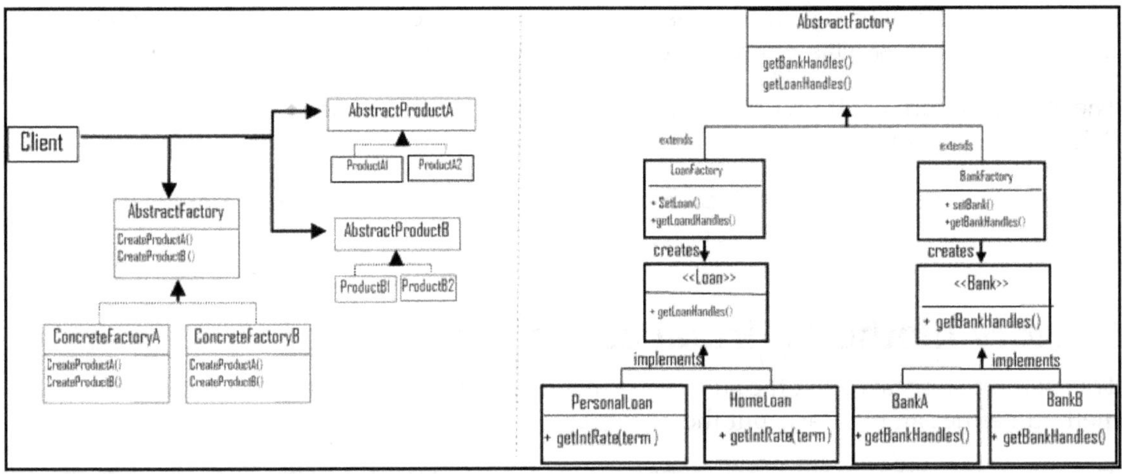


The preceding class diagram depicts the **AbstractFactory** class structure and a real-time implementation of an abstract factory pattern for an application that combines a different set of (heterogeneous) products from two different groups (**<<Bank>>** and **<<Loan>>**).

The benefits of this are the following:

- Isolating concrete classes
- Making exchanging product families easy
- Promoting consistency among products

Impact is such as; supporting new kinds of the product is difficult.

## Builder

The builder is intended to separate the construction of a complex object from its representation so that the same construction process can create different representations. In other words, use this pattern to simplify the construction of complex object with simple objects in a step-by-step manner:

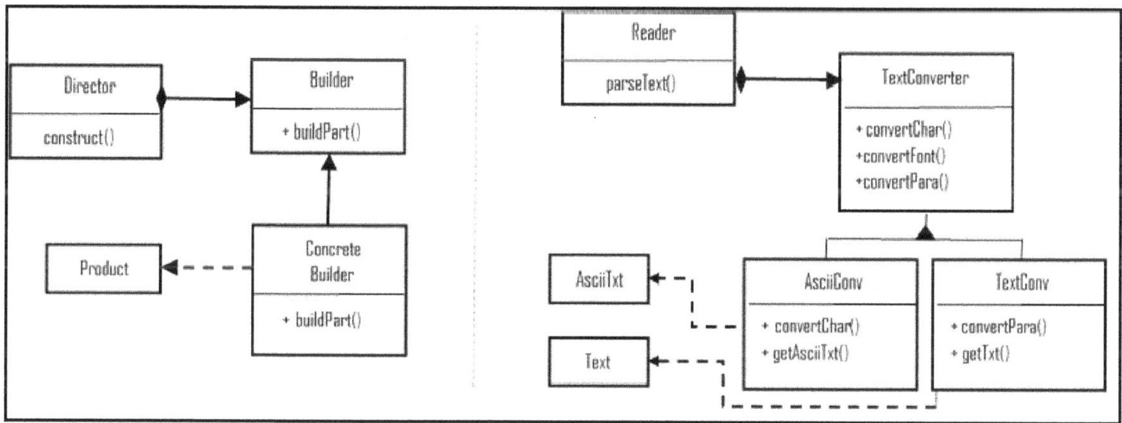


The class diagram depicts a typical builder pattern structure and a sample implementation classes for the **Builder** pattern. The **Builder** (**TextConverter**) is an abstract Interface that creates parts of a product page. The **Concrete Builder** (**AsciiConv**, **TexConv**) constructs and assembles parts by interface implementation, the **Director** (**Reader**) constructs an object with the builder interface, and the **Products** (**AsciiTxt**, **Text**) are under construction complex objects.

The benefits are as listed:

- Allows changing the internal representation and defines new kind of builder
- Isolates code for construction and representation
- Provides finer control over the construction process

Impacts are as listed:

- Leads to creating a separate concrete builder for each type of product
- Leads to mutable **Builder** classes

## Prototype

Prototype pattern suggests copying or cloning the existing object and customizing it if needed rather than creating a new object. Choose this pattern when a system should be independent of its products creation, compose, and representation:

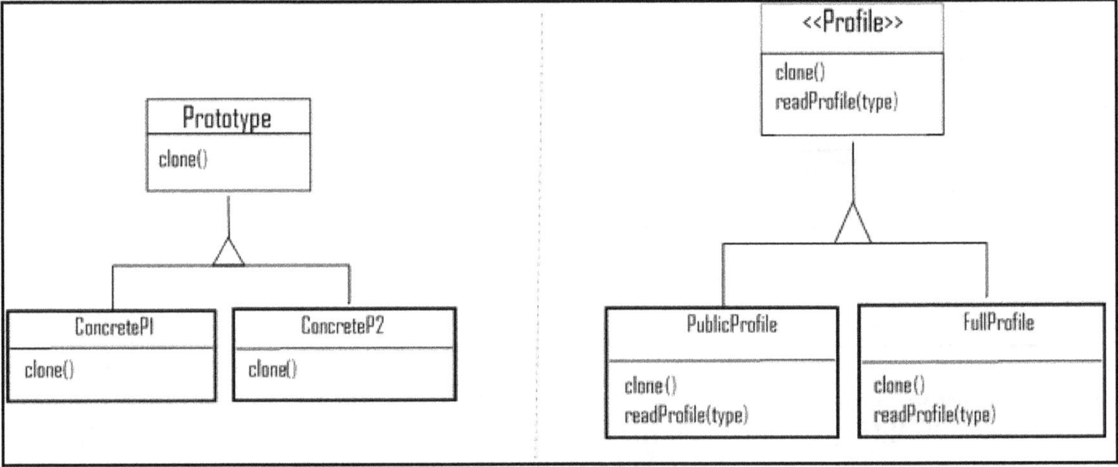


We can create a copy of **PublicProfile** (limited information) or **FullProfile** at runtime. Those two classes share a few combination of states, so it is good that we design as a prototype.

Let's take a look at its benefits:

- Adding and removing products at runtime
- Specifying new objects by varying values and structures
- Reduced subclasses
- Dynamic class configuration to an application

The impact is, each subclass must implement clone operation, and it is not possible to clone circular reference classes.

# Singleton

This pattern suggests that you create one and only one instance and provide a global point of access to the created object:

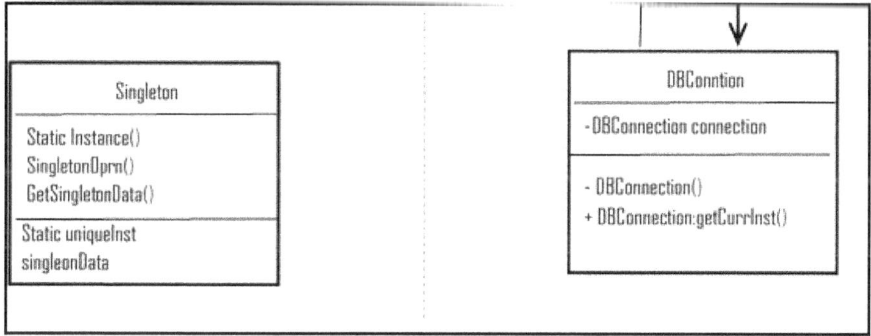


The DB connection in the preceding diagram is intended to be a singleton and provides a getter for its only object.

Here are its benefits:

- Controlled access to a sole instance
- Reduced namespace
- Flexibility to refinement of operations and representations
- More flexible than class operations

Impacts are as follows:

- Carry states for the whole lifetime of the application, creating additional overhead for unit tests
- Some level of violation of single responsibility principle
- By using singleton as a global instance, it hides the dependencies of the application; rather, it should get exposed through interfaces

# Structural design patterns

The structural patterns provide guidelines to compose classes and objects to form a larger structure in accordance with the OO design principles.

The structural class pattern uses inheritance to compose interfaces or implementations, and structural object patterns advocate ways to compose objects and realize the new functionality.

Some focus areas of Structural design pattern are as follows:

- Providing a uniform abstraction of different interfaces (Adapter)
- Changing the composition at runtime and providing flexibility of object composition; otherwise, it is impossible with static class composition
- Ensuring efficiency and consistency by sharing objects
- Adding object responsibility dynamically

The following section describes each structural pattern with standard structure and sample implementation structure as a diagram as well.

## Adapter class (wrapper)

Convert one interface of a class into another interface that the client wanted. In other words, the adapter makes heterogeneous classes work together:

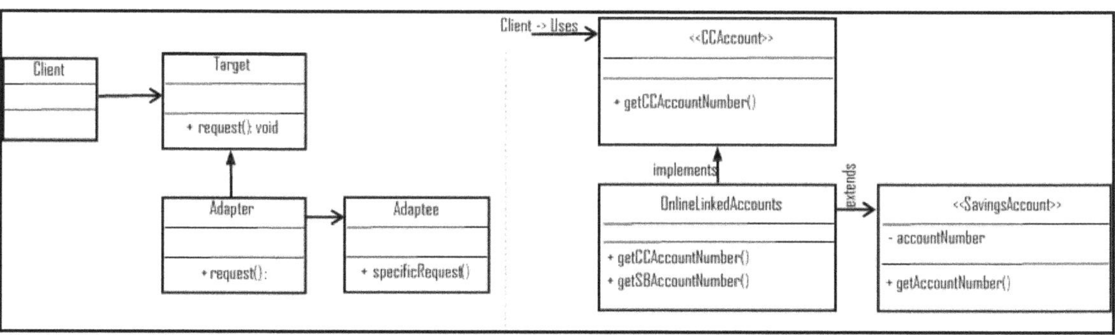


The preceding class diagram depicts an adapter called **OnlineLinkedAccounts** that adopts a savings account's details and a target interface called **credit card details**, and combine the results to show both account numbers.

## Adapter (object)

An adapter object relies on object composition, and when we need to use several of the existing subclasses, we can use object adapter to adapt the interface of the parent class:

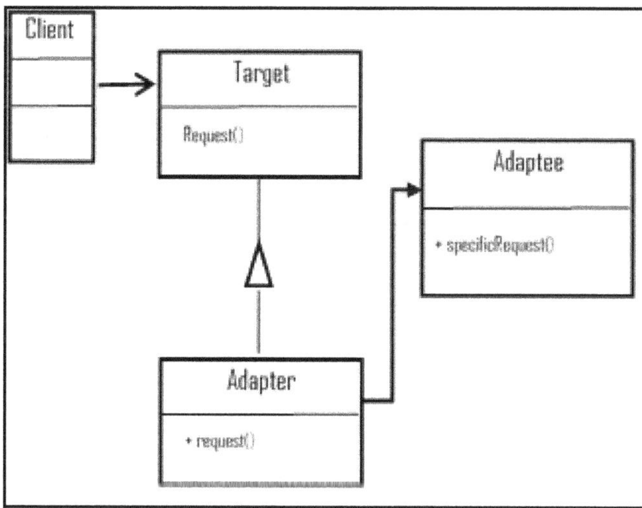


The preceding diagram depicts the formal structure of an **Adapter**.

These are the benefits:

- Saves time during development and testing by emulating a similar behavior of different parts of the application
- Provides easy extensions for new features with similar behaviors
- Allows a single adapter works with many adaptees (adapter object)

Impacts are as follows:

- Leads to needlessly duplicated codes between classes (less usage of inherited classes' functionalities)
- May lead to nested adaptions to reach for intended types that are in longer chains
- Make it more difficult to override adaptee behavior (adapter object)

# Bridge (handle/body)

Bridge pattern intent is to decouple the abstraction from its implementation, so abstraction and implementation are independent (not bound at compile time, so no impact to the client):

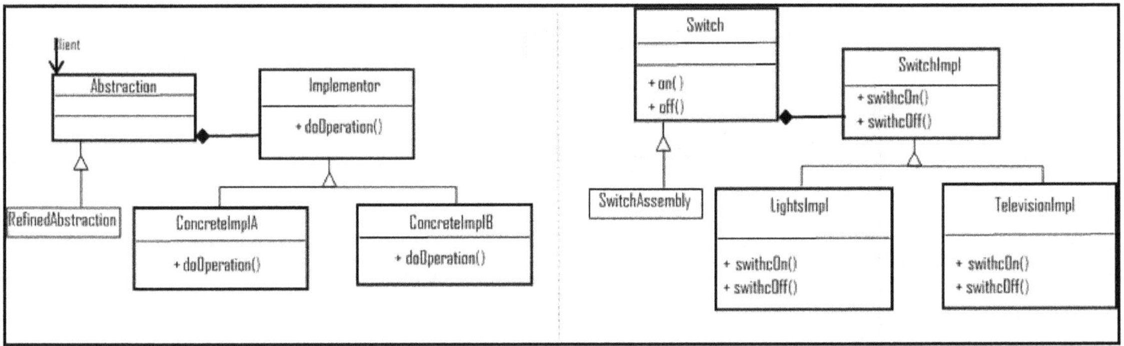


The benefits are as mentioned:

- Decoupling interfaces from the implementation
- Configuring the implementation of an abstraction at runtime
- Elimination of compile-time dependency
- Improved extensibility
- Hiding implementation details from the client

The impact is, introducing some level of complexity.

# Composite

**Composite** objects let clients treat individual objects and composition of objects uniformly. **Composite** represents the hierarchies of objects as tree structures.

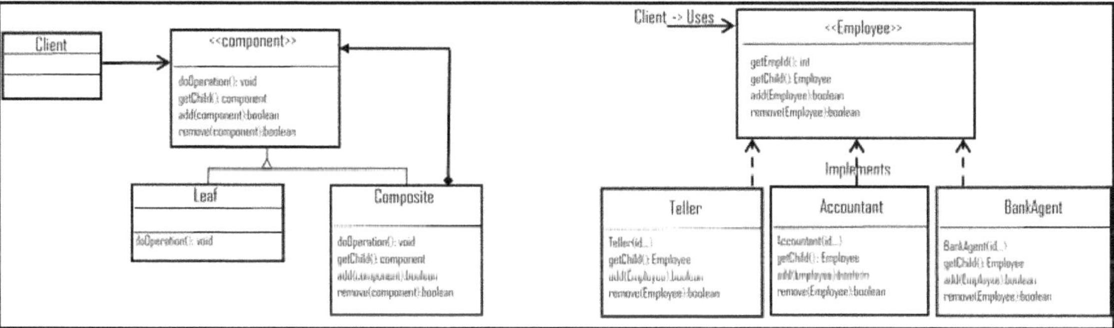


The preceding diagram depicts the standard structure of the **Composite** pattern and an implementation of a part-whole hierarchy (employee part of agent, **Accountant**, and teller), and to the **Client,** all objects are **Composite** and structured uniformly.

These are the benefits:

- It simplifies the client code by hiding the complex communications (leaf or composite component)
- It is easier to add new components, and client does not need a change when new components get added

The impact is such that it makes the design overly general and open as there are no restrictions to add any new components to composite classes.

# Decorator

The decorator pattern attaches additional responsibilities to an object dynamically. It provides an alternative way (by composition) to subclass and to extend the functionality of an object at runtime.

This pattern creates a decorator class by wrapping the original class to provide additional functionalities without impact to the signature of methods.

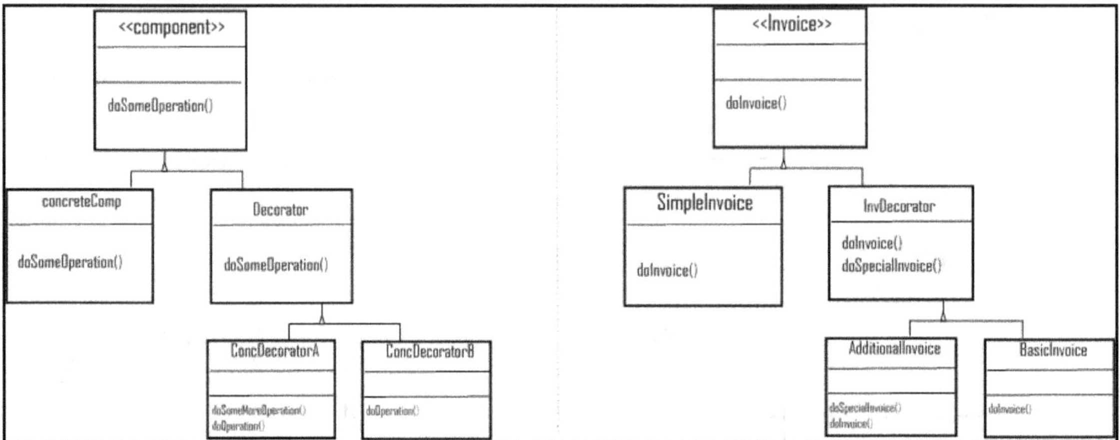


Observe the preceding diagram as it depicts invoice functionalities extended by composition dynamically (runtime).

Let's list the benefits:

- It reduces time for upgrades
- It simplifies enhancing the functionalities from the targeted classes and incorporates behavior into objects (changes class responsibilities, not the interface)

Impacts are as follows:

- It tends to introduce more look-alike objects
- It leads to debugging difficulties as it is adding functionality at runtime

## Façade

Façade suggests providing a high-level interface that unifies set of interfaces of subsystems, so it simplifies the subsystem usage.

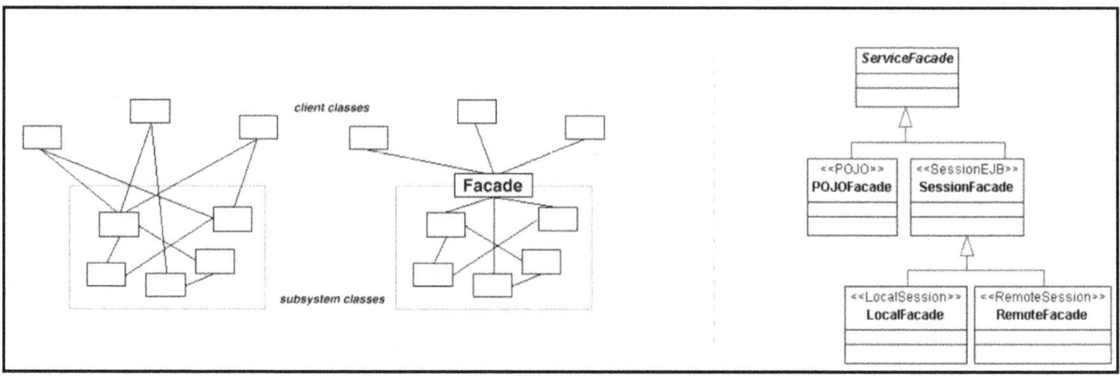


A sample implementation of a service façade as in the preceding diagram, the session subsystem are unified with session façade (local and remote).

Let's look at the benefits:

- It promotes loose coupling (between clients and subsystems)
- It hides complexities of the subsystem from the clients

The impact is such that it may lead to façade to check whether the subsystem structure changes.

# Flyweight

**Flyweight** suggests using the shared support of a vast number of fine-grained objects. We can use the **Flyweight** pattern to reduce the number of objects created (by sharing) and thereby reduce the memory footprint and improve the performance.

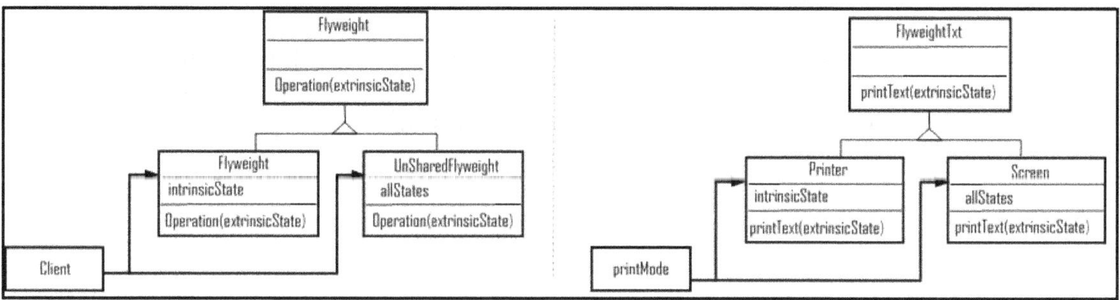

The preceding diagram depicts the general structure of the **Flyweight** pattern and a sample implementation. Consider a massive object that is shared across printer and a screen; **Flyweight** is a good option and can be cached as well (say for printing multiple copies).

Here are the benefits:

- It leads to good performance due to reduction in the total number of instances (by shared objects)
- It makes implementation for objects cache easy

The impact is such that it may introduce runtime costs associated with transferring, finding, or computing foreign (extrinsic) state.

## Proxy

The proxy pattern suggests providing a placeholder (surrogate) for another object to control and get access to it. It is the best fit for lazy loading of objects (defer the creation and initialization until we need to use it).

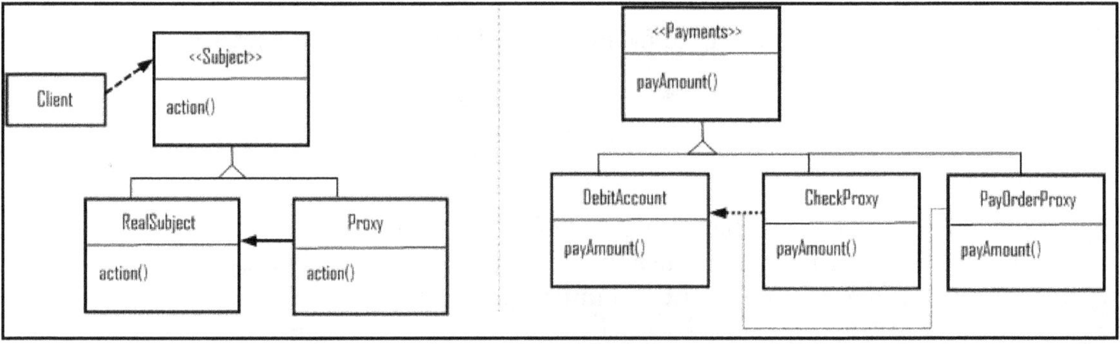


The preceding diagram shows a sample implementation of a proxy pattern for a payment class, and the payment can be either by check or by pay order. However, the actual access would be to **DebitAccount** object, so **PayOrderProxy** and **CheckProxy** are both surrogates for Debit Account.

The following are the benefits:

- It introduces the right level of indirections when accessing an object (abstraction of an object that resides in a different space)
- Creating objects on demand
- Copy-on-write (may reduce the copying of heavy objects if not modified)

The impact is such that it can make some implementations less efficient due to indirections.

# Behavioral patterns

Behavioral patterns provide guidelines on assigning responsibilities between objects. It does help with ways to implement algorithms and with communication between classes and objects.

Behavioral pattern focuses on the following characteristics:

- Communication between objects and classes
- Characterizing the complex control flow; flow of control in software programming (otherwise, it is hard to follow at runtime)
- Enforcing object composition rather than inheritance
- Loose coupling between the peer objects, and at the same time, they know each other (by indirections)
- Encapsulating the behavior in an object and delegating request to it

There are various design patterns available to enforce the above said behavioral focusses and characteristics. We will see details of those behavioral patterns in this section . We also provided a sample implementation structure as a diagram for some of the patterns.

## Chain of responsibility

This pattern suggests avoiding coupling the client object (sender of requests) with the receiver object by enabling objects (more than one) to handle the request.

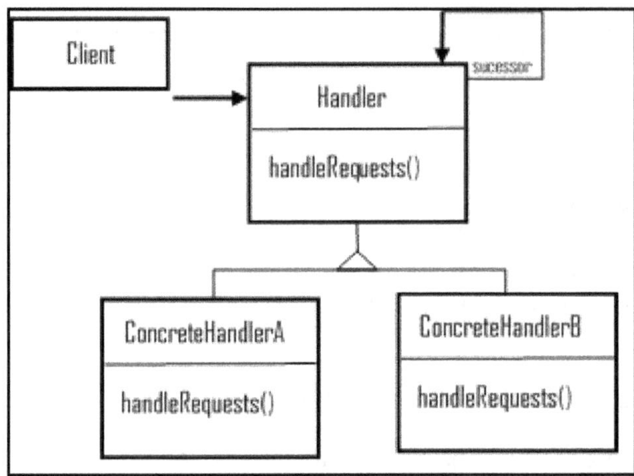


The preceding diagram depicts the typical structure of the chain of responsibility; the handler is the interface to define the requests and optionally express the successors along with concrete handlers that can handle the requests and forwards the same if needed.

Here's a list of the benefits:

- Reduced coupling (objects do not know which other objects handle the requests)
- Additional flexibilities in responsibilities assignments (of objects)

The impact is, no handshakes between the request handlers, so no guarantee of handling the request by other objects, and it may fall off from the chain unnoticed.

## Command (action/transaction)

This pattern suggests encapsulation of requests as an object, parameterizing clients with different requests; it can placed over message queues, can be logged, and supports undo operations.

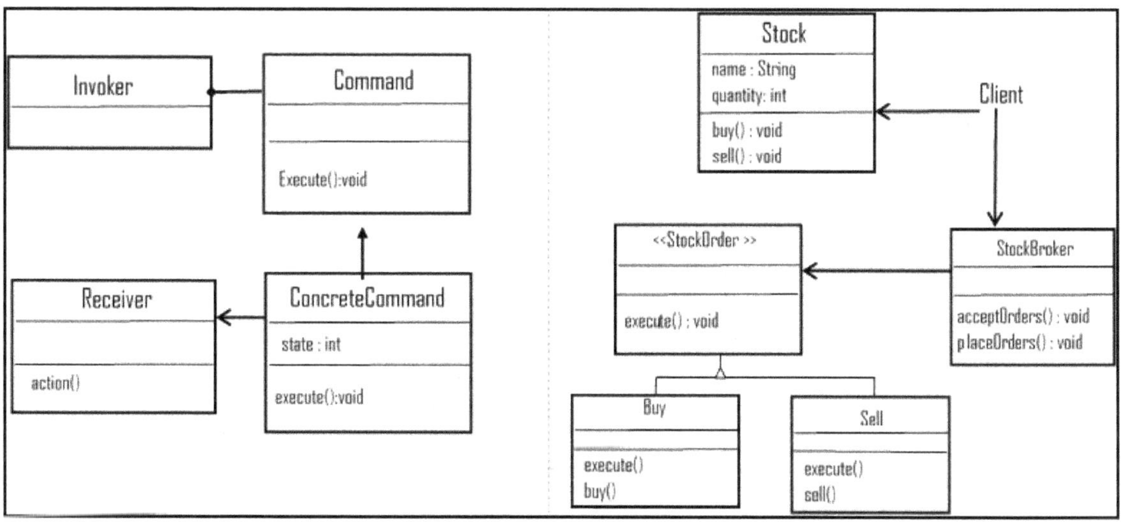


The preceding diagram depicts the structure of a command pattern and a sample implementation for a stockbroker application classes. **<<StockOrder>>** interface is a **Command**, and **Stock** concrete class creates requests. **Buy** and **Sell** are concrete classes implementing the **<<StockOrder>>**. The **StockBroker** is an invoker, and its objects execute specific commands depending on the type that it receives.

Here are the benefits:

- Encapsulation of object facilitates the changing of requests partially (by changing a single command) and no impacts to the rest of the flow
- Separates the invoking object from the actual action performing object
- Easy to add new commands without any impact to the existing classes

The impact is, the number of classes and objects increases over time or depends on the number of commands (concrete command implementations).

## Interpreter

This pattern suggests defining grammar along with an interpreter that uses representations so that the system can interpret any given sentences of a language.

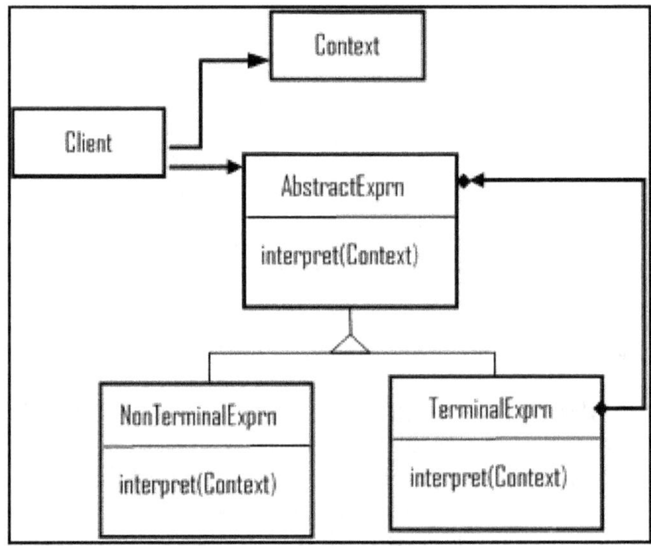


Abstract expression or regular expression declares interpret operation, terminal expressions or literal expressions implements symbols in the grammar, and non-terminal expressions (alternate, sequence, repetition) has nonterminal symbols in the grammar.

Let's look at the benefits:

- It is easy to change and extend the grammar
- Implementing the grammar is easy as well
- Helps introduce new ways to interpret expressions
- Impacts
- Introduces maintenance overhead for complex grammars

# Iterator (cursor)

This pattern suggests providing an approach to sequentially access the elements of an aggregate object and, at the same time, hide the underlying implementations.

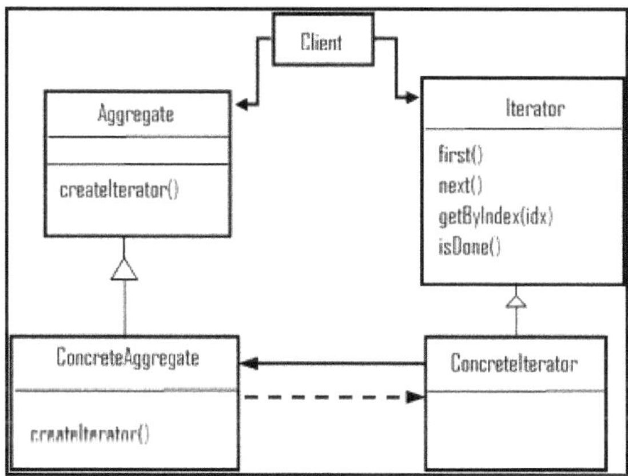


The preceding diagram depicts the structure of the iteration pattern in which the iterator interface defines traversing methods, and the concrete iterator implements the interface. Aggregate defines an interface for creating an iterator object, while a Concrete aggregate implements the aggregate interface to create an object.

Here are the benefits:

- It supports variations in the aggregate traversals
- Iterators simplify the aggregate interfaces
- It may have null iterators and helps handle boundary conditions better
- Impacts
- It may introduce additional maintenance cost (dynamic allocation of polymorphic iterators)
- It may have privileged access and thus introduces complexities to define new traversal methods in iterators

## Mediator

The **Mediator** pattern advocates defining ways of interactions between encapsulated objects without depending on each other by explicit reference.

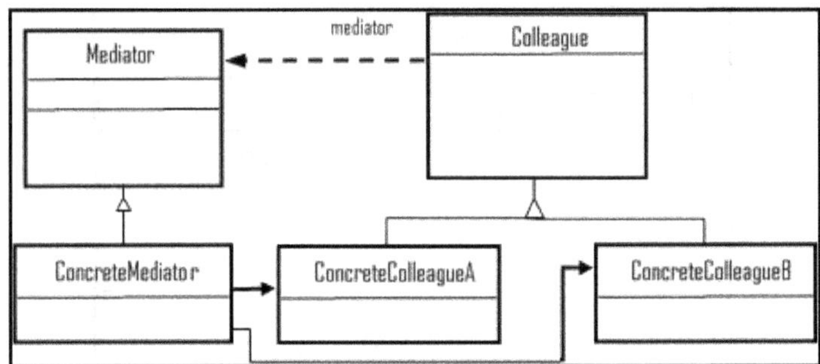


The preceding diagram is a typical structure of the **Mediator** pattern, where **Mediator** or dialog director defines an interface to communicate with other colleague objects; concrete mediator implements cooperative behavior by coordinating colleague objects.

Let's look at the benefits:

- Limits subclassing (by localizing behavior and restricting the distribution of behaviors to several other objects)
- Enforcing decoupling between colleagues objects
- Simplifying object protocols (replaces many-to-many interactions to one-to-one)
- Providing clear clarification on how objects should interact

Impacts is centralized control, leading to more complex and monolithic systems.

## Memento

This pattern suggests capturing and externalizing an object's internal state without violating encapsulation principles; so, we can restore the captured object.

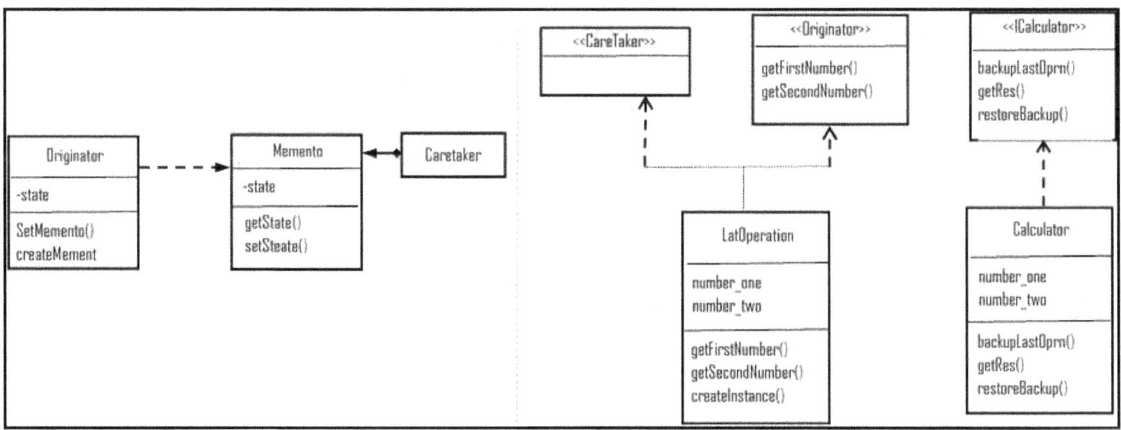


The preceding diagram depicts the structure of the memento pattern and a sample implementation for a calculator application. The **Caretaker** interface helps restore the previous operation that's handled in the **<<Calculator>>** concrete class.

These are the benefits:

- It preserves encapsulation boundaries by exposing information limited to the originator
- It simplifies the originator

Impacts are as follows:

- Memento implementation might be expensive, as it needs to copy large amounts of data to store into the memento
- It may be difficult to implement (through some programming languages) and ensure that only the originator is accessing the memento's state
- It might incur hidden storage and maintenance costs at the caretaker implementations

# Observer (dependents/publish/subscribe)

The **Observer** pattern suggests that when one object changes the state, it notifies its dependents and updates automatically. When implementation is in need of one-to-many dependencies, you would want to use this pattern.

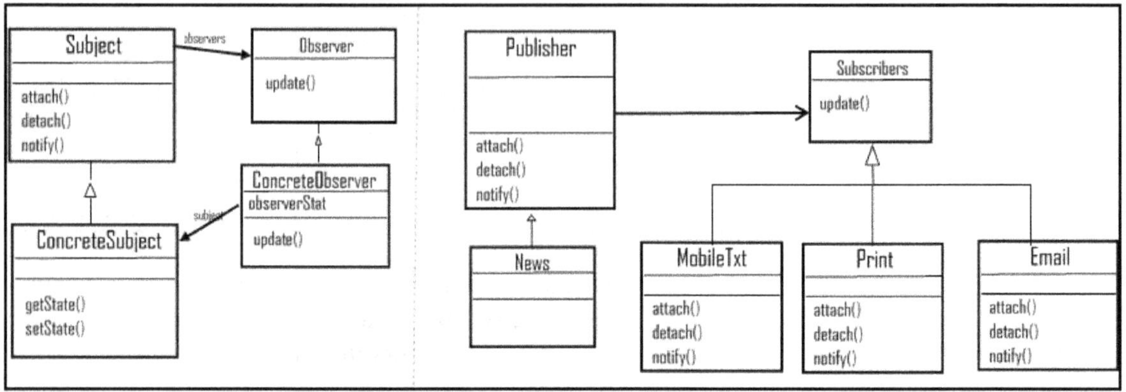


The preceding diagram depicts **Observer** pattern structure and a sample implementation of the same for a publications app; whenever an event occurs, subscribers need to be informed. The subscribers have a different mode of publishing (SMS, print, and emailing) and may need to support new modes as well in the future, so the best fit is **Observer**, as we just saw.

Let's go through its benefits:

- Enables easy broadcast of communication
- Supports loose coupling between objects as it's capable of sending data to other objects without any change in the subject
- Abstract coupling between subject and observer (changes in the observer do not impact subject)
- Can add or remove Observers any time

Impacts are as follows:

- Accidental or unintended updates impact the system heavily as it cascades to the observer down the layers
- May lead to performance issues
- Independent notifications may result in inconsistent state or behavior (no handshakes)

## State (objects for states)

These allow an object to alter its behavior when its internal state changes, and it appears as the class changes.

Use state pattern when an object's behavior depends on its state and change at runtime depends on that state.

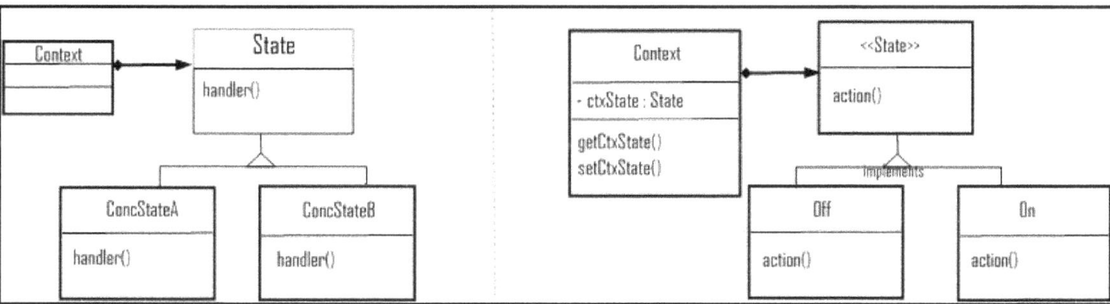


The diagram depicts both structure of State pattern and a sample implementation; Context class carries states, and **Off** and **On** classes implement State interface so that context can use the action on each concrete class's off/on.

Listed are the benefits:

- Suggest localizes state-specific behavior and partitions behavior for different states (new states and transitions can be added easily by subclass definitions)
- Makes state transitions explicit
- State objects are shareable

The impact is, it may make adding a new concrete element difficult.

## Strategy (policy)

Strategy pattern, also known as policy, defines a family or set of algorithms, encapsulates each one, and make them interchangeable. Strategy lets the algorithm vary independently of the clients that use it. When a group of classes differs only on their behavior, it is better to isolate the algorithms in separate classes and provide the ability to choose different algorithms at runtime.

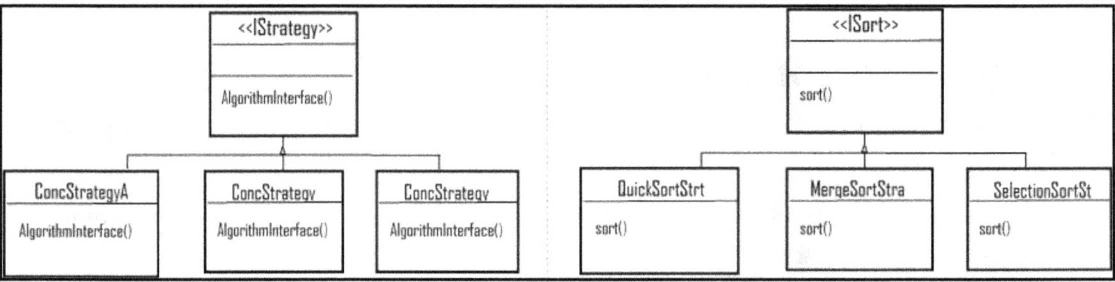


The preceding diagram shows the strategy structure, and implementation of sorting algorithms (as a family) and depends on the input depends on the volume for sort, then the client can use the intended algorithm from the Concrete strategy sorting classes.

The benefits are as listed:

- Enables open and closed principle
- Enables large-scale reusability
- Eliminates conditional statements (leads to clean code, well-defined responsibilities, easy to test, and so on)

Impacts are as follows:

- Clients need to be aware of different strategies and how they differ
- Communication overhead between strategy and context
- Increased number of objects

# The template method

This suggests providing a skeleton of an algorithm in operation, and deferring a few steps to subclasses. The template method lets subclasses redefine a few specific actions of a defined algorithm without changing the algorithm structure.

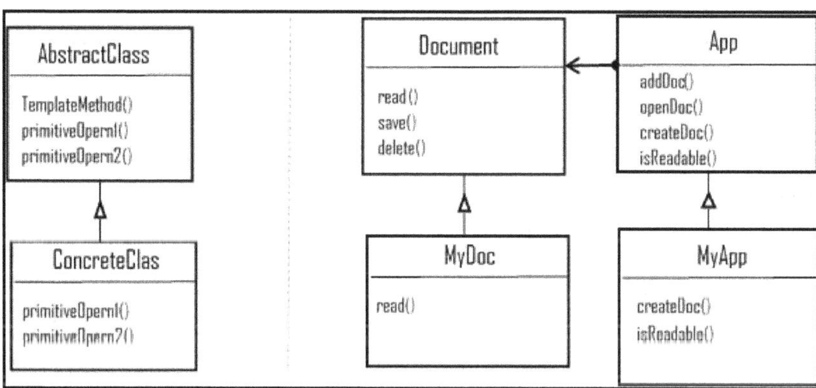


The following are the benefits:

- Fundamental technique for code reuse
- Allows partial implementation of business process while delegating implementation-specific portion to implementation objects (flexible in creating prototypes)
- Helps implement the Hollywood principle (inverted control structure, *Don't call us, we will call you*)

Impacts are as follows:

- Sequence of flow might lead to confusion
- High maintenance cost and impacts are high on any changes to the code

# Visitor

The visitor pattern represents an operation performed on the objects. It lets us define a new operation without changing the class elements on which it operates. In simple words, we use the visitor class to alter the execution of an algorithm as and when the visitor varies.

>

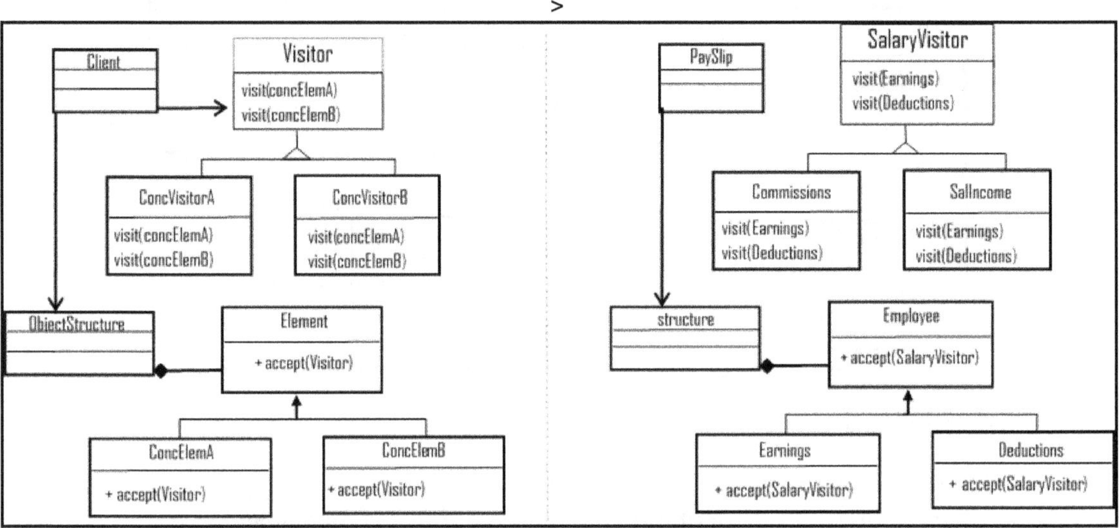


Here are the benefits:

- Adding new operations over an object structure is straightforward and easy (by adding a new visitor)
- Visitor separates unrelated operations and gathers related operations

Impacts are as follows:

- The visitor class hierarchy can be difficult to maintain when a new concrete element class gets added
- Implementation often forces to provide public operation that accesses an element's internal state (leads to compromising its encapsulation)

# Concurrency patterns

In software paradigm, the ability to perform multiple tasks at the same time (concurrency) by a software application is a critical factor; most software applications have some or other sort of concurrency. Keeping this in mind, let's briefly touch upon on a few concurrency patterns here, as other chapters in this book cover many (concurrency) related patterns in detail.

# Concurrency design pattern

In many situations the automated system may have to handle many different events simultaneously called concurrency. OOP provides an adequate means (abstraction, reusability, sharing of distributed persistent data, parallel executions and so on) of dealing with concurrency. This section will cover few concurrency patterns in brief.

## Producer-consumer

The producer-consumer pattern decouples the produce consume data processes. The process may handle data at different rates. Producer and consumer pattern's parallel loops are broken down into two categories as those that produce data and those that consume the produced data.

Data queues are used to communicate data between loops in the producer/consumer design pattern. These queues are offered data buffering between the producer and consumer loops.

## Active object

The active object pattern enforces decoupling of method execution from the method invocation and so enhances the concurrency and simplifies synchronized access to the objects that reside in their (own) threads of control.

We use this pattern where an application handles multiple client requests simultaneously to improve its quality of service.

## Monitor object

This pattern suggests synchronization on concurrent method execution to ensure that only one method runs within an object at a time. Monitors also allow an object's methods to execute scheduled sequences cooperatively.

We use this pattern (implement synchronization) when multiple threads are invoking methods of an object that modify its internal state. Contrary to active objects, monitor object belongs to the groups of passive objects; monitors are not having its (own) thread of control.

# Concurrency architectural pattern

**Half-sync/Half-async**: In concurrent systems, decoupling of synchronous and asynchronous service processing brings programming simplicity without reducing the performance. Half-sync/Half-async introduces two intercommunicating layers, one for synchronous and another for asynchronous service processing, with a queuing layer in-between.

This pattern enables the synchronous and asynchronous processing services to communicate with each other and helps those processes to decompose into layers.

**Leader/Followers**: If we need an efficient concurrency model where multiple threads need to take turns sharing a set of event sources that detect, de-multiplex, dispatch, and process event-sources' service requests, then the best choice is to implement the Leaders/Followers pattern in our system.

The aim of this pattern is to provide an elegant solution to process multiple events concurrently, such as in multithreaded server applications.

# Summary

The design patterns have evolved since 1992, and even today, it is inevitable in solving many software design problems in a proven technique and practices called design patterns. It is not difficult to see any specific pattern as a solution or technique that can be analyzed, implemented, and reused, but it is difficult to characterize the problem it solves and the context in which it is the best fit. It is critical to know the purpose of the patterns, as it helps understand the existing design of any given system.

With this chapter, we touched upon the key elements of OOD, abstraction, encapsulation, modularization, and hierarchy along with a few additional items such as typing, concurrency, and persistence.

Also, we discussed the design principles, hoping that the readers get a *SOLID* understanding of what OO principles offer to OO software designers. We believe that the SOLID principles are the fundamental training material for anyone who wants to step into software design and development even in today's world.

We touched upon three broad categories of OO design patterns: creational, structural, and behavioral. We also discussed the benefits and impacts of each pattern so that the readers will be able to easily characterize the problems it solves and the context it best suits as a software solution.

We also added a section, hoping readers to get a fair amount of introduction about concurrency (design and architectural) patterns as well.

# References

The following table refers to cross-reference of OO software design patterns:

| | | Scope | |
|---|---|---|---|
| | | **Class** | **Object** |
| **Purpose / Type** | **Creational** | (1) Factory Method | 1. Abstract Factory<br>2. Builder<br>3. Prototype<br>4. Singleton |
| | **Structural** | (2) Adapter (class) | 5. Adapter (Object)<br>6. Bridge<br>7. Composite<br>8. Decorator<br>9. Façade<br>10. Flyweight<br>11. Proxy |
| | **Behavioral** | (3) Interpreter<br>(4) Template Method | 12. Chain of Responsibility<br>13. Command<br>14. Iterator<br>15. Mediator<br>16. Memento<br>17. Observer<br>18. State<br>19. Strategy<br>20. Visitor |

Reference books are as follows:

- Design Patterns: Elements of Reusable Object-Oriented Software by Erich Gamma, Richard Helm, Ralph Johnson and John Vlissides
- *Object-Oriented Analysis and Design with Applications (2nd Edition)* by Grady Booch

Other references for this chapter:

- `http://www.oodesign.com/`
- `https://www.tutorialspoint.com/design_pattern`
- `https://sourcemaking.com/design_patterns/`
- `http://www.blackwasp.co.uk/GofPatterns.aspx`
- `http://www.mif.vu.lt/~plukas/resources/DPBook/`
- `www.dzone.com`
- `http://www.javaworld.com`
- `https://sudo.ch/unizh/concurrencypatterns/ConcurrencyPatterns.pdf`
- `http://www.cs.wustl.edu/~schmidt/POSA/POSA2/conc-patterns.html`
- `https://en.wikipedia.org/wiki/Concurrency_pattern`

# 4

# Enterprise Integration Patterns

This chapter is going to cover deeper topics of enterprise integration patterns. These topics are as follows:

- Need for integration patterns
- Integration scenarios in enterprises
- Main challenges in enterprise integration
- Getting started with messaging patterns

## Need for integration patterns

Present day enterprises are comprised of thousands of applications. Many of them are commercial, off-the-shelf applications; some of them are in-house applications, and some others are legacy applications that have been part of the enterprise for a very long time. Though there will be thousands of applications, it is impossible for employees to access each one of them separately using separate consoles.

Why are so many applications required in an enterprise? The answer to that question is that each enterprise has thousands of business functions that are impossible to be performed by a single application. Even an application such as an ERP can do very limited functions when compared to the actual needs of the enterprise.

Another reason for multiple applications is that spreading various functions across multiple applications ensures a better level of business continuity in the sense that even if one application fails; others will continue to run without causing impediment to business functions.

Vendors in the market have also learned the art of developing applications that are focused on catering to the needs of specific business functions. However, with the change in dynamics of the various business functions, vendors are trying to integrate multiple functions into a single business application. For example, many billing system applications started to incorporate additional functions for accounting. So in short, in the present scenario, it is not possible to define clear boundaries for applications.

Users, such as customers and partners, tend to access various functions without much of a concern about the underlying applications that are involved in performing the function. All these parameters warrant the need for a proper integration mechanism across various applications that are part of the enterprise ecosystem. In the past, integration used to be confined only to applications that exist within an organization.

In the present-day scenario, there are a host of new paradigms such as social media applications, **Internet of Things** (**IoT**) based applications, cloud-based applications, microservices-enabled applications, and so on, to name a few prominent ones. To enable seamless data sharing and support business process across the enterprise, it is necessary for enterprises to ensure that all the applications are integrated. The diverse types of applications have created a need for the enterprises to develop a robust set of capabilities for their integration platform so that they can continue to remain competitive in the present-day dynamics of agile enterprises that are in a constantly changing mode to suit the customer demands and expectations.

There is no shortcut for enterprise integration. It is a very broad and difficult area to handle, but inevitable for the present-day enterprise. Enterprise integration patterns do not provide any ready-made code that can be used for integrating applications. In fact, they suggest proven and tested approaches for solving enterprise integration problems. If used correctly, enterprise integration patterns can help organizations fill up the huge gap that exists between their integration vision and its actual implementation.

In the next section, we will examine the diverse types of scenarios that demand integration in enterprises.

# Integration scenarios in enterprises

The concept of integration is a very broad area. However, some of the most common integration scenarios in enterprises are the following:

- Information portals
- Data replication

- Shared business functions
- Service-oriented architectures
- Distributed business processes
- Business-to-business integration

There could be several other scenarios in enterprises based on the nature of the business and the domain handled by them. We will examine some of the prominent integration scenarios now.

# Information portal

Many users in an organization will have the need to access more than one application to perform a single business function. For example, an HR professional may have to access several applications, such as talent acquisition, compensation and benefits, learning and development, talent branding, and so on, to pull out details pertaining to various aspects of talent management. This scenario makes it extremely difficult for them to carry out their daily business functions at pace. This is where the concept of information portals comes to their help. An information portal can access information from diverse systems, aggregate, and present them in a single view. Simple information portals divide the display screen into several zones. Each zone will display data from a specific application. These information portals also have the capability to provide drill down information in one zone based on the information selected by the user in the other zone. An example of an information portal is as follows:

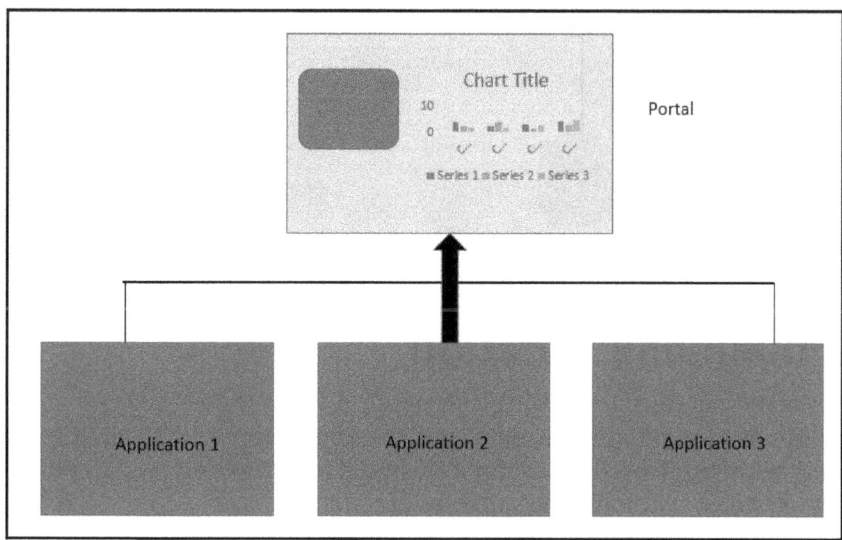

# Data replication

In an enterprise, many applications will have a copy of the same data. For example, customer details could be there in the order management system, billing system, advertising and promotions system, and so on. So, if the address is updated in one system, it is mandatory to ensure that it is updated in other systems also. Replication is one of the techniques to ensure this required consistency. How is data replication done? Many organizations define policies that will ensure that there is continuous synchronization and replication of data at regular intervals of time to ensure that data stays up to date on all the systems. Another technique is to export data into files and import them to other systems. Another technique, called **message-oriented middleware**, is used to embed data records into messages and send them to other applications for synchronization purposes:

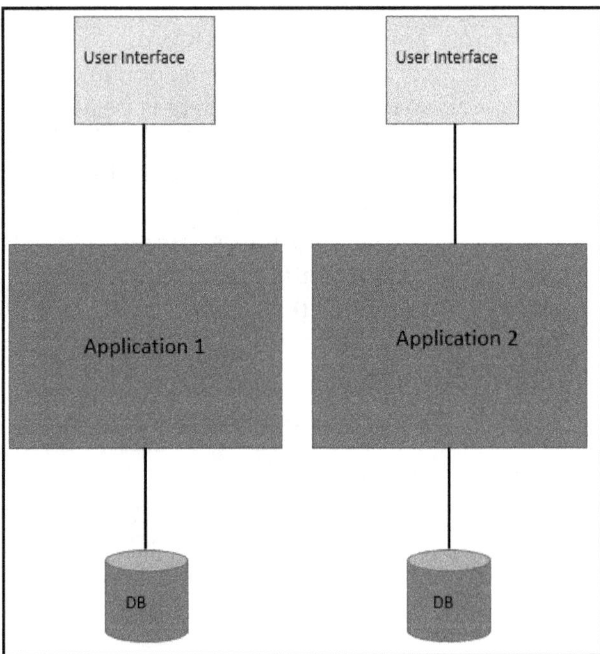


# Shared business function

If the same set of data is stored in multiple systems, it leads to redundancy of data. The functions that are used to handle this data (such as a customer address in the previous example) could be implemented as a shared business function once and exposed as a service to other systems that have the same set of data.

A **shared business function** can be used as a good functionality to replace redundant data. For example, let us take the case of a customer address that is stored in multiple systems across the organization. Instead of storing the same data in multiple systems, a business function called `GetCustomerAddress` could be used by a system to fetch the data from other systems instead of permanently storing it.

The trade-off between the use of redundant data versus shared business functions is based on several criteria. Some of the parameters that define the criteria are the following:

- Amount of control over the systems where the data is present (in some situations, invoking a `shared` function could be a more intensive task than loading data into the database)
- Rate of change of data under consideration (for example, a customer address may be needed very frequently whereas it may change only infrequently)

The diagram depicting the use of a `shared` function is as follows:

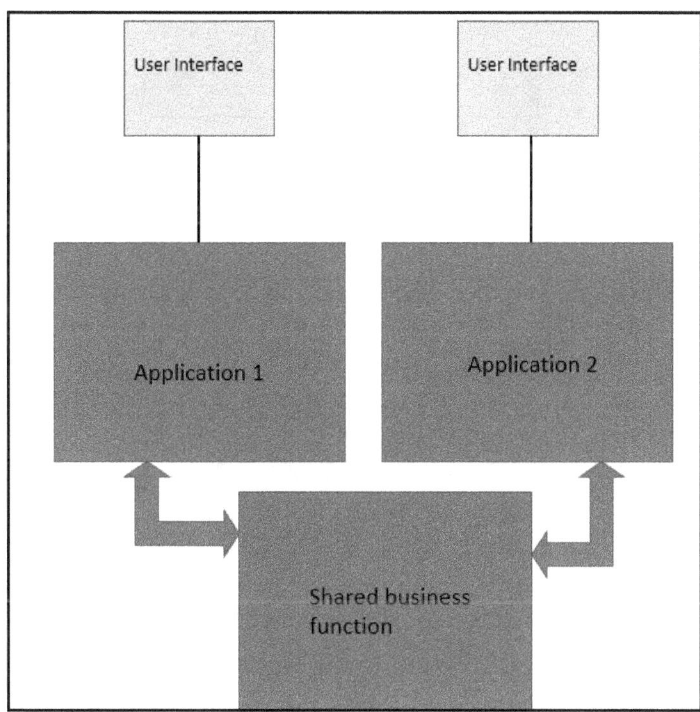

# Service-oriented architecture

Shared business functions, which we discussed earlier, are commonly referred to as *services*. A service is typically a well-defined function that is universally available to perform a specific operation. These services are made available for use by other systems that act as service consumers. Once a set of services are created, it is very important to ensure that they are maintained and made available to other systems in an appropriate manner. The two important aspects of service management are the following:

- **Service discovery**: All services are made available in a centralized service directory through which the other applications can discover them
- **Service negotiation**: Each service must describe its interface in such a way that other applications in the enterprise can negotiate and set up a communication contract with them

**Service-oriented architecture** (**SOA**) is also a mechanism for application integration, which in turn blurs the line between integration and distributed applications. The SOA was discussed in detail in `Chapter 7`, *Service-Oriented Architecture (SOA)*. The block diagram depicting SOA is as follows:

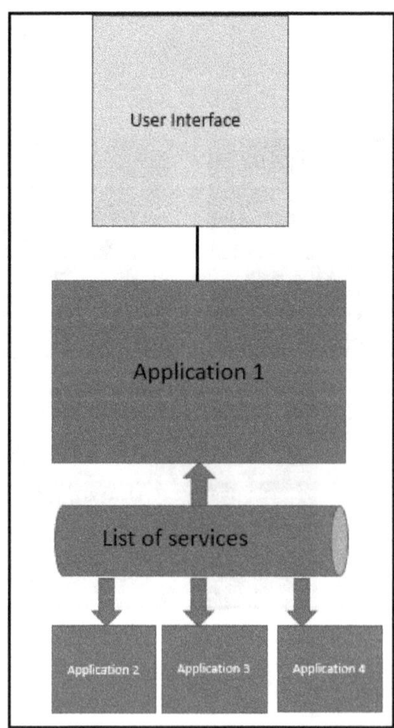

Another important aspect of service-oriented architecture is the concept of **enterprise service bus** (**ESB**), which provides connectivity between the sender and receiver components of the SOA in a loosely coupled manner.

# Distributed business process management

As we have already discussed, a single business function can be spread across several applications present in an enterprise. In such situations, it is very important to ensure coordination between the various applications. This can be done by implementing a business process management system. The business process management system will coordinate with all relevant applications that are part of a specific business function and ensure seamless execution. However, in this context, it is important to remember that there exists a very blurred line between business process management and SOA. There is always a possibility that all services are made available as services, and a business process function can be made available as an application to access all services through SOA. The diagram of a distributed process management system is depicted as follows:

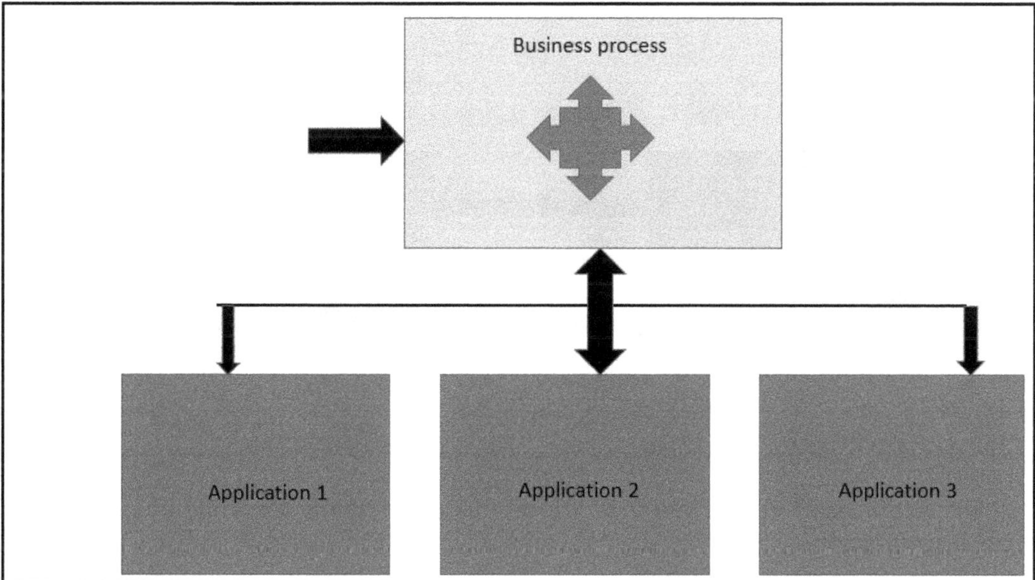

# The business-to-business integration

As discussed at the start of the chapter, present-day enterprises need to interact with several components that are external to their ecosystem, such as customers, partners, and so on. These external elements need access to many applications that are a part of the enterprise. For example, in the case of a product organization, there will be several partners who implement the services that are part of the product. In such cases, it is very important for partners to get access to some critical enterprise applications to stay up to date with the new product features, updates, learning resources, product user forums, and groups. The reverse is also true in the sense that the enterprise also relies heavily on certain external organizations for some of their functions, and hence it is important to ensure the flow of data from certain external applications to the enterprise. Such scenarios give rise to situations that warrant a business-to-business integration. This is not a very straightforward situation like an integration of applications within an enterprise. This is primarily due to the fact that when it comes to business-to-business integration, several other aspects of security, legal implications, and governance need to be considered to enable smooth integration. The graphic depicting a business-to-business integration scenario is as follows:

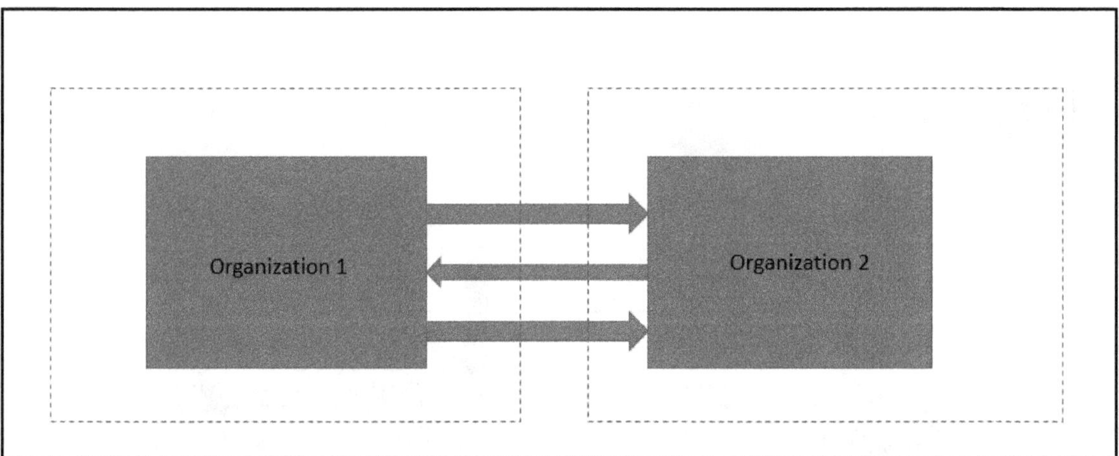


In the next section, we will analyze the various challenges that exist while integrating enterprise applications.

# Main challenges in enterprise integration

Some of the main challenges associated with enterprise application integration are as follows:

- **Networks are slow and unreliable**: Enterprise integration applications need to transfer data from one application to another. These applications may reside in different states, countries, or continents. In such situations, data needs to be transferred through a LAN or a WAN, or a combination of both. Transferring data through diverse network topologies and protocols introduces significant transmission delays and other types of interruptions that become a stumbling block in enterprise application integration.
- **Heterogeneous application platforms**: While integrating multiple applications, it is important to keep in mind that each application will have its own platform and operating system. To ensure seamless integration between such applications, it is vital to ensure that data transfer between applications happens in a format that can be understood by all the applications that are involved. For this to happen, there should be a middleware component that converts data into a generic format understandable by all the applications.
- **Application updates and upgrades**: Applications that are integrated will constantly keep getting upgraded due to system updates. In some situations, some system upgrades will introduce drastic changes in the overall application. This may impact all other applications that are involved in the integration. It is important for integration solutions to minimize dependencies between various applications that are part of the integration. One of the ways to achieve this is by ensuring loose coupling between the applications.
- **Security**: Certain applications in domains such as healthcare and insurance are bound by stringent security policies and frameworks. If such applications are involved in the integration process, it is important to adhere to the security guidelines. Otherwise, it will lead to the violation of legal guidelines.

Some of the key techniques that are used to overcome the aforementioned challenges are the following:

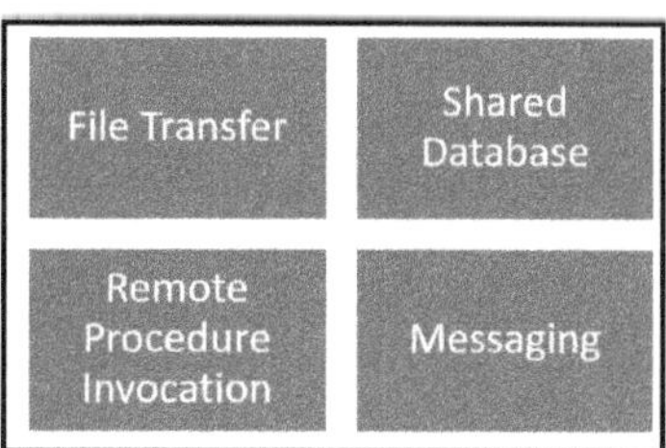

Let's discuss these techniques briefly.

# File transfer

Here, file is the basic mode for transfer of data between applications that need to be integrated. One application will perform a write operation on a file that will be read by the other application. However, for this to happen successfully and create the necessary impact, it is important for the involved applications to agree upon the following parameters about the file:

- Filename and location
- Format of the file
- Time at which the file will be written and read
- How the file will be deleted

# Shared database

In this case, the database becomes the point at which integration happens. Multiple applications that need to be integrated share a common database schema, which is in the same database. This prevents duplicate data storage and prevents the need for data transfer from one application to another.

# Remote procedure invocation

In this case, integration of applications happens through some functionality that is exposed by one application. The other application(s) access these functionalities remotely as a remote procedure. The process of invoking these functionalities as a remote procedure is called **remote procedure invocation**. Remote procedure invocation occurs in real time and is a synchronous communication.

# Messaging

In this case, integration of applications happens through messaging. One of the applications publishes a message to a message channel that can be accessed by all other applications. Other applications access the message channel and reach the message at some later point in time. The only criteria here is that the applications that are involved should have a predefined agreement on the message channel and the format of the message that is sent to the channel. In the next section, we will dive deep into the concepts of messaging and how enterprise applications can be integrated using the concept of messaging. In the next section, we will dwell deep into the various types of messaging patterns.

# Getting started with messaging patterns

Messaging is a reliable technique that is used for interconnecting applications using the concept of packets called **messages**. These packets are sent to channels, which are logical pathways providing interconnection between the various applications. These channels are also called **queues**. Several messages can be queued up in a channel and can be made accessible to multiple applications at the same point in time. There are two main types of applications in messaging, they are:

- Sender/producer
- Receiver/consumer

A sender is an application that sends a message to the channel. A receiver is an application that reads the message that is sent to the channel. Messaging is an asynchronous mode of communication, meaning it is not necessary that the receiver should read the message from the channel as soon as it reaches the channel.

A message could be any kind of data structure, such as an array, string, or object. Every message contains two parts:

- Header
- Body

The header contains metadata about the message, such as details of the sender, receiver, timestamp, and so on. This information is used by the messaging system but is usually ignored by the applications. The message body contains the actual data that is sent by the application. The body of the message is ignored by the messaging system but is used by the applications.

Messaging capabilities are provided to a system by a specialized software application called **message-oriented middleware** (**MOM**). MOM is also called a **messaging system**. MOM is required to ensure smooth transmission of messages across applications. One of the main reasons for the existence of MOM is the unreliable state of networks that interconnect the systems. Even if a message is sent by an application, it is not necessary that it reaches the intended destination if the network is not proper. MOM helps to overcome this network-related limitation and other limitations, and ensures that a message is repeatedly transmitted until it reaches its destination. The communication of applications through messaging is depicted in the following diagram:

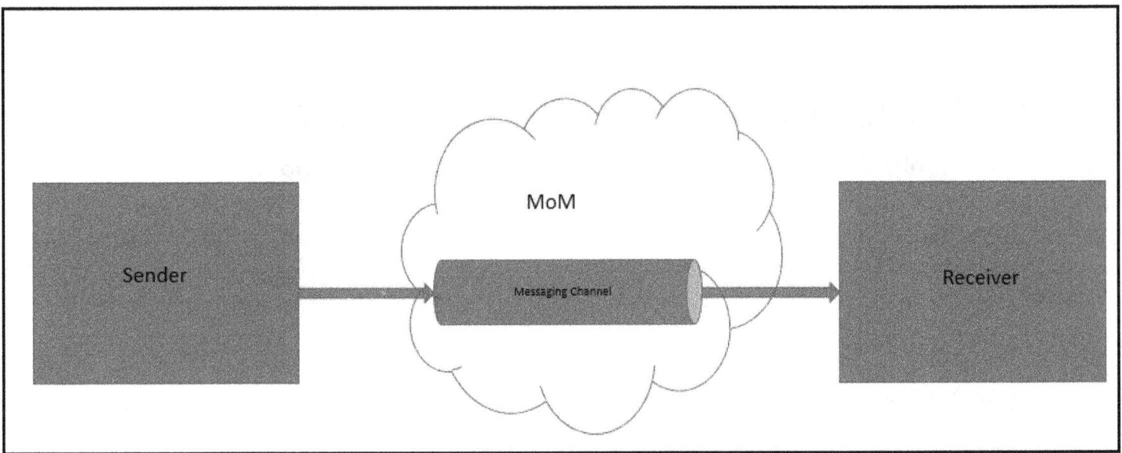


The following are the five steps involved in message transmission:

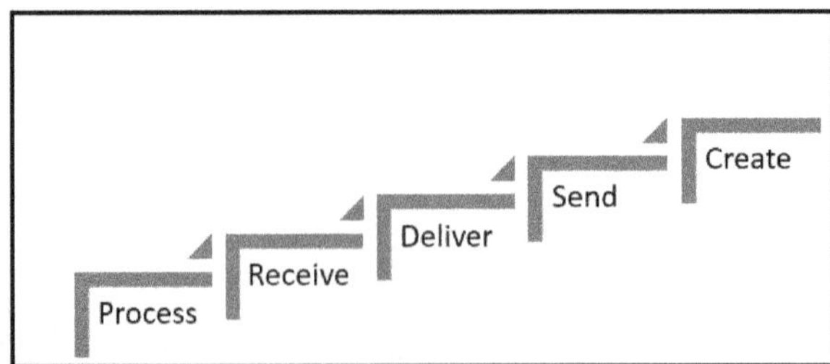


In each of these steps, the following activities are performed:

1. **Create**: In this step, the sender or producer adds a header and data and creates the message
2. **Send**: In this step, the sender sends out the message to the channel

3. **Deliver**: In this step, MOM moves the message from the sender's system to the receiver's system making the message available for the receiver
4. **Receive**: In this step, the receiver or consumer reads the message from the channel
5. **Process**: In this step, the receiver extracts the data from the message

In the next section, we will examine the prominent messaging patterns that are used in the design of enterprise systems.

# Pipe and filter pattern

In many situations, a single event could trigger a series of actions and each will perform a specific function. So, pipe and filter patterns are used to handle such situations that require complex processing of messages while maintaining flexibility and independence. A large task is split into a series of smaller, sequential, independent tasks (filters) that are connected by channels (pipes). The diagram of the pipe and filter pattern is depicted as follows:

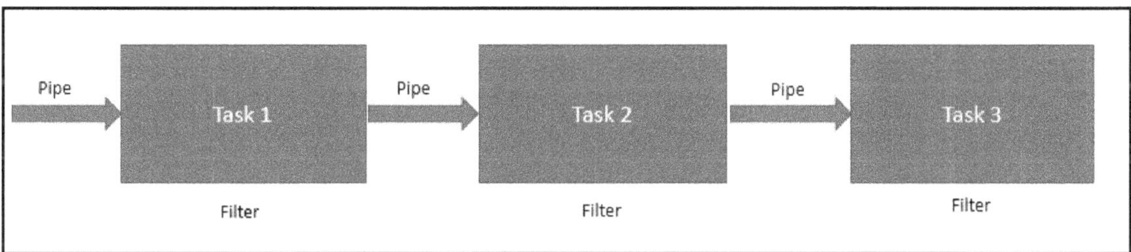


Each filter has a simple interface that consists of an inbound pipe that receives, processes, and publishes the result to the outbound pipe. The role of a pipe is to connect one filter to the next. In the case of the pipe and filter pattern, all components use the same external interface, and hence they can be present in different solutions. These solutions can be interconnected by means of different pipes. The connection outlet that provides a connection between the pipe and filter is called a **port**. Typically, each filter has one input port and one output port.

# Message router pattern

This pattern is used in situations where sequential execution of steps may not always be possible. In some situations, the output of a filter may have to be passed to one of the several pipes based on the fulfillment of certain criteria or conditions. In such situations, message router patterns are used. The diagram depicting the message router pattern is as follows:

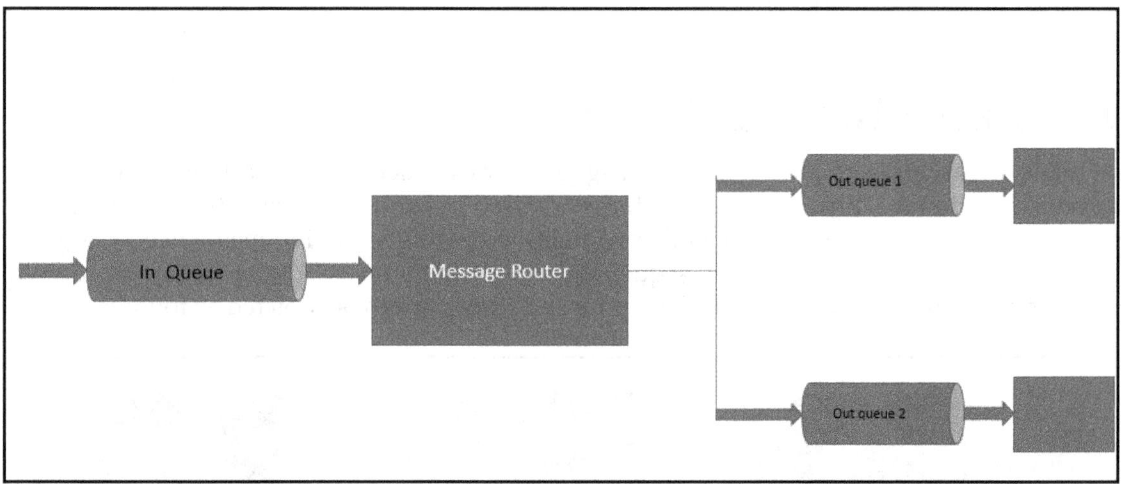


# Message translator pattern

In the beginning of the chapter, we discussed scenarios where there could be a need to integrate certain third-party applications/partner applications to some of the applications that are part of the enterprise. These applications will use diverse data models and may sometimes use totally different data formats for communication. For present-day agile enterprises, it is necessary to use patterns that can interconnect diverse types of applications by converting data from one format to another. This is where the **message translator pattern** plays a key role. The message translator pattern acts as a special filter between other filters or applications and translates data from one format to another. The diagram depicting the message translator pattern is given as follows:

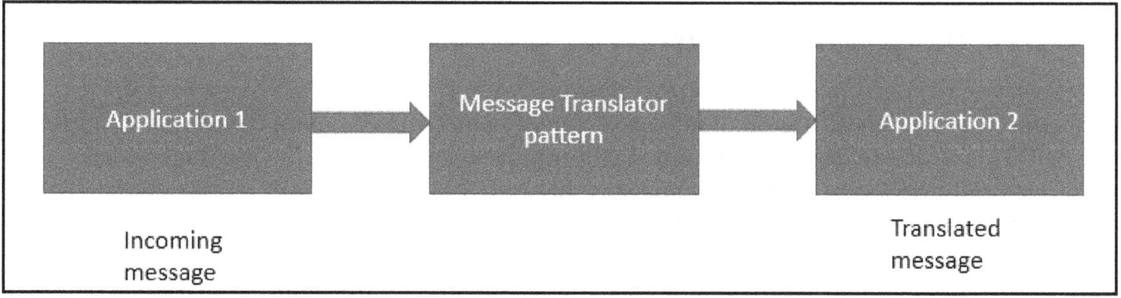


## Message endpoint pattern

Applications in an enterprise communicate with each other by sending messages through a message channel. But the next issue is that there needs to be a mechanism in place that will help applications to connect to the message channel. This is applicable for the sender application to send messages and for the receiver application to receive messages. This is where the message endpoint pattern comes into the picture. The message endpoint acts as a client of the messaging system, which the sender and receiver application can use to send and receive messages. Message endpoint code is accessible to both the application and the MOM's client API. The remaining application knows nothing about message formats, messaging channels, or any other details of the applications with which it is communicating through messaging. It just knows that it has sent some data to another application or that it will receive data from another application. Message endpoint code takes the data, converts it into a message, and sends it to the correct messaging channel. Similarly, on the receiving end, the message endpoint receives the message, extracts the contents, and gives it to the application. The diagram depicting the message endpoint pattern is as follows:

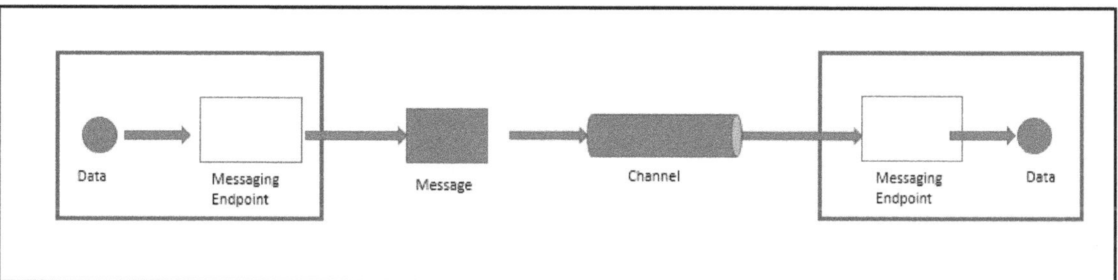

# Point-to-point channel pattern

Consider the scenario in which an application is using messaging to make a remote procedure call. In this situation, it is necessary to ensure that only one receiver will perform the call. This is where the **point-to-point channel** pattern helps us. If a message is sent through a point-to-point channel, it ensures that only one receiver will receive the message. In case the channel has multiple receivers, only one of them will be able to receive the message. If multiple receivers try to consume the message, the channel will make sure that only one of them will be successful in their attempts. But this does not prevent the channel from having multiple receivers and them receiving multiple messages concurrently. The only criteria here is that only one receiver will receive a specific message:

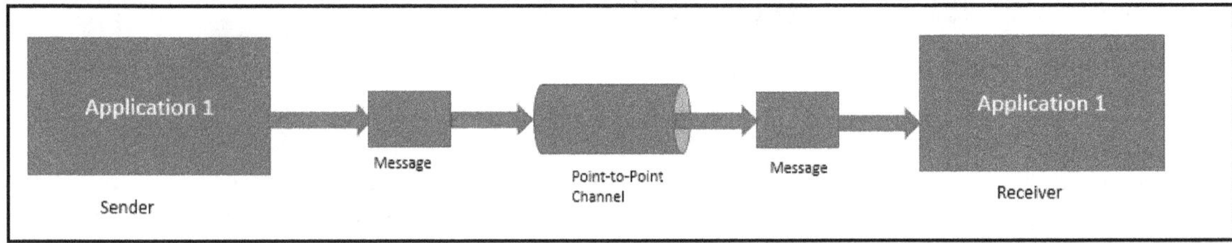


# Publish-subscribe channel pattern

This pattern will be of use for applications that use messaging to announce events. The announcement of events will involve sending messages to multiple receivers simultaneously. If the message is sent on a publish-subscribe channel, a copy of the message will be sent to each receiver:

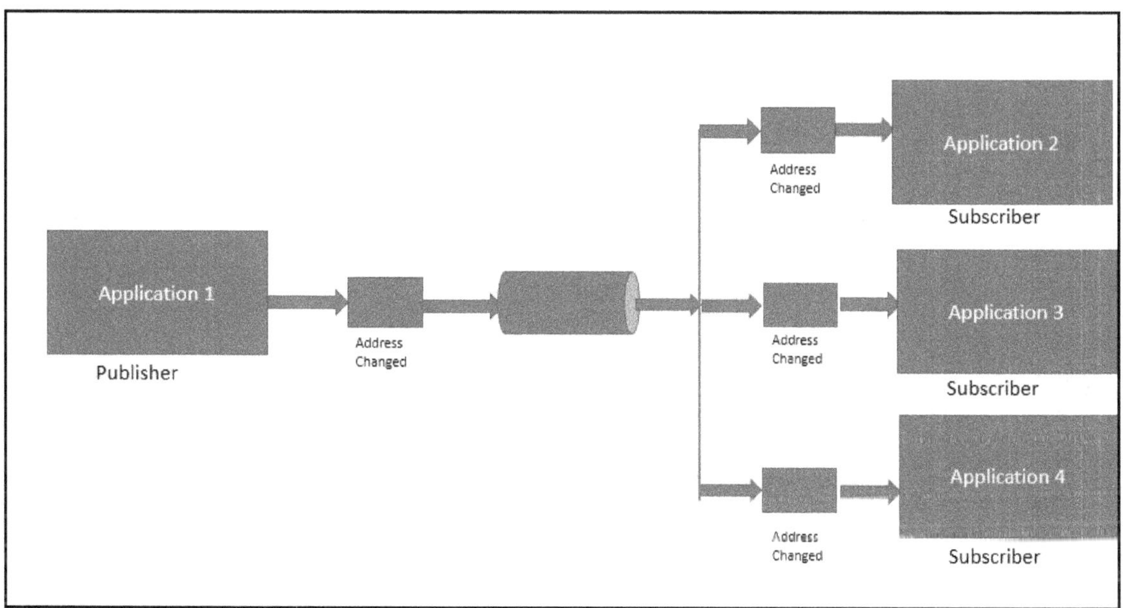


A publish-subscribe channel works basically like a broadcast mechanism. It has one input channel which is split into several output channels, one for each subscriber. When an event is published in the channel, a copy of the message is delivered to each of the output channels that are attached to it. Each output channel has only one subscriber attached to it. Each subscriber can consume the message only once. In this way, each subscriber gets a message only once and the message copies disappear from the channel once they are consumed.

# Datatype channel pattern

If several types of data are transmitted through a channel, it is important to differentiate the various formats of data. This is where the datatype channel pattern comes in handy. The diagram of a datatype channel pattern is depicted as follows:

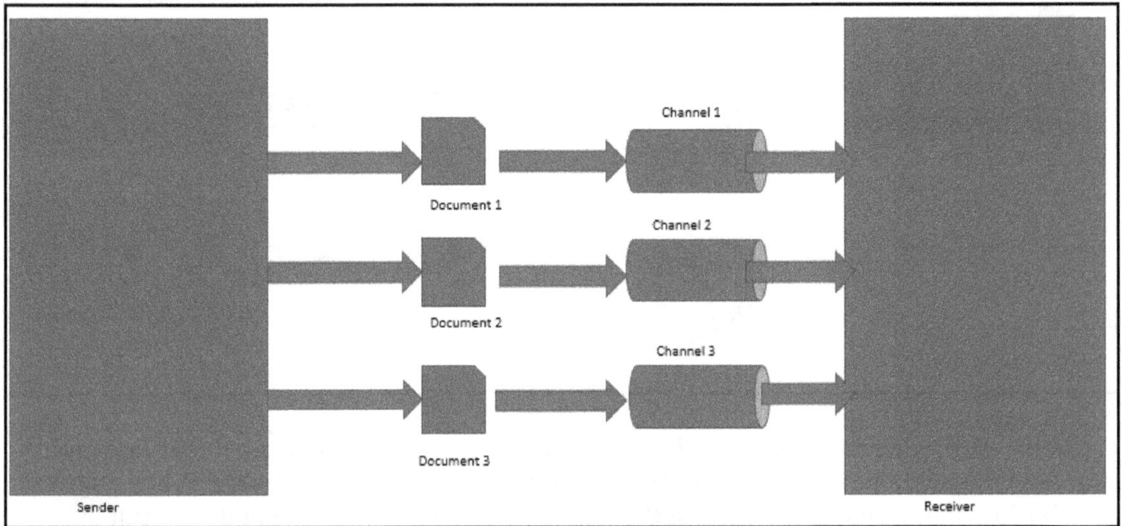


If a datatype channel is used for each type of data, messages on a specific channel will contain only the same type of data. The sender should know the type of data and send it through the appropriate channel for that type of data. The receiver should be able to know the type of data based on the channel from which it received the data.

# Message bus patterns

In enterprises, there will be several disparate systems. These systems should be able to communicate and share data with one another and operate seamlessly for the effective functioning of the enterprise. This is where the message bus pattern comes in handy. The architecture of the message bus pattern is depicted in the following diagram:

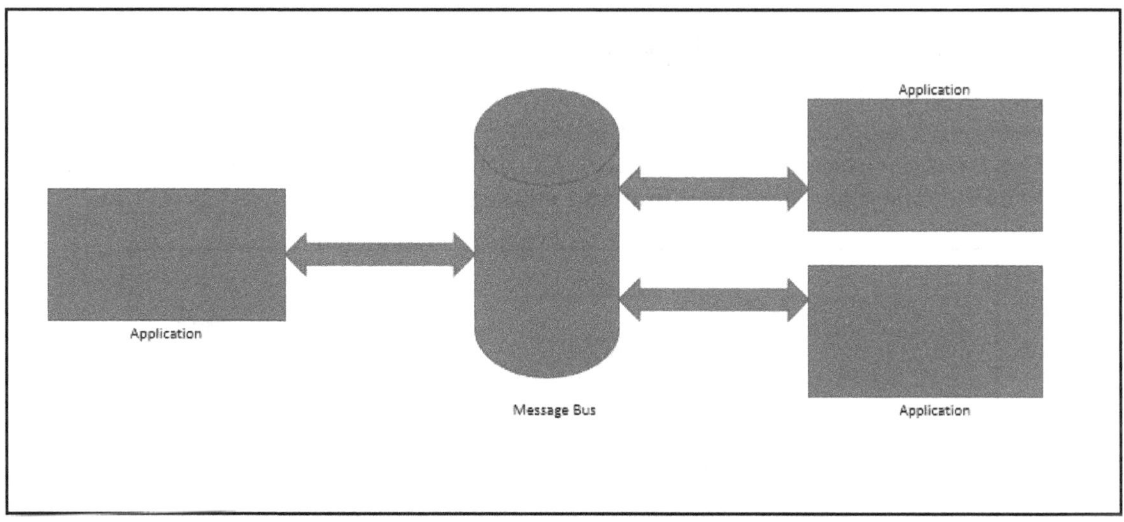


If the various applications are interconnected using a message bus, it allows them to communicate seamlessly using messages. The following are the main components of a message bus:

- **Common data model**
- **Common command set**
- **Messaging infrastructure**: This component allows the various systems to communicate using a shared set of interfaces

The concept of a message bus is very similar to that of a communication bus which is used in a computer. The communication bus facilitates communication among the various components of a computer such as CPU, memory, peripheral devices, and so on.

# Command message patterns

If an application wants to invoke the functionality provided by another application, the most commonly used method is remote procedure invocation. But if remote procedure invocation has to be used along with the concept of messaging, command message patterns are very useful. The diagram of the **command message** pattern is depicted as follows:

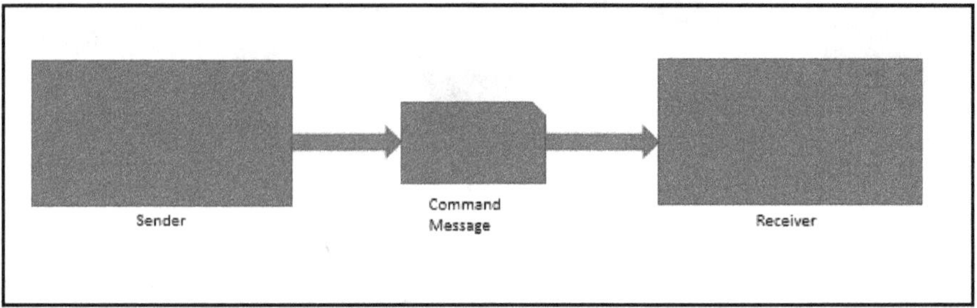


A command message is a message that is reliably used to invoke a procedure that is running in another application. There is no specific type for a command message. Command messages are normal messages that have a command embedded in them.

# Event message patterns

Several applications communicate with one another using events. If event-based communication happens from using messages, then event message patterns are used. The event message pattern is depicted in the following diagram:

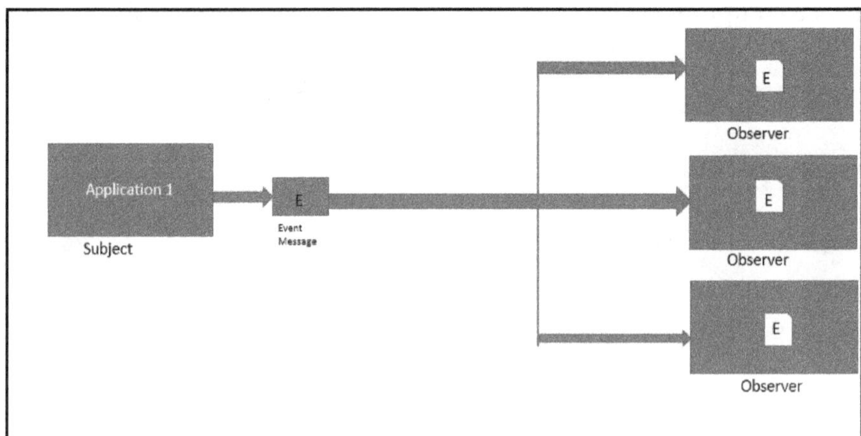

In an event message pattern, if the subject has to announce an event, it will first create an event object. This object is then wrapped in a message and sent on a channel. The observer will receive the event from the channel and process it. Messaging in events does not alter the event notification; it just ensures that the notification reaches the observer.

# Request-reply pattern

When applications communicate through messaging, it is typically one-way communication. Suppose if the applications want a two-way communication, then a request-reply pattern is used. In a request-reply pattern, the request message and the reply message will have their own channels. The diagram of a request-reply pattern is depicted as follows:

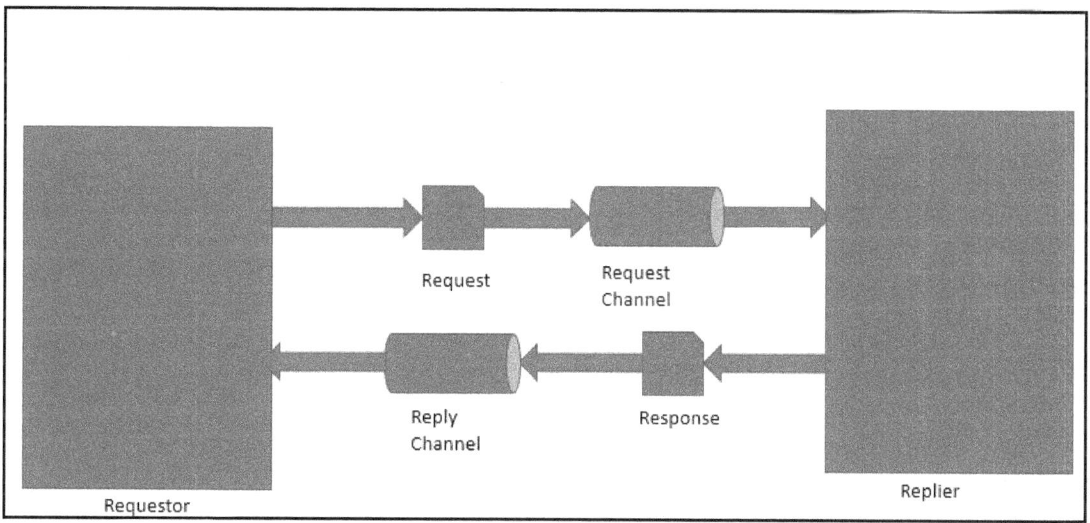

# Content-based router pattern

In many enterprises, a single function is spread across several systems. In such situations, it is important to ensure that the message goes through each of the systems that contain the function. In such situations, the content-based router pattern becomes very helpful. The content-based router pattern is depicted as follows:

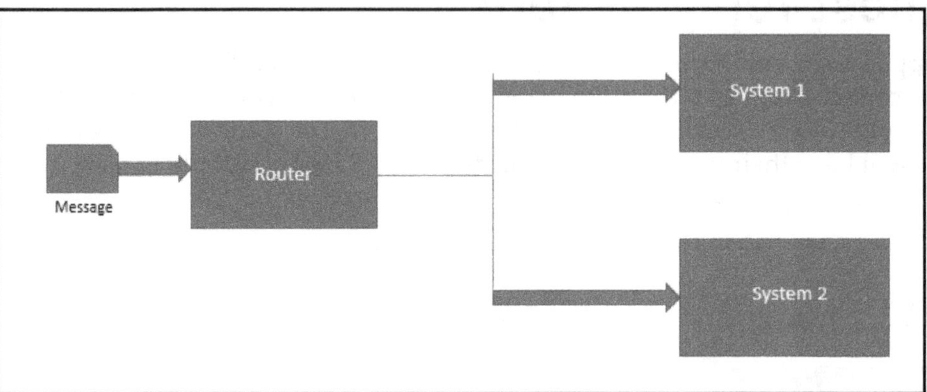


The content-based router pattern examines the content of the message and then routes the message onto the correct channel based on the data that is contained in the message. The parameters on which the message is routed could be one of the following:

- Existence of certain data values in specific fields
- Presence or absence of certain fields in the message

It is very important to ensure that in a content-based router, the routing function that is implemented in the router should be easy to maintain. It is also possible to maintain a content-based router in the form of a rules engine that calculates the destination channel based on a set of pre-configured rules.

# Message filter pattern

In many scenarios, there will be situations in which we are interested in receiving some kind of promotional messages/discounting messages, say for example from an e-commerce website based on a certain product that you may be interested in buying. But this may not be applicable to all messages. So in such situations, it is important to ensure that the unwanted messages get blocked or filtered. In such situations, the message filter pattern becomes very useful. The diagram depicting the message filter pattern is given as follows:

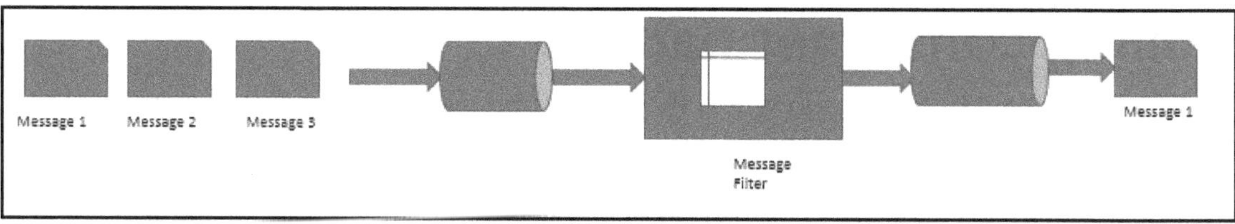


The message filter has only a single output channel. If the data present in the message matches the specific output criteria that are mentioned by the message filter, the message is routed to the output channel, else it is discarded.

# Resequencer pattern

When a message routing pattern is used, messages get routed through several systems based on the fulfillment of certain criteria or rules. But when messages pass through several systems, there is a likelihood that they get out of order. In these situations, the **resequencer** pattern comes in handy. The diagram depicting the resequencer pattern is given as follows:

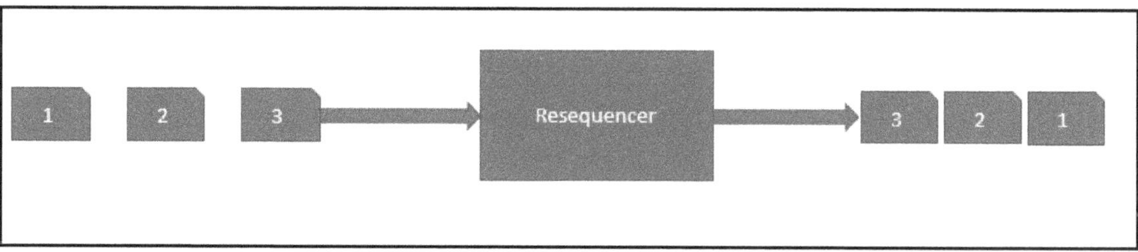

The resequencer is a stateful filter that can be used to reorder messages so that they can be published in a specific sequence to the output channel. The resequencer contains an internal buffer that stores a sequence of messages until the complete sequence is obtained. The in-sequence messages are published immediately to the output channel. The out-of-sequence messages are kept in the internal buffer until they are placed in sequence and then they are sent to the output channel. The resequencer just makes the message in-sequence; it does not generally modify the contents of the message.

# Polling consumer pattern

There will be several situations in which the application may not always be ready to consume messages. In such situations, the application would like to reach a state of readiness before it starts consuming messages. In such situations, the polling consumer pattern becomes very helpful. The diagram of a polling consumer pattern is depicted as follows:

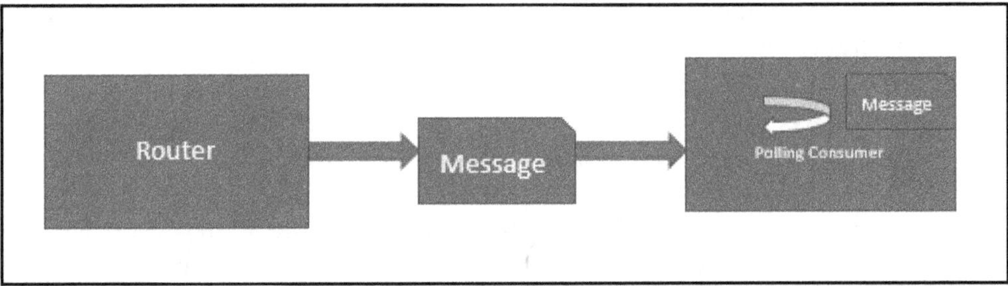


In this pattern, the application uses a polling consumer, which makes a call as and when it is ready to receive a message. The polling consumer is also known as a **synchronous receiver**. This is because the receiver thread is in a blocked state until a message is received. Most of the messaging APIs provide a `receive` method, which blocks until a message is delivered.

# Channel adapter

If applications communicate with the help of messaging, it is necessary to ensure that the applications can connect to the messaging system to send and receive messages. This is where the **channel adapter** is helpful. The diagram depicting the channel adapter pattern is shown as follows:

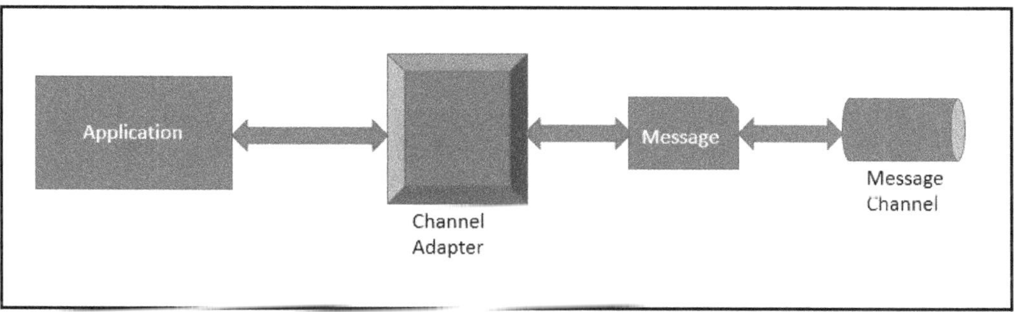


A channel adapter should be able to access the application's API or data and publish messages on a channel based on this data. It should also be able to invoke the functionality inside the application and receive messages. The adapter ideally acts as a client to the messaging system. The channel adapter invokes the functions of the application through an interface that is supplied by the application. This helps an application to remain integrated with a messaging system if it has a proper channel adapter. In the next section, we will focus on mobile integration patterns, that is, patterns that are used for integrating mobile devices to enterprise systems.

# Mobile integration pattern

We need a faster way for mobile devices to integrate with enterprise services, and this necessitates the need for a mobile integration pattern. When we talk about the integration of mobile services with enterprises, there are two main possibilities that could arise during the integration:

- A mobile application that is integrated with some function of the enterprise sends a request message to the enterprise system and gets a response in return
- An enterprise system sends a push notification message to a mobile application

This flow is shown in the following diagram:

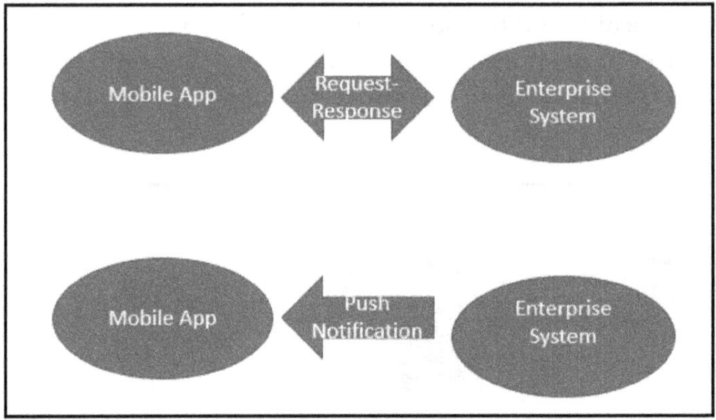


## Request-response pattern

To define a request-response pattern, it is necessary to ensure that mobile-ready interfaces are present in the enterprise services that are created in the ESB. This pattern provides support for the integration of mobile services in an ESB architecture. A special type of adapter customized for mobile services called a **mobile integration adapter** helps to integrate mobile applications with the mobile-related services that are running in the ESB. The major steps involved in this mobile integration are depicted in the following diagram:

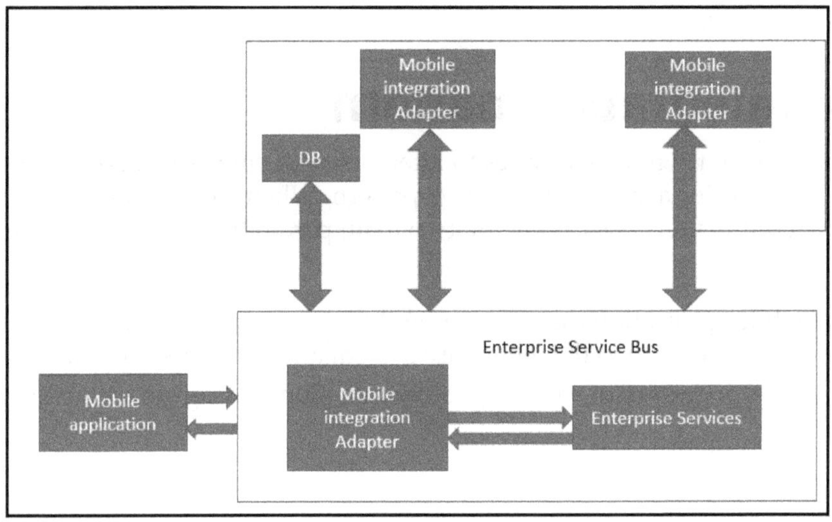

Here is how the integration happens:

1. As a first step, the mobile adapter sends the inbound request directly to the enterprise service.
2. Then the enterprise service present in the ESB establishes a connection with the required backend systems to process the inbound request. The ESB also works with the backend systems to get a response.
3. At last, the ESB sends the response to the mobile adapter which in turn passes the response back to the mobile application.

# Defining a push notification pattern

Push notification patterns are used if an enterprise application wants to send push notifications to the mobile devices. The steps involved in defining the push notification are depicted in the following diagram:

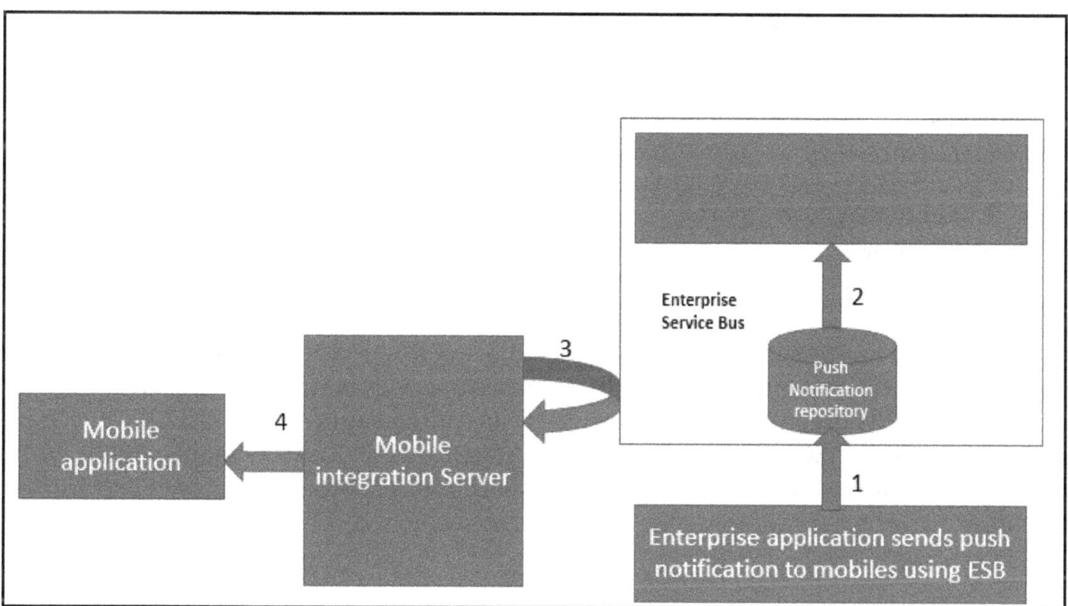

Enterprise applications typically use a backend service that is running on the mobile integration server to push the notification messages to devices. The following are the main steps in the workflow of the process:

1. The enterprise application sends a push notification to the mobile device using the ESB and mobile backend service
2. Once the ESB receives the notification, it calls the mobile backend service to send push notifications to the mobile device
3. Messages pass through the mobile integration server to reach the mobile application and the mobile device

At the start of the chapter, we discussed several types of external applications getting integrated with the enterprise systems. In the next section, we will have an overview of the API management pattern. In this section, we will focus briefly on the integration aspects while using microservices/API-based design concepts in architecture.

# API management pattern

The API management pattern integrates applications with enterprise systems and other cloud-based services using APIs. The following are the main components of the API management pattern:

- API management portal
- API user
- Enterprise services

The consumer of each API service first sends a request to the API management portal. The API management portal interacts with the enterprise service before sending a response to the consumer. APIs use industry-standard formats for messages such as SOAP for web services and XML or JSON for representational state transfer. The API management portal acts as a simple proxy and helps to forward request and response messages to and from the backend.

# Summary

At the start of the chapter, we examined several types of integration scenarios that exist in enterprises. Some of the key integration scenarios that exist in enterprises are the following:

- Information portals
- Data replication
- Shared business functions
- Service-oriented architectures
- Distributed business processes
- Business-to-business integration

After covering these topics, the main challenges faced in application integration were discussed. The techniques to overcome these challenges were also discussed. In the next section of the chapter, we discussed several types of messaging patterns at length. After messaging patterns, prominent mobile integration patterns were discussed. We concluded the chapter with a brief discussion of the API management pattern, which is the most recent trend in the industry.

# 5

# Domain-Driven Design (DDD) Principles and Patterns

Most of the commercial software application is created with a set of complex business requirements to solve the specific business problems or needs. However, expecting all the software developers/architects to be experts on business domains and expecting them to know entire business functions is also impractical. On the other side, how do we create software that brings value and get consumers with automated business needs to use the software? Software applications cannot just be a showpiece of technical excellence, but in most cases, they also have to have a real ease of automated business excellence. The domain-driven design and models are the answers to our questions.

This section will cover most of DDD aspects and patterns that can help successful implementations of DDD-based software.

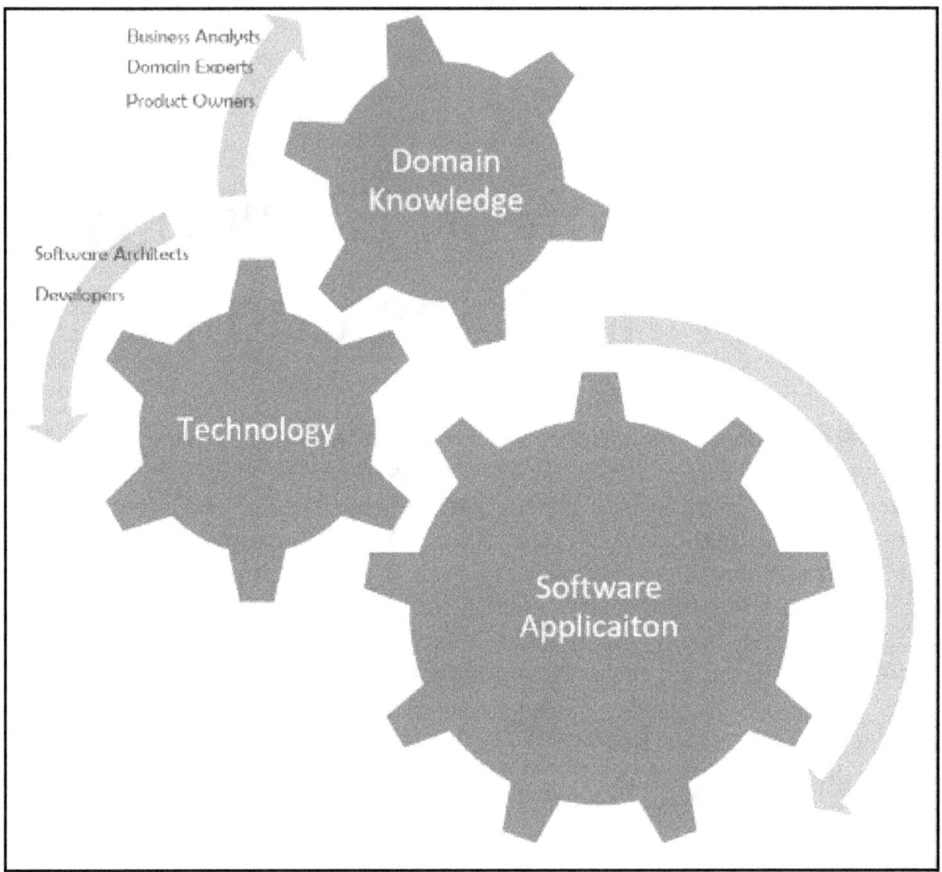


The preceding diagram is an attempt to visualize a domain-driven software model driven by collaborated effort from domain and technology experts.

DDD concepts, principles, and patterns bring technology and business excellence together to any sophisticated software applications that can be created and managed. DDD was coined by Evan and most of the content of this chapter is the influence of his book *Domain-Driven Design - Tackling Complexity in the Heart of Software* and also from the book *Pattern-Principles-And Practices* by Scott Millett and Nick Tune.

This section intends to cover a few essential aspects of DDD and also discuss a few common domain-driven design patterns in detail.

# Principles, characteristics, and practices of DDD

Before we delve into various design patterns, let us touch upon the fundamental principles of DDD, then few primary characteristics constituents, and also few best practices that help teams to adopt and follow DDD.

## Principles

The fundamental principles of DDD are described in the following sections.

### Focusing on the core domain

This principle suggests product development teams to focus more on the core domain, that is, the parts that are most important to a business and which need more attention than others. So, we need to identify the core domain by distilling and decomposing a big problem domain into subdomains. For instance, when designing a retail banking software, we should focus on the credit and debit accounting instead of the manufacturing and distribution of credit cards and debit cards as they support functions and they can be outsourced as well.

### Collaborate and learn

As we mentioned in the introduction section, software experts may not know the domain, and the domain analysts may not know the technology and software implementations. So, collaboration and learning from each other is inevitable for DDD aspects, without which the software design or development won't happen at all. For instance, to develop a back office software application for an investment bank, the risk management experts and Software experts need to work together to learn the systems, applicability, usability, banking customer's intentions, and so on.

In recent days, traditional banks are collaborating with financial technology startups aka fintech, as they see significant benefits of data analytics, AI, and machine learning into core banking systems as they would be able to take accurate decisions, innovate faster along with solving banking industry's everyday problems.

## Model the domain

As we now understand the collaboration and learn principle from the previous section, the collaboration, deep learning, and get insights of the core domain along with fundamental functions, this is inevitable. The output expected out of model the domain principle is a domain model, which is well-organized and structured knowledge of the problem in the core domain space along with fundamental concepts, vocabulary, issues, and relationships among the involved entities. You can seek contributions from different stakeholders such as analysts, domain experts, business partners, tech savvy users, and core developers and build these domain models, so everyone in a team understands the functional concepts and definitions and also how the current problem is tackled and solved.

## Evolve

Another critical aspect of the domain model is evolution. Domain models need to evolve over time through iterations and feedback. The design team starts with one significant problem and traverses through different scopes of the core domain along with generated models with incremental changes iteratively. It is critical as models need to adjust to feedback from domain experts while delivering domain models dealing with complexity.

## Talk in ubiquitous language

Collaborating, learning, and defining a model brings a lot of initial communication barriers between software specialists and domain experts. So, evolving domain models by practicing the same type of communications (discussions, writings, and diagrams) within a context is paramount for successful implementations, and this sort of conversation is called ubiquitous language. It is structured around the domain model and extensively used by all the team members within a bounded context. It should be the medium or mode to connect all the activities of the team during the development of software.

The design team can establish deep understanding, and connect domain jargons and software entities with ubiquitous language to keep discovering and evolving their domain models.

# Characteristics

The following characteristics are the primary constituents and may serve as a glossary of items that we will discuss in this chapter. You will see that many of these are factored into the patterns that we present in this section:

- **Domain model**: Organized and structured knowledge related to the specific problem.
- **Bounded context**: A system fulfils the fundamental goals of the real-world complex business problems, provides a clear and shared understanding of what can be consistent, and what can be independent.
- **Entities**: These are mutable objects, which can change their attributes without changing their identity (for example, the employee's ID doesn't change even when their email ID, address, and name changes).
- **Value objects**: These are immutable objects (unlike entities), distinguishable only by the state of their properties. The equality of value objects is not based on their identity. (Two location objects can be the same by their long and latitude values.)
- **Encapsulation**: Fields of an object are exposed only for private access, in other words, detected only through accessor methods (setters and getters).
- **Aggregate**: This is a collection of entities (for example, a computer is an aggregate of entities such as software and hardware). The aggregate may not work without those objects.
- **Aggregate root**: This is an entry point to aggregates, and only known reference to any outside object. This helps to create the precise boundary around aggregates.

# Best practices

We have listed a few best practices for a team that intends to dwell in DDD for their software product development:

- Gather requirements and capture required behaviors
- Focus on what stakeholders want, when, and why
- Distill the problem space
- Be a problem solver first, technologist comes second
- Manage the complexity with abstraction and create subdomains

- Understand the reality of the landscape with context maps and bounded contexts
- Model a solution, tackle ambiguity, and carve out an area of safety
- Make implicit concepts explicit

# DDD patterns

In this section, we will browse through a set of patterns to build enterprise applications from the domain models. Applying these design patterns together with OO concepts to a system helps meet the business needs.

This section covers significant aspects of DDD design patterns grouped as strategic design patterns and tactical design patterns of DDD.

## Strategic patterns

The primary aim of this group is to bring understanding and consensus between the business and the software development teams with more emphasis on business interests and goals. The strategic patterns help software development team members focus on what is more important and critical to the business by identifying a core domain. The core domain is a particular area of the company or even a specific slice that is critical.

Few primary constituents of strategic patters are ubiquitous language, domain, subdomain, core domain, bounded context, and a context map. We will see how one can integrate the disparate systems via the strategic design patterns such as bounded context, messaging, and REST discussed in this chapter with those constituents.

## Ubiquitous language

A model acts as a universal language to manage communication between software developers and domain experts. The following table shows the example of ubiquitous languages and their equivalent pseudo code:

| **Ubiquitous language** | **Equivalent pseudo code** | **Comments** |
|---|---|---|
| We administer vaccines | `AdministerVaccines {}` | Not a core domain—need some more specific details |
| We administer flu shots to patients | `patientNeedAFluShot()` | Better, may be missing some domain concepts |
| Nurse administers flu vaccines to patient in standard doses | `Nurse->administer vaccine(patient, Vaccine.getStandardDose())` | Much better, and may be good to start with |

## Domain, subdomain, and core domain

Domain refers to a problem space that software teams try to create a solution for, and represents how the actual business works. The vaccines example from the table can be seen as domain, with the end-to-end flow, managing vaccinations, preventive medicines, dosages, side effects, and so on. Core domain is the core business that the organization does not want to outsource. So, the core domain here in this context is vaccination, and other functions like patients management, cost of vaccines, vaccination camps, and so on are subdomains and are outside of the core domain. Core domains interact with subdomains.

## Bounded contexts

Bounded contexts are distinctive conceptual lines that define the boundaries and separate the contexts from other parts of the system. A bounded context represents refined business capabilities, and it is the focus of DDD. It deals with large distributed models and teams by dividing them into different bounded contexts and being explicit about their interrelationships.

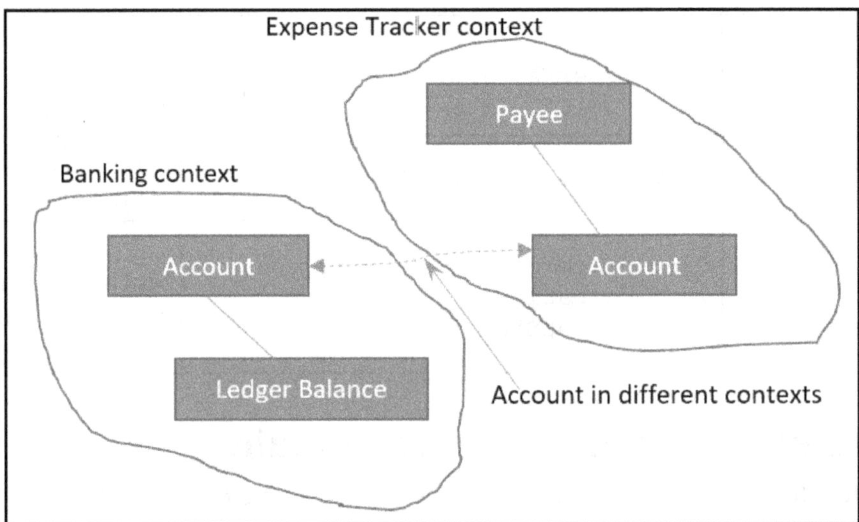


Before we go deeper into patterns, let's refresh the idea about bounded contexts. The preceding diagram depicts account in both contexts; though the account doesn't differ, the contexts do. The following sections deal with patterns that help integrate the bounded contexts for any DDD solution.

# Integrating bounded contexts

The Bounded contexts help in identifying the  relationships between subsystems and so one can choose the communication methods between those subsystems. Selecting appropriate communication and establishing relationships with the established communication is the responsibility of the designers, which helps them too to ensure there is no impact on project delivery timelines and efficiency. An example of integration and establishing communication reflecting explicit models could be integrating a payment system with an e-commerce sales system. Choosing the communication method is critical, and we will see more of integrating bounded contexts in the following sections.

# Autonomous bounded context

To ensure atomicity, design loosely coupled systems with fewer dependencies; solutions can also be developed in isolation.

# The shared-nothing architecture

While guaranteeing bounded contexts to be self-reliant, retaining the integrity of the bounded context is also critical. The shared-nothing pattern suggests that each bounded context has its own data stores, codebases, and developers, as shown in the following diagram:

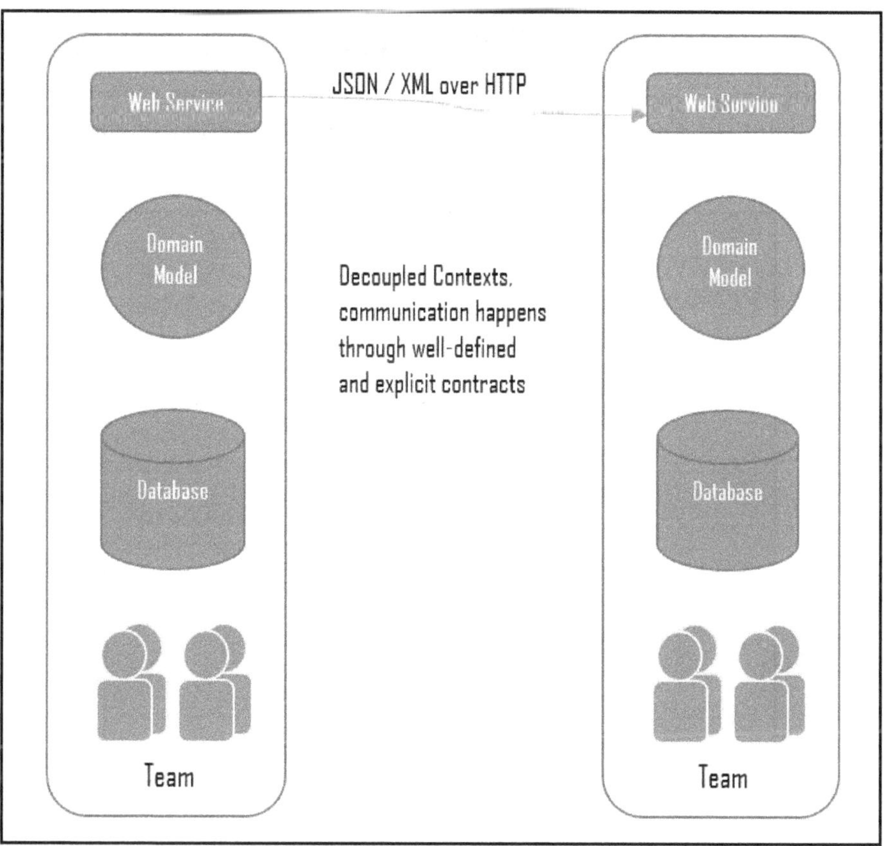

As each bounded context is physically isolated, it can evolve independently for internal reasons, resulting in uncompromised domain model with super-efficient and faster delivery of business values.

## Single responsibility codes

It's a best practice to partition the software systems according to their business capabilities, that is, by isolating separate business capabilities into different bounded contexts. For example, the shipping code of the business is not affected by a new shipping provider that got added to Sales.

## Multiple bounded contexts (within a solution)

Depending on the code (language), deployments, and infrastructure, there are situations where different bounded context resides in the same code repository or a solution with combined contexts to depict one big picture of full business use cases.

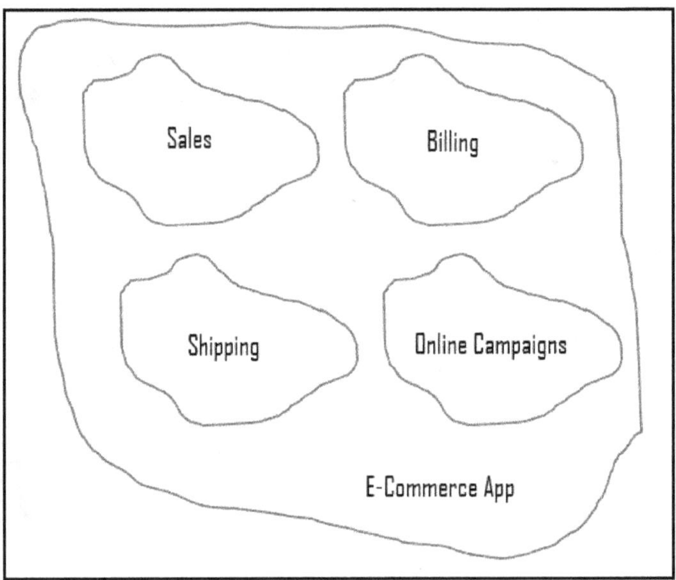

To maintain the different contexts within a solution, this pattern suggests keeping namespaces distinct or recommends projects to keep bounded contexts separate.

## Adoption of SOA principles

Build highly scalable systems using DDD with SOA concepts and patterns. Build bounded context as SOA services to solve the technical and social challenges (integrating teams and developing at a high velocity) of bounded context integration. Please refer to `Chapter 7`, *Service-Oriented Architecture (SOA)*, for more details on SOA's principles and practices.

# Integrating with legacy systems

Legacy systems is always a case in the real world, and they come with exciting challenges while we try to incorporate the latest industry improvements into them. In DDD, this problem is more interesting to address as there are many handy patterns available that help limit the impact of the legacy on the other parts of the system, manage complexity, and save designers from having to reduce explicitness (against DDD philosophy) of their new code to integrate into legacy modules or components.

We will touch upon bubble context, autonomous bubble context, and expose legacy systems as services in this section.

## The bubble context

If a team wants to start applying the DDD to the legacy systems but it is not yet familiar with DDD practices, then the bubble context pattern can be considered. As the bounded context in the legacy may be an isolated codebase, the bubble context pattern provides clarity, and directions that to the team to create domain models and evolve as well. The bubble context reflects the best of the DDD philosophy of iteration, and it progresses by having full control over the domain model.

It is considered as the best fit to facilitate frequent iterations and get insights even when legacy code is involved.

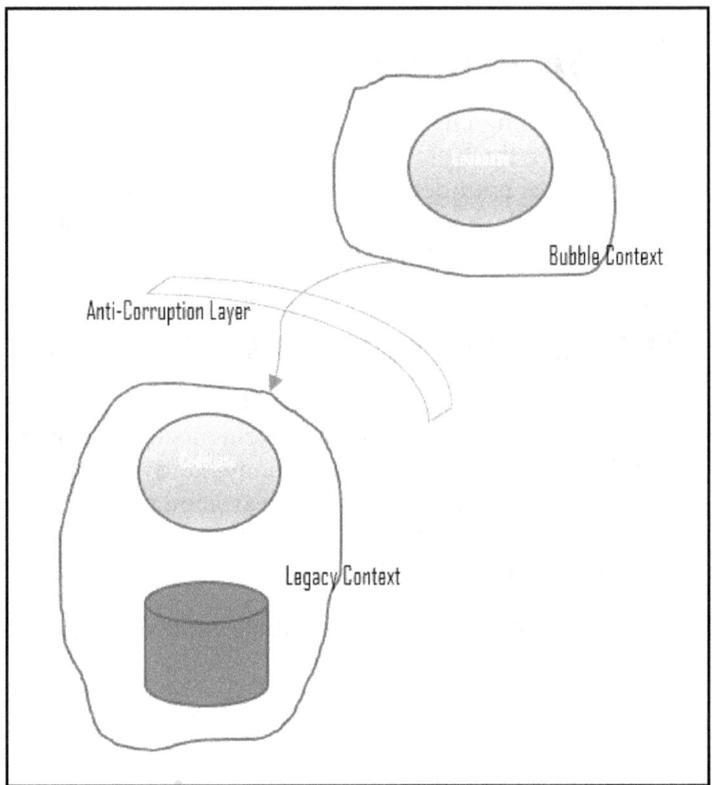


When you need to integrate with legacy code but do not want to create any dependency or tight coupling with a legacy system, as bubble context does, this pattern suggests using an anonymous bubble called **autonomous bubble context**. Bubble context gets all its data from the legacy system, whereas the autonomous bubble context has its own data store and is able to run in isolation of the legacy code or other bounded contexts.

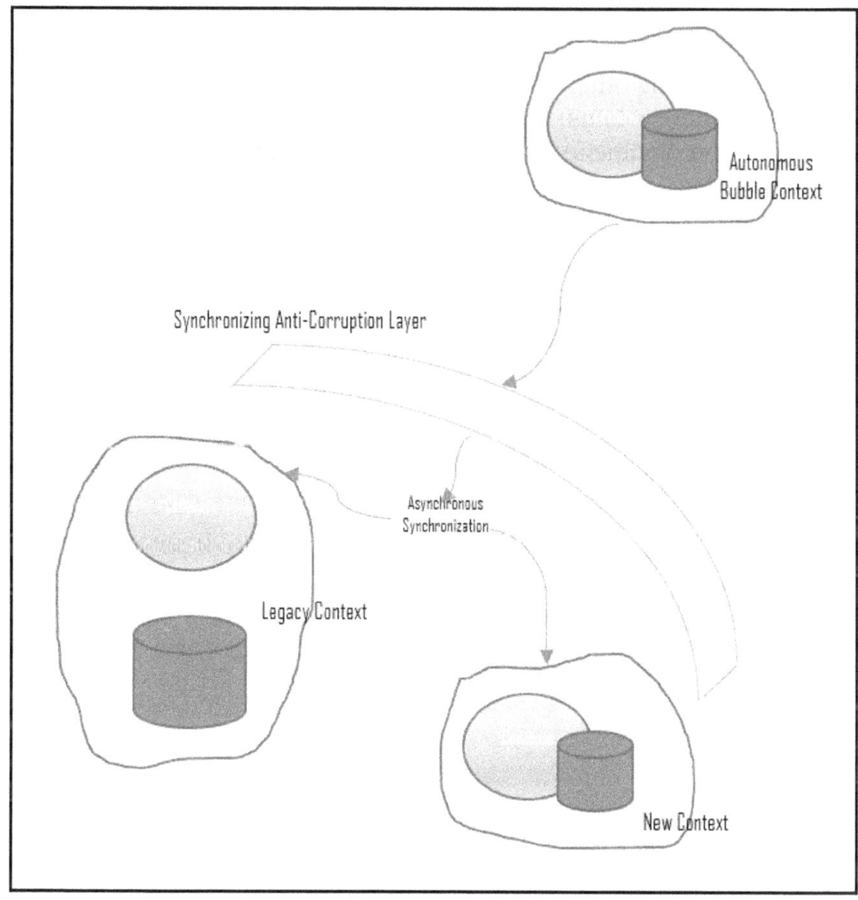


The preceding diagram depicts the autonomous bubble context, and you may notice that the bubble context has dependencies with legacy context. However, the autonomous bubble context has its own storage, and so it can run in isolation.

## The anti-corruption layer

An isolating layer talks to the other systems through its existing interface with little or no modifications (to the other systems) and provides clients with the functionality of their own domain. This layer is responsible for translating communication between the two models in both directions, as needed.

## Expose as a service

It may be a good idea to expose legacy system as a service, especially when the legacy context needs to be consumed by multiple new contexts. This pattern is also known as the **open host pattern**.

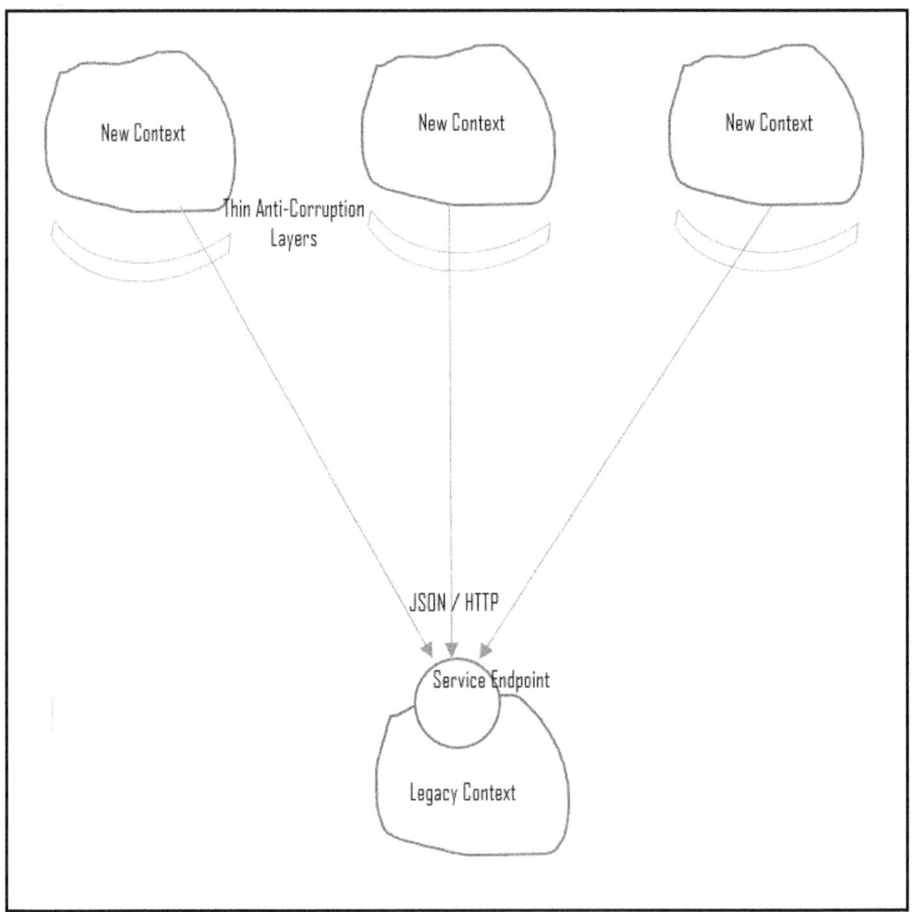

Each new context still has to translate the response from the legacy to its internals; however, with simplified open host APIs, one can mitigate the translation complexity.

With this pattern, there is a need for some modifications to the legacy context (unlike the bubble context); also, standardization of consumable API SLAs may be challenging as it has multiple consumers.

We can clearly justify that a lot of legacy systems in the real world would like to adopt DDD; however, with the lack of right patterns and given the cost and impacts, there are genuine reasons and hesitations to move toward DDD. Recognizing and harnessing these models should ease the situations and encourage organizations to adopt DDD for their legacy systems and progress toward faster delivery.

# Distributed bounded context integration strategies

Distribution is inevitable in the modern world for various reasons, and primarily for system abilities such as availability, scalability, reliability, and fault tolerance. This section briefly touches upon a few integration strategies for the distributed bounded context, such as Database integration, Flat file integration, Messaging, and REST. We will cover how those patterns help integeratting distributed bounded contexts. Also, we will see (briefly) how reactive solutions help in integration strategies.

# Database integration

The database integration pattern is one of the conventional approaches of using a single data source that lets an application write to a specific database location and lets another application read from it. The access by another application can be made as polling with some frequency. This pattern might come in handy for prototypes or even for **most viable product** (**MVP**) delivery.

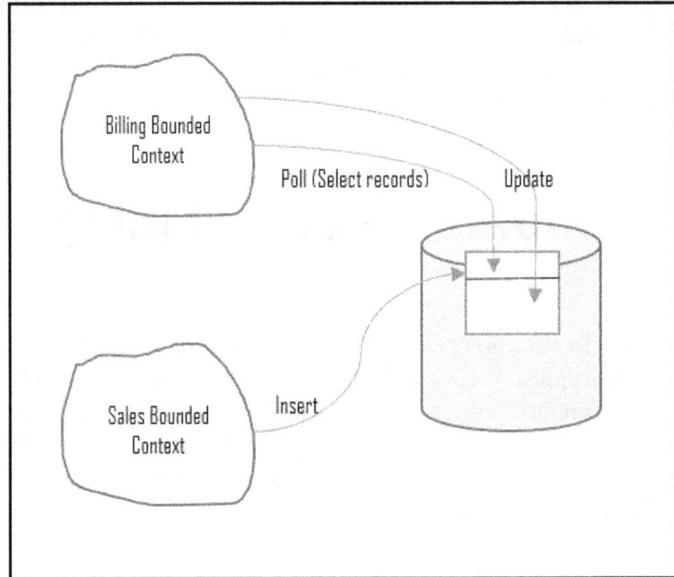


The preceding diagram depicts an example of database integration, where the sales team inserts the records and the billing context polls to the same data source. If it finds the sales record, it processes and updates the same row.

While this pattern has advantages of loose coupling, it also has a few drawbacks, such as single point of failure, and needs a mechanism for efficient fault handling and so on. DB down scenario is a SPOF example, and to mitigate, one may need to go with a clustered DB, buy more hardware to scale, or consider the cloud infrastructure, and so on.

# Flat file integration

The flat file integration pattern is similar to database integration; however, instead of having a database to integrate two components, it suggests using flat files. The updates, inserts, and polling are needed just as we would in another pattern, but this is a little more flexible. However, this comes with some disadvantages like managing the file formats, concurrency, and locks, among other things, would need more involvement and effort, leading to scalability and reliability issues.

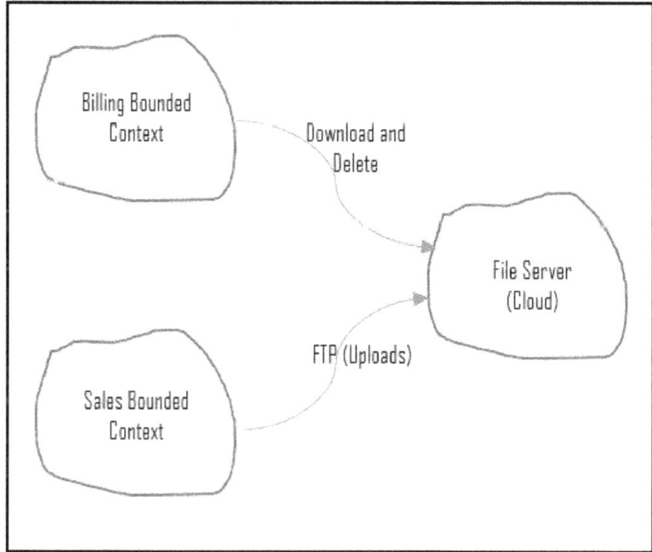


This diagram is the sample implementation for flat file integration and involves polling, update, and delete.

# Event-driven architecture and messaging

Messaging and event-driven architecture pattern bring the best out of modeling communication between bounded contexts with distributed systems. This section under DDD intends to ensure you understand the significance of EDA and messaging patterns within the context of DDD. And also to emphasize the benefit of implementing asynchronous messaging and EDA patterns for communication between the contexts. The benefits include increased reliability even on failures of subsystems. We have covered most of the EDA and messaging patterns well and in-depth in `Chapter 8`, *Event-Driven Architecture Patterns*, and `Chapter 9`, *Microservices Architecture Patterns*, and we encourage you to refer to those chapters and get insights about event-driven and messaging patterns.

# Tactical patterns

Tactical patterns help manage complexities and provide clarity in behaviors of domain models. The primary focus of these patterns is to protect models from corruption by offering protection layers.

In this section, we will touch upon the few of the common patterns that help in creating object-oriented domain models.

At the end of this section, we will also briefly cover the emerging patterns of event sourcing and domain events.

# Patterns to model the domain

This section will discuss few tactical patterns, and explain how they represent the policies and logic within the problem domain. They express elements of models in the code, the relationship between the objects and model rules, and bind the analysis details to the code implementation.

We will discuss the following patterns in details:

- Entities
- Value Objects
- Domain Services
- Modules
- Aggregates

- Factories
- Repositories

The following diagram depicts various tactical patterns and their logical flow:

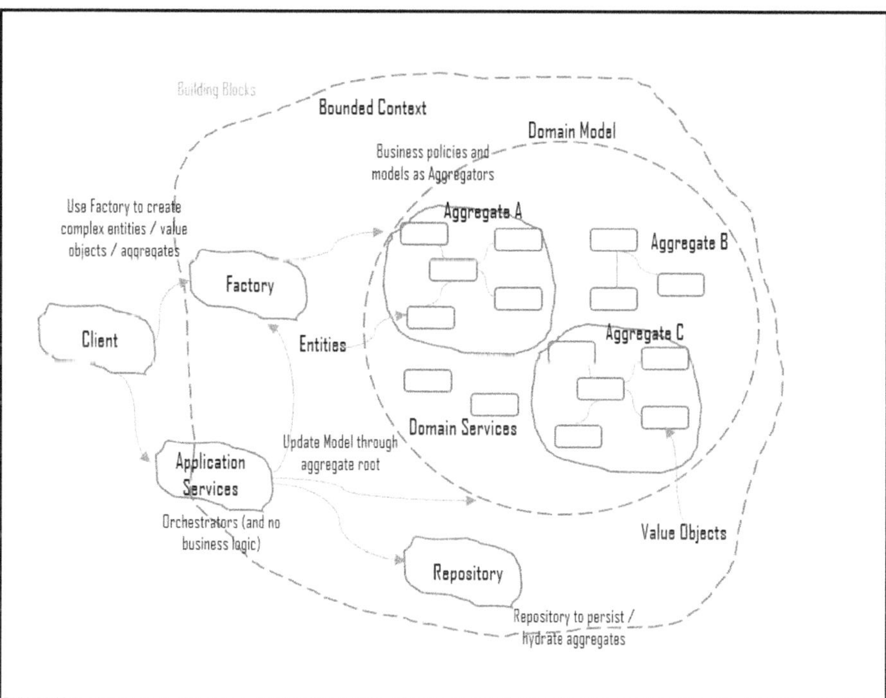


# Entities

As stated in the introduction section, an entity is a mutable object. It can change its attributes without changing its identity. For example, a product is an entity, which is unique and won't change its ID (distinctiveness) once it is set.

However, its price, description, and so on, can be changed as many as times it needs to.

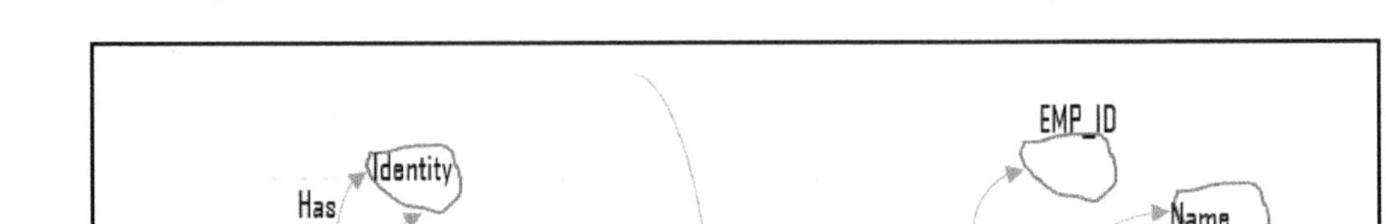

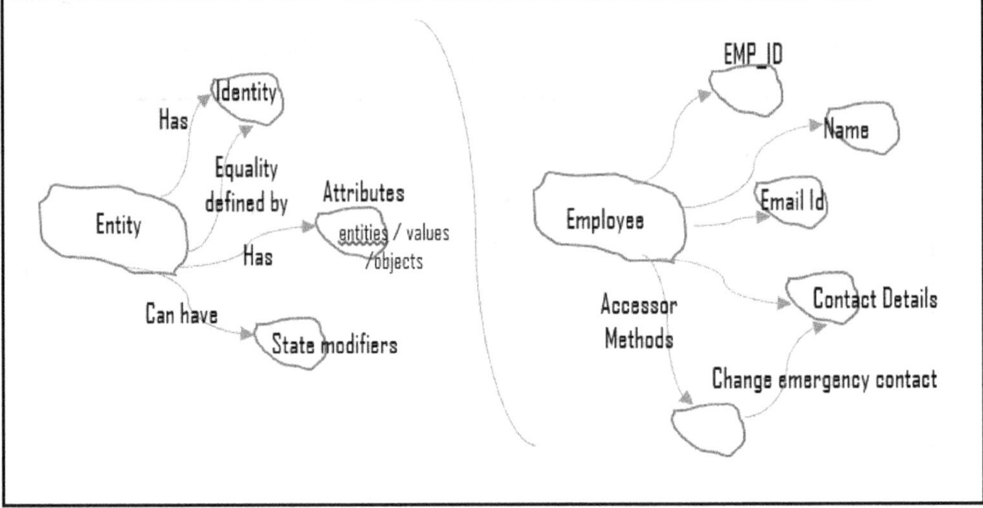


The preceding diagram depicts an entity along with an example. An employee ID is unique and never changes. However, there is a contact detail that can be modified by accessor methods.

Entities have the following properties:

- They are defined by their identity
- The identity remains the same throughout its lifetime
- They are responsible for equality checks

# Value objects

Unlike entities, value objects are immutable and used as descriptors for model elements. They are known to the system only by their characteristics, and they don't need to have unique identifiers. They are always associated with other objects (for example, Delivery Address in the sales order can be a value object) and it is consistently associated with sales order context; otherwise, it doesn't have any meaning.

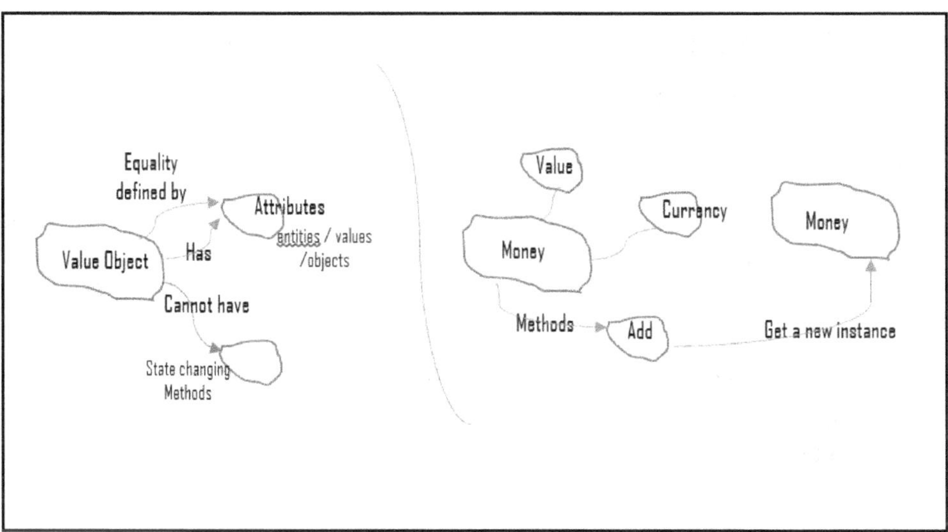


The preceding diagram depicts the basic concept of a value object along with an example, and the following diagram is a sample class representation of entity and value object:

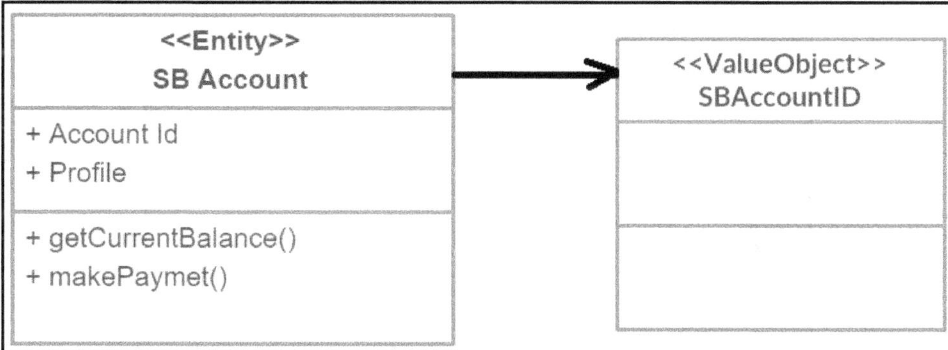


The following list describes the characteristics of value objects:

- They describe the properties and characteristics within a problem domain
- They do not have an identity
- They are immutable, that is, the content of the object cannot be changed; instead, properties modeled as value objects must be replaced

# Domain services

In ubiquitous language, there are situations where actions cannot be attributed to any specific entity or value object, and those operations can be termed as **domain service** (not an application service).

Domain services encapsulate the domain logic and concepts that may not be modeled as entities or value objects, and they are responsible for orchestrating business logic using entities and value objects. The following are a few characteristics/features of domain services:

- Domain services neither have identity nor state
- Any operation performed by the domain services does not belong to any of the existing entities
- Any domain operation in the domain service carry specific objects of the domain model

The following class diagram depicts a sample money transfer operation from one account to another. As we won't be knowing in which object we can store the transfer operation, we choose domain service for this operation:

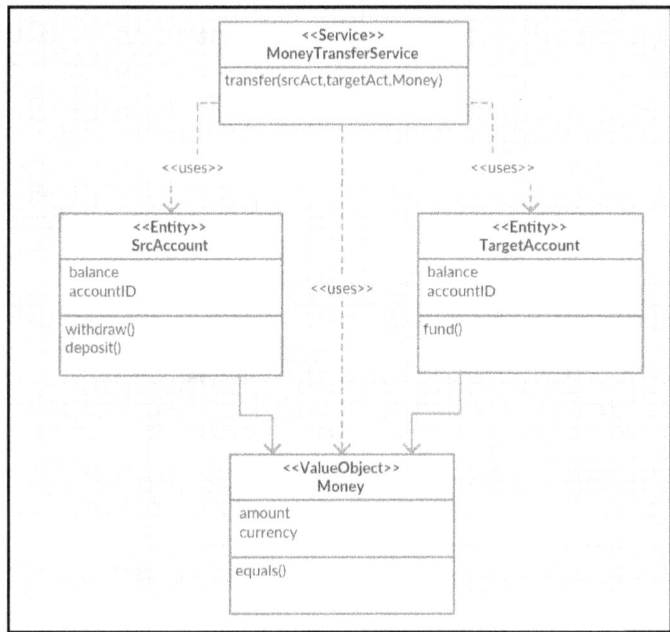

# Modules

Modules are used to decompose the domain model. Naming the modules is part of the ubiquitous language, and they represent a distinct part of domain models and enable clarity when in isolation. Modules help developers to quickly read and understand the domain model in code before deep diving into class development. Note that decomposing domain models is different from subdomains' decomposition of the domain and bounded context.

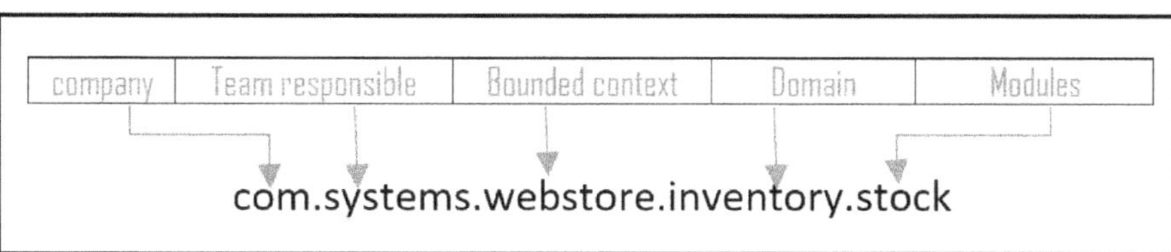


The preceding diagram depicts a sample module name and a sample template to follow.

# Aggregates

In DDD, the concept of an aggregate is a boundary that helps in decomposing larger modules into smaller clusters of domain objects, and so the technical complexities can be managed as a high level of abstraction. Aggregates help in doing the following:

- Reducing and constraining relationships between domain objects
- Grouping objects of the same business use cases and viewing them as a unified model

Every aggregate has a specific root and border, and within that particular border, all the possible invariants should be satisfied. Domain invariants are statements or rules that always need to be adhered to and help preserve consistency (also known as **atomic transactional coherence**).

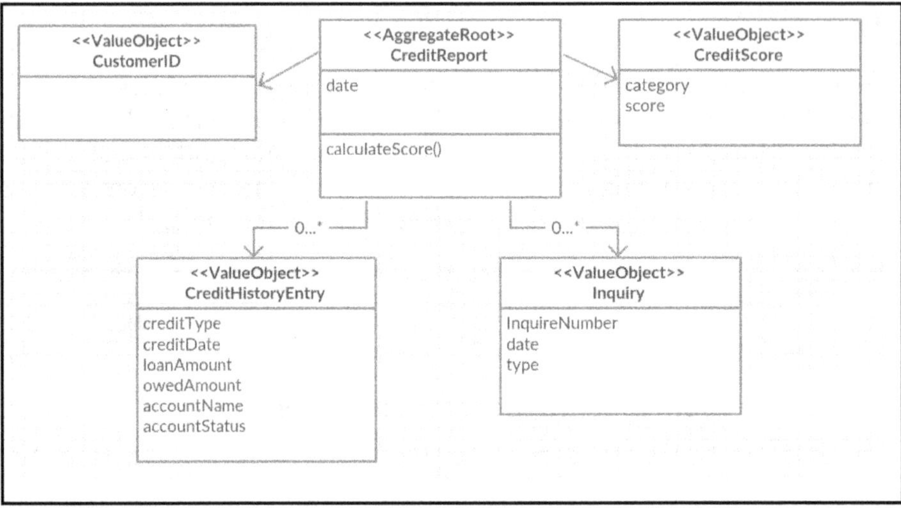


The preceding diagram represents an aggregator sample implementation and brief information about each class and its characteristics associated with aggregates context as follows:

- **CreditReport**: This includes user information and links, and saves and stores external linkage by **Customer ID** (identifier).
- **CustomerID**: This an independent aggregate that preserves user information
- **CreditScore**: This holds credit rating estimation rule and act as invariants. This invariant gets modified/impacted based on credit modifications history.
- **CreditHistoryEntry**: This helps achieve transactional coherence when it's modified.
- **Inquiry**: This can handle specific credit score requests from third-party organizations.

# Factories

Factories are a pattern to separate the use (of the object) from the construction (of the object). Aggregates, entities, and value objects create some level of complexity within a domain model, especially with larger domain models. Factories help to express the (creation and use of) complex objects in a better manner.

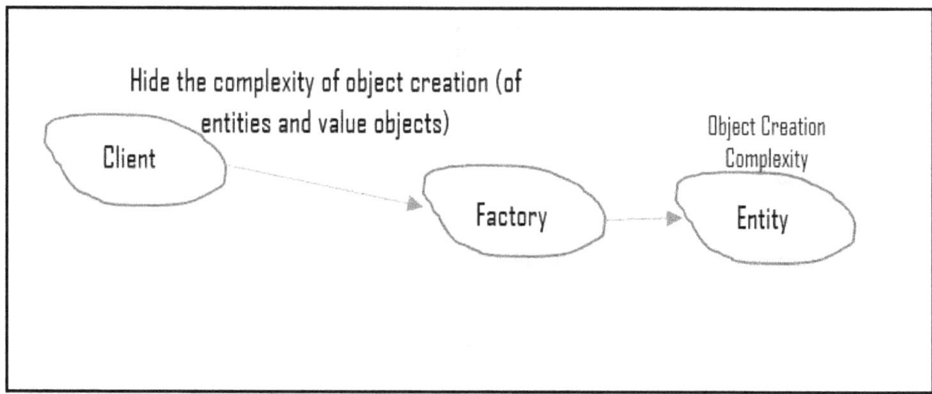


The preceding diagram might help grasp a quick detail about factory creation from the DDD perspective. The following are some characteristics of factories that we would want to be refreshed with:

- Separating use from construction
- Encapsulating internals (and avoid exposing the internals of aggregate)
- Hiding decisions on the creation type-domain layer factories to abstract the type of class to be created
- Decluttering complex domain models

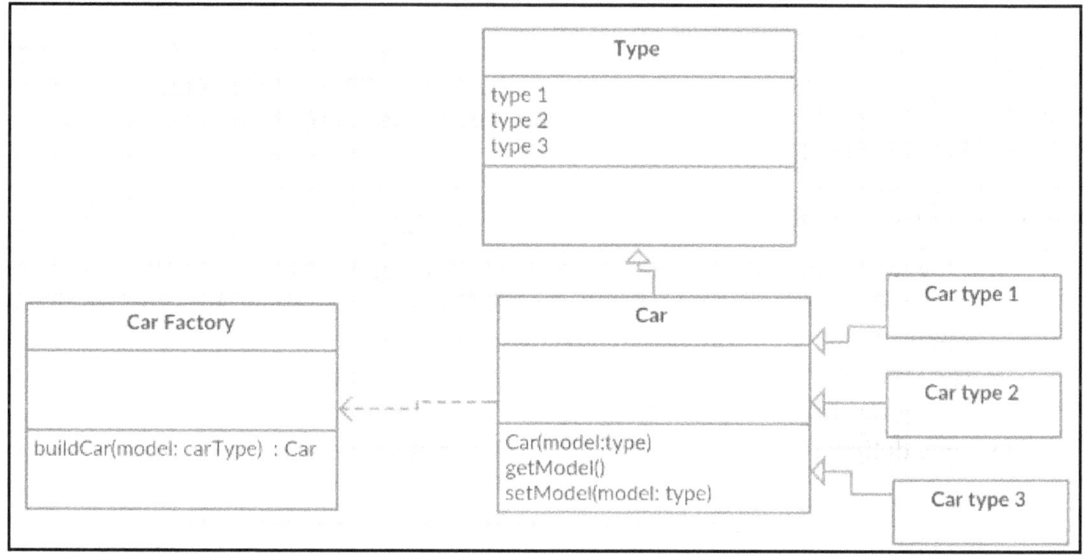

The preceding class diagram intends to give a sample view of the factory implementation for car models to be created; the creation complexity is abstract to the domain.

# Repositories

Repositories are patterns to manage aggregate persistence and retrieval while ensuring a clear separation between the data model and the domain model. Repositories are mediators that act as a collection of facades for storage and persistence.

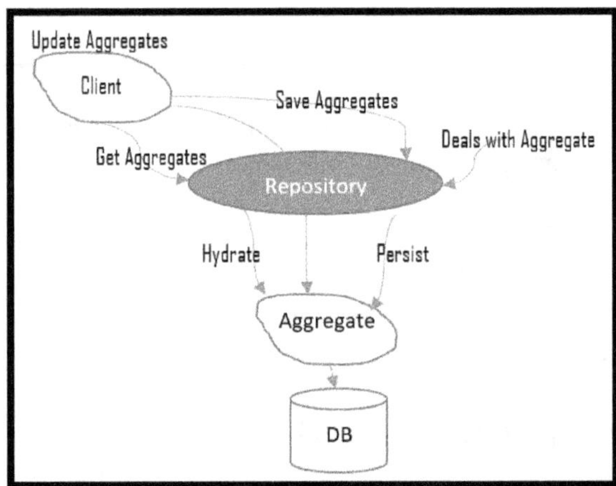


The preceding diagram depicts a sample structure of a repository model. It shows the client operation of save and update (persistence) with aggregates, through repository, while there is a separate access to the repository (**Deals with Aggregate** in the above diagram); a clear separation between the domain and data model.

Repositories differ from traditional data access strategies in the following three ways:

- They restrict access to domain objects by allowing the retrieval and persistence of aggregate roots while ensuring that all the changes and invariants are handled by aggregates
- They hide the underlying technology used for persistence and retrieval of aggregates from the facades
- They define a boundary between the domain model and the data model

We have the following two types of repositories:

- Repositories as collections
- Repositories as permanent data storage

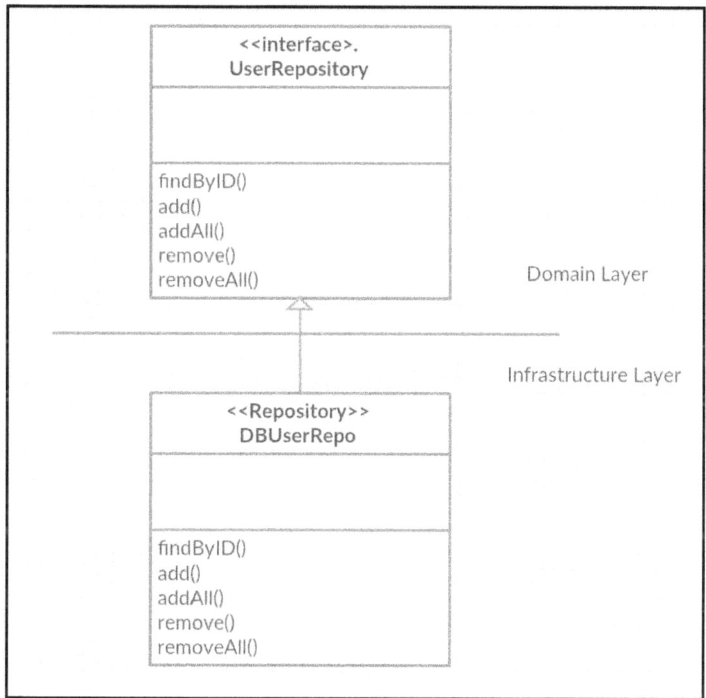


The preceding class diagram depicts a sample structure of a repository class and its underlying layer. The repository is within the infrastructure layer and extends the domain layer interface (restrict access).

# Emerging patterns

In this section, we will cover the following two emerging patterns:

- **Domain events**: They enforce consistency between multiple aggregates of the same domain
- **Event sourcing**: This is a way of persisting the application's state and finding the current state by traversing through the history of those saved states

# Domain events

The domain event pattern is a preferred a way to trigger side effects across multiple aggregates within the same domain. A domain event is an event that occurs in a particular domain, which the other parts of the same domain (subdomain) should also be aware of and may need to react to it as well.

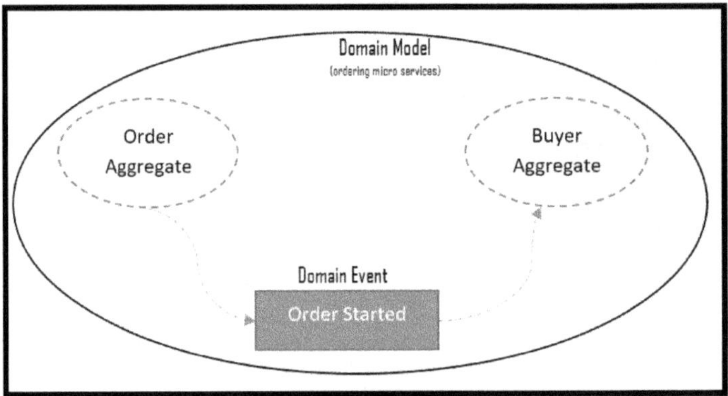


A domain event pattern helps to do the following:

- Express the side effects of an event in a domain explicitly
- Maintain consistency of the side effects (either all the operations related to the business task are performed or none of them are)
- Enable a better separation of concerns among classes within the same domain

# Event sourcing

Event sourcing provides simplification of various events, and it is a way of persisting an application's state and finding the current state by traversing through the history of those saved states. An example could be a seat reservation system that scans the completed bookings and finds out how many more seats are available when a new booking request arrives.

The seat allocation depends on various events (booking, cancellations, modifications, and so on), and it can be handled differently with the event sourcing pattern. This is of immense help in some domains where the audit trail is a critical requirement, (accounting, financial transactions, flight reservations, and so on), and also the pattern helps achieve better performance as events are immutable and support append-only operations.

The following requirements may hint where we need to use event sourcing as a pattern:

- A simple standalone object to access complex relational storage module
- Audit Trails (these are a critical requirement)
- Integration with other subsystems
- Production troubleshooting (by storing the events and replaying)

We need to be aware of a few general concerns as follows about event sourcing so that we can have trade-offs and mitigation plans:

- **Versioning**: As event sourcing systems are append-only models, they face unique versioning challenges. Imagine we need to read an event that was created/written years ago into the event-sourcing system. So versioning is necessary to change the definition of a specific event type or aggregate at some point in the future, and one needs to have clear and definite plans and strategies for managing multiple versions for event-source models.
- **Querying**: This is a little expensive as it gets deeper. It depends on the level and period of the states to be retrieved.
- **Timeout**: This is the time taken to load the domain object state by querying the event store for all the events related to the state of the aggregate.

# Other patterns

Before concluding this chapter, take a look at the following list of patterns that are important as a part of DDD, however, not covered in this chapter. You are encouraged to review our references section to get an insight into the following topics:

- Layered architecture
- Service layers
- Application services
- Refactoring toward deeper insight
- Supple design
- Making behavior visible (intention revealing interfaces)
- Side-effect-free functions
- **Representational state transfer** (REST)

# Summary

Sometimes, software design experts get into confusion when to and when not to use domain models. The following points might help you get an insight into DDD for efficient decision making and decide to implement DDD or not:

- Business cases and requirements are particular, specific to domains, and not related to technology implementations
- As an independent team, they wanted to go to DDD when:
    - The team has never done earlier that sort of business cases
    - The team need help from domain experts
    - The business cases are more complex
    - The team need to start from ground zero, and there are no previous models exists
- When the given design problem is important to your business
- Skilled, motivated, and passionate team to execute
- Have greater access to domain experts who are aligned with product vision
- Willing to follow iterative methodology
- Nontrivial problem domain that is critical to business
- Great understanding of vision
- Business goals, values, success and failure factors, and how is it going to be different from earlier implementations

To summarize, this chapter has short introductions to core principles, characteristics, and best practices for a team to get a head start and adopt DDD. Then, we introduced strategic patterns such as ubiquitous language, domain, subdomain, core domain, and bounded context in detail. We also covered the most essential aspects of DDD, such as autonomous bounded context, shared nothing architecture, single responsibility codes, multiple bounded contexts, and a bit of thought process about SOA principles concerning DDD aspects as part of integrating bounded contexts. We also saw the bubble context, autonomous bubble context, and expose as a service as part of the significant real-world problem of integrating with legacy systems. We introduced you to database integration, flat file integration, and event-driven messaging as part of distributed bounded context integration strategies.

As part of tactical patterns, this chapter covered entity, value objects, domain services, modules, aggregates, factories, and repositories and also discussed two emerging patterns: domain events and event sourcing.

# References and further reading materials

For more information, you can refer to the following books:

- *Domain-Driven DESIGN - Tackling Complexity in the Heart of Software* - Eric Evans (Pearson)
- *Patterns, Principles, and Practices of Domain-Driven Design* - Scott Millet with Nick Tune (Wrox)

You can refer to the following online resources, too:

- DDD quickly: `https://www.infoq.com/minibooks/domain-driven-design-quickly`
- Framework and tools: `https://isis.apache.org/documentation.html`
- Three guiding principles: `https://techbeacon.com/get-your-feet-wet-domain-driven-design-3-guiding-principles`
- Getting started with DDD: `https://dzone.com/storage/assets/1216461-dzone-rc-domain-driven-design.pdf`
- Model evaluation and management: `https://arxiv.org/ftp/arxiv/papers/1409/1409.2361.pdf`
- `https://www.infoq.com/articles/ddd-in-practice` (characteristics of DDD)
- `https://www.codeproject.com/Articles/1158628/Domain-Driven-Design-What-You-Need-to-Know-About-S`
- `https://www.codeproject.com/Articles/1164363/Domain-Driven-Design-Tactical-Design-Patterns-Part`
- `https://www.slideshare.net/SpringCentral/ddd-rest-domain-driven-apis-for-the-web`
- `https://www.infoq.com/presentations/ddd-rest`
- `https://ordina-jworks.github.io/conference/2016/07/10/SpringIO16-DDD-Rest.html`
- `https://www.slideshare.net/canpekdemir/domain-driven-design-71055163`
- `https://msdn.microsoft.com/magazine/dn342868.aspx`
- `http://mkuthan.github.io/blog/2013/11/04/ddd-architecture-summary/`

# 6
# Enterprise Architecture Platforms and Tools

This chapter contains two main sections.The objective of the chapter is to provide an overview of the two prominent enterprise patterns which are used in the industry nowadays. Some of the prominent Enterprise Architecture platforms and tools are also covered in this chapter. The first section focuses on the two popular enterprise architecture framework that are used nowadays:

- **The open group architecture framework** (TOGAF)
- Zachman framework

In the second section, we will focus on the prominent **enterprise architecture** (**EA**) platforms and tools that are used by organizations. We will cover the following popular platforms:

- Enterprise architect
- Dragon1
- ABACUS

# Overview of enterprise architecture frameworks

An **enterprise architecture framework** (**EAF**) helps to map all the software-related development processes within an enterprise to fulfill the goals and objectives of the enterprise. EAF also provides a framework for the organizations to analyze and understand their weaknesses and inconsistencies. There are many popular and well established EAF frameworks that exist in the industry today. Some of them were developed for specific areas, whereas others have a broader scope. Some of the EAF frameworks that exist in the market are the following:

- **Department of defense architecture framework** (**DoDAF**)
- **Federal enterprise architecture framework** (**FEAF**)
- **Treasury enterprise architecture framework** (**TEAF**)
- **The open group architecture framework** (**TOGAF**)
- Zachman framework for enterprise architecture

Though there are four or five prominent EAFs in the industry, the most popular and widely used ones are TOGAF and Zachman framework for enterprise architecture. Hence in this chapter, our discussions will be focused only on these two frameworks.

# Getting started with TOGAF

TOGAF is an extremely popular architecture framework that is used to design an enterprise architecture. It offers all the toolsets and techniques that are used in the design, production, and maintenance of enterprise architecture. It is developed based on a process model that uses industry best practices and a set of reusable architecture assets.

As per TOGAF, **architecture** is defined as *the fundamental organization of a system, embodied in its components, their relationships to each other and the environment, and the principles governing its design and evolution* (you can refer to `http://pubs.opengroup.org/architecture/togaf9-doc/arch/` for more information). In short, the architecture of a system provides an elaborate plan for its implementation. The architecture also highlights the various components that are present in the system and the interrelationships that exist among them.

TOGAF is designed to support four architecture domains of enterprise architecture. These four domains are highlighted in the following diagram:

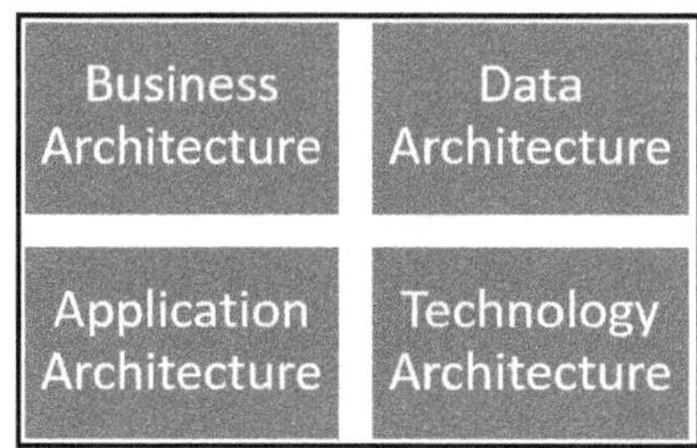


Each of the architecture domains listed in the previous diagram plays a vital role in defining the architecture of an enterprise. The roles are listed as follows:

- The **business architecture** provides a blueprint of the overall business activities, such as the business strategy, organization, core business processes, and so on.
- The **data architecture** provides a blueprint of the organization's data assets, be it logical or physical. It also specifies the various data management resources of the organization.
- The **application architecture** provides a blueprint for the various applications that must be deployed in the organization, along with their interactions and dependencies on the various business processes that are present in the organization.
- The **technology architecture** provides a high-level description of the hardware and software assets that are required to support the various data, application, and business services that are needed in the organization. Technology architecture focuses mainly on the infrastructure components, processing standards, and so on.

# Architecture development method (ADM)

The core of the TOGAF architecture is the ADM. It provides a set of tested and repeatable processes for developing enterprise architectures.

The following are the key activities that are captured in the ADM:

- Establish a framework for architecture
- Develop content for architecture
- Provide guidance for realization of architectures

All the ADM activities follow an iterative cycle, which includes both architecture definition and realization. This helps the organizations to transform their architectures in a step-wise manner that is aligned with their business goals and opportunities. The phases of an ADM are shown in the following diagram:

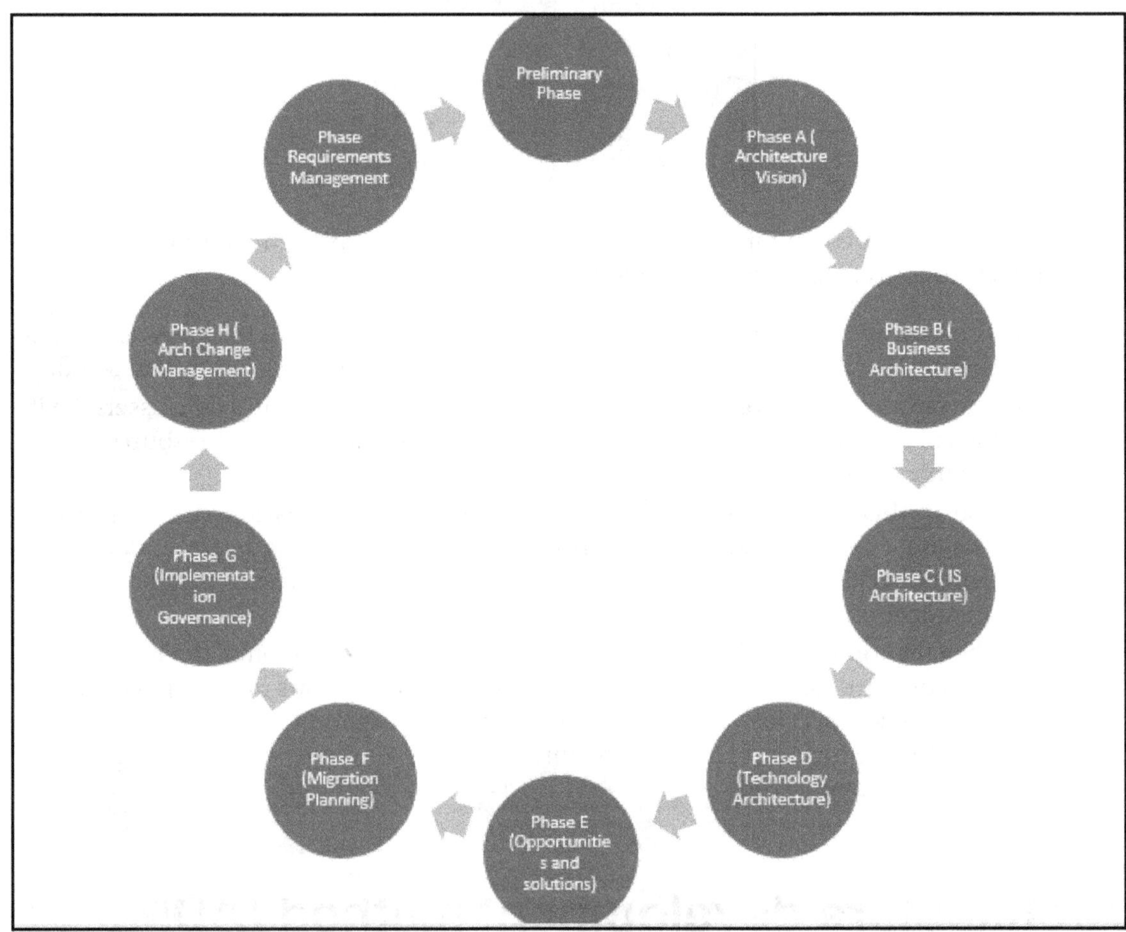


Activities that happen in each phase within the ADM are explained as follows:

- **Preliminary phase**: The main initiation activities that are required for architecture capability building are done. Some examples of activities that are done in this phase are customization of TOGAF, the definition of principles to be used for architecture design, and so on.

- **Phase A - Architecture vision**: In this initial phase, the key actors are involved in the definition of scope. Some other activities are stakeholder identification, getting all necessary approvals for architecture design and development, and so on.
- **Phase B - Business architecture**: In this phase, an agreement is made to develop a business architecture that is aligned with the architecture vision of the organization.
- **Phase C - Information systems architecture**: In this phase, an agreement is made to develop an information system architecture that is aligned with the architecture vision of the organization.
- **Phase D - Technology architecture**: It mainly deals with developing a technology blueprint that is aligned with the architecture vision of the organization.
- **Phase E - Opportunities and solutions**: It deals with doing the initial implementation planning and identification of different formats of architecture delivery.
- **Phase F - Migration planning**: It mainly deals with the steps involved in moving from a baseline to final target architectures. The various steps involved in migration are generally captured in an implementation and migration plan.
- **Phase G - Implementation governance**: It provides an overview of the implementation.
- **Phase H - Architecture change management**: It deals with carving out a change management plan to handle changes that come up in the architecture.
- **Requirements management**: It deals with managing the architecture requirements that evolve throughout the various phases of ADM.

# Deliverables, artifacts, and building blocks

Throughout the execution of an ADM, several types of outputs are produced. Some of them are process flows, project plans, compliance assessments, and so on. TOGAF provides an architecture content framework that offers a structural model for the architectural content. This structural model allows several types of work products to be defined, structured, and presented in a consistent manner.

The architecture content framework basically uses three types of categories to denote the specific type of architectural work product under consideration. They are the following:

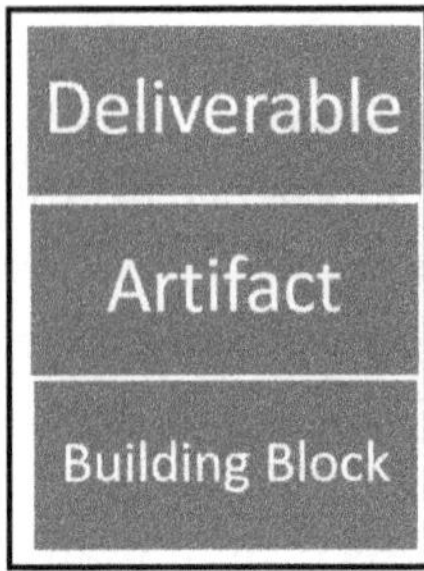


A **deliverable** is a type of work product that is reviewed and agreed upon formally by the stakeholders. Deliverables are typical outputs of projects and they are in the form of documents. These deliverables are either archived or transferred to an architecture repository as a model standard at the time of completion of the project.

An **artifact** is a type of work product that describes some specific aspect of an architecture.

Some important categories of artifacts are as follows:

- Catalogs (list things)
- Matrices (show relationship between various things)
- Diagrams (depict pictures of things)

Some common examples are a requirements catalog, use-case diagram, interaction diagram, and so on.

A **building block** denotes a fundamental component of IT or architectural capability that can potentially be combined with other building blocks to develop and deliver architectures.

Building blocks can be specified at various levels of detail based on the stage at which architecture development of the system has reached. For example, at very initial stages, the building block could be just a name that may later get involved into a complete specification of the component and its design.

There are two types of building blocks, they are:

- **Architecture building blocks** (**ABBs**): They describe the capability that is expected from the architecture. This capability then describes the specification that will be used for making the building blocks of the solution. For example, customer service could be an example of a capability that is needed within an enterprise, which may have several solutions blocks such as applications, processes, data, and so on.
- **Solution building blocks** (**SBBs**): They denote the various components that will be used in the implementation of the required capability.

The relationships between deliverables, artifacts, and building blocks are depicted in the following diagram:

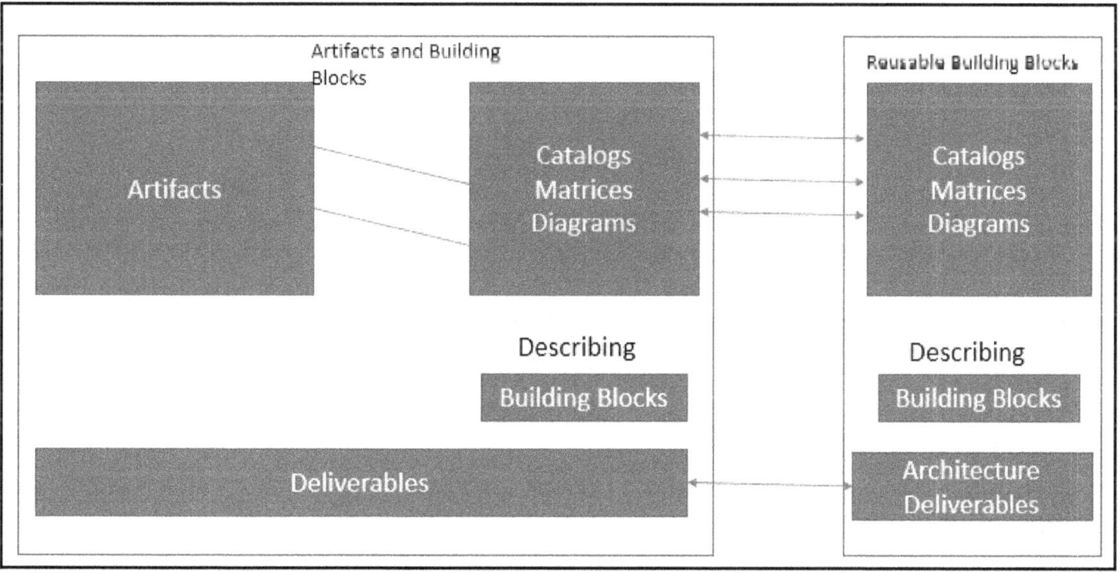

All the artifacts pertaining to architecture are interrelated in some way or the other. A specific architecture definition document may refer several other complementary artifacts. The artifacts could belong to various building blocks which are part of the architecture under consideration. The following example pertains to the target call handling process. The various references to other building blocks are depicted in the following diagram:

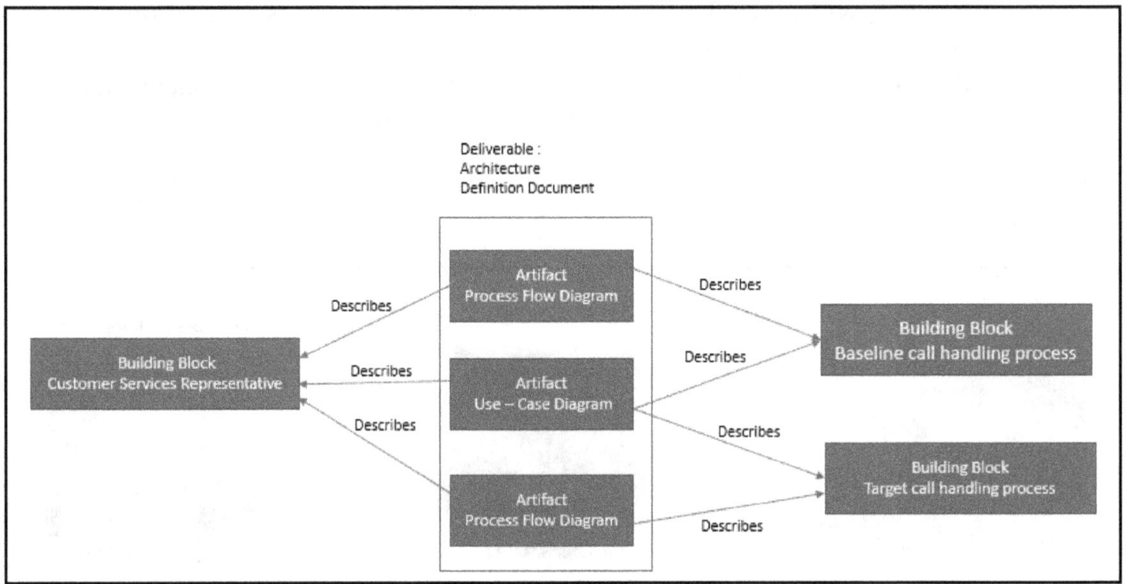


# Enterprise continuum

TOGAF includes a concept called **enterprise continuum**. This concept explains how certain generic solutions can be customized and used as per specific requirements of an organization. Enterprise continuum provides a view of the architecture repository that provides ways and techniques for classifying architecture and other related artifacts as they transform from generic architecture to specific architectures that are suitable for specific needs of the organization. Enterprise continuum has two complementary concepts associated with it, they are:

- Architecture continuum
- Solutions continuum

The architecture of enterprise continuum is depicted in the following diagram:

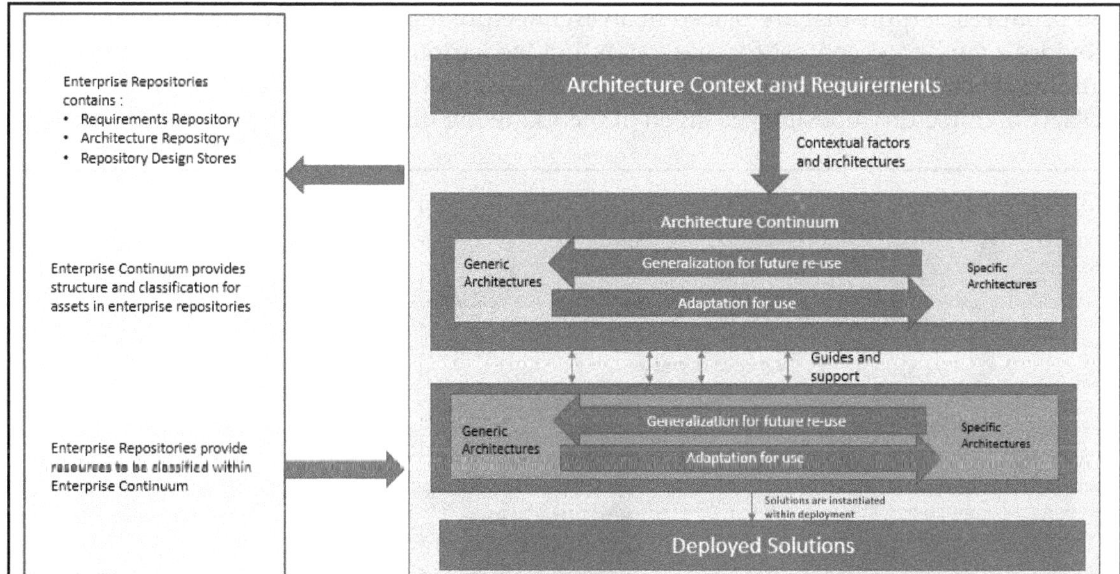


# Architecture repository

Another important concept of TOGAF is architecture repository. This can be used to store diverse types of architectural outputs, each at varying levels of abstraction; these outputs are created by ADM. This concept of TOGAF helps to provide cooperation and collaboration between practitioners and architects who are working at various levels in an organization.

Both enterprise continuum and architecture repository allow architects to use all architectural resources and assets that are available in an organization-specific architecture.

In general, TOGAF ADM can be considered typically as a process lifecycle that operates at various levels in an organization. ADM operates under a holistic governance framework and produces outputs that are placed in an architecture repository. Enterprise continuum provides a very good context for understanding the various architectural models, the building blocks, and the relationship of the building blocks to each other. The structure of TOGAF architecture repository is given in the following diagram:

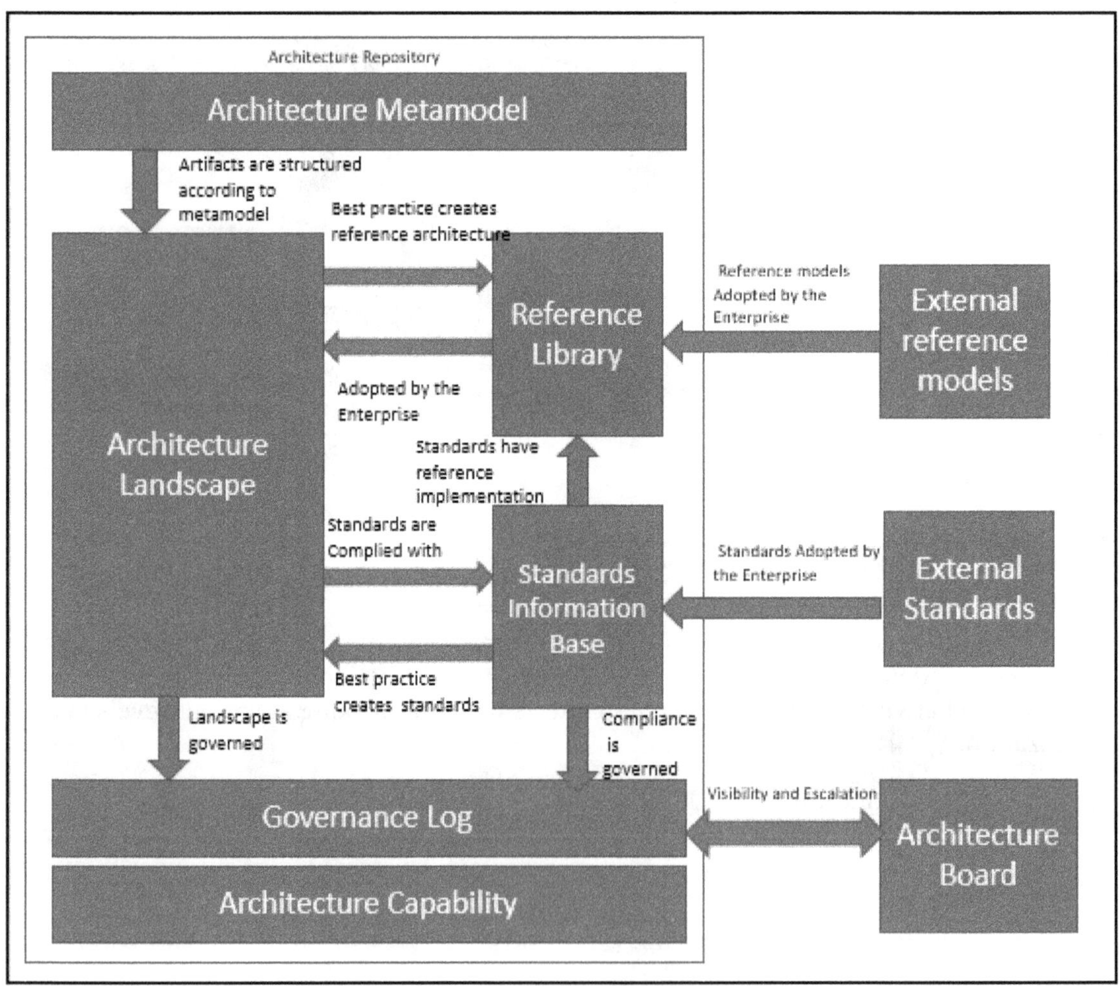

The following list shows major components of an architecture repository and the functionalities provided by those components:

- **Architecture metamodel**: This component describes the architecture framework, which is tailor-made as per the needs of the organization.
- **Architecture capability**: This component describes parameters, processes, and so on that support governance of the architecture repository.
- **Architecture landscape**: This is the representation of architectural assets that are deployed within an organization at any point in time. There is always a possibility that the landscape exists at various levels of abstraction, which are aligned to different sets of architecture objectives.
- **Standards information base**: This component describes the standards to which new architectures must comply. Standards in this context may include industry standards, standards from products and services that are deployed in the organization, and so on.
- **Reference library**: This component provides guidelines, templates, and so on that can be used as a reference to create new architectures for the organization.
- **Governance log**: This component maintains a log of governance activity that happens across the enterprise.

# Advantages of using TOGAF

The following are the main benefits of using TOGAF for EA design:

- The TOGAF framework provides a good understanding of the techniques to be used to integrate architecture development with strategies that are aligned with the objectives of the organization
- The framework provides well-defined guidelines on the steps to integrate architecture governance with IT governance
- The framework provides many checklists on how to support IT governance within the organization
- The framework provides a lot of reusable artifacts that can be used to create diverse types of architecture for organizations based on the varying requirements
- The framework provides a lot of options to reduce IT operating costs and helps in the design of portable applications

# Limitations of TOGAF

There are certain limitations too, which are listed as follows:

- The framework plays the role of a design authority in an enterprise and offers very few features for the architects to maintain enterprise-wide descriptions, standards, principles, and so on
- The framework provides very limited guidance to solution architects
- The framework assumes that enterprises will have their own processes that will be integrated with TOGAF
- It is just a framework, not a modeling language or any other component that could be treated as a replacement for architect skills
- It is not very consistent with the metamodels it supports

In the next topic, we will examine the details of the Zachman framework, which has also gained a lot of popularity and traction in the enterprise architecture domain.

# Zachman framework for enterprise architecture

*The* Zachman framework was published by John Zachman for EA in 1987. Zachman was motivated by increased levels of complexity involved in the design of information systems, which forced him to think of a logical construct for designing the architecture of enterprises, which in turn led to the development of the Zachman framework for enterprise architecture. The framework does not focus much on providing any form of guidance on sequence, process, or implementation. The core focus is to ensure that all views are well established, ensuring a complete system regardless of the order in which they were established. The Zachman framework does not have any explicit compliance rules as it does not belong to the category of a standard written by a professional organization.

The Zachman framework was initially developed for IBM but now has been standardized for use across enterprises. The main motivation behind the Zachman framework is to derive a simple logical structure for enterprises by classifying and organizing the various components of an enterprise in a manner that enables easy management of enterprises and facilitates easy development of enterprise systems such as manual systems and automated systems. The simplest form of the Zachman framework has the following depictions:

- Perspectives depicted in the design process, that is owner, designer, and builder.
- Product abstractions, such as what (material it is made of) and how (a process by which it works).
- Where (geometry by which components are related to one another), who (operating instructions) is doing what kind of work, when (timing of when things happen), why (engineering aspects due to which things happen). In some of the older versions of the framework, there were some additional perspectives present such as planner, sub-contractor, and so on.

The various perspectives that are typically used in the Zachman framework, as well as their roles in the enterprise architecture landscape, are as follows:

- **Planner**: A planner positions the product in the context of its environment and specifies the scope
- **Owner**: An owner will be interested in the business benefits of the product, how it will be used in the organization, and the added value it will offer to the organization
- **Designer**: A designer will carve out the specifications of the product to ensure that it meets the expectations of the owner. All aspects of product design are taken care of by the designer
- **Builder**: A builder manages the process of assembling various components of the product
- **Sub-contractor**: A sub-contractor incorporates out-of-context components that are specified by the builder

Please note that perspectives with respect to the Zachman framework keep changing as per the enterprise landscape.

The simplest depiction of the framework has the following components:

| | What | How | Where | Who | When | Why | |
|---|---|---|---|---|---|---|---|
| Planner | | | | | | | Scope |
| Owner | | | | | | | Concepts |
| Designer | | | | | | | Logic |
| Builder | | | | | | | Physics |
| Implementer | | | | | | | Technology |
| Operator | | | | | | | Product |
| | Material | Process | Geometry | Instructions | Timing | Objectives | |

# Advantages

The following are the main advantages of the Zachman framework:

- It provides a framework for improving several types of professional communication within the organization
- It provides details about the reasons and risks of not using any architectural perspective
- It provides options to explore and compare a wide variety of tools and/or methodologies
- It has options that will suggest the development of new and improved approaches for producing various architectural representations

# Restrictions

The Zachman framework has the following limitations:

- It can lead to a process-heavy/documentation-heavy approach as there is a lot of data that needs to be filled out in the cells that are used to capture the data pertaining to the framework
- It does not provide a step-by-step process for designing a new architecture

- It does not provide any guidelines for assessing the suitability of a future architecture for an organization
- It does not provide a framework for implementing governance in an architecture

# Guidelines for choosing EAF

Given an option to choose the architecture that is best suited for your enterprise, what are the parameters you will use to make a decision? The following table helps you to choose one based on some common parameters that are prominent in the industry landscape (in a five-point scale):

| Criteria | Zachman | TOGAF |
|---|---|---|
| Taxonomy Completeness | 4 | 2 |
| Process Completeness | 1 | 4 |
| Reference model guidance | 1 | 3 |
| Practice Guidance | 1 | 2 |
| Maturity Model | 1 | 1 |
| Business Focus | 1 | 2 |
| Governance Guidance | 1 | 2 |
| Partitioning Guidance | 1 | 2 |
| Prescriptive Catalog | 1 | 2 |
| Vendor Neutrality | 2 | 4 |
| Information Availability | 2 | 4 |
| Time to Value | 1 | 3 |

Some key terms used in the table are as follows:

- **Process completeness**: This criterion helps to find the level of step-by-step guidance provided by the framework for architecture implementation
- **Business focus**: This criterion helps us to find the technology choice flexibility which in turn will help in alignment with business objectives
- **Partitioning guidance**: This criterion helps to judge the flexibility offered by the framework for partitioning of the enterprise to manage complexity effectively
- **Time to value**: This criterion provides guidance on the time taken by a solution built using this framework to deliver business value to the organization

In the next section, we will examine the prominent platforms and tools that are available for deployment/design of enterprise architecture.

# Enterprise architecture platforms and tools

The following are some of the main parameters to be considered by enterprise architects while choosing an enterprise architecture platform:

- **Innovation**: Enterprise architects will need a lot of features that will enable them to think and work in an innovative manner. At the same time, they should have access to all tools and features that are available in any EA environment.
- **Visualization**: Most of the EA tools also perform the function of business support tools. In such a scenario, it becomes necessary that the tool offers a lot of rich visualization and animation features, which are expected as a part of normal business support activities.
- **Mapping and modeling**: One of the most important feature requirements of EA tools is modeling. The tools should be able to provide diverse types of modeling such as contextual modeling, logical modeling, and physical modeling. The need for advanced modeling capabilities becomes more prominent in the context of present-day digital businesses with a lot of customer centricity.

- **Analysis and design**: One of the key requirements of any EA tool is to support analysis and design. Now, because of the changes in the enterprise landscape, it becomes necessary for the tools to support advanced features such as business intelligence.
- **Speeding time to value**: EA tools should be able to provide features that enable easy integration with a lot of third-party tools and interfaces. These capabilities will help them to deliver business value quickly.
- **Business architecture design**: EA tools should offer features that help in accommodating rapidly changing features as a part of architecture design. They should also provide features to develop new types of business models quickly.

In the next section, we will examine some popular platforms and tools that are available for the design and development of enterprise architectures.

# Enterprise Architect from Sparx Systems

It is a comprehensive enterprise architecture platform that offers the following core capabilities pertaining to enterprise architecture design:

- Analysis
- Modeling
- Design
- Construction
- Testing and management

This tool offers integrated support and full traceability between all tasks, phases, components, domain, and lifecycle management of enterprise architecture. Enterprise Architect combines the rich UML toolset with a high performance and interactive user interface to provide an advanced toolset for the enterprise architects.

The intuitive user interface of the Enterprise Architect tool is depicted in the following screenshot:

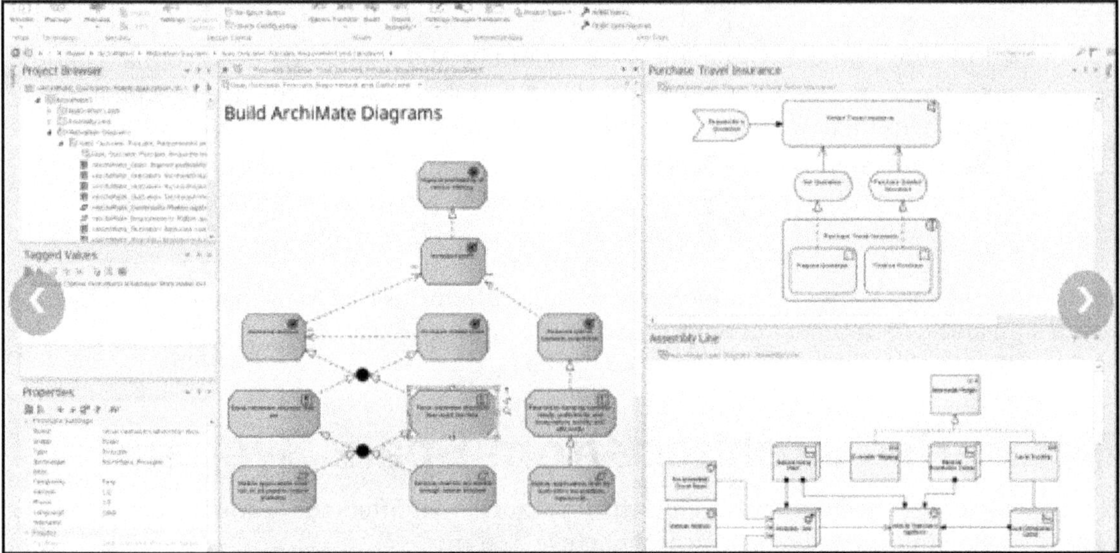


The following are the main industries supported by the Enterprise Architect tool:

- Aerospace
- Banking
- Web development
- Engineering
- Finance
- Medicine
- Military
- Research and academia
- Transport
- Retail
- Utilities

Enterprise Architect is also a tool that is widely used by standard organizations across the world to organize their knowledge, models, and messages. This tool has been continuously updated as per the changes in the UML standards.

Enterprise Architect is a proven, scalable, effective, and affordable full life cycle development platform for:

- Strategic modeling
- Requirements gathering
- Business analysis
- Software design
- Software profiling
- Software testing and debugging
- Modeling and simulation of business processes
- Systems and software engineering
- enterprise architecture design
- Database design and engineering
- Design and development of XML schemas
- Project management activities for various stages of enterprise architecture design and development
- Testing and maintenance of applications
- Reporting

Enterprise Architect is optimized for the following activities, which are involved as a part of enterprise architecture design:

- Creating, capturing, and working with a rich and diverse set of architecture requirements from multiple stakeholders
- Modeling, designing, and architecting a wide range of software systems as per the requirements of the organization
- Business analysis, modeling the business process, and strategic modeling as per the needs of the organization
- Modelling of systems, modeling of system architecture, and component design
- Comparing, designing, constructing, modeling, and updating database systems
- Defining and generating schema based on XSD and other standards
- Creating architecture designs based on domain-specific modeling languages such as UML

- Simulating and visualizing a wide range of systems, tasks, and associated processes
- Designing, developing, executing, debugging, and testing codes written in a wide variety of software languages
- Simulating behavioral processes and designing state machines and their various interactions
- Building executable codes for types of state machines based on the architectural design and providing an environment that supports simulation of these executables
- Collaborating and sharing information
- Providing the capabilities for quality control and testing of complex architectural systems
- Project managing tasks that are associated with enterprise architecture design and development
- Team-based collaboration features using the concept of cloud-based repositories that are optimized for access over diverse types of LAN and WAN networks

# Dragon1

Dragon1 is a very popular enterprise architecture platform that offers the following features, which are mandatory for the design and development of enterprise architecture:

- Technology roadmaps that can be used to derive architectures aligned to business objectives of the organization
- Heat maps that show the pain points for architecture design in an organization
- Capability maps that provide a blueprint of the capabilities that exist in an organization
- Glossary of terms used in architecture design and development
- Architecture description document
- Decision matrix sketches of total concepts
- Drawing on architecture principles
- enterprise architecture blueprints
- Application landscapes
- Models atlas

Dragon1 offers features that can be used by individuals at various levels of an organization. The main groups that will benefit from using Dragon1 in an organization are:

- **Analysts**: Helps them to do impact analyses
- **Architects**: Helps diverse types of architects such as business, enterprise, information, IT, and so on, for creating architecture designs as per their domain
- **Designers**: Helps them to create both functional and technical designs
- **Managers** (IT and business): Provides toolsets that help them to monitor and manage operations visually through features such as dashboards
- **Program and project managers**: Monitoring and managing changes in their schedules on a real-time basis visually
- **CxOs** (CIO, CEO, CFO, and so on): Dashboard view of various organization domains in an easy to understand manner

Some of the core capabilities of Dragon1 are the following:

- **Publishing and reporting**: Any type of document/information can be uploaded, stored, and published using Dragon1
- **Data management**: Provides support for storage, updating, and deletion of any type of data
- **Requirement management**: Provides exhaustive features for requirements gathering from diverse types of stakeholders
- **Process, application, and metamodelling**: Offers capabilities and features to build models for any type of entity class, such as process, application, and so on
- **System design**: Provides a rich set of features that allows systems to be designed at conceptual, logical, or physical level
- **User management**: Provides role-based features that can be used by employees at various levels in an organization
- **Architecture visualization**: Offers extensive graphical features that help in the creation of rich visualizations
- **Dashboards and scenarios**: Offers rich features that enable the creation of dashboard features and scenario analysis

To learn more, you can visit `https://www.dragon1.com/products/enterprise-architecture-tool-comparison`.

# ABACUS from avolution software

Avolution's ABACUS suite is one of the best EA modeling tools as per Gartner's magical quadrant. It comes with a large library of architecture frameworks and patterns for most of the common platforms. It also provides support for data imported from a broad range of modeling solutions and third-party sources.

ABACUS comes in two variants; they are as follows:

- Standard
- Professional

ABACUS's standard suite of products offers only architecture modeling functionality, whereas ABACUS's professional suite provides architecture modeling and scenario analysis capability. ABACUS provides enterprise modeling capability based on components, constraints, and connection framework. It also has features for assigning properties for connections and components that can be accessed through a tabular view in the user interface.

# Architecture of ABACUS

ABACUS consists of metamodels and multiple architectures along with a view for each architecture. The solution provides a large set of libraries that are derived from industry standard frameworks such as TOGAF and several others. ABACUS has an XML-based file format that acts as an objects database. Any new file format that is added to ABACUS is stored as another object in an objects database. This feature is extremely helpful for the creation of new architecture models or adding enhancements to the existing metamodels, because these aspects can be done with the help of right-clicks and do not need any changes to the internal database as required by several other EA tools in the market.

The ABACUS approach that is used to define metamodels basically uses three key units, they are:

- Component
- Connection
- Constraints

These key units conform to the IEEE1471 standard. ABACUS ships with different libraries that contain these key units. The list of libraries that are present in ABACUS includes more than 50 prominent architectural patterns. The flexibility of Avolution provides support for a larger number of architectural frameworks when compared to other EA platforms that are available in the market. ABACUS has features that allow users to create new libraries or merge existing libraries to create a new one within a matter of minutes.

Apart from the tools that were discussed in this section, Gartner's magic quadrant, shown in the following image, provides the list of enterprise architecture platforms that are prominent in the enterprise architecture landscape. This could be used by any Enterprise Architect as a basis for decision making. For more on this, visit `https://www.gartner.com/doc/reprints?id=1-2Q45NIBct=151020st=sb`.

# Summary

In the first section of the chapter, we discussed the Zachman framework and the TOGAF framework, which are prominent nowadays. The components of these frameworks and the advantages and disadvantages of each of them were examined. Finally, we provided a set of metrics that could be used to evaluate and choose the best EA framework for an organization based on various parameters. Next, we examined the various popular EA platforms and tools that are used for the design and development of enterprise architecture. We concluded the chapter by providing a list of EA tools that are supported by Gartner's magical quadrant.

# References

`https://www.sparxsystems.com.au/products/ea/`

`https://www.avolutionsoftware.com/downloads/ABACUS%20TA001910ITM.pdf`

# 7
# Service-Oriented Architecture (SOA)

You might have wondered about many websites having different kinds of dashboards showing distinct yet relevant contents, and how in this world it is possible to combine a weather report and stock market quotes in one display.

Weather reports and stock quotes are functionally different systems; one is the meteorological area and the other one is the national stock exchange, yet they can be combined and shown in a single dashboard.

So, if we need to define what a web service is, then a*ny reusable, custom-developed software code that lets heterogeneous applications talk to each other and disparate systems get integrated in a cost-effective manner* could be our definition.

We can design a software system that integrates disparate data sources and different ecosystems that can evolve and mature over time in a better and cost-effective way by adopting fundamental SOA principles and characteristics in every service design.

In this chapter, we will cover the following topics as part of SOA:

- Web services and SOA
- Introduction to SOA
- Life cycle of SOA
- Primary characteristics of SOA
- Principles of SOA
- SOA design patterns

# Web services and SOA

The first step for any web service design is to start with strict adherence to SOA characteristics and principles. Basic building blocks and stepping stones for any web service design are the SOA architecture patterns.

SOA is the most favorable and proven architectural design style that helps to solve a few key problems within modern software systems to handle ever-changing user expectations efficiently.

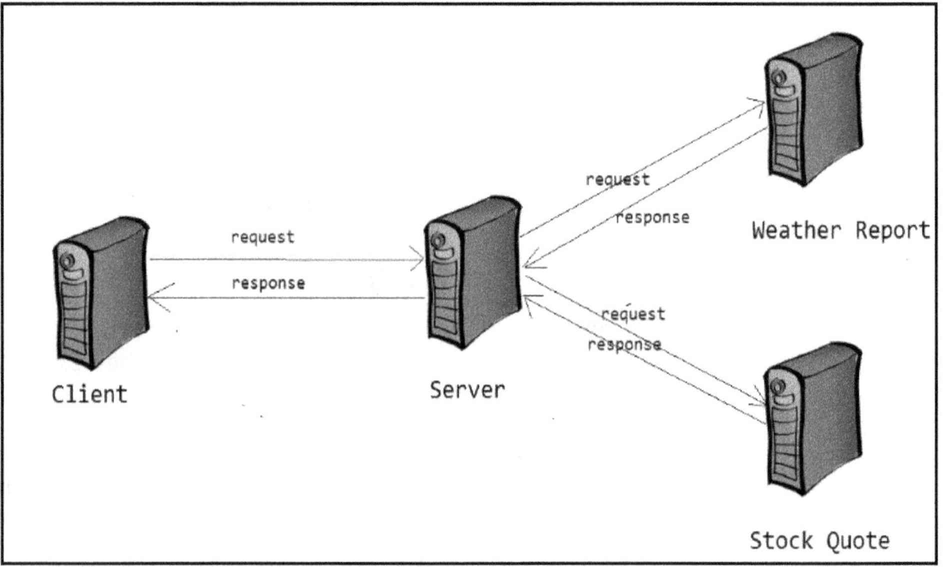


Recently, in many real-time cloud applications, SOA has become the foundation of cloud efforts, and a lot of convergence with the private and public cloud as well. Certainly, SOA is playing a significant role in the background with virtualization, event processing, business process management, and much more in real-world applications.

# Introduction to SOA

SOA is an architectural style of services and not a technology or any programming language. It defines standards and ways to design and develop a service.

Service is the logical representation of repeatable business activities* that have a specified outcome. It is self-contained, Provides guidelines to combine a service with other services. It is also an abstract or black box to the consumer who consumes it.

*The following are a few examples of business activities with specific outcomes:

- Get city's weather report
- Get stock quote of given stock code
- Get hotel booking details by booking ID
- Get user profile information for given user ID

In short, SOA is essentially a collection of services, and those services communicate with each other, and a service is an operation or a function that is well-defined, self-contained, and independent of other service contexts and states.

# Life cycle of SOA

Let's first touch upon the life cycle of SOA, and briefly discuss each stage in the life cycle, before we get into the characteristics of SOA.

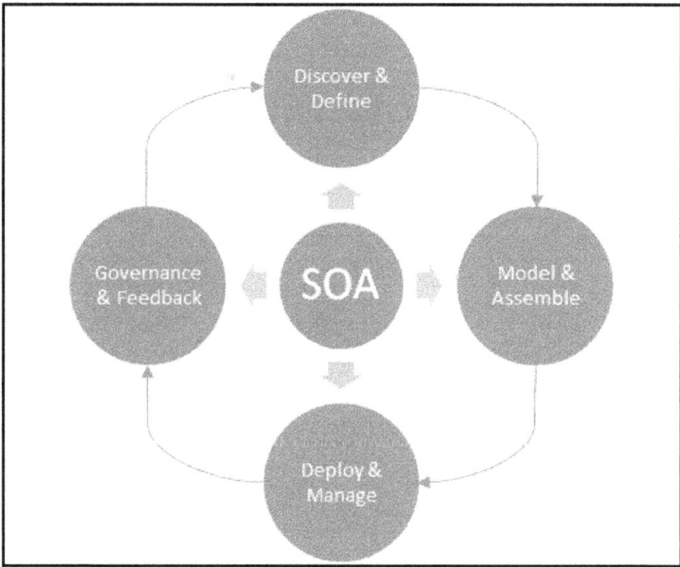

Any services are discoverable by having a clear set of communication standards such as WSDL, SOAP, REST, and so on, and therefore they are picked up for consumption.

Service design is the next critical item in which we need to find a proper pattern and deliver services as model-driven, business function-specific, testable in isolation, and so on, and the most common patterns are discussed in detail later in this chapter.

For any business or organization, after the functional design phase, it is important to have services that are developed, deployed, and consumed. However, unlike waterfall methodology (customer waits until all the components are developed), it is better if the service development and deployment happen in an iterative and agile fashion, so customers meet ROI in short-term.

Governance and feedback are crucial for any evolving service, as they play a critical role in service adoption and help businesses to achieve ROI as soon as possible.

# Primary characteristics of SOA

Any functional system or component that is SOA-based has its unique characteristics. However, in this section, we will cover fundamental elements that are uncompromising in any SOA-based designs.

## Service interconnectivity with well-defined interfaces

Interoperability or interconnectivity between the two involving systems is a critical aspect of SOA. To achieve interoperability, architects should analyze the system deeper and come up with a greater level of detail so that they can define well-defined interfaces. Those interfaces in SOA embody interaction points between the system and its boundaries, which should be standardized, explicit, behavior predictable, scalable, and sustainable.

## Standard interfaces and Service level agreements

The interfaces should be well-thought and standardized. The response of a weather report can evolve faster without any changes in the client's request (payload). In the weather forecast web service, the city name can be a key element; however, the city can have different climatic conditions within the city, and to get precise weather conditions, the interface needs longitude and latitude along with the city name.

## Event-driven and messaging

Loose coupling is one of the essential primary characteristics of SOA, and it can be easily achieved by having event-driven and messaging as part of a service's design. The services that we design should represent a business function or domain and consider an application that needs to send an email to the user immediately after booking a hotel and assume we have a hotel booking service that can book a hotel and send a confirmation email to the user. As per the business functions, we can have two different services; one that takes care of the hotel booking, and another one that takes care of the post-booking process such as email, mobile confirmations, and so on. The email service can receive events from the booking service, or it can listen for any messages from other systems, depending on its event-driven design or message-driven design.

## Flexible

Repeatable and Reusable is another essential characteristic of SOA, so services should be flexible with fewer constraints in the policies and accomplish reusability and repeatability with no impact on the clients who are already consuming the services. In these situations, designers would get concerns about service optimizations and performance improvements. However, the flexibility should be given preference over optimizations.

Let's get some insights about flexibility. Consider a client (consumer) access a weather report for a given city by its name, there are chances that the given city can respond with more than one results (City's airport, downtown and so on), so potentially the results can be more than one. In that situation how do we design a payload to respond with only one row, maybe the request payload should have a placeholder to accept longitude and latitude as seen in the below XML snippet and so the response of the service shows only one result, not many?

```
▼<definitions xmlns:SOAP-ENV="http://schemas.xmlsoap.org/soap/envelope/" xmlns:xsd=
 xmlns:SOAP-ENC="http://schemas.xmlsoap.org/soap/encoding/" xmlns:tns="http://grapt
 xmlns:soap="http://schemas.xmlsoap.org/wsdl/soap/" xmlns:wsdl="http://schemas.xmls
 targetNamespace="http://graphical.weather.gov/xml/DWMLgen/wsdl/ndfdXML.wsdl">
  ▼<types>
    ▼<xsd:schema targetNamespace="http://graphical.weather.gov/xml/DWMLgen/wsdl/ndf
       <xsd:import namespace="http://schemas.xmlsoap.org/soap/encoding/"/>
       <xsd:import namespace="http://schemas.xmlsoap.org/wsdl/"/>
      ▼<xsd:complexType name="weatherParametersType">
        ▶<xsd:all>...</xsd:all>
       </xsd:complexType>
     </xsd:schema>
   </types>
  ▼<message name="NDFDgenRequest">
     <part name="latitude" type="xsd:decimal"/>
     <part name="longitude" type="xsd:decimal"/>
     <part name="product" type="xsd:string"/>
     <part name="startTime" type="xsd:dateTime"/>
     <part name="endTime" type="xsd:dateTime"/>
     <part name="Unit" type="xsd:string"/>
     <part name="weatherParameters" type="tns:weatherParametersType"/>
   </message>
```

In another scenario, assume the consumer wanted to search weather conditions for a city called Dover, which is a duplicate name across the world (more than 50 cities name is Dover around the world), so to find unique Dover, the payload should also have the flexibility to mention State and Country or Zip code.

To achieve flexibility, one should not hard-wire any elements in the client payloads that are prone to change, and also evaluate alternate approaches that yield advantages and greater flexibility for the services and its' centralized functions.

How do we justify flexibility over service optimization? If we consider the service need to respond with weather conditions for the city name Dover, there may be multiple calls involved; one to find a list of cities by name Dover, the second one to call specific Dover with intended State, and Country or Zip code. So expected results for the consumer is vital than reducing the number of calls to the services. So in this kind of situations, considering the flexibility over optimization is a better approach.

# Evolution

The beauty of software product development is that *any software product can be given for consumption once it reaches the minimum viable stage in real quick while product development keeps introducing more and more features*.

This seamless feature usage may not be possible in other major industries. For instance, in the automobile sector, we may not have the luxury of releasing the product before its completion in all the aspects. As we cannot manufacture wheels or engines and start using them, we have to wait until it comes out as a car and is quality certified.

In software development, it is so beautiful that we can create financial systems with just a few features for a customer to use, while we keep developing and deploying new features into production so that more and more functionalities can be consumed by the customers seamlessly. SOA designs can create a perfect example of software and system evolution.

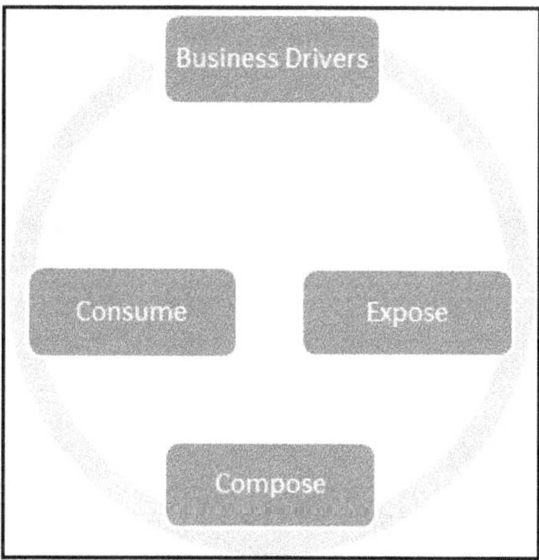

Let's pick our same weather report example; the services can start by accepting a city name and zip code, later enhanced with longitude and latitude, then with IP addresses, and then the location from where it is searched, with not just current weather details, but with hourly, daily, and weekly forecasts. In our introduction section, we mentioned that *to handle the ever-changing and high demand of user expectations very effectively,* services should be evolved and flexible in order to manage the demands and not force the client to modify their way of consuming services.

Other common characteristics of evolution are as follows:

- Services are transport independent
- Services are software platform independent
- Choreography versus orchestration of services
- Explicit calls
- Services represent a business function or domain
- Location of services are transparent, discoverable, and support introspection

However, we are not covering all of those in detail, and we encourage readers to refer to other materials on all these design principles for more detailed discussions.

Many authors and references point out that service orientation can be related to the separation of concern principles, and that is true as long as it does not share the states between the entities and maintains the atomicity of the services.

One must have faced challenges implementing these practices especially with legacy, non-service based monolithic systems. They may be still consumable and making money. However, they are not scalable and incurs high maintenance. So how can we change those legacy systems into independent, scalable, high-performance services?; It can be done by following SOA principles, practices and with suitable SOA patterns. So let us learn deeper and get insights into SOA principles and Patterns in the following sections.

# Principles of SOA

Though there are no specifications or standards that are comprehensive of SOA principles, we can define some tenets as a core principle of SOA that helps to realize all the characteristics of SOA. Adherence to these principles is evident to stand up any service and for its consumptions.

We will touch upon those principles rather briefly in this section, and in addition to that, there is a handy matrix that depicts relationships of the SOA life cycle, characteristics, and principles at the end of this chapter.

# Standardized service contract

Standardization is a fundamental principle of any SOA. Services exhibit their functions and their capabilities through a service contract, forcing the SOA designer to focus on service granularity, data types to be exposed, purposes of services, service optimization, service versions to be exposed, service endpoints, and more, of all service standardizations. **Service level agreement** (**SLA**) for any services are established with this principle to provide clear vision and direction of consumptions, governance, security, versioning, requests, and responses. Standardization ensures, service contracts are well defined and way the path for rest o f the principles and leads to more and more service consumptions.

# Service interoperability

Interoperability is another important principle of SOA. The ability to share information between services is interoperability, and it helps applications to realize efficient communications across distributed services on various software platforms. Interoperability applies on different levels such as operational (business process), informational, and technical architecture stages that determine how systems can communicate with each other at each level.

# Service abstraction

Providing a simplified view of services by hiding internal details (complexity) helps better explain the function and operation of services, helps the consumer to focus on the core business logic of the services, and protects internal implementations from unintentional changes. Abstractions can be applied at every level from language implementation to the service level. Earlier in this chapter, the stock quote services talked only about getting quotes of a given stock ID and nothing else, it does not say how it interacts with details of the company that the customer asked for, neither how it connects to the stock exchange's dynamic data, nor how new business details get added to the system. What they all need to know as a consumer of a service is whether the service can pick the quote for their favorite company, not how you get it.

## Service autonomy

Autonomy is a way of achieving isolations of a service's executions from its shared resources, and releasing the services with no impact on the client who is already using the earlier version of the service. Services can be developed, versioned, tested, and deployed, while consumers continue to use previous versions or seamless changes to the service that they consume, and this brings enormous benefit to the customers.

## Service composability

Services are useful composition participants regardless of size and complexity of the composition. Services can be the orchestrator of different other services, and that orchestrator service adheres all the SOA characteristics.

Service compositions are often applied to legacy software applications to avoid the risk of retrofit; applying customized solutions and continuous operation of the production by retaining the existing software solutions.

If you observe this principle, it warrants a separation of concern to be exercised. In the life cycle of services, we understand clearly that the services evolve with more and more functionalities. With applying loose coupling as well as service reusability, it is inevitable that we need to keep providing more and more additional requirements or solve more and more problems for the customer. Recall the point of our evolution characteristic, and this principle is related to evolution.

## Service discoverability

Services lose their purpose if they are not exposed or published to internal or external entities. Services are rated by their usage and by the number of customers using the service, regardless of its consumption by external or internal customers. It is challenging to find the available services even within internal teams, but with utmost care and effort, we can bring best practices on discoverability. Standardization of services also helps to achieve better discoverability.

If the services are not exposed or published to internal or external entities, then they have lost their purpose. Services evaluated by their usage and number of customers using the service could be internal or external. Challenges still exist in finding the available services to consume even within internal teams, and utmost care and effort to bring best practices to ensure this principle is followed is the key so that the services evolve and the organization keeps getting its ROI iteratively.

# Service loose coupling

Loose coupling is one of the core design principles that help the services to realize automaticity, test in isolation, and so service can evolve with no impact on the service functionalities. This principle intends to apply various aspects of loose coupling at different levels, and it may vary according to the application contexts as well.

Let's take our email service as an example. The booking service sends a notification to the email service once it completes the hotel reservation, and regardless of the email server status (it may be even down, but the booking service doesn't need to wait until the email servers come up). So, the email service can decide when to send an email; it may be during off-peak hours, there may be different scheduled times, maybe once the email server is up and running after its scheduled maintenance, perhaps resending the failed deliveries, and so on.

So, the design of email services handles the loose coupling principles as in this context, it is most elegant and preferable. Most of us would agree that it is not always in all the designs and at all the levels that we can bring this principle, as it may not help the business functions. For instance, in the email service and booking service, the booking and email services can be independent and loosely coupled; the email service is dependent on the email server and applying the loose coupling principle is not feasible. Our other service that provides the weather report is dependent on the location service, and in this context, coupling may be an acceptable design.

# Service reusability

Service reusability is one of the core principles and brings a realization of flexible and evolution characteristics of services-oriented architecture. The design aspects should consider a set of business functions or logic that can be made available without duplicating the code to numerous internal or external clients.

Reuse is a strong OO principle, and it is imperative in the service level as well. With agnostic functional contexts, the services are resources, and so can be reused at maximum level; more the reuse, more the ROI.

In our examples, location services, email services, weather report services, and stock quote services are all reusable and logical separations of business functions.

## Service statelessness

Services should be stateless as much as they can. Statelessness is another important principle that helps services to lower the consumption of resources, test in isolation, and reusability. To implement statelessness in the email service, it needs all the necessary information explicitly for sending emails, and so it does not need to pick up additional information from a database or any other resources as its focus is on the business logic of setting up schedules to send emails. The schema can have more details (message, email IDs, subject) explicitly, rather that just booking ID, and make an email service to pick up additional information from the database for that booking ID.

# SOA design patterns

In the current software design world, we already have time-tested software solutions for specific recurring problems. Best practices and the way that software design solves the repeatable problems in a quick and cost-effective manner creates reusable patterns over time, and it is a rule of thumb that we should be able to pick up and use the right ones for our design problems.

SOA deals with a number of design patterns, and numerous materials discuss each one in depth. We would like to touch upon a few of the most important ones that real-time software solutions often require.

We will deal with the following patterns in this chapter:

- Service messaging
- Message screening
- Agnostic services
- Atomic service transaction
- Authentication broker

- Message origin authentication
- Service façade
- Multiple service contracts
- Service callback
- Event-driven messaging
- Service refactor
- Metadata centralization

# Service messaging

Service messaging provides a communication platform through which messages are transmitted and routed as independent units. It brings the efficient execution of loosely coupled service interactions and data exchanges.

Off the shelf, **message-oriented middleware** (**MOM**) queues are the best example of service messaging. MOM queues can have a single sender or receiver or multiple senders and receivers, and some applications even require to use of multiple Queues will help in decoupling discreet and distinct components of a system.

Most SOA implementations use MOM queues, and it is hard to find an SOA-compliant system without a messaging system.

The benefits of service messaging are as follows:

- A service messaging pattern in your design makes your design solution a best fit and elegant for any clients who want to communicate to services asynchronously
- It is an implementation of loose coupling and one of the core principles of SOA
- With service messaging, the following are made easy and elegant:
    - Fail-safe and loop back in services
    - Versioning of services
    - Record, defer, and replay
    - Multiplexed messages
- Best fit for concurrency models as immutable messages are thread safe

The impacts of service messaging are as follows:

- Asynchronous communications lead to reliability concerns in some cases, unlike the services that receive the client response immediately
- As service messaging involves Asynchronous communication to other systems, there may be a need to engage further systems that manage and supports the service process and executions (more systems to be operated and maintained).
- Need to rely more on messaging systems (dependency on messaging systems)

# Message screening

The services are susceptible to injection attacks: injecting malicious data into services that leads to undesirable behavior. The services can prevent any harmful message content by screening data when it is received at the server side, even before the service uses it.

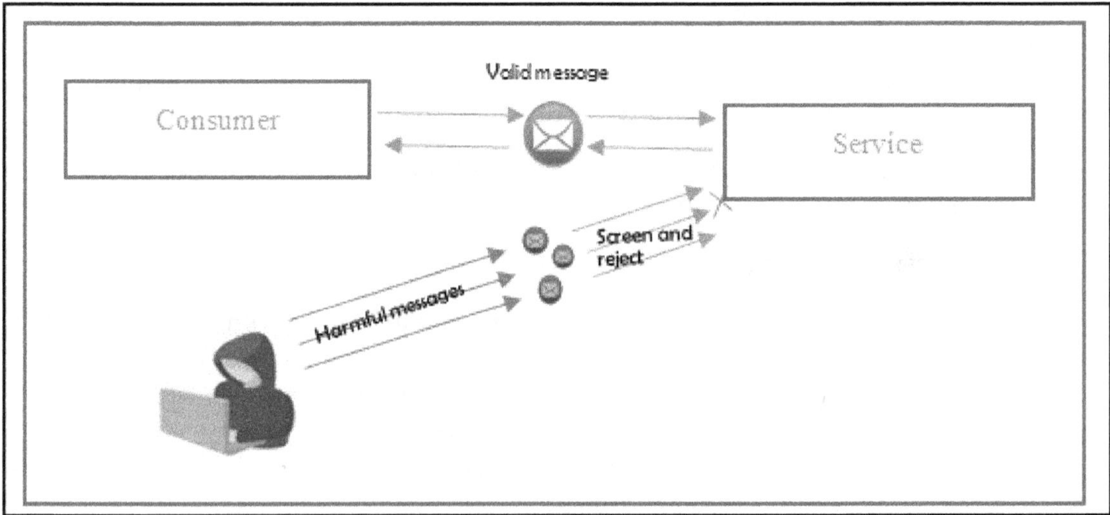


The services should assume that all input messages it receives are harmful, and therefore all those messages should undergo various checks to find any presence of malicious content and protect the services from any harmful content.

The benefits of message screening are as follows:

- Eliminates different types of injection attacks
- Prevents resource exhaustion due to injection attacks
- Service is protected from malicious content even before its consumption
- Service validates messages regardless of whether the client validated it or not

The impacts of message screening are as follows:

- Screening logic for each message incurs additional runtime
- Processing binary messages or binary attachments needs to have specialized logic for screening
- It is hard or even impossible to find and limit all potentially harmful content by message screening

# Agnostic services

Consider various functions of financial banking such as account management, life insurance, lending or loan management, wealth management, and so on. Each service might need to share the abilities of other services, rather having them as duplicated rather then reused.

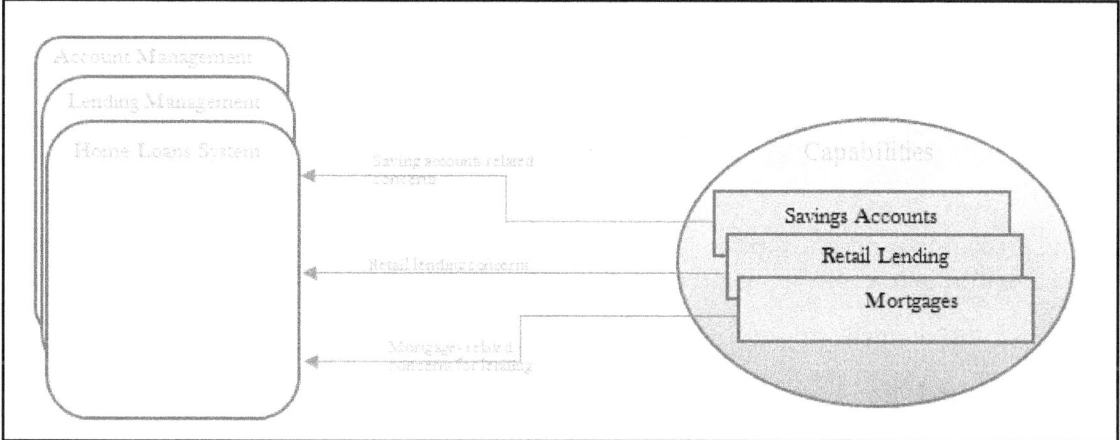

Consider a home loan management service that needs to know the savings account details of the borrower, other retail lending information for credit reports, and mortgage information from property management. So, those capabilities are common concerns for any lending service that can be defined and used by not only the home loan systems but by any other major system such as credit cards, life insurance products, account management services, investment management services, and so on.

Implementing business logic for a set of well-defined capabilities that address major common concerns and are certainly not specific to one problem but common to multiple business problems, are called agnostic services.

The separation of agnostic business logic or capabilities into discrete services helps enterprises with service reuse and composability.

```
<?xml version="1.0" encoding="utf-8"?>
<soap:Envelope xmlns:xsi="http://www.w3.org/2001/XMLSchema-instance"
xmlns:xsd="http://www.w3.org/2001/XMLSchema" xmlns:soap12="http://www.w3.org/2003/05/soap-
envelope">
  <soap:Body>
   <GetMortgagePayment xmlns="http://www.webserviceX.NET/">
    <Years>15</Years>
    <Interest>12</Interest>
    <LoanAmount>2000000</LoanAmount>
    <AnnualTax>5</AnnualTax>
    <AnnualInsurance>1000</AnnualInsurance>
   </GetMortgagePayment>
   <GetLoanAccountProfile>
            <AccountNumber>1203493</AccountNumber>
            <AccountType>SB/LA</AccountType>
   <GetLoanAccountProfile>
  </soap:Body>
</soap:Envelope>
```

As the preceding example depicts, having the services explicitly state that they are agnostic helps the imminent consumers and designers to reuse the existing agnostic services.

The benefits of agnostic services are as follows:

- Exercising service reusability and composability
- Consumers benefit from iterative refinements of service capabilities beyond initial service definitions
- Enables multi-purpose capabilities, and those would be the most preferred conventional capabilities

The impacts of agnostic services are as follows:

- Improvement of a service's abilities through its advantages of preliminary analysis takes a lot of time and considerations, and more iterations are needed for development
- Arriving at a universal consensus on service functions might be challenging as business functions of services might be too vague or too generic
- Need more design planning and considerations, as agnostic services design push us to consider many design parts those are not necessarily need to be deliberated for short-term or mid-term delivery, and so may lead us to end up in missing delivery commitments

# Atomic service transaction

The rollback of operations is so important in a distributed environment. When any one of the runtime activities that span across multiple services fails, then all the transactions that have happened so far should be rolled back, otherwise the distributed services may compromise the integrity of the software solution.

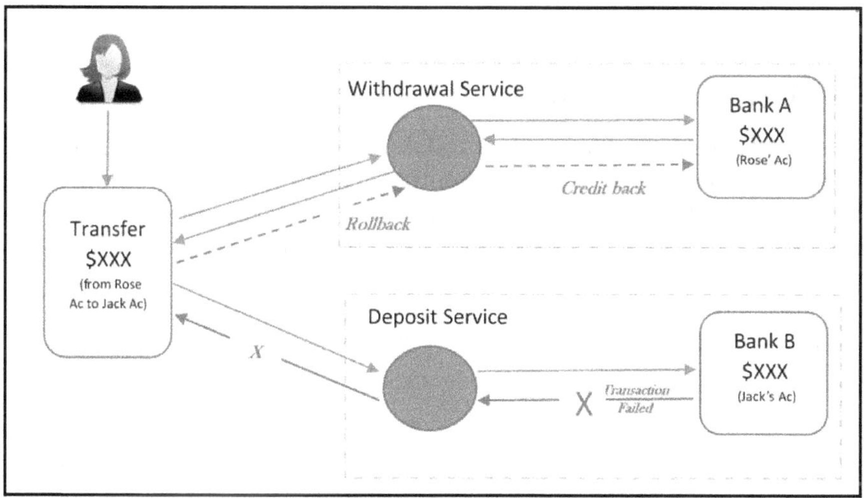

In a typical online savings account transaction, the banking system would have withdrawal and deposit services, and if either one of the service calls fail for any reason, the bank system would end up in an inconsistent state regardless of the sequence of the service calls (first withdrawal or deposit, or vice versa).

The preceding diagram shows a failed transaction of credit to the target account, which leads to the rollback of a debit transaction from the source account.

So, as an implementation, the runtime service activities are wrapped in a transaction with explicit reversal logic, ensuring all actions and changes are rolled back in case of the current operations failing.

The benefits of atomic service transactions are as follows:

- Helps to propagate the rollback mechanism across message-based business services
- Effective implementation of the stateless principle

The impacts of atomic service transactions is that it might need more memory resources depending on the number of transactions to be preserved its original state until commit or rollback notification.

# Authentication broker

A service consumer uses a mechanism to validate an identity to the called resource, and a caller's identity is verified based on the credentials presented by that caller. Credentials can be passwords, the digital certificate provided by a certificate authority, biometrics, ATM PIN, or combinations of any of these types.

In most cases, authentication is the first step to determine the eligibility of access to the web service, and the second phase is to verify that the user is authorized to access the web service.

For identity-based authorization, one can verify the claims contained within the authenticated user's credentials. Depending on the privileges provided to the client, the service can either grant or deny access to the underlying resources. The token authentication mechanism is a useful authentication model of fine-grained authorization.

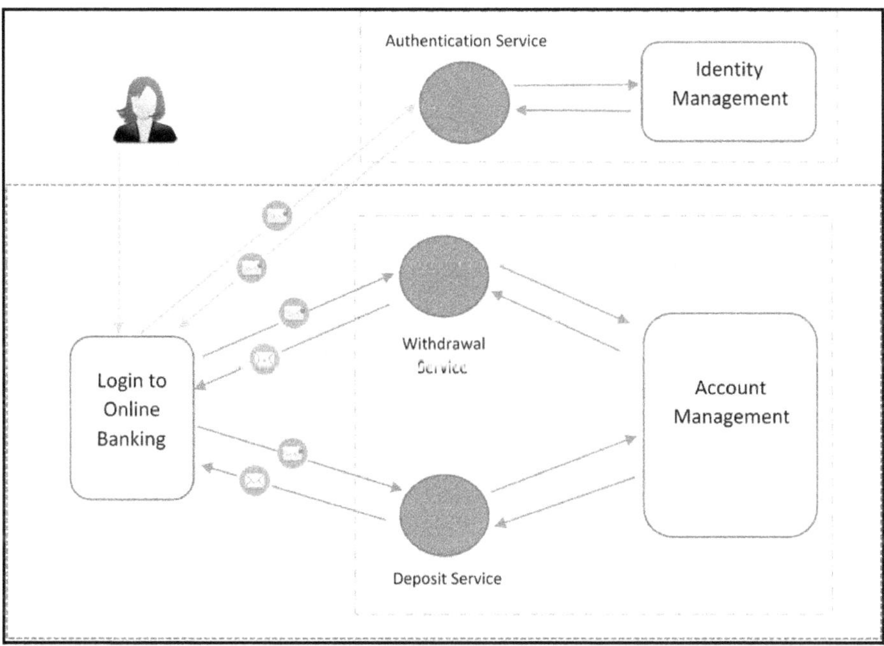


The preceding diagram depicts an online banking user who gets access to online banking debit transactions by contacting the authentication services, which authenticates against the central identity store. Then, the service responds with the token so that the user can consume the withdrawal service and the deposit service.

The authentication broker pattern helps to realize the authentication and authorization by a centralized identity store. The authentication services assume complete responsibility and provide a token that the consumer can use to access the service.

The following example shows a digital signature and x509 information and messages to be validated for authentication and authorization of its content. The authentication service uses that information and validates the messages for any tampering, then the authentication service will not generate a valid token, and so the application denies access to the feature:

The benefits of the authentication broker are as follows:

- Centrally managed trust (authentication) and so helps to eliminate the need for each client and service to manage their authentication independently
- Easy to accomplish agreements and updates happen at one place without impacting any clients
- Participants of brokered authentication do not require prior knowledge of one another to communicate
- Security tokens can be used across organizational boundaries and provide autonomous security domains

The impact of the authentication is, it sometimes create a single point of failure, and any security breach could impact the entire service across inventory.

# Message origin authentication

Imagine a situation where Rose is doing an online money transfer from her bank account to Jack's account. However, Jack did not receive the amount to his account, but Rose's account is showing that the amount is deducted. So, what would've happened to the money that Rose transferred?

It is possible that Jack's account number got modified or tampered with by an intruder's account number in intermediate layers, and so all the money got credited to the different account.

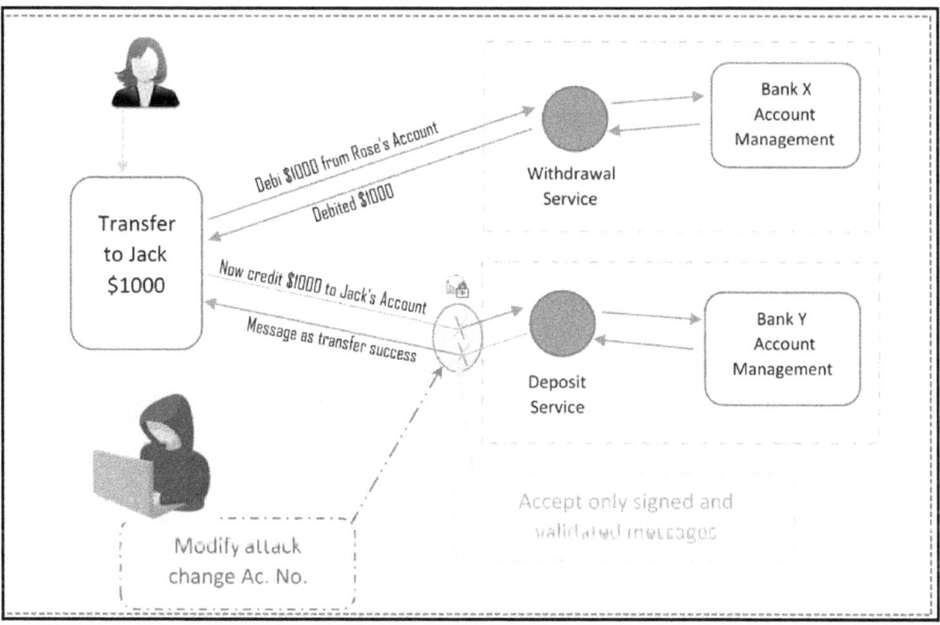


The message sent by a service consumer gets processed by one or more intermediate layers such as routers, message queues, and so on. The attacker could manipulate the messages in any of the intermediate layers and influence the service behavior for the evil purpose.

Message origin authentication (or data origin authentication) suggests to use a digital signing mechanism for transmitting sensitive messages, and so the service can verify the signature to ensure received messages are initiated by the originator, and has not been tampered with on the way.

Applying the digital signature algorithm to the payload as proof of origin provides tamper-proof messages. Services that receive this information verify the signature by using an algorithm, and it should match. If it does not match, then the service rejects the messages.

So, the message origin authentication validates two important aspects of security:

- **Data integrity**: The message has not been modified or tampered with on the way to the service
- **Authenticated**: The received message at the service side is originated from the intended sender and not from anyone else

The benefits of message origin authentication are as follows:

- Detect tampering of received messages
- Trace the origin of the messages to an identifiable source

The impacts of message origin authentication are as follows:

- Performance issues due to cryptographic implementations
- Choice of digital signing algorithm and variations in number and type of the key would be an additional overhead
- Selection of digital signing algorithm can affect the level of security achieved as it varies according to the degree of security the application needs

# Service façade

Imagine a building that needs to undergo maintenance work. The outer wall of the building is replaceable without impacting the internal structure, and it is called a façade. The exterior walls are torn off and replaced at one wing of the building at a time, while the other wing is in use.

Roughly, we can relate the same concept to the service façade in SOA. While some clients use the existing services, any enhancements to the services can be carried over with no impacts to consumer contracts as they continue to use an older service version.

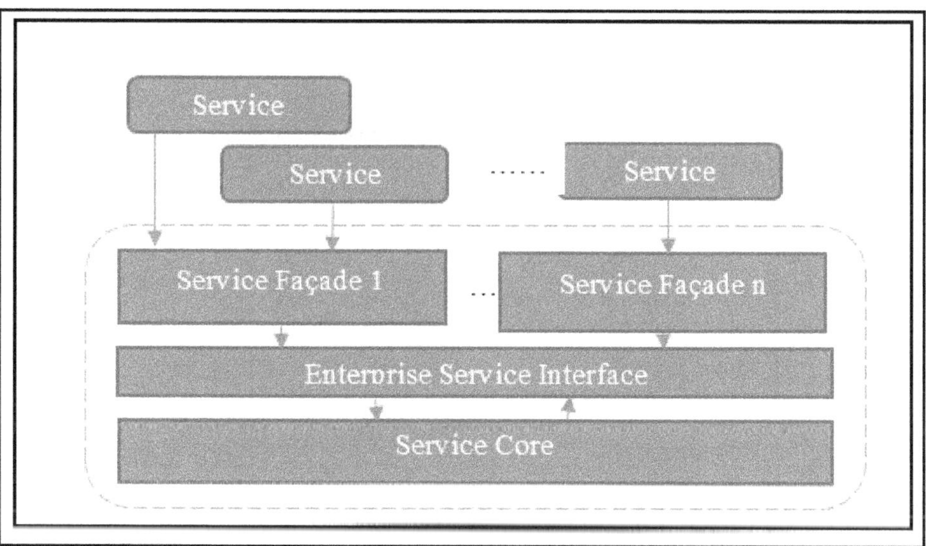


The pattern of segregating the core logic of services from the service contracts is called the service façade. The service façade facilitates loose coupling between the client contracts, thereby, in case of any changes to the services, it does not affect its customers and they do not need to modify their code.

When designing a service, the architect needs to watch out for any negative coupling, such as the contract to logic that creates dependencies upon the contract, and so whenever the service changes, the contract is also likely to change, so impacting all the service consumers who do not expect any impact.

The service façade eliminates this sort of coupling by establishing an interface between the core service logic and the service contract. The service façade logic allows contracts to remain decoupled from the underlying logic and further shields it from its core business logic. It applies to both functional and behavioral changes and so helps the services to evolve.

The service façade sits between the service and the service contract. Service façades can support multiple contracts. Note that multiple service contracts talk to the same service façade and only the service façades are coupled to the contract, not actual services, thus the services are independent and loosely coupled. If a contract changes, it minimizes the changes to the service.

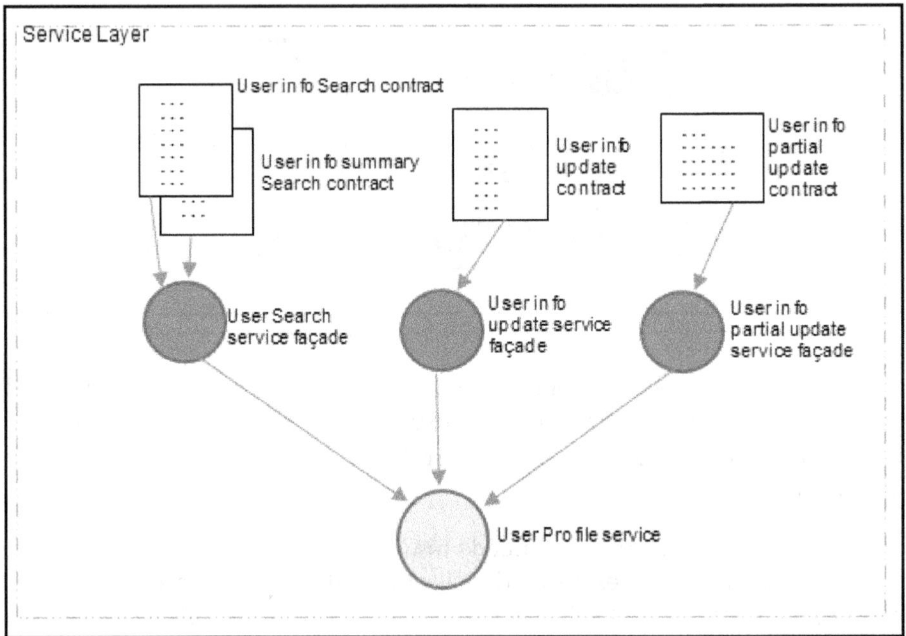


The preceding diagram depicts a service that serves multiple contracts for different business functions. The *user info summary search* and *user info partial update* are good examples of a contract-specific service façades having specific business logic to serve the clients without having any impacts on the client or services.

The benefits of the service façade are as follows:

- Façade shields the services and consumers of the services from the changes in the canonical model
- Façade hides the complexities of the canonical model
- Façade returns data representations agreed by the consumer
- Façade makes your design elegant

The impacts of the service façade are as follows:

- Due to the service façade having very user-specific business logic, it incurs additional development and maintenance costs
- Façades tend to create an extra physical distribution of services that lead to more complexity and additional processing overhead

# Multiple service contract

One standard contract may not be suitable or applicable for all the potential service consumers. For instance, one service contract should be allowed to update complete profile information, while another contract should not be allowed a full update, but only partial updates are allowed. Though a profile update is one single service, two different consumers need two separate contracts. The multiple service contract pattern helps to exercise the preceding options. The service façade and the multiple service contract are related, and the service façade helps the systems to realize multiple or concurrent contracts.

Multiple contracts or concurrent contracts serve two purposes. One is to support backward compatibility of a service, and the other one is to bring different views of a service for various uses.

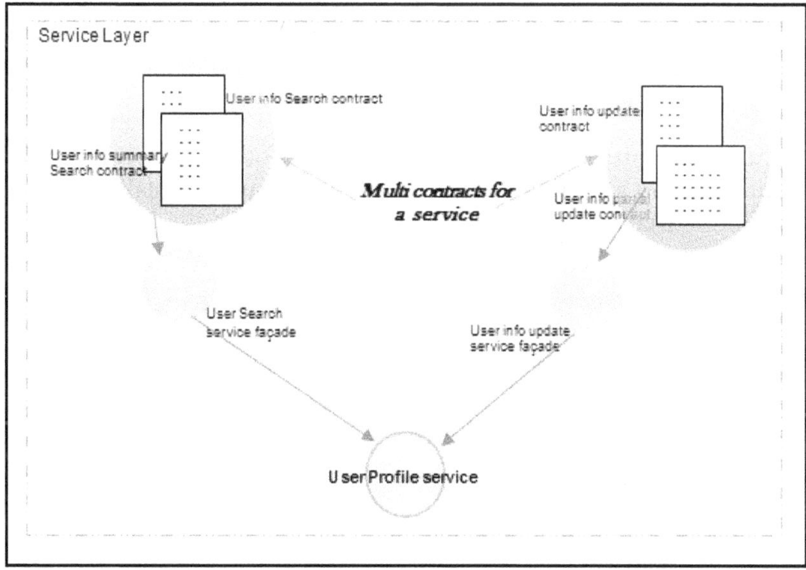

The encircled rectangles in the preceding diagram represent multi-service contracts, and both connect to the same service but for two different purposes. In the preceding example, one service contract is allowed to update only a few fields of a profile, while another contract can update all the fields of a profile. So, multiple contracts for the same service helps different consumers use the services for distinct purposes.

The benefits of the multiple service contract are as follows:

- Can support backward and forward compatibility
- Multiple version management keeps the customer end with no impact on any new changes to the services

The impact of the multiple service contract is such as this pattern considers as many contracts, however, each new contract, ends up in new service endpoint to inventory and might hamper the service governance and high maintenance.

# Service callback

Assume you are calling a customer care center from your telephone. Once connected, you hear an automated message saying that all of their customer care executives are busy, and so ask you to wait on the line. You may even be one of many waiting for the same service executive (concurrency and multiple threads). Now, you have two options to choose from; one is to hold the line and wait for someone to speak to, and two is to hang up and try again after some time. However, trying again after some time may have you ending up in the same situation.

How about the customer care executive calls you back? You dial the number, the system picks up your number, and says that it will call you back automatically when the customer care executive is free so that you do not need to wait.

Imagine a web service that takes a longer time to complete its tasks, but the caller or the consumer of the service does not want to wait for all the tasks to be completed, and also the consumer needs to know once all the process/tasks get completed. This is similar to our earlier example of a client calls a customer care executive but do not want to wait in the queue either.

Service callback pattern implementation is the best approach to fulfil such requirements.

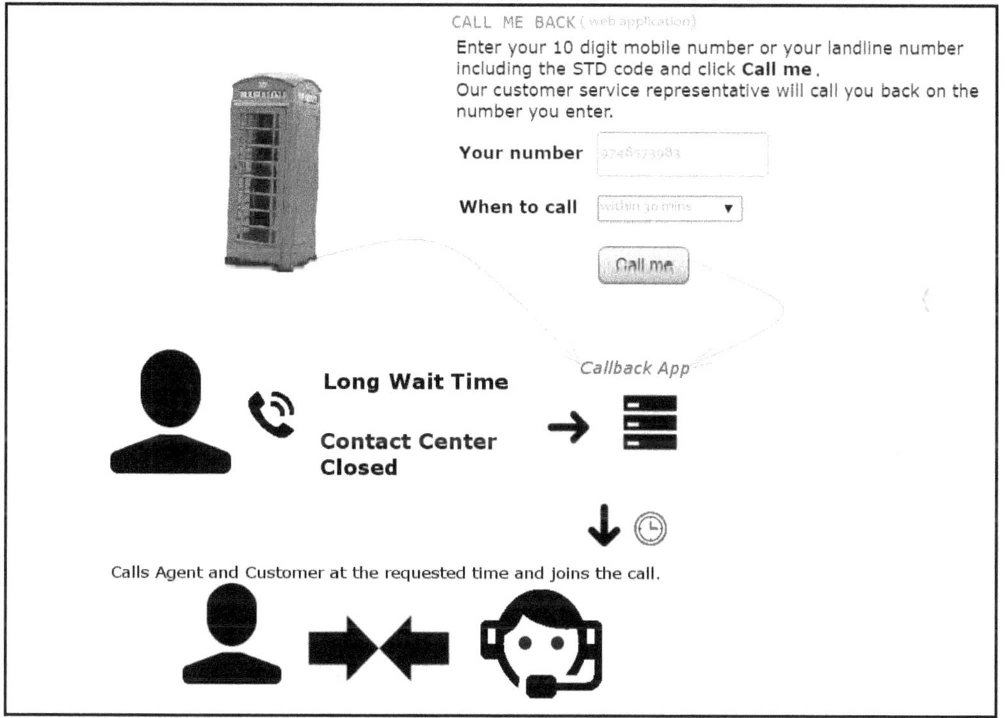

The preceding diagram depicts various calling systems (a web page, telephone, and contact center app) using a callback app that exercises the service callback pattern.

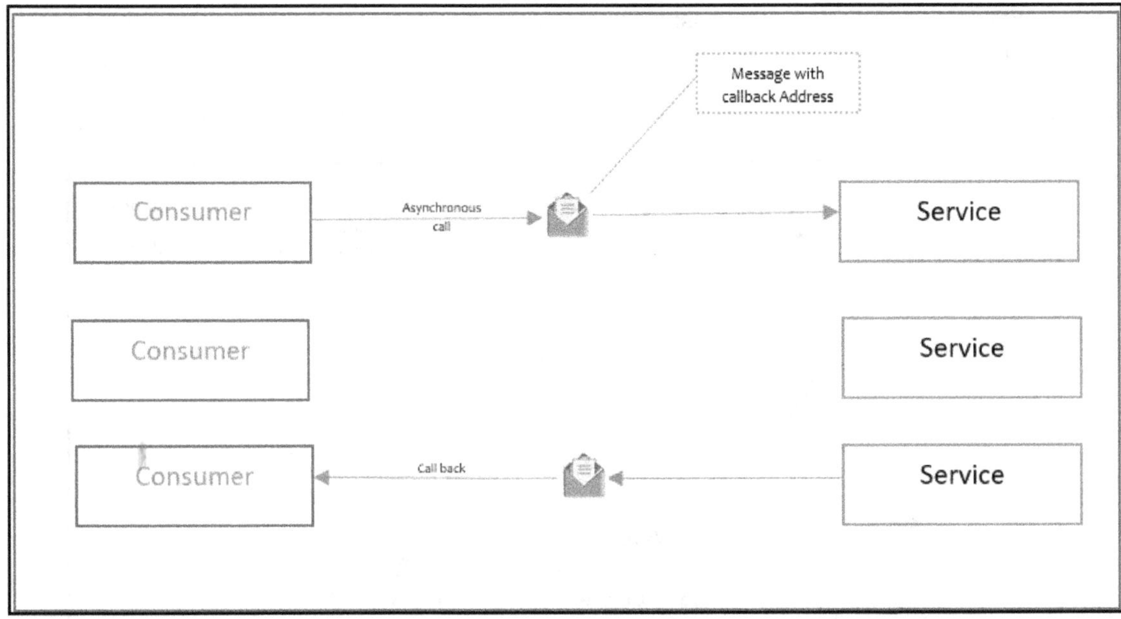


The service callback pattern suggests that the consumers of services communicate asynchronously with the services and make sure to provide callback addresses in the message, with which services can use the same callback address to communicate back with the client.

The preceding diagram depicts a scenario of a consumer calling the service asynchronously through the message. The message contains the callback address, so once the service completes its process, it uses the callback address to communicate and respond back. The service callback address can be a phone number, an email address, or it can be another service endpoint that can do further business logic and respond to consumers.

```
<soapenv:Envelope soapenv:encodingStyle="http://schemas.xmlsoap.org/soap/encoding/"
      .......
      .......
  <soapenv:Header>
    <con:StartHeader soapenv:actor="http://schemas.xmlsoap.org/soap/actor/next"
     soapenv:mustUnderstand="0"
     xmlns:con="http://www.openuri.org/2002/04/soap/conversation/">
    <con:conversationID>[123456]:myServer/myAppNotify</con:conversationID>
        <con:callbackLocation>
         http://myServer/myAppNotifyCallback
        </con:callbackLocation>
      </con:StartHeader>
  </soapenv:Header>
  <soapenv:Body>
      ..........
      ..........
      ..........
  </soapenv:Body>
</soapenv:Envelope>
```

In our first example, the callback address is the client's phone number, which the service would call. The second example may contain an email address or callback URL (of the same or even another service) with the status of upload as a response.

The benefits of the service callback are as follows:

- Extremely useful in cases where the request needs to wait for a longer response time
- Best implementation of loose coupling of services
- Best choice for message broadcast requirements

The impacts of the service callback are as follows:

- As this patterns mostly deals with asynchronous communication, it may introduce reliability concerns
- May require more infrastructure upgrades to support the necessary callback correlation
- Handling request and response errors is usually more challenging

More examples of a service message with the service callback pattern design are as follows:

- A software system that needs a service to load a large file and read its content line by line then upload to the database probably after validating each line. As it is typically massive in size and the caller of the system cannot wait for the longer process to complete, at the same time, a notification is sent to the caller once the upload is complete.

- Stock trading system and stock quote ticker services.
- Booking complete status, email notifications, and so on.

# Event-driven messaging

One of the core patterns of event-driven architecture is event-driven messaging; services (publishers) notify their consumers (subscribers) with relevant events when they happen, while customers are not necessarily waiting or aware of that event.

Imagine a stock trading service notifying its users whenever a particular stock price goes up:

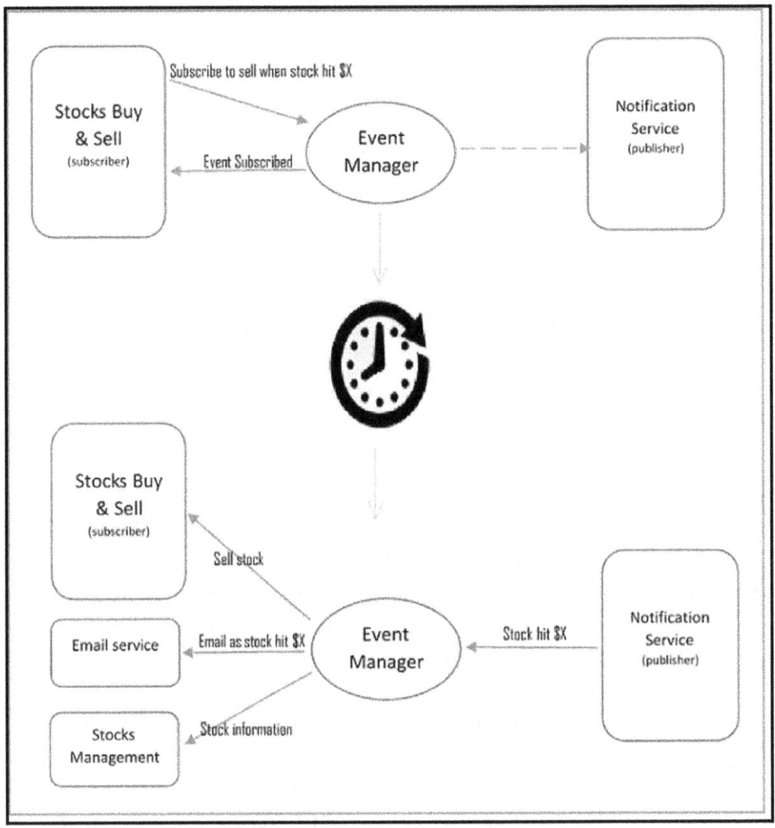

The preceding diagram depicts a cycle of notification process kicks in when a stock price hit a particular threshold; the subscriber lets event manager knows the intention, and the publisher publish (informs) when the event occurs. The $X is the predefined limit or sale price, and it is the event here. The following diagram depicts a sample pay load of the same.

```
...........
<edms:events>
  <edms:event name="StockOrderEvent" uid="StockOrderEventUID" version="1.0">
    <edms:header name="cbe" element="cbe:CommonBaseEvent" use="optional"/>
    <edms:body name="order" element="exs:Order" use="required"/>
    <edms:body name="details" element="exs:ProcessingDetails" use="optional"/>
    <edms:fault name="orderFault" element="exs:OrderFault"/>
    <edms:fault name="processingFault" element="exs:OrderProcessingFault"/>
  </edms:event>
</edms:events>
...........
```

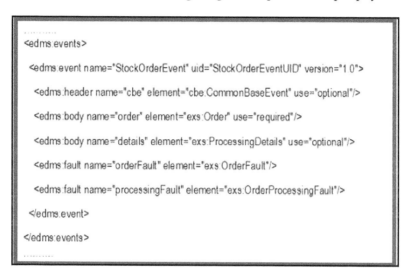

The benefits of event-driven messaging are as follows:

- Best pattern for integration intentions between cross-functional boundaries and services
- Achieve a higher degree of automation of process with less complexity

The impacts of event-driven messaging are as follows:

- Creates additional complexity while incorporating message exchanges as part of atomic services
- Depends on publisher and subscriber services availability
- Needs to address ripple effects of reliability issues by combining other relevant patterns in event-driven messaging design

# Service refactoring

In many situations, the services undergo many changes without any impact to the service contracts. It could be a simple software update improving the performance of a system, database updates, programming version upgrades, and so on.

Service refactoring helps to improve the service by changing the internals without changing its behavior, and so causing no impact on service contracts.

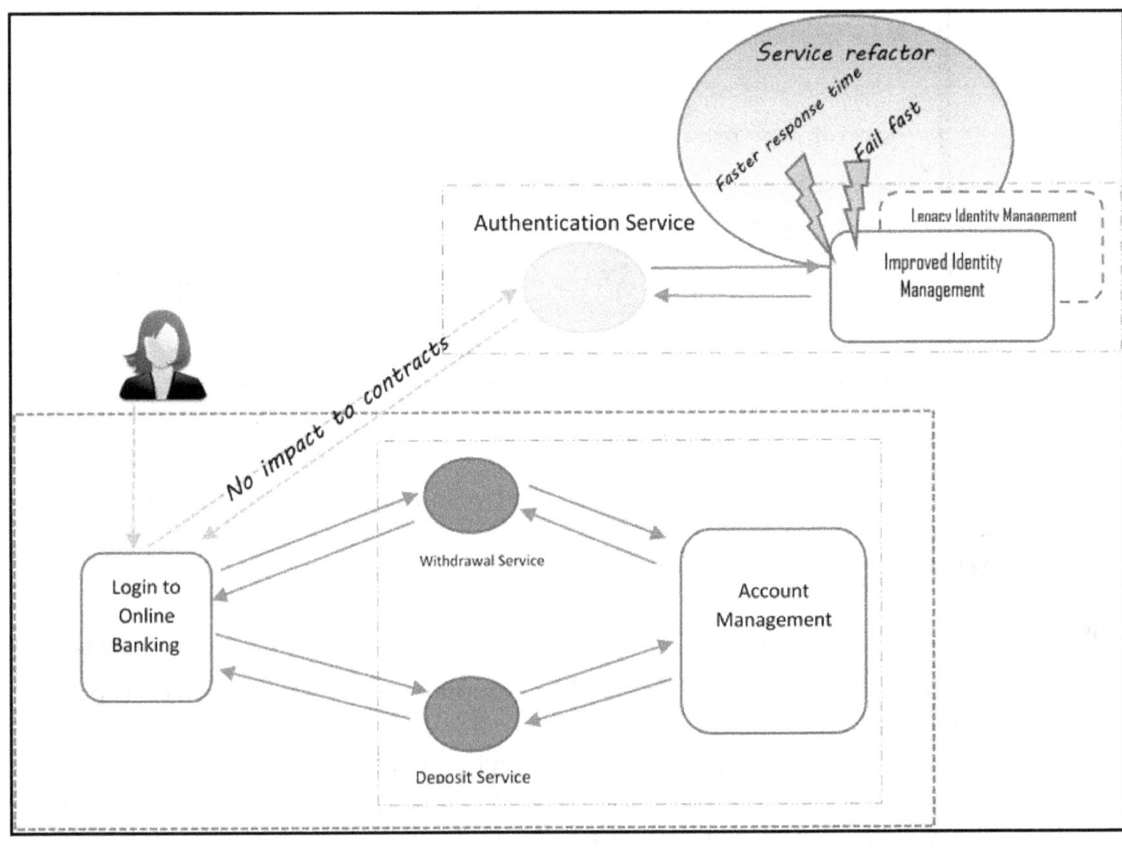

In the preceding diagram (encircled at the top-right as service refactor), the identity management system has undergone refactoring to improve the performance of its response time and has been upgraded with fail fast capabilities. There is no impact on the banking client, and it continues to use the same authentication services but with improved service capabilities.

The benefits of service refactoring are as follows:

- Easy update of heavily dependent services without affecting any of its consumers
- No changes to functional behavior after upgrades
- With limited scope minimizes adverse impacts to the service consumers

The impacts of service refactoring are as follows:

- May lead to add more governance efforts
- Might introduce potentially adverse side effects (improved performance but handling of concurrent requests could lead to lower availability)

# Metadata centralization

Having a centralized service catalog and providing a formal process of service registration and discovery is inevitable to any organization, and so limiting the risk of building services or functionality that already exists, or that is already under development.

The following diagram depicts a service registry that holds the information of published services, and so the service consumers would look up and bind those registered services for a runtime bind and invoke:

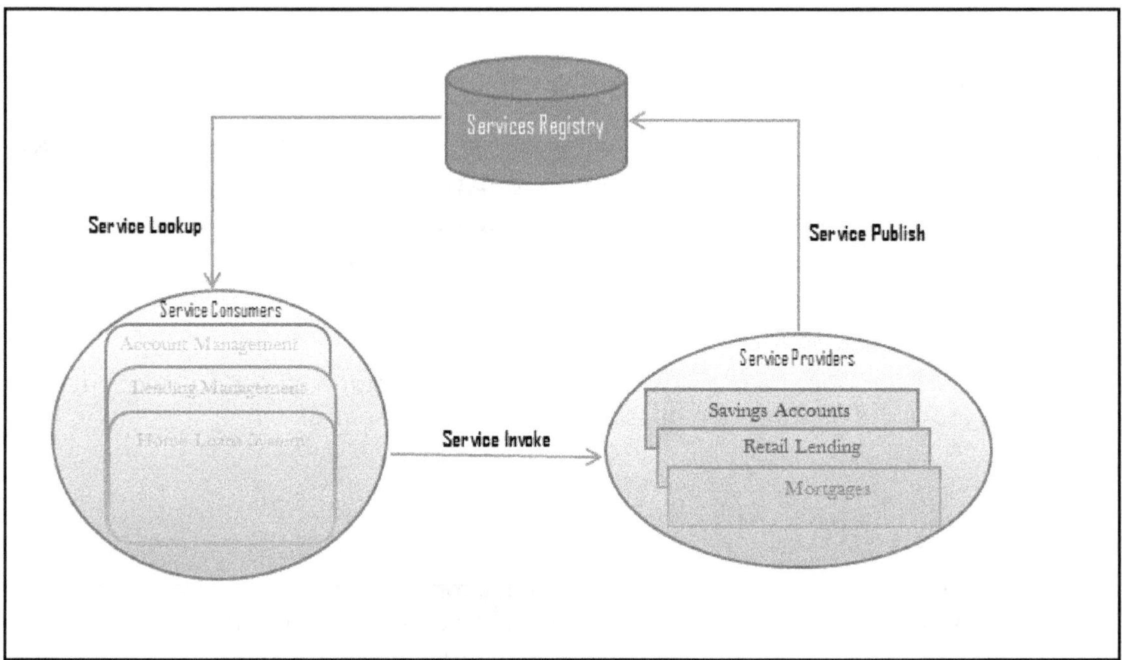


The information of the services and its functionalities are available to benefit the enterprises with

- Services discoverability
- Inventory normalization
- Standardization for service reusability
- Provide ways to minimize the risk of redundancy.
- Publish services with functional and QoS meta-data.

This pattern applies to one-domain service inventories, or even to several inventories.

```
<Catalog ....>
        <system systemId=http://sample.org/sb?wsdl uri="SBService.wsdl" />
        <public publicId="......" uri="wsdl/sb/sbApp.wsdl"/>
</Catalog>
```

```
<businessEntity businessKey="....."   operator="..../uddi"   authorizedName="...">
 <discoveryURLs>  <discoveryURL useType="businessEntity">.........</discoveryURL>  </discoveryURLs>
      <name>XMethods</name>
    <description xml:lang="en">service resources </description>
 <businessServices>  <businessService serviceKey="......"        businessKey="......">
   <name>Stock Quotes</name>
   <description xml:lang="en">stock quotes</description>
   <bindingTemplates>      <bindingTemplate bindingKey=".."      serviceKey="..">
      <description  xml:lang="en">stock quote binding   </description>
      <accessPoint URLType="http">http://.../soap       </accessPoint>
    </bindingTemplate>    </bindingTemplates>
  </businessService>  </businessServices>
</businessEntity>
```

The benefits of the sample catalog are as follows:

- Minimizes the risk of building functionality that already exists
- Helps in service normalization
- Helps in compelling discovery and interpretation
- Runtime discovery and binding
- Ensures metadata standardization

The impacts of the sample catalog are as follows:

- Due to metadata standardization, the documentation and registration need to be part of the service delivery lifecycle (additional governance)
- Service registry needs to be adequately mature and reliable to lead to strict governing and maintenance

# Principles and patterns cross reference

The following table has references to SOA principles and related SOA patterns for each principle. This matrix might come in handy when you want to refer to a common design pattern and its associated SOA design principle:

| **Principles** | **Patterns** |
|---|---|
| Standardized service contract/service interoperability | • Service messaging<br>• Message screening<br>• Agnostic services<br>• Multiple contracts<br>• Event-driven messaging<br>• Service callback<br>• Service façade<br>• Service refactoring |
| Service abstraction | • Service refactoring |
| Service autonomy | • Event-driven messaging<br>• Service messaging |
| Service composability | • Agnostic services<br>• Message origin authentication<br>• Service callback<br>• Authentication broker |
| Service discoverability | • Metadata centralization |
| Service loose coupling | • Service messaging<br>• Event-driven messaging<br>• Service callback<br>• Service façade<br>• Multiple contracts |

| Service reusability | • Agnostic services<br>• Multiple contracts |
|---|---|
| Service statelessness | • Atomic service transaction |

# Summary

In this chapter, we have learned about what *SOA* is, and its fundamental characteristics such as service interconnectivity, event-driven and messaging, flexible, service evolution, along with a few other common characteristics. In later sections, we covered SOA principles such as service contract standards, interoperability abstraction, service autonomy, service composability, reusability, and statelessness in detail.

We also learned about the most common SOA design patterns and where those patterns can be applied so that one can build SOA-compliant services. The patterns that we touched upon are service messaging, message screening, agnostic services, atomic service transaction, authentication broker, message origin authentication, service façade, multiple service contract, service callback, event-driven messaging, service refactoring, and metadata centralization.

# 8
# Event-Driven Architectural Patterns

Why do organizations need **event-driven architecture** (EDA)? Organizations across the world are operating in an agile manner and changing their structure frequently. They are evolving into business structures that can operate as independent service providers and consumers. These service providers and consumers need not necessarily exist within the organization. Some business services are outsourced to external business partners and other business services within the organization are looking to provide their services to external organizations in addition to internal business lines. All these emerging trends necessitate process architectures that have high levels of autonomy, or in other words, loose coupling between various application components that exist within an organization. The need for loosely coupled architecture with high levels of autonomy led to the evolution of EDA. Using EDA, organizations can rapidly reorganize their structure without changing their application constructions. Now, let us get started with the details of EDA.

An event in a generic sense refers to any change in state that is of interest to an organization/business/end user. The signal in a car indicating that the gas is low, the ringing of a mobile phone, and the ringing of a smoke alarm in a house are all examples of some real-world events that we come across in our everyday lives. Understanding the concept of an event is easier with the help of an example, as depicted in the following diagram:

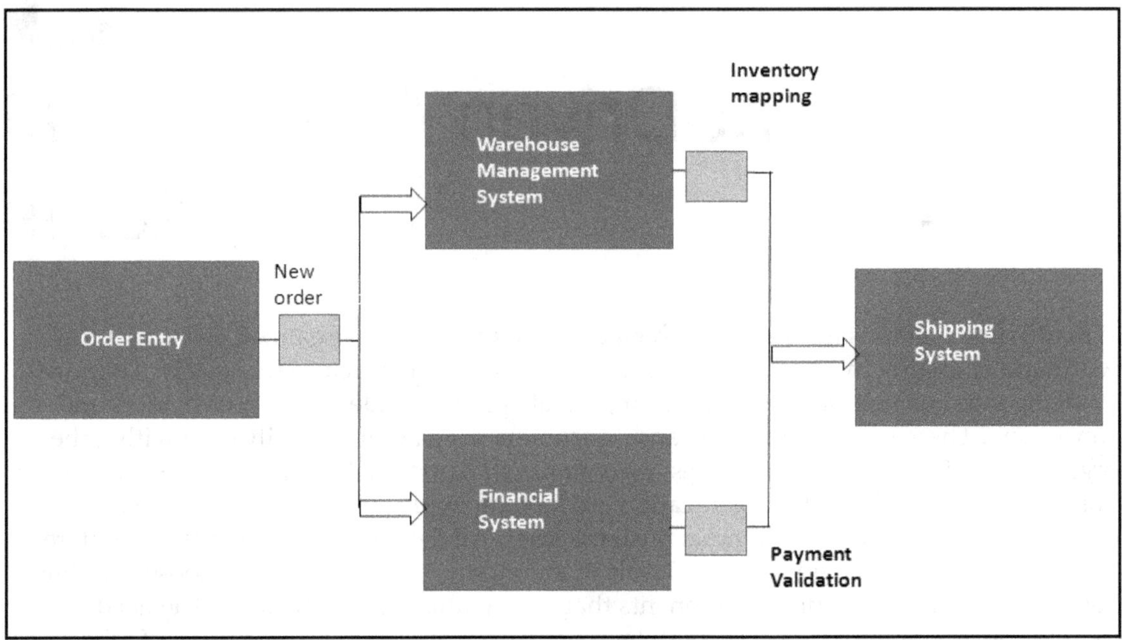


The diagram depicts the flow of actions in an order management system. As soon as an order management system receives an order from a website or from an order entry system, the next step would be to notify other systems about the order. In this step, receiving an order is an event. This event needs to be published to other systems that would be interested in this event. In this example, the other systems that would be interested in this event are a warehouse management system that would check the order item in the inventory stored in the warehouse to ensure its availability and a finance system that would check the credit balance or the payment mechanism that is associated with the order.

Each of these systems will, in turn, publish an event to other systems that are required to complete the next step in order processing. Accordingly, the warehouse system may publish an inventory allocated event and the financial system may publish a payment validated event to the shipping system. The shipping system will, in turn, make necessary arrangements to ship the order to the customer. In this specific flow of events, these are the component systems that are a part of the event flow. But there could be several other systems that could form a part of the event flow based on the outcomes of event processing at each step. For example, if the warehouse management system detects low inventory levels for the item placed in the order, it will trigger an event to the procurement system to procure the item. Similarly, if the financial system detects a low credit balance or an incorrect payment option, it will trigger an email notification to the customer that the credit balance is low or the payment was not completed successfully.

From this example, we understand that the crux of EDA is the concept of **publish/subscribe.** In the preceding example, the order management system publishes the order event to two other interested parties that have subscribed to the event warehouse management system and financial system. These two systems, in turn, publish events to shipping systems and so on. The three important definitions in the context of the EDA pattern are the following:

- **Event**: An event is a runtime operation, executed by a software element to make some information (including the information that it occurred) available for potential use by software elements not specified by the operation.
- **Publisher**: To trigger (or publish) an event is to execute it. A software element that may trigger events is a publisher. A software element that may use the event's information is a subscriber.
- **Context**: In event-driven design, a context is a Boolean expression specified by a subscriber at registration time, but evaluated at triggering time, such that the registered action will only be executed if the evaluation yields true.

The event-driven pattern is a class of patterns that has gained a lot of traction of late because of the rapidly changing industry paradigm. Many folks get easily confused between **service-oriented architecture** (**SOA**) and EDA patterns. In the next section, we will try to analyze and understand the differences between the two.

# Service-oriented architecture and event-driven architecture (SOA versus EDA)

Organizations across the world are changing their structures rapidly and are moving toward on-demand business models. There is an increase in the movement toward setting up network-oriented business structures that will have autonomous service providers and consumers. Outsourcing is also very prominent as many parts of the business process will also be outsourced to external business partners. Various departments and business units who are present within organizations are taking on the role of service providers. The focus of these service providers is to increasingly provide services to the external market entities. This necessitates organizations being agile enough to quickly respond to changes or events that happen in the external environment. All these aspects demand a paradigm shift from a command-driven, tightly coupled, service-driven SOA concept to a more loosely coupled model that is driven by events. EDA is a publish/subscribe type of pattern. In the context of EDA, the publisher is completely unaware of the subscriber, and vice versa. Components of the EDA pattern are so loosely coupled that only the semantics of the message is shared between them. Now, the decision that needs to be made is when to use SOA and when to use EDA.

There is a common tendency to use EDA and SOA interchangeably because of the nature of their working. But that should not be the case. There are clear differentiators between the two architectural options. For situations that demand a strong cohesion in the business processes, SOA is the ideal choice of architecture. The following are the various scenarios in which a command/control style of SOA could be an ideal choice of architecture for organizations:

- If there exists a vertical interaction between the various hierarchical layers of functions that exist in an organization
- If there are functional request-and-reply processes such as man-machine dialogues where the user feeds a question and waits for an answer
- If there are processes that are transactional in nature that requires commit and rollback features
- If data enrichment is required in a message for it to be published to its full content in a formal format

EDA is the preferred style for organizations that require a loose coupling between their various processes. EDA is the choice of architecture in federated and autonomous processing environments. The following are some of the scenarios in which EDA is an ideal choice of architecture for organizations:

- If there exists a horizontal communication between various tiers that are part of process chain
- If there are workflow types of processes in an organization
- If there exist processes that involve cross-functional borders of organizations, for example, a B2B process

Aiming for loose coupling in architecture always provides the flexibility and the agility that is necessary for present-day organizations. So, the rule of thumb to be followed while designing architectures for organizations is use loose coupling whenever possible and use tightly coupled architectural options only if required. Other aspects of design, such as performance, response time, and so on, should also be taken into consideration while making architectural design choices. In a typical enterprise-level organization, the bifurcation and the relationship of processes with regard to EDA and SOA architecture are depicted in the following diagram:

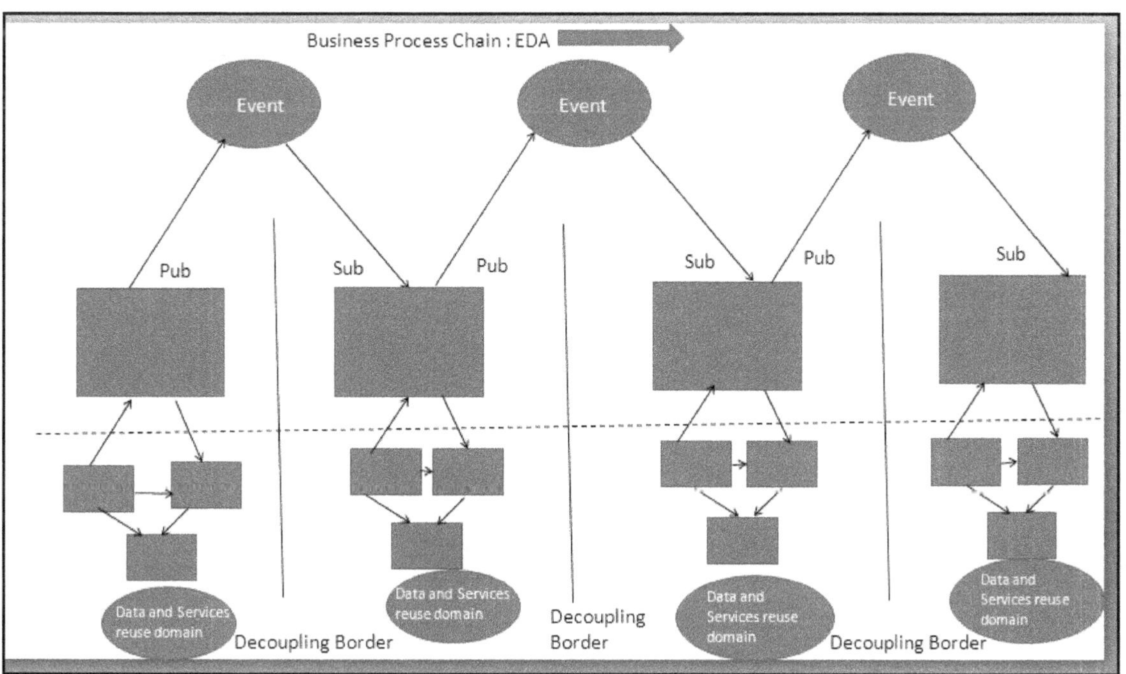

In the diagram, the circles at the top denote loosely coupled systems, which are good candidates to be chosen as decoupling points or events. At these decoupling points, the various system components can be connected or disconnected without altering the connected peer systems. Data exchange between various domains in an organization takes place only at these decoupling points and not at the lower levels of systems that are tightly coupled. Within the reuse domain (indicated at the bottom of the figure), a fine-grained EDA implementation would be required to decouple the components because of their tight integration. The more fine-grained the EDA implementation is, the greater the flexibility of IT systems will be, but this would also reduce the scope of reuse of domains.

In the preceding diagram, if web services technology is used at decoupling points along with a common infrastructure backbone such as an enterprise service bus, it is very easy to establish connectivity between heterogeneous systems. Systems that are present downstream need not be SOA alone; they can also be SOAP-wrapped legacy systems, **commercial off-the-shelf software** (**COTS**), or other applications such as ERP. The following diagram shows the integration of EDA and SOA . In this diagram, components are connected through decoupling points, which are events:

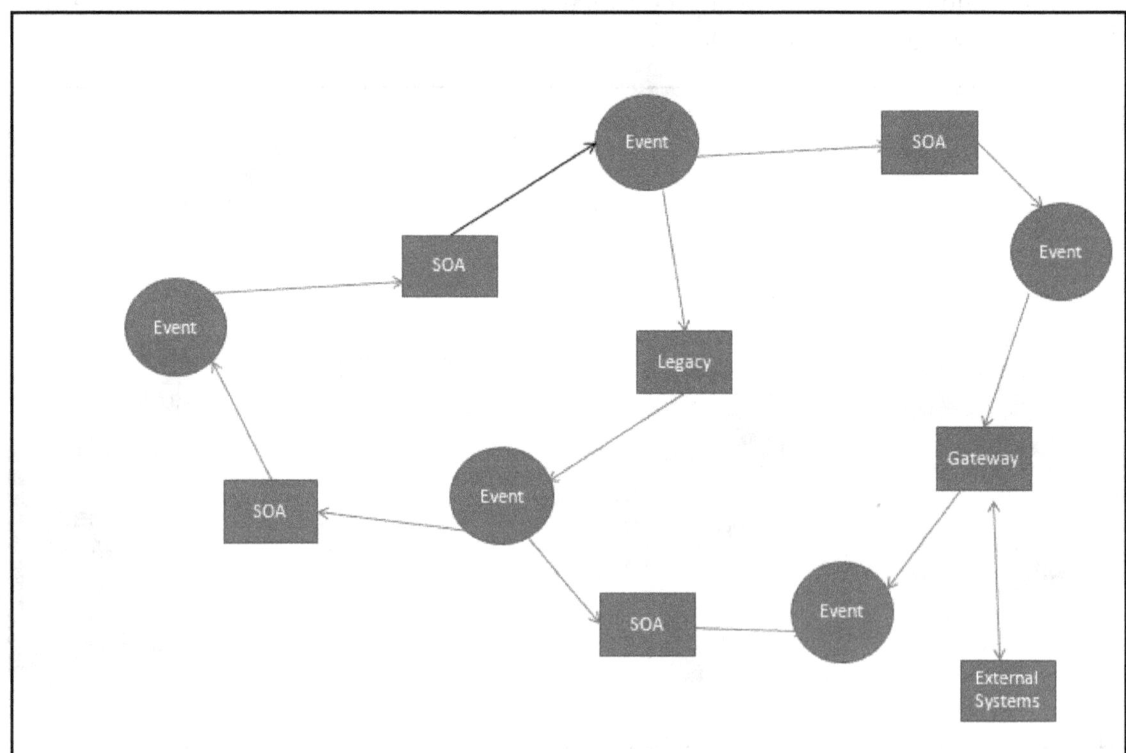

Now, we have clearly learned the differences between EDA and SOA. In the next section, we will learn the components of an EDA pattern. These components should be part of any architecture that uses EDA patterns.

# Key characteristics of event-driven patterns

If there is a component in a system that publishes and accepts events, can you consider that as an example of an EDA pattern? The answer to the question is a clear no. In this section, we will examine the characteristics of EDA patterns. Their main characteristics are the following:

- **Multicast communications**: The publishers or the participating systems have the capability to send events to multiple systems that have subscribed to it. In other words, it is not a unicast communication in which one sender can send data only to one receiver.
- **Real-time transmission**: Publishers publish the events as and when they occur in real time to the subscribers. In other words, the mode of processing or transmission involved here is real time and not batch processing.
- **Asynchronous communication**: The publisher does not wait for the receiver to process an event before sending the next event.
- **Fine-grained communication**: Publishers keep publishing individual fine-grained events instead of waiting for a single aggregated event.
- **Ontology**: EDA systems always have a technique to classify events in terms of some form of a group/hierarchy based on their common characteristics. This gives flexibility to the subscribers to subscribe to a specific event or specific category of events.

# Components of an EDA pattern

The main components of the EDA pattern are the following:

- Event specifications
- Event processing
- Event tooling
- Enterprise integration
- Sources and targets

All these components and the various other subcomponents are summarized in the following diagram:

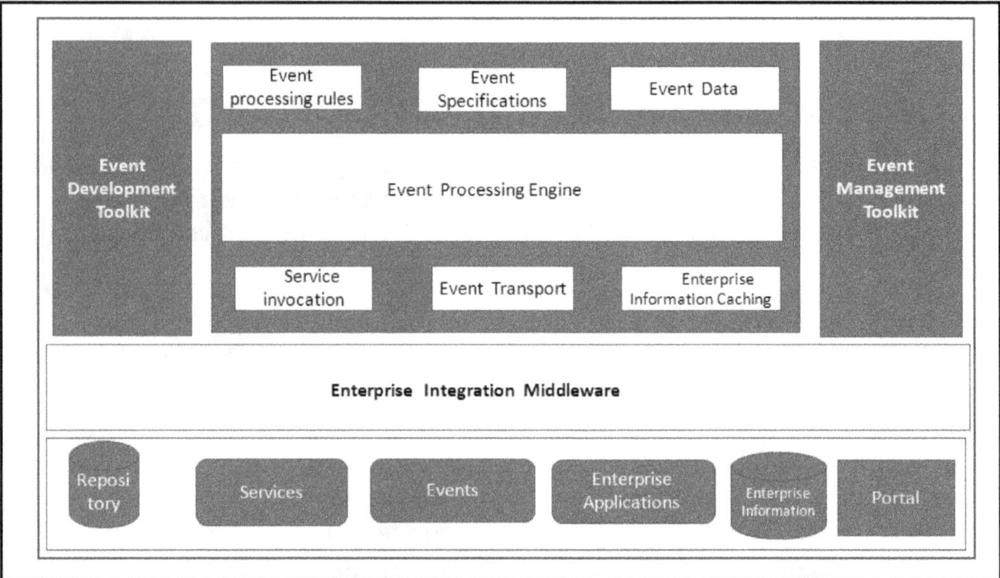


The core component of any EDA is strong metadata architecture. The core components of event metadata architecture are the following:

- **Event specifications**: These event specifications should be made available to event generators, event processing engines, and event transformers. There is no industry-approved standard for event definition and processing at the moment; they are just in the evolving phase.
- **Event processing**: This is a technique for processing and analyzing streams of data about events with an objective of deriving some kind of a conclusion from them, for example, a weather prediction system whose main function is to predict the onset of cyclones. For the system to derive this conclusion, it should take into consideration several patterns, such as wind speed, the direction of flow, atmospheric pressure, moisture content, and so on. All these parameters constitute the event data, and this data should be processed by an event engine in order to arrive at specific conclusions. So, the essential components that are required for any event processing are the following:
    - Event engine
    - Event data

- **Event tooling**: Event development tools provide the following key functions with regard to the processing of events:
    - Define event specifications
    - Define event processing rules
    - Manage event subscriptions

  They also provide add-on functions such as monitoring of event processing infrastructure and event flows.

- **Enterprise integration**: This has a pivotal role to play in EDA design. Some of the necessary integration services that are required are the following:
    - Event preprocessing
    - Event channel transport
    - Service invocation
    - Publication and subscription
    - Enterprise information access
- **Sources and targets**: Sources refer to the components of the enterprise that generate events. This could refer to systems, services, automated agents, or even people who are responsible for creating events. Targets refer to the components that perform an action based on the occurrence of events or based on the event outcomes. The topology of sources and targets of events are governed by several parameters, such asthe following:
    - Event flows
    - Event occurrence volumes
    - Location of sources and targets and so on

Event flows are a very important component of EDA architecture. In the next section, we will see the various logical layers that are present in an event flow. These logical layer components need to be carefully chosen and designed for successful implementation of EDA patterns.

# Event flow layers

The four logical layers present in the event flow are the following:

- Event generators
- Event channel
- Event processing
- Downstream event-driven activity

## Event generators

The sources from where events are generated are called **event generators**. The source could be an application, service, business process, sensor, database, or even a human being. An event that is generated is evaluated for notability by an event filter, and if the evaluation is successful, leads to the generation of a notable event. Since there are diverse sources for the generation of events, not all generated events will be in a format that is suitable for processing. For such events, it is necessary to ensure that they are converted into a compatible format before they are sent to the event channel.

## Event channel

This acts a transmission medium and messaging backbone for EDA. It receives standard formatted events from the event generator and sends them to other event generators, event processing engines, and downstream subscribers.

## Event processing

Once the events are received, they are processed and evaluated based on some rules that are stored in the event processing engine. Based on the results of the evaluation, a specific course of action is initiated. The event rules are created based on the criteria specified by the organization and/or other interested parties. Event processing could result in several courses of action, such as notifying a certain system/agency, taking an alternate course of action, initiating a business process, and so on.

## Downstream event-driven activity

Any event can trigger a sequence of downstream activities that could be a response to the event. The event could be a push notification by the event processing engine or pull notifications by the subscribers. Subscribers in this context could refer to an application, humans, services, or business processes.

# Design considerations for event-driven patterns

In this section, we will explain the various design considerations that need to be kept in mind before choosing EDA patterns for architecture implementation. The main considerations are the following:

- **Agility**: Agility refers to the ability to cope with the rapid changes that happen in the environment. In the EDA pattern, components are loosely coupled. This ensures that changes that happen to one component do not affect the other components in the system. Hence, the degree of agility offered by the EDA pattern is high, making it an ideal choice for the design of systems that require continuous changes without any downtime.
- **Ease of deployment**: The EDA pattern components are loosely coupled in nature, which makes their deployment very easy. For solutions that require maximum ease of deployment, event broker topology is a better option than event mediator topology. This is due to the fact that in event mediator topology, there exists a relatively tight coupling between the event mediator and event processor.
- **Testability**: Unit testing of EDA pattern components is difficult because of the fact that it requires special test clients and test tools to generate events that are required for testing purposes.
- **Performance**: EDA has the capability to perform asynchronous operations in parallel, which provides very high performance for the architecture, irrespective of the time lag involved in queuing and dequeuing messages.
- **Scalability**: EDA offers a high level of scalability because of the highly decoupled nature of the components.
- **Ease of development**: Ease of development using this pattern is low because of the asynchronous nature of the pattern.

Though there are well-defined components for an EDA pattern, the implementation style of the pattern varies based on the type of system functionality and complexity. In the next section, we will learn about the various styles in which EDA patterns are implemented.

# Implementation variants of EDA patterns

The various styles in which EDA patterns are implemented are the following:

- Simple event processing patterns
- Event stream processing patterns
- Complex event processing patterns

## Simple event processing patterns

These patterns are used to measure events that are related to specific measurable changes in conditions. These patterns are used in scenarios that demand real-time flow of work to be triggered without any other constraints or considerations. Parameters such as lag time and costs related to business are not taken into consideration while using simple event processing patterns in architecture. Some scenarios for usage of this type of pattern could be a detection of temperature/pressure changes by a sensor. Let us explain simple event processing with the help of the order management system example we used at the beginning of the chapter. The diagram is repeated here for quick reference:

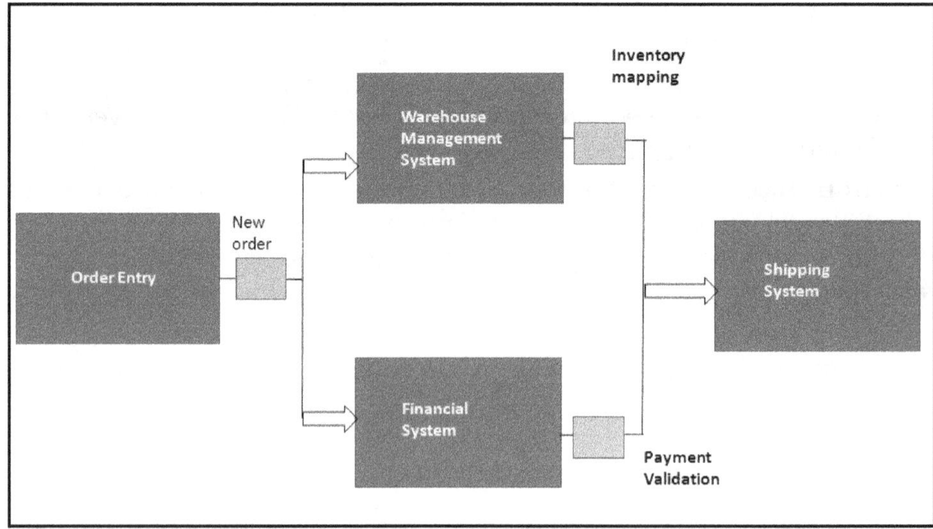

In this example, after the order enters the order management system, the first event is triggering a notification to the warehouse management system for checking inventory levels and to the financial system for payment validation. For simplicity, we will consider only one flow of events: the events related to the warehouse management (related to inventory check). Once the order enters the warehouse management system, the items in the order are checked against the inventory present in the warehouse using the check inventory service. The check inventory service allocates the inventory pertaining to the items present in the order and then checks the remaining inventory for optimal levels of inventory threshold. If the stock in the warehouse falls under the available threshold, the check inventory service generates a low inventory threshold event. This event is received by the simple event processing engine, as depicted in the following diagram. The event processing rules in this example will initiate two sets of events to handle the low inventory threshold situation: the first one would be a process to reorder the inventory, and the second one would be for publishing the event for consumption by the subscribers. In this particular example, the subscribers are inventory buyers and a notification to the inventory controller would also be generated. All these activities are depicted in the following diagram:

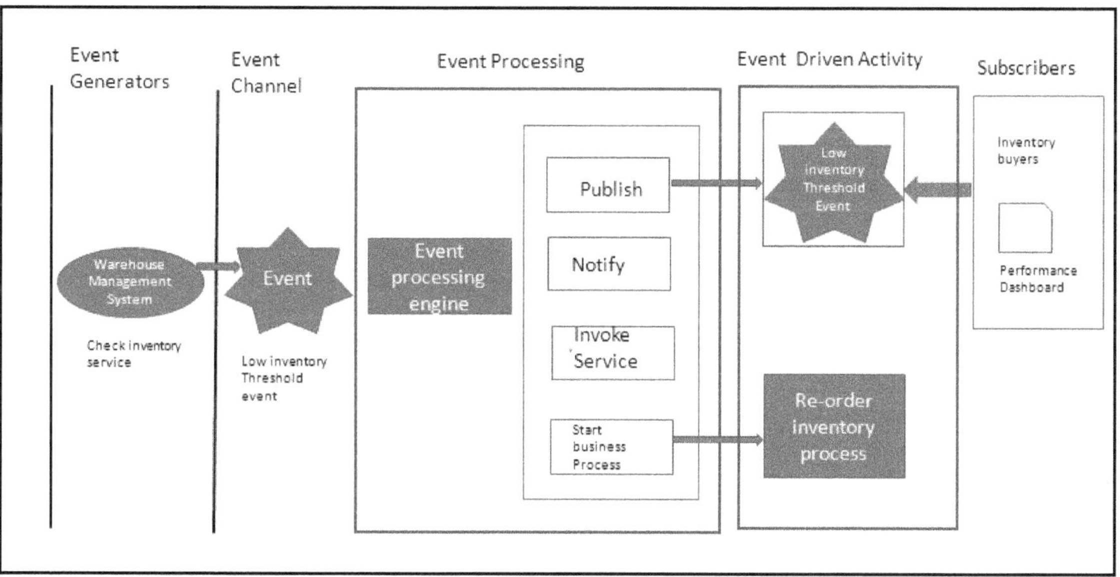

# Event stream processing patterns

In event stream processing, ordinary events that occur are filtered for notability and sent to subscribers. This style is used in order to ensure that real-time information flows in and around the enterprise. This pattern facilitates real-time decision-making.

Let us demonstrate this type of event further with the help of the order processing example that we have been discussing in this chapter. In the order processing example, if we consider the sequence of events at the warehouse, the RFID sensor generates an event for each product that moves out of the warehouse. In this scenario, suppose, for example, a retailer wants to be informed when high-value products leave the warehouse. To meet this requirement, a local event filter has been designed, which has rules to filter out events for items priced less than $5,000. Suppose there is a purchase of a high-value item for $6,000. This event, which is a high-value event, is reformatted to a standard event format and placed in the event channel. The event processing engine receives the event maps it to the rules for high-end products leaving the warehouse, and publishes it. The subscribers who have subscribed to this event receive it; in this example, it could be an inventory manager's dashboard.

# Complex event processing (CEP) patterns

In CEP, a combination of simple and ordinary events is taken into consideration in order to judge it a complex event has happened. The various events that are taken into consideration may be evaluated over a long period of time. The event correlation between the various events may occur in various dimensions, such as temporal, causal, and spatial. For this evaluation to happen, CEP requires the following components:

- Event interpreters
- Event pattern definition
- Event pattern matching
- Event correlation techniques

CEP is generally used to respond to anomalies in business, and in order to assess the opportunities and threats.

EDA patterns come in two different flavors or topologies. Each topology needs to be implemented only in specific scenarios as their features and characteristics are different. Hence, it is very important to understand these topologies so wise decisions can be made regarding their choice and implementation. In the next section, we will understand the various EDA pattern topologies.

# Types of event-driven patterns

There are two types of topologies for event-driven patterns:

- Event mediator topology pattern
- Event broker topology pattern

The mediator topology pattern is used when it is required to orchestrate multiple steps that are part of an event with the help of a central mediator. The broker topology is used when it is required to chain multiple events together without the need for a central mediator. The architecture and components of each of these patterns are discussed next.

# Event mediator topology pattern

The mediator topology pattern is used to design systems/processes that will need some level of coordination/orchestration in order to process the event. The ideal example of this scenario could be the order processing example, where there are multiple steps, such as order entry, inventory validation, finance validation, and so on. All these steps require some level of orchestration in order to assess whether they can be performed serially or in parallel. There are four main components within the mediator topology:

- Event queue
- Event mediator
- Event channels
- Event processors

All these components are depicted in the following diagram:

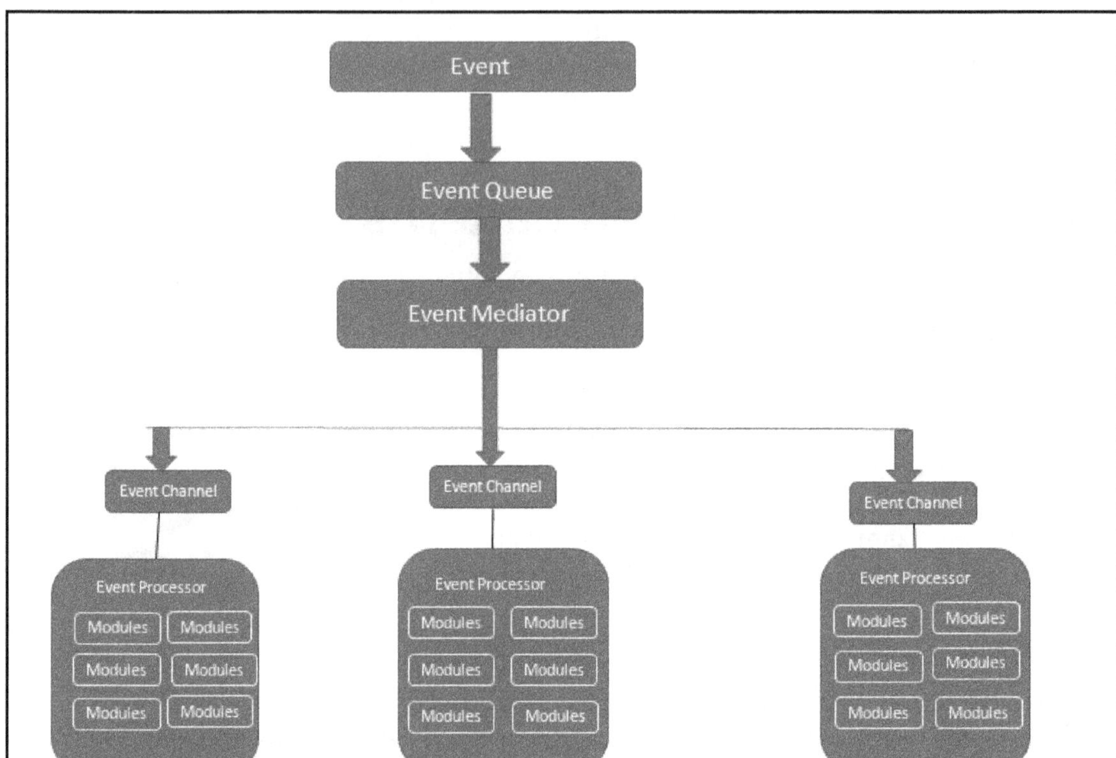


The client sends an event, which is then received by the event queue. The event queue transfers the event to the event mediator. The event mediator receives the event and orchestrates it. This is done by sending additional asynchronous events to the various event channels, which in turn will execute each step of the process. Event processors receive the event from the event channel and apply business logic to process the event. There can be any number of event queues in an EDA. An event queue can be implemented as a message queue, web service component, or in any other form that is suitable for the system under consideration. There are two types of events that are provided by this pattern:

- **Initial event**: This refers to the original event that is received by the mediator
- **Processing event**: This refers to the events that are generated by the mediator and are sent to the event processing components

The event mediator is mainly responsible for performing orchestration of the various steps that are present within the initial event. In order to perform each step in the initial event, the event mediator sends a specific processing event to the event channel. This processing event is received and processed by the event processor. Event channels are used to pass processing events associated with each step to the event processors. Event channels can either be in the form of message queues or in the form of message topics. The application logic that is required for processing the events is present in the event processor. Event processors are typically highly decoupled architectural components that are associated with a specific task in the system.

# Event broker topology pattern

The event broker topology pattern is used in scenarios where the event flow is relatively simple in nature and does not require any central event orchestration. The two main components of the event broker topology pattern are the following:

- Broker
- Event processor

The components of an event broker topology pattern are depicted in the following diagram:

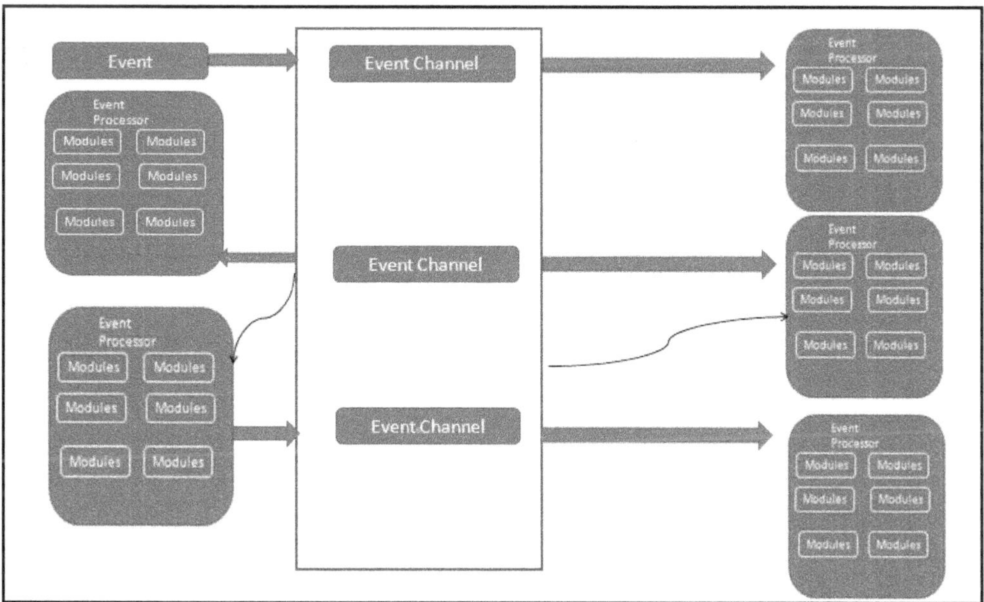

The event broker component contains all the event channels and can be designed in a centralized or federated manner. The main difference between the event broker topology pattern and the event mediator topology pattern is the absence of an event mediator component which controls and orchestrates the event. Instead of an event mediator, the event processor performs that role of processing and publishing each event, indicating that the particular action is just completed. The broker component can be centralized or federated and contains all of the event channels that are used within the event flow. The event channels contained within the broker component can be message queues, message topics, or a combination of both.

In the next section, we will discuss some of the variants of event-driven patterns.

## Hub and spoke pattern

The hub and spoke pattern is a variant of the event broker topology pattern. In the hub and spoke architecture, the hub acts as the centralized broker and the spoke act as adapters that connect applications to the hub. The spoke establishes a connection with an application and converts application data into a format that the hub understands. The hub translates the incoming data into a format that is understood by the destination system and performs routing of messages accordingly. The presence of a single hub makes this architecture easy to manage, but at the same time imposes limits on the scalability of the architecture:

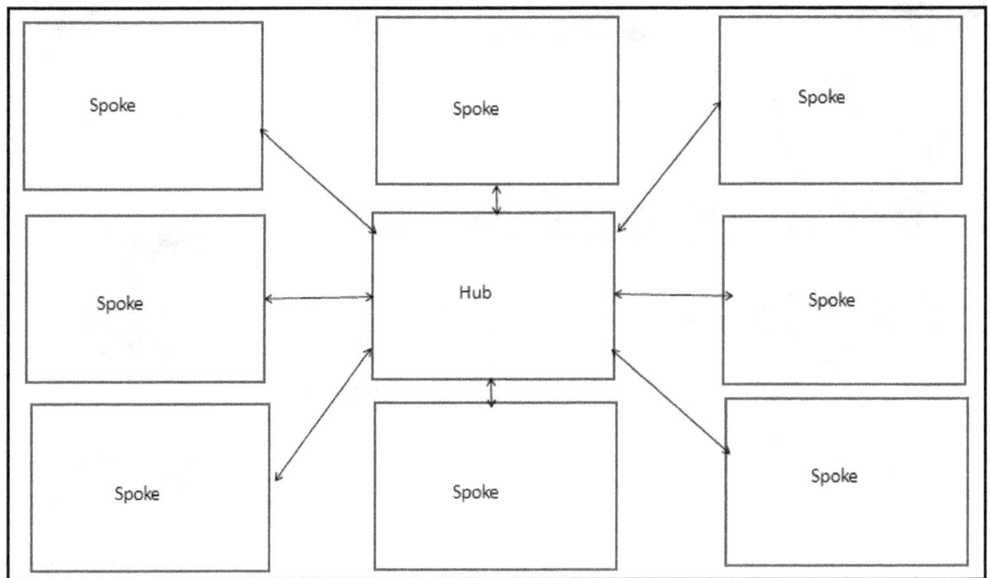

In order to overcome this limitation, the concept of the federated hub and spoke architecture has evolved. In the federated hub and spoke architecture, multiple hubs are present. Each hub has a local metadata and rules, as well as global metadata. Any changes to the global metadata and rules are automatically propagated to other local hubs. The federated hub and spoke architecture provides scalability and also flexibility by facilitating centralized management of hubs.

# Broadcast pattern

In a broadcast pattern, also a called **publish/subscribe** broadcast pattern, information is sent to all the parties that are present in the network. Only interested parties receive the message; the others discard the message. If the systems in a network have the efficiency to discard unwanted messages, then this pattern works very well for the design of such systems. When it comes to implementation of this pattern at the network level, a variant of **Internet Protocol** (**IP**) called **User Datagram Protocol** (**UDP**) allows us to send a piece of information to all computers that are part of a network. This is a variant of the event broadcast pattern that is applicable to networks.

# Polling pattern

In this pattern, subscribers contact the publishers to find out whether they have anything that is of interest to them. This is not used much as it involves a lot of wastage of system resources. Imagine a subscriber polling a publisher 50 times when it has nothing new for them.

Event-driven patterns of late are implemented in a slightly different manner in an attempt to adapt to the changing technology landscape. In the next section, we will understand the actual implementation of event-driven patterns in systems.

# EDA pattern implementation in systems/processes

In this section, we will discuss the implementation of event-driven patterns in processes. The main components that are involved in this implementation are the following:

- Event queue
- Event log
- Event collectors
- Reply queue
- Read versus write events

Each of these components and the overall functioning of this architecture will be explained in this section. The core component for this implementation is a central event queue. All events are inserted into a central event queue before they are processed. The following diagram depicts this queue-based architecture:

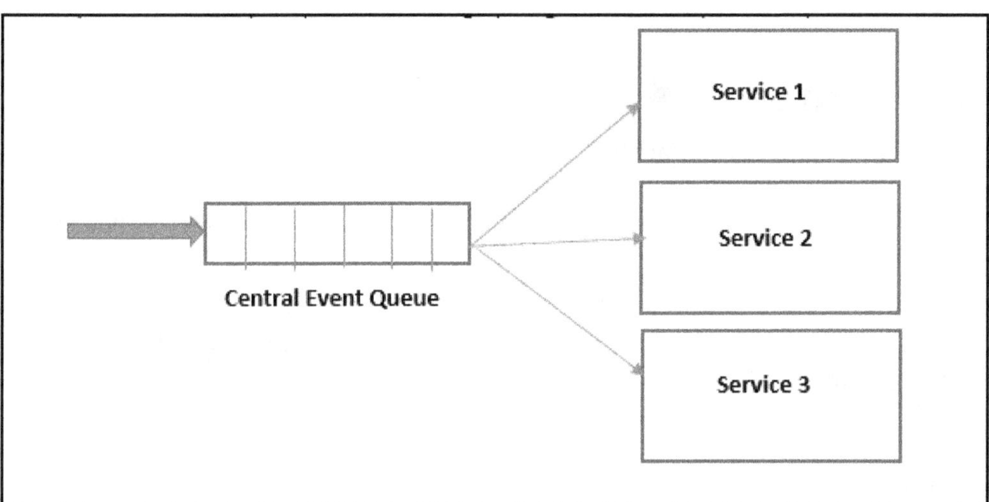

Events are placed in an order when they are inserted into the queue so that it is possible to track the sequence in which the system responds to events.

# Event log

There needs to be a backup and recovery mechanism for the messages that are added to the central event queue. This is done by writing all the event details to an event log, which is typically placed in a disk. In the event of a system crash, the system's state can be rebuilt by recovering its state from the event log. So, the main purpose of an event log is to ensure that events persist. In order to make the backup mechanism stronger, backups of the event log can be taken, which is equivalent to taking a backup of the system's state. These backup copies can also be used to do pilot performance tests on new releases before they are actually deployed in production. The diagram of the event log is as follows:

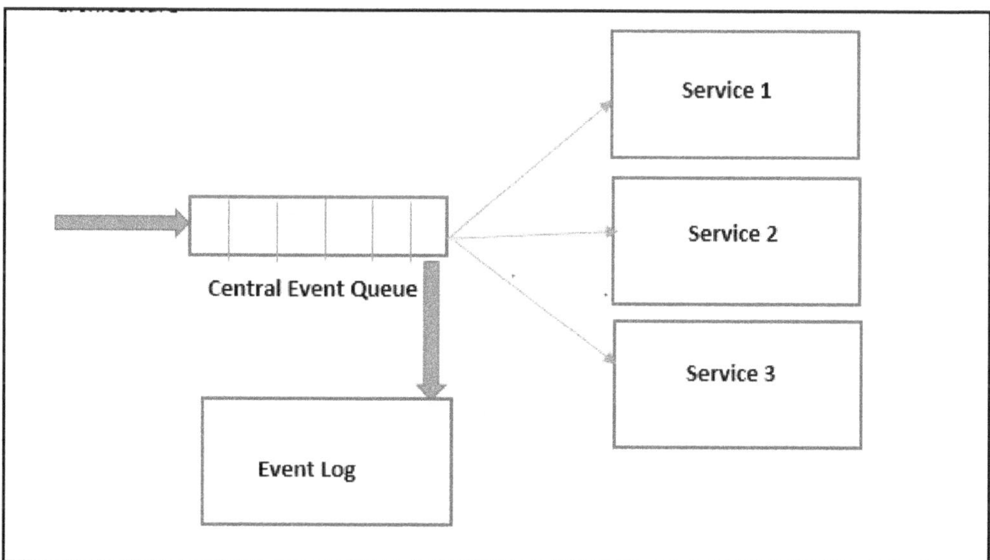

## Event collectors

Event requests originate from different types of sources, and they reach the system through some network in the form of HTTP requests or in some other formats. These events are collected from diverse sources using event collectors. The following diagram depicts the EDA with collectors:

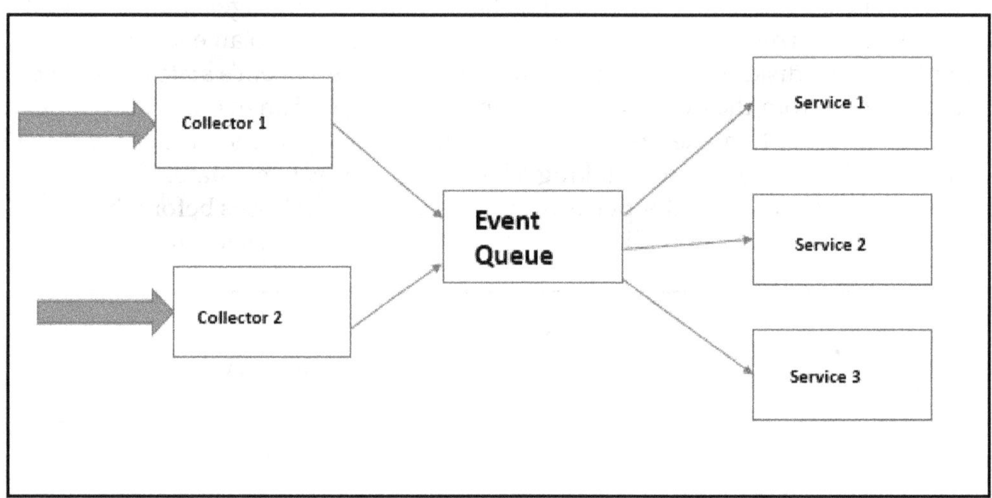


## Reply queue

In some scenarios, it is required to send a response back to an event request. In such situations, it is required to have a response or reply queue to provide support. The following diagram depicts one such example. From the diagram, it is clear that the response needs to be sent back to the appropriate event collector. For example, if the incoming request is in HTTP format and is sent by the HTTP collector into the event queue, then the response has to be sent back to the source through the HTTP collector only. The point to be noted here is that the responses are not recorded in the event log:

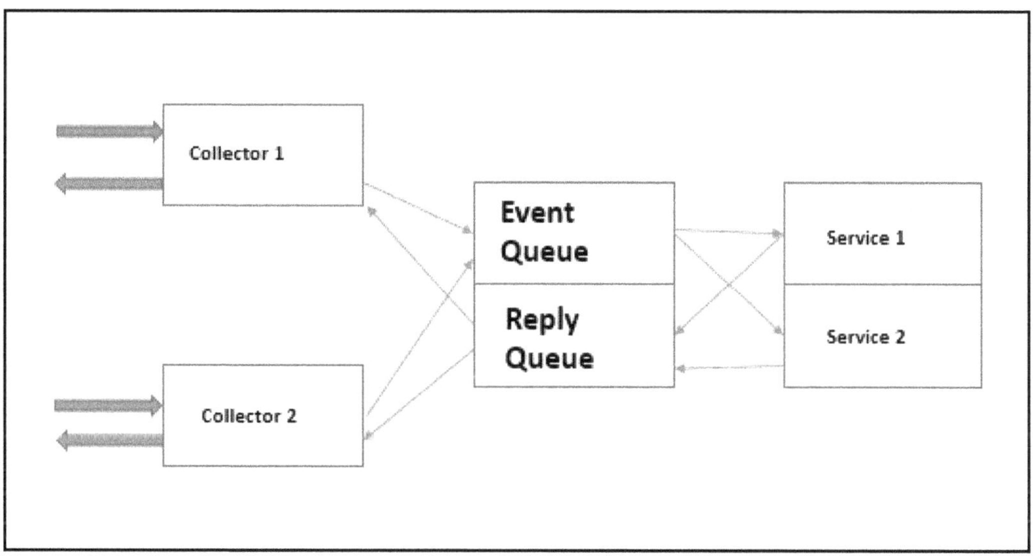


# Improving the performance of EDA-based processes/systems

In the case of persisting events, all events that are pushed to the event queue are persisted to the event log. This makes the system slow. In order to improve the performance of the system, there should be a mechanism to persist only events that have the capability to alter the state of the system, that is, read events do not alter the state of the system whereas write events will alter the state. So, there should be a mechanism in place to persist only write events.

This can be made possible with the event collectors by differentiating read events and write events. There should also be separate queues to handle read and write events. Using this mechanism, it is easy to ensure that events in the read event queue are not persisted and only the events in the write event queue are persisted. This concept is depicted in the following diagram:

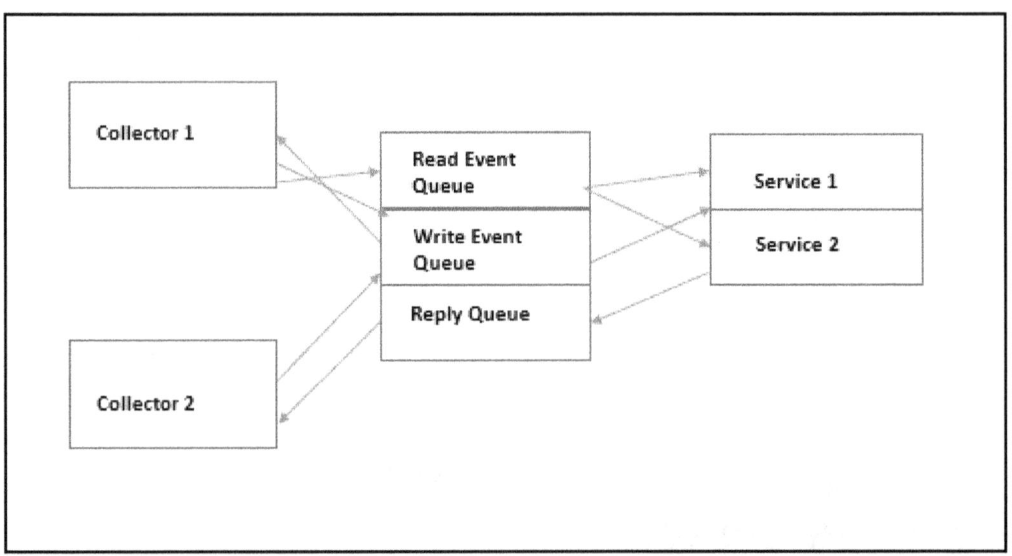


So in practice, there will be three queues: the read event queue, the write event queue, and the reply queue. Though it looks complex, from the implementation perspective it is fairly simple.

The ability to recreate system state from the event log is the most important benefit of systems that use EDA.

Most of the EDA pattern implementations are done in the form of COTS products and/or home-grown solutions. In the next section, we will see IBM WebSphere MQ, which is one of the most prominent EDA products on the market.

# IBM WebSphere MQ

IBM WebSphere MQ is used to provide messaging support for applications. It has the capability to transmit messages across diverse networks. The application can connect to IBM WebSphere MQ whenever there is a need to send or receive a message. IBM WebSphere MQ can handle diverse types of processors, operating systems, subsystems, and other communication protocols while transferring the message between systems. Another feature is that while transferring a message, if it finds that a processor is not available, it can place the message in a queue and transfer it later once the processor or system becomes available. The following are the different modes of operation supported by IBM WebSphere MQ, which is considered a messaging and queuing application:

- Point-to-point transfer
- Publish/subscribe
- File transfer

The key features of WebSphere MQ are explained as follows:

- **Messaging**: Processes communicate with each other by sending messages, and not by means of calls.
- **Queuing**: Messages that are sent are placed in queues and then processed in order so that the different processes can work independently without having any direct connection and the associated overhead.
- **Point-to-point**: It is possible to send multicast/broadcast messages to a list of queues. So it is necessary for the sender to know the destination name, but not necessarily the location of the destination.
- **Publish/subscribe**: All the applications that are interested in specific types or categories of messages will subscribe to those messages that are published by specific applications/processes.
- **Multicast**: This speeds up the pace at which messages are transmitted. It gives the capability to a publisher to send messages to multiple subscribers in the network at the same time.

- **Telemetry**: IBM WebSphere MQ Telemetry is designed to support messaging for devices. It sets up a connection between device and application messaging. It provides connectivity between the various components, such as the application, internet, services, and so on, with networks of instrumented devices. IBM WebSphere MQ Telemetry comes with a very efficient protocol that provides messaging support for a large number of devices that are connected over a network. This messaging protocol is published so that it can be added to the devices.

# Emerging trends in EDA

In this section, we will examine some of the very recent advancements in the field of event-driven architectural patterns.

## Event-driven microservices

Most organizations are moving away from the present siloed monolithic applications to the concept of microservices in order to achieve agility and also gain a competitive edge in the market. One of the main issues that arise with the use of microservices is distributed data management. Each microservice has its own private database. Designing business transactions that update entities that are owned by multiple microservices in multiple diverse databases is a major concern. This poses great difficulties in maintaining the consistency of data that is present in databases. This is depicted in the following diagram:

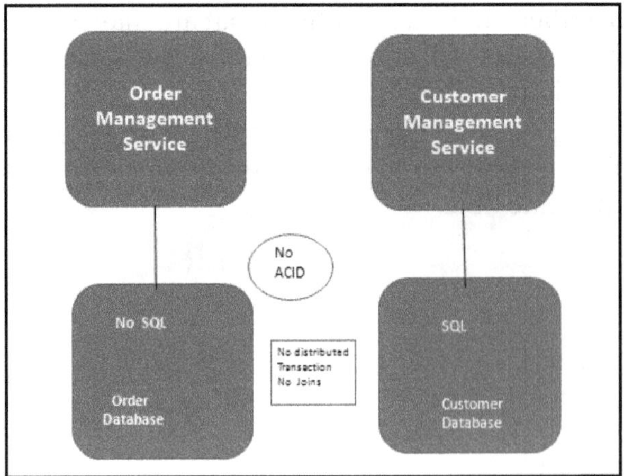

EDA provides a solution for this issue that occurs in distributed databases while using microservices. In an EDA, a service publishes events when there is a change. Other services that would be of interest would have subscribed to these events. As and when an event is received, the service typically updates its own state and also publishes more events that in turn might get consumed by other services. The event-driven approach provides the features to implement consistent transactions. The following diagram depicts how EDA helps in the implementation of consistency in business transactions that are used by multiple services. The example in the diagram refers to the order management example that we used at the start of the chapter:

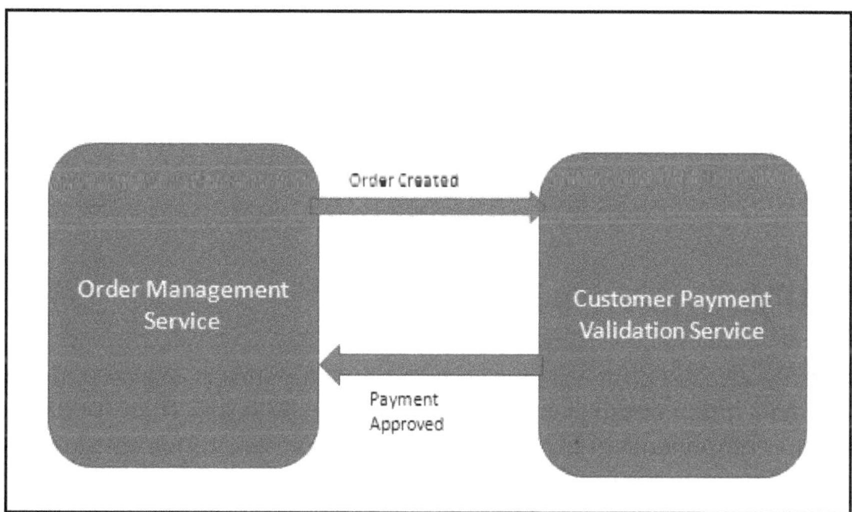


## Complex event processing

Of late, many interesting use cases have evolved around complex events. Statistical functions such as event correlation and aggregation along with computational algorithms are being applied to event data to uncover meaningful patterns that provide valuable use cases for several domains/industries. One of the prominent use cases is in the field of banking to detect frauds in transactions. Another promising use case is in weather forecasting, where several atmospheric parameters are correlated to predict cyclones, earthquakes, and so on. Many of the command centers that are used for weather forecasting across the world work on the basis of EDA.

# Internet of Things (IoT) and EDA

IoT refers to the interconnection of all objects around the computing devices that are embedded in them, which in turn helps them to send and receive data. In this scenario, any object around us will become a smart object and can keep sending messages to other objects that have subscribed to receive its messages. Using IoT, 3 trillion objects are expected to be interconnected by 2020. All these objects in turn function with the help of EDA architecture. This goes to show the huge potential that EDA has in years to come.

# References

`http://tutorials.jenkov.com/software-architecture/event-driven-architecture.html`

`https://www.ibm.com/support/knowledgecenter/en/SSFKSJ_7.5.0/com.ibm.mq.pro.doc/q001020_.htm`

# Summary

In this chapter, we discussed the various aspects of EDA patterns. We started with the definition and description of the event and event-driven patterns. Then we discussed in detail the various components of EDA. EDA patterns have two topology variants and each of them has specific usage scenarios based on the system requirements. These patterns and their components were discussed in detail.

There are multiple variants of EDA patterns. These patterns and their features were discussed in detail in the chapter. EDA patterns have multiple layers in which they work. These layers and the components that are present in each layer were discussed in the chapter. SOA and EDA are related concepts and they complement each other. Their similarities, differences, and usage scenarios were discussed in detail in this chapter. The chapter concluded with a discussion about the emerging trends in the EDA space.

# 9
# Microservices Architecture Patterns

Microservices architecture (**MSA**) is being proclaimed as the most powerful architectural pattern for designing, developing, deploying, and delivering next-generation software applications. Microservices are clearly emerging as the prime building block for constructing enterprise-grade and mission-critical applications. Microservices are fine-grained, typically single-purpose, and loosely-coupled services facilitating easy and independent deployment and horizontal scalability. Microservices are self-defined, cleanly isolated, and autonomous, and intrinsically support the popular polyglot model. The polyglot paradigm represents multiple programming languages, data transmission protocols, and persistence mechanisms. The idea is to build and run highly reliable, scalable, available, resilient, message-driven, and secure microservices. Microservices are interoperable, technology-agnostic, and composable to produce process-centric applications. Microservices and the Docker-enabled containerization go hand in hand in agile software engineering and rapid IT service delivery. There are a variety of best practices, key guidelines, design and evaluation metrics, and enabling patterns being unearthed by many accomplished professionals in order to speed up the process of migration from monolithic workloads to microservices-based workloads. Besides, there are API gateways, integrated platforms for service integration and orchestration, deployment and delivery environments such as Docker containers, and so on for increasing the MSA adoption rate. Product vendors, system integrators, cloud service providers, DevOps engineers, and other IT professionals are teaming up for accelerating the use of services in realizing highly flexible, extensible, elastic, and sustainable applications. This chapter is dedicated to illustrating all the existing and emerging patterns in this new field for our readers.

# Microservices patterns

Several IT professionals, based on their extensive experiences, have come out with a number of enabling patterns for producing microservices-based applications. Further on, there are patterns exclusively for building fresh services from the ground up. Not only for development, but also for testing, deployment, and delivery, exquisite patterns are being unearthed and popularized. One strategic impact of MSA is on the risk-free translation of legacy applications into MSA-based modern applications. There are facilitating patterns of decomposition of massive and monolithic applications into several microservices. In the following sections, we will discuss the prominent patterns in detail. There are mainly two patterns: architecture and design patterns.

# Decomposition patterns

Patterns are vital for any new paradigm to thrive. The microservices paradigm too has to be accordingly enabled with many novel and value-adding patterns in order to sustain and simplify its long and arduous journey. Whether designing, developing, deploying, and delivering newer microservices, or dismantling legacy and monolithic applications into a myriad of interactive microservices, the role and relevance of architecture and design patterns is extremely high. Without an iota of doubt, the IT team of every company across the world is burdened with a number of inflexible, closed, expensive to maintain, and largely sized software applications. Having understood the significant benefits being envisaged through the MSA proposition, worldwide corporates are keenly exploring the possibility of leveraging it with all the clarity and confidence for modernizing current applications. This technology-induced transition and transformation empower every business house to be ready for the digital economy and era. Microservices are being touted as the way forward to realize the dream of digital enterprises, and there is a clarion call for unearthing powerful and game-changing patterns to speed up the setting up and sustaining microservices-centric applications. Let us start with a few interesting decomposition patterns.

The microservices architecture pattern corresponds to the *y* axis scaling of the scale cube, which is a 3D model of scalability as shown in the following diagram:

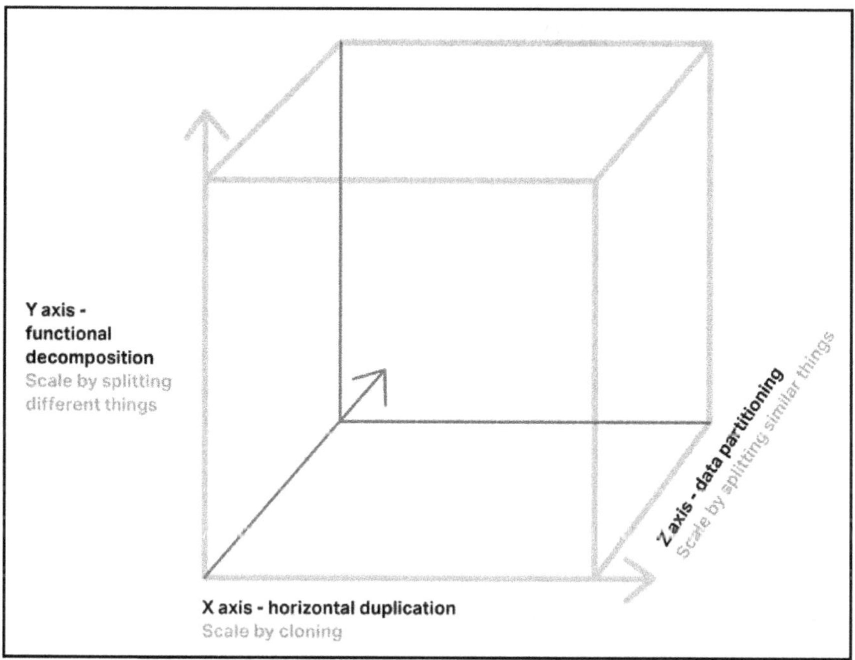


The *x* axis scaling is for running multiple cloned copies of an application behind a load balancer. This is the most common way of achieving horizontal scalability. The *y* axis scaling represents an application that is split by a function, service, or resource. Each service is responsible for one or more closely related functions. The *z* axis scaling is commonly used to scale databases because the data is partitioned across a set of servers. Each server runs an identical copy of the code and each service request is routed to the appropriate server. The *z* axis scaling, like *x* axis scaling, improves the application's capacity and availability. However, to solve the problems of increasing development and application complexity, the *y* axis scaling is recommended. The *y* axis scaling splits the application into multiple services.

## Decomposition by use case pattern

There are many bases and causes for segmenting big applications into a dynamic pool of smaller and cooperative components. As we all know, software packages and libraries are being constructed in order to automate and accelerate multiple use cases. Hence, this pattern unambiguously specifies the ways and means of expertly partitioning massive applications into many small modules; each of them will accomplish at least one use case. We know that there are breakthrough business and technical cases for any technology to survive by beating all kinds of competitions at the increasingly knowledgeable market. However, use cases are typically the benefits being accrued by users (humans), user agents/services (software), or IoT and I/O devices while using any technology-sponsored applications and services. In this pattern, it is all about starting, identifying, and prioritizing use cases. Use cases are definitely the crucial factor and the turning point for developing new applications as well as modernizing existing applications. This pattern helps to produce next-generation applications by producing fresh services and by extracting the hidden microservices encapsulated inside big applications.

## Decomposition by resources pattern

In this pattern, it is defining microservices based on the resources (server machines, storage appliances, network components, software infrastructures, databases, and so on) that they access or control. This allows the creation of a set of microservices that function as channels for access to individual resources. We are envisioning the days of application-aware infrastructures and infrastructure-aware applications. For microservices to exhibit their special capabilities, the underlying resources play an important role, which cannot be sidestepped.

## Decomposition by business capability pattern

Functionality is another option to decompose monolithic applications into many interoperable microservices. These functions or responsibilities are generally business-specific or agnostic. That is, these vertical, as well as horizontal functions, can be easily used by more than one part of the application. These functions are coarse-grained in the sense that many fine-grained services can be born out of these bigger functionalities/responsibilities. This is an interesting pattern for the MSA era.

Increasingly, business applications are becoming sophisticated and complicated. A myriad of third-party applications is getting integrated. Monolithic and massive-scale applications are the most prevalent and prominent these days. **Service-oriented architecture** (**SOA**) patterns are majorly leveraged for establishing and sustaining seamless and spontaneous integration between different and distributed applications using specific wrappers and service-oriented interfaces. That is, enterprise and cloud application integration is being enabled through SOA techniques and tips. Having understood the strategic significance of the MSA pattern, business behemoths are strategizing to smoothly go in the MSA way to be right and relevant to their customers and clients. Besides partitioning the large-scale application into a dynamic collection of easily manageable, lightly coupled, and relatively simple services, the MSA paradigm is to accelerate software development by enabling continuous delivery/deployment.

For achieving the aforementioned benefits, the decomposition of the application into microservices has to be done very carefully. A useful guideline for the **object-oriented design** (**OOD**) world is the **single responsibility principle** (**SRP**) that defines a responsibility of a class as a reason to change and states that a class should only have one reason to change. Another useful principle from OOD is the **common closure principle** (**CCP**); things that change together should be packaged together to ensure that each change affects only one service.

The promising solution approach is as follows. Define services corresponding to business capabilities. A business capability is something that a business does in order to generate value. A business capability often corresponds to a business object, for example:

- Order management is responsible for orders
- Customer management is responsible for customers

This sort of business capability-based decomposition of monolithic applications is to benefit businesses in the long run. Also, bigger and better business capabilities can be realized through the orchestration of business capability services. There are API gateways, partitioning best practices, Docker containers to host microservices, orchestration tools, and governance engines in order to derive process-aware composite applications at runtime on a need basis.

## Decomposition by subdomain pattern

For bringing up modular software applications, application components and services need to be loosely coupled (each service has an API that encapsulates its implementation, the implementation can be changed without affecting its clients) and cohesive (a service should implement a small set of strongly related functions). With component-based software assembly and **service-oriented architecture** (**SOA**) approaches, setting up and sustaining modular applications has been the case. These components and services are typically coarse-grained. With the surging popularity and pervasiveness of service architectures, creating fine-grained services is gathering momentum. The principal goal of MSA is to quickly take software solutions to the market by enabling continuous integration, deployment, and delivery. Hence, the systematic and sagacious decomposition of applications and coarse-grained services is acquiring special consideration. In the aforementioned pattern, we discussed that business capability is the base for disintegrating applications.

This pattern recommends decomposing by subdomains. It is recommended to define services corresponding to **domain-driven design** (**DDD**) subdomains. DDD refers to the application's problem space (the business) as the domain. A domain consists of multiple subdomains. Each subdomain corresponds to a different part of the business. The subdomains of an online store application include:

- Product catalogue
- Inventory management
- Order management
- Delivery management

The resulting service architecture is quite stable since the subdomains are relatively stable. The challenge is to precisely identify the subdomains. Decomposition follows the *Divide and Conquer* paradigm. With the digital era all set to dawn, the software complexity is to rise, and hence bring the technique of decomposition into the picture. Big and packaged applications need to be divided in order to gain a decisive and deeper understanding.

# Microservices deployment pattern

There is a myriad of ways and means for deploying microservices. There are a few runtime and execution environments including **bare metal** (**BM**) servers, **virtual machines** (**VMs**), and containers. Therefore, the deployment options have increased. Then, there are one or more instances of the same microservice to be accommodated in one server. The deployment pattern choices are not straightforward and instead depend on various parameters.

## Multiple service instances per host pattern

Microservices are generally small in size and hence are quickly built, tweaked, composed, and deployed. The availability and throughput of microservices are important. Redundancy is one widely used aspect for guaranteeing high availability and throughput. That is, each service is deployed as a set of service instances.

The beauty of microservices is that services can be implemented using different programming languages and frameworks. As articulated in the beginning, microservices can be independently deployable and horizontally scalable. Service instances have to be clearly isolated from one another to ensure the safety and security of services. The resources (processors/cores/threads, memory, storage, and so on) consumed by service instances need to be minutely monitored, measured, and managed in order to ensure the optimized utilization of different IT resources.

It is possible to run multiple instances of different services on a physical or virtual server. It is possible to deploy each service instance as a JVM process, and it is also possible to deploy multiple instances in the same JVM. With higher density, the utilization of resources, as well as services, is bound to go up. The issues alluding to this pattern are the competition for resources, resource dependencies, and resource monitoring.

## Single service instance per host pattern

This is another service deployment pattern. There are requirements and scenarios wherein multiple instances of a service are deployed on a single server. On the other hand, there are needs for deploying only one instance and running it on a host machine. The benefits of this approach include:

- Service instances are fully isolated from one another
- There is no competition for resources and the issues being associated with dependencies are no more

- A service instance can consume at most the resources of a single host
- It is easy to monitor, manage, and redeploy each service instance

The drawback is that the resource utilization may decrease.

## Service instance per VM pattern

There are a few options for service instance deployment. BM servers,VMs, and in the recent past, Docker containers are the mainstream deployment and runtime environments. This pattern specifies the deployment of a service in a VM. Cloud environments are increasingly virtualized and hence VM-hosted services are flourishing. The auto-scaling facility being supplied by **cloud service providers** (**CSPs**) helps to provision fresh VMs quickly and concurrently to scale the number of service instances horizontally. This mechanism ensures the required performance level and the service availability. The service isolation happens at the VM level. The typical issue here is that VM provisioning consumes a couple of minutes.

## Service instance per container pattern

Every software module is being containerized through the Docker packaging format and the open-source platform, and the resulting Docker image of that particular application or service is being stocked in publicly discoverable and accessible hubs. When a Docker image gets committed, it automatically becomes a Docker container that can be immediately deployed and run. The container starts to deliver the implemented service to the outside world to be subscribed and consumed. The original and open-source Docker platform is being speedily strengthened through a host of pioneering tools, engines, and frameworks to bring all-around automation. There are Docker machines, container cluster management platforms, orchestration and networking tools, container monitoring tools, and so on in order to proclaim the Docker-enabled containerization as a production-level technology. The pivotal convergence of microservices and Docker paradigms is to lay a solid and stimulating foundation for producing bigger and better software applications.

Unlike VMs, container creation and running is quite fast. That means, through the leverage of containers, it is possible to achieve real-time scalability. As a best practice, every container is to host a service instance. Through multiple containers, it is possible to have multiple instances of a service. Generally, due to the lightweight nature of containers, there can be tens or even hundreds of application containers running comfortably on a physical host.

## Serverless deployment pattern

Serverless computing, alternatively termed as **Function as a Service** (**FaaS**), is attracting a lot of mind and market shares. Development, debugging, deployment, delivery, and decommissioning of application services are the major portion of any **application lifecycle management** (**ALM**) process. That is, there is a need for operational guys to set up and sustain optimized infrastructures for deploying and running software applications.

This serverless deployment pattern recommends a kind of deployment infrastructure that hides the concept of servers (whether physical or virtual). The infrastructure takes the application service's code and runs it. The user has to pay for each of his requests based on the resources consumed. The performance, scalability, and availability requirements are being automatically met. Almost all the established cloud service providers are providing this new deployment pattern. This is a new cloud service ensuring every function is being delivered as a service.

For an example, start with an AWS Lambda function, which is a stateless component to handle events. To create an AWS Lambda function, the user has to package his NodeJS, Java, or Python code for his service in a ZIP file and upload it to AWS Lambda. When an event occurs, AWS Lambda finds an idle instance of the function and launches one if none are available and invokes the handler function. AWS Lambda can run more instances automatically on a need basis to handle extra users and payloads.

There are four ways to invoke a lambda function. One option is to configure the lambda function to be invoked in response to an event generated by an AWS service. The examples of events include the following:

- An object being deposited in an S3 bucket
- An item is created, updated, or deleted in a DynamoDB table
- A message is available to read from a Kinesis stream

Another way to invoke a lambda function is to configure the AWS Lambda Gateway to route HTTP requests to the lambda function. AWS Gateway transforms an HTTP request into an event object, invokes the lambda function, and generates an HTTP response from the lambda function's result.

It is also possible to invoke the lambda function using the AWS Lambda Web Service API. The application that invokes the lambda function supplies a JSON object, which is passed to the lambda function. The web service call returns the value returned by the lambda. The final and fourth way to invoke a lambda function is periodically using a cron-like mechanism. It is possible to tell AWS to invoke the lambda function every five minutes.

The advantages are many; the infrastructure provisioning, setting up and administering time, and treasure and talent get reduced significantly. Software engineers can coolly focus on their core strengths without any botheration of the readying infrastructure to run their applications. However, there are a few limitations. AWS Lambda at this point in time supports a few languages. It is only suitable for deploying stateless applications that run quickly and respond to requests. Running long-running stateful applications such as a database or message broker in the serverless model is not possible. If an application takes a long time to start, then the application is not a good fit for serverless deployment. Similarly, legacy monolithic and massive applications are not suitable for serverless computing. Serverless deployment is typically reactive, not proactive, and hence the issue of high latency can arise.

# Service deployment platform pattern

There are a few automated software deployment tools on the market. IBM UrbanCode Deploy is an application release automation solution. This software allows for seamlessly deploying to distributed data centers and cloud environments on demand or on schedule. It is possible to scale up to enterprise-class deployments handling thousands of servers. The other popular software deployment automation solutions include:

- Docker orchestration frameworks including Docker swarm and Kubernetes (`http://kubernetes.io/`)
- Serverless platforms such as AWS Lambda
- PaaS including Cloud Foundry

Deployment, release, and delivery activities are increasingly being automated through a bevy of tools. For faster software delivery to the market, the tools-supported continuous integration, deployment, and delivery are indispensable, and the aforementioned patterns come in handy for software architects and designers.

# Microservices design patterns

Designing competent microservices that can work with other services seamlessly and spontaneously is essential for the intended success of the MSA. Similarly, designing the architecture of cloud, enterprise, mobile, IoT, analytical, operational, and transactional applications through the power of microservices has to be done elegantly and expediently. As enunciated previously, microservices can be realized through multiple technologies and tools. Also, the resplendent MSA paradigm is futuristic in the sense that any new technology can be easily used for producing next-generation microservices that are easily findable, accessible, assessable, maneuverable, replaceable, substitutable, and so on. The ensuing section will list all the dominant design patterns for progressively journeying toward the projected MSA era.

Design patterns are typically fine-grained and immensely contribute to building individual as well as composite microservices. Not only business logic, but also design patterns help in attaching data connectivity and persistence logic. Design patterns are therefore comprehensive for supplying the envisaged success of the MSA paradigm. The following section enumerates and explains the key design patterns.

## Aggregator microservice design pattern

Service and data aggregation are very vital for the intended success of the MSA pattern. As services are relatively micro in size and typically a microservice implements a single task, multiple distributed and decentralized services need to be identified and aggregated to serve a fully-fledged business functionality and feature. The aggregator pattern is therefore essential for the MSA era. Since each service is exposed using the lightweight RESTful interface, an application, which comprises many microservices, can retrieve the data from different services and process/display it accordingly by using this aggregator pattern.

There are viable options to bring in the required business logic if there is a requirement for a kind of processing on the retrieved data before the data gets displayed:

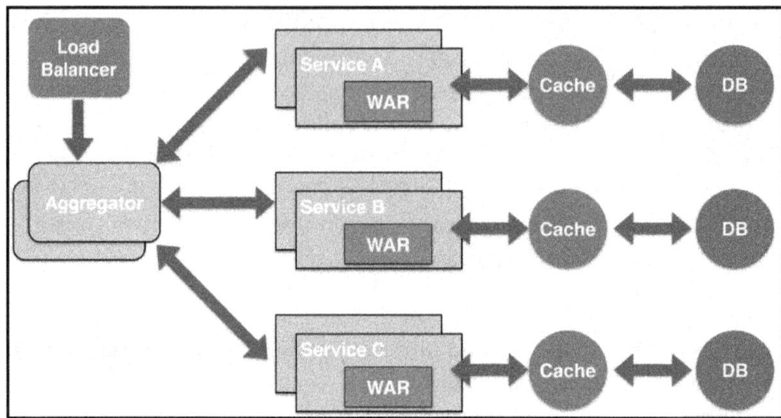


If the aggregation has to happen at the service level to create composite services, then the aggregator would just collect the data from each of the participating services, apply the ordained business logic to it, and aggregate and publish it using a composite REST endpoint. This process-centric composite service can then be consumed by other services that need it. All the microservices may have their own cache and database. The composite service can also be blessed with its own caching and database layer. An aggregator can scale independently on the *x* axis and *z* axis as well.

## Proxy microservice design pattern

This pattern is a slight variation of the aggregator. In this case, the client is not involved in the aggregation activity. Based on business needs, different microservices can be invoked. The proxy pattern can scale independently on *x* axis and *z* axis as well. The idea is that each microservice need not be exposed to the consumer. The proxy may be a dumb proxy, in which case it just delegates the request to one of the services. Alternatively, it may be a smart proxy where some data transformation is applied before the response is served to the client. With the explosion of different IoT and I/O devices, this proxy pattern is a beneficial one.

## Chained microservice design pattern

This is for producing a single consolidated response to a request. In this case, the request from the client is received by Service A, which is then communicating with Service B, which in turn may be communicating with Service C. All the services are likely using a synchronous HTTP request/response message. The key concern here is that the client is blocked until all the services in the chain finish the processing. That is, the chain of Service A to Service B and then Service B to Service C gets completed. The chain has to be short and small, otherwise, the synchronous communication may lead to a delay.

## Microservice chassis pattern

Cross-cutting concerns are many and also repeated across the source code of any application. The aspect-oriented programming model through a unique fashion was the first one to tackle these cross-cutting concerns that are prevalent in an enterprise-class application. The well-known examples include identity and access, network locations of databases and messaging platforms, logging, data encryption, evaluation metrics, and so on. As we all know, microservices are small in size and quick in development, testing, debugging, deployment, and delivery. That is, a small team of developers can build a service in a day or two. As per the MSA pattern, such small-scale services from multiple development teams are picked up purposefully and blended to form mission-critical applications instantaneously. The whole process of generating process-aware, microservices-based applications are completed in a short span of time. Herein, wasting a lot of additional time to attach all kinds of cross-cutting concerns is not a logically sound proposition. Therefore, the microservices chassis framework gets formulated and recommended to build microservices in the application perspective. Developers, when leveraging the MSA pattern, also have to incorporate the MSA-specific cross-cutting concerns, such as service registration and discovery and circuit breakers for reliably handling partial failure. Therefore, the best solution approach is that when creating a microservice, it is crucial to add the lean and clean code for handling the aforementioned cross-cutting concerns. This way of embedding cross-cutting concerns is the smartest way forward for the MSA world.

## Externalized configuration pattern

Any enterprise-grade application typically uses one or more infrastructures and third-party services. For example, the application has to use a few common infrastructure services such as service registry, authentication, authorization and audit services, message broker and queue, filesystem, database, knowledge visualization platform, security, and so on. Further on, there are several third-party applications and services such as payment gateway, email server, and so on. Thus, any production-grade application has to be directly or indirectly attached to local as well as remote services to exhibit a highly integrated capability. Another pertinent question is, how do we enable a service to run in multiple environments without any modification?

Generally, a service must be provided with configuration data that tells it how to connect with other services. For example, for connecting to a database, the database network location and credentials have to be attached to the configuration data. Also, there are variations such as a QA database versus a production environment database. The prominent solution approach is to externalize all application-centric configuration information so that a service reads the configuration details from the external source to complete its functionality perfectly. The advantage of this pattern is that application services run in multiple environments without modification and/or recompilation.

# Microservices database patterns

Data persistence is an important factor in any microservice. There have been new database management systems in the recent past for stocking raw and processed data. There are big, fast, streaming, IoT data, and various data processing types such as batch, real-time, interactive, and iterative processing. Fresh data capture, ingestion, storage, processing, mining, analytics, and visualization technologies and tools are emerging and evolving in order to support data-driven insights and insight-driven decisions. There are several data-related patterns in the MSA world, and this section is specially prepared for discussing them.

## Database per service pattern

The MSA pattern is being embraced by mission-critical applications, and such MSA-compliant applications invariably provide a variety of business, technical, and user advantages. Having realized the strategic significance of the MSA idea, worldwide businesses, organizations, and institutions are keenly formulating workable and winning strategies and plans for leveraging the distinct capabilities of the MSA paradigm. As we know, microservices can be coded using multiple languages, and the data persistence needs of microservices can be served by multiple systems including **database management systems** (**DBMS**), filesystems, and so on. Further on, there are SQL, NoSQL, NewSQL, in-memory, in-database database management systems. Thus, microservices support the polyglot capability. This pattern recommends the leverage of a database for each service.

There is a growing family of data-intensive applications such as e-commerce, business, supply chain management, and so on, and these get segmented into a pool of interacting services. Herein, each service needs to persist its own data. Therefore, each microservice has to be accordingly enabled through its own data persistence mechanism. There are challenges when each microservice uses its own database. Complex business transactions have to work across multiple services, and hence, multiple databases. Further on, some business operations must update data owned by multiple services. There are occasions wherein there is a demand to query data that is owned by multiple services. Databases must sometimes be replicated and shared in order to scale.

For ensuring the much-needed isolation for utmost data security, API-driven access is being insisted. The service's database is effectively a part of the implementation of that service. The database cannot be accessed directly by other services. APIs are the way forward for database access. There are a few different ways to keep a service's persistent data private. Firstly, a separate table can be built and allocated for each microservice. Secondly, a separate schema can be generated for each microservice. Finally, a separate database server can be allocated for each service. Having a database per service ensures that microservices are loosely coupled and the best database solution can be chosen for every service based on its task. For example, a microservice performing text searching can be given a text mining and search engine. Similarly, a microservice performing social media analytics can be empowered with a graph database such as Neo4j.

However, as we all know, NoSQL databases do not support the ACID properties, and hence distributed and nested transactions are not suitable for microservices that involve NoSQL backend systems. The option here is to use an eventually consistent and **event-driven architecture** (**EDA**). Service producers publish their messages into message queues in the form of topics, whereas service consumers subscribe to those topics and use them. Some queries mandate to join data from multiple databases. The way forward is to empower applications to do the join operation rather than being accomplished at the database. For example, the API gateway or a kind of composition service could retrieve a customer, and his/her orders from the customer and order microservices. Then, the *join* action can be done by the API gateway or the composition service. Another option is to leverage the **command query responsibility segregation** (**CQRS**) pattern.

## Shared data design pattern

Microservices are self-defined and autonomous. That is, microservices have all the modules (presentation logic, business logic, integration logic, data connectivity, and persistence logic) to run in an independent fashion. Further on, services can easily draw upon the strength of proven technologies and tools to be fully polyglot. That is, nowadays, there are several database management systems such as SQL, NoSQL, NewSQL, and so on, and microservices can choose any one of them for the data persistence they need to be extremely and elegantly contributory to the originally expressed and envisaged business goal.

Organizations modernize their legacy applications to become microservices-enabled, modern applications. One standout challenge here is the database normalization. That is, each microservice has to have the right amount of data. In this design pattern, some services, likely in a chain, may share caching and database stores. This is logical if there is a strong coupling between the two services. This pattern may be categorized as an anti-pattern because microservices postulate and propose the share-nothing phenomenon. For greenfield microservices-centric applications, this pattern is undoubtedly an anti-pattern. This pattern can be leveraged as a temporary aspect during the transition phase from the monolithic to microservice.

## Shared database pattern

There are several unique factors for the runaway success of microservices architecture. We have been well-versed with shared databases. Now, in the big data and webscale applications era, a variety of new and differently abled databases have emerged and are doing well for several new-generation applications. The previously discussed pattern, therefore, has recommended dedicated databases for different services. However, there are certain requirements such as the ACID-centric transactions and transactional applications. The solution approach is to use a single database that is shared by multiple microservices. Every microservice is comfortably and conveniently able to access data owned by other microservices. The shared database ensures utmost data consistency. The management and operational complexities of a single shared database are on the lower side.

As usual, there are a few drawbacks being associated with the shared database pattern. The first and foremost is the tight coupling between services and the database. The second one is the issues associated with the data sharing. The traditional SQL databases do not support horizontal scalability, and hence, the surge in data volumes cannot be handled by SQL databases that are shared across.

## Command-query responsibility segregation (CQRS) pattern

In the microservices world, implementing queries that join data from multiple services and their own databases is a real challenge. The solution approach is to split the application into two parts; the command side and the query side. The command side handles create, update, and delete requests and emits events when data changes. The query side handles queries by executing them against one or more materialized views that are kept up to date by subscribing to the stream of events emitted when data changes. The advantages are many. This pattern is especially necessary for an **event-driven architecture** (**EDA**) environment. This gives improved separation of concerns and supports multiple denormalized views.

# Microservices integration patterns

Microservices are autonomous and self-defined. Still, distributed and decentralized services ought to talk to each other in order to produce powerful process-centric and business-critical applications. This section is specially allocated for letting you know about the brewing integration patterns in the MSA environment.

# Remote procedure invocation (RPI) pattern

Microservices have to interoperate with multiple microservices in order to complete any complex functionality. For this purpose, services use an inter-process communication protocol. The solution approach is to leverage the RPI for any inter-service communication and collaboration. The client uses a request/reply-based protocol to make requests to a service. The well-known RPI technologies include REST, gRPC, and Apache Thrift. This pattern is easy to implement and there is no need for any intermediate broker for facilitating the intended communication. However, there are a few critical drawbacks being associated with this pattern. That is, services are tightly coupled and have to be online to find, bind, and interact. Other prominent interaction types such as notifications, request/asynchronous response, publish/subscribe, and publish/asynchronous response are not supported here.

# Messaging design pattern

Messaging is typically asynchronous in nature and is used extensively for inter-service communication. Services talk to one another by exchanging standardized messages over messaging channels. There are message brokers, hubs, and queues (Apache Kafka, RabbitMQ, and so on) in the market. This pattern has the following benefits:

- Messaging enables loose and light coupling between participating and contributing services. The dependency hell gets eliminated here.
- Message brokers typically buffer messages until the subscriber/consumer is able to receive and process them. This intermediary-based message storage enhances the message availability. This pattern supports a variety of communication patterns such as fire and forgets, polling, publish, and subscribe.

Asynchronous communication through messaging middleware solutions turns out to be the messiah for the distributed computing era.

# Asynchronous messaging design pattern

Message-based asynchronous communication is insisted on setting up and sustaining reliable and resilient microservices. The loose and light coupling between microservices and the interactions happening through passing standardized messages are being touted as the success formula for the MSA pattern. The highly popular REST design pattern is typically synchronous and hence blocks the client service. The much-needed asynchronous interaction is still possible through the RESTful protocol, but it has to be achieved at the application level. Therefore, the leverage of message brokers and queues has gone up significantly in the MSA world. Further on, there is a mix of both synchronous and asynchronous communications. For example, Service A may call Service C synchronously, which is then communicating with Service B and D asynchronously using a shared message queue. By using WebSockets, Service A can talk to Service C in an asynchronous manner to achieve the mandated scalability. Precisely speaking, a combination of the request/response (REST) and pub/sub messaging may be used to accomplish any unique business needs.

# Domain-specific protocol pattern

There are a wider variety of inter-process communication protocols. For certain scenarios, domain-specific protocols are being recommended for inter-process communication. For email services, SMTP and IMAP are the preferred ones. For media streaming requirements, RTMP, HLS, and HDS are being used.

# API gateway pattern

There are several challenges in the MSA world. Microservices are generally fine-grained and each of them is blessed with a granular API. The other characteristics include different services are being coded using different languages and many data transmission protocols and data persistence methods. In short, services support the polyglot architecture. Further on, there are several client options such as desktop, mobile, wearable, portable, and fixed devices. There are telling scenarios that consume data and application logic from different and distributed microservices and data services. Precisely speaking, we are heading into the days of distributed computing. Microservices need to find the appropriate services to interact with and contribute to completing the desired business functionality and goals in a time-bound and SLA-compliant manner.

Network topologies and technologies also play a vital role in shaping up MSA applications. The latency of different methods such as WAN, MAN, LAN, CAN, PAN, and BAN differs. That is, the latency is lower in personal area networks, whereas it is on the higher side for wide area networks. Microservices can quickly access nearby microservices multiple times, whereas, in the case of remote services, the number of service access is lower and time-consuming.

The viable and value-adding solution approach is to have an API gateway as the **single point of contact** (**SPOC**) for all kinds of services in order to interact with local as well as remote services. All kinds of connectivity, mediation, brokerage, aggregation, message enrichment, protocol and data format translations, and so on are being taken care of by this standardized API gateway solution. Multiple services and data sources are neatly found and composed by this API gateway service that can also expose a unique API for each client. The security requirements of the data and messages flowing through the network channels are also accomplished by this product.

# Backend for frontend pattern

This pattern recommends and defines a separate API for each kind of client. Typically, apart from the traditional web interface, mobile and management interfaces are common these days. An API gateway has the capability of providing different APIs for different client types. The API gateway insulates the clients from the application, which can be partitioned into multiple cooperative microservices. This way, any kind of application refactoring, re-platforming, and retrofitting does not have any sinister impact on approaching clients. The optimal APIs can be chosen and used for the appropriate client. The API gateway enables clients to retrieve data from multiple services and sources with a single round-trip operation. Fewer requests also mean less overhead and improve the user experience. Multiple backend microservices and data sources can be orchestrated on a need basis to produce bigger and better applications. This transformation gives a unique experience for user agents. The API gateway intrinsically takes care of all kinds of data and protocol translations.

# Microservices registration, discovery, and usage patterns

Services need to be registered in a publicly available service registry in order to enable services to be found at runtime and leveraged accordingly. In a dynamic and distributed environment, services move around, so the task of runtime service discovery has to be facilitated through such network-accessible registries and repositories. Not only services, but also their instances, have to be registered to simplify the goal of high availability of services.

# Service discovery pattern

Microservices have to find one or more appropriate microservice to initiate a kind of conversation towards fulfilling the identified business functionality. As we all know, there are several service discovery mechanisms, service registries, and repositories. In the traditional web service world, we used to play around with WSDL and UDDI for service interfacing, discovery, and initiation. In the earlier era too, we were tinkering with RPC, RMI, CORBA, EJB, Jini, and so on. In the recent past, RESTful service interactions are the most common way of establishing service connectivity and service fulfillment.

However, microservices are quite distinct in the sense that they are more dynamic, varied, and versatile and many in numbers. Further on, services are predominantly made to run inside virtual machines and containers. Virtualized and containerized environments are dynamic with the inherent ability to provide live-in migration of virtualized resources and workloads. The API gateway is one solution for appropriately enabling services to discover services to correspond and complete the business functionality. The service registry is to have all the required information such as location, host, port, and so on of all the participating and contributing services. This sort of mechanism aids in sharply reducing the number of network hops for services trying to involve other services.

For enterprise-class services, the connectivity typically happens through a clustered load balancer. The location of the load balancer is predefined and determined. Services send the request to the load balancer, which in turn queries a service registry, which may be built into the load balancer. The load balancer then forwards the service request and query to an available instance of the particular service.

The popular clustering solutions such as Kubernetes (`https://github.com/GoogleCloudPlatform/kubernetes/blob/master/docs/services.md`) and Marathon (`https://mesosphere.github.io/marathon/docs/service-discovery-load-balancing.html`) run a proxy on each host. The proxy actually functions as a server-side discovery router/load balancer. In order to access a service, a client service connects to the local proxy using the port assigned to that service. The proxy then forwards the request to a service instance running somewhere in the cluster. Routers, **application delivery controllers** (**ADCs**), load balancers, and other network solution modules are made available in large-scale IT environments such as clouds.

# Service registry pattern

Service registries and repositories are very vital for any software development organization. With microservices emerging as the next-generation application building block, the relevance of services and their one-stop registry is on the climb. A service registry has all the right references for each of the services in the environment. That is, each service, once developed, has to be registered with the service registry in order to be found, bound, and to contribute immensely. Thus, any service wanting to connect with other services has to first connect to the service registry to collect all the discovery, access, and leverage details of the services. A service registry might invoke a service instance's health check API to verify that it is able to handle requests. The well-known service registry technologies are:

- Apache Zookeeper
- Consul
- Etcd

A service registry is very critical in the service world and it has to be highly available. If it is not available even for a short time, then the business continuity is in danger.

# Service registration pattern

We have discussed the importance of the service registry. Because of the dynamism being exhibited by microservices, the role of the service registry acquires special significance. Every single service has to be registered with the service registry in order to be extremely beneficial for businesses. That is, the details of each service instance must be registered with the service registry when each instance begins its long and arduous journey. On the other hand, the service instance gets unregistered on getting decommissioned or shut down.

Microservices can register themselves or a third-party solution can be assigned to register each service instance. For the first case, microservices are solely responsible for registering themselves with the service registry. On start-up, the service registers itself (host and IP address) with the service registry and makes itself available to be discovered and hooked. Not only services, but also each instance of those services has to register methodically with the service registry. If one service instance fails, the other service instances come in handy in sustaining the business operations, offerings, and outputs. For the second case, third-party solution and service providers can be contracted to set up a service registry to register each service instance.

# Event-driven architecture (EDA) patterns

With the emergence of legions of digitized items/smart objects/sentient materials, along with the scores of connected devices in our everyday environments, everyone is going to be significantly sagacious in his or her decisions, deeds, and deals. In the projected IoT world, a lot of decisive and deeper automation is bound to happen. Any tangible thing in our midst is internally as well as externally empowered in time to proactively and pre-emptively act on all kinds of noteworthy events. That is, every single entity in and around us is going to be event-driven. The role of IT in the projected event-driven world is paramount and path-breaking. The IT systems and business applications/services have to capture, buffer, process, mine, and analyze all incoming events to spit out insights. The days ahead are definitely digital, and our everyday systems ought to be adequately and adroitly empowered to be *sense* and *react*. Herein, the role and responsibility of EDA in enabling our IT and business systems to be innovative, disruptive, and transformative are bound to grow further.

Database per service is the predominant solution approach in the MSA world. But there are specific requirements wherein the ACID transaction is mandatory for guaranteeing the goal of data consistency. The way forward is to use the proven and potential event-driven architecture to attain the data consistency. That is, each service publishes an event whenever it updates its data. Other services subscribe to those published events and accordingly update their own databases. This guarantees data consistency across multiple microservices without going through the traditionally distributed transactions.

To fulfil the promise of faster delivery cycles, teams need autonomy. Dependence across teams is a recipe for slow progress. This is why monolithic architectures progress slowly. Isolation between services is how teams can retain autonomy - maintaining this isolation is critical.

Each team must be empowered to make independent decisions even about their data layer without impacting or becoming dependent on any other team. Even the choice of the types of data store should be independent—this concept is known as polyglot persistence. How the data is modeled should also be an autonomous decision, local to each service. The team should have full control over making schema changes, that is, adding or dropping tables and entities, or columns and attributes. What about modifying, adding, or deleting classes and objects? In autonomous teams, these need to be non-breaking changes for other teams, to protect each team's autonomy. The safest way to ensure that each team has the independence to make their own data layer choices is to not share the data store across microservices.

The isolation between services sets boundaries around each microservice, while the event-driven mechanism addresses how services communicate. The role of the event-driven system is critical to the overall operation of the architecture.

# Event sourcing pattern

Event sourcing is an architectural pattern in which the state of an application is determined by a sequence of events. Each event in the sequence is recorded in an append-only event store or stream. Conventionally, most software applications work with data and the application has to maintain the current state of the data by updating it as users work with the data. A typical data process is to read data from the store, make some modifications to it, and update the current state of the data with the new values. The transaction is one that changes the data value. However, this way of data update and keeping up the data consistency has many inherent limitations. It requires a **two-phase commit** (**2PC**) when accomplishing distributed transactions. Any 2PC commit reduces the throughput of transactions substantially. When there are many concurrent users, there is a possibility for data update conflicts because the update operations take place on a single item of data. Further on, there is a need for an additional auditing mechanism, which records the details of each operation in a separate log, otherwise, the history is lost.

Event sourcing achieves the much-needed atomicity without the complex 2PC process by using the event-centric approach. Rather than storing the current state of an entity, the application stores a sequence of state-changing events. That is, whenever the state of a business entity changes, a new event is created and appended to the list of already captured and stored events. Since saving an event is a single operation, it is inherently atomic. The software application can then easily reconstruct an entity's current state by replaying the events.

Software applications and services classically are persisting events in an event store (a database of events) and the event store exposes an API for adding and retrieving a business entity's events. The event store also behaves like a *publish and subscribe* message broker. Subscribers can subscribe to particular events. Whenever there is a new event, the event store delivers it to all the rightful subscribers. Further on, an application can periodically save a snapshot of an entity's current state. To reconstruct the current state, the application takes the most recent snapshot and the events that have occurred since that snapshot. Thus, sourcing and storing events acquires special significance in the event-driven world.

# Transaction log tailing pattern

This is another option for achieving distributed transactions. The idea is to tail the database transaction log and publish each change as an event. The benefit with this pattern is that there is no change required at the application level; everything happens at the database level. Avoiding duplicate publishing is a bit difficult. This pattern ensures low-level DB changes, but it is quite difficult to determine the business-level events.

# Publishing events using the database trigger pattern

This is another solution approach for the challenge and concern of distributed transactions among multiple microservices. One or more database triggers insert events into an `EVENTS` table, which is polled by a separate process that publishes the events to a message broker, and the required microservices and their databases consume them and get updated accordingly.

# Application publishes events pattern

The application inserts events into an `EVENTS` table as a part of the local transaction. A separate process polls the `EVENTS` table and publishes the events to a message broker. The key concerns being associated with this pattern is that appropriate changes have to be enacted on the application.

It is going to be an event-driven world. Events in formalized and standardized forms are going to be the real differentiators for the futuristic systems to be sensitive, responsive, and resilient in their actions and reactions. With the IoT era fast dawning, there will be trillions of events and the IT systems, plus the business applications, that have to be accordingly defined and designed. Herein, the role of microservices in setting up and sustaining such kinds of adaptive, people-centric, process-optimized, service-oriented, and event-driven applications is remarkably growing. The EDA pattern is turning out to be an extremely rightful entity for the IoT world. Microservices are capable of capturing and processing event messages for producing rightful outputs. The message-based asynchronous communication model is also supported by microservices.

# Testing and troubleshooting patterns

Performing service verification and validation for understanding its ability to provide its assigned functionality, as well as the **non-functional requirements** (**NFRs**), is an important parameter and factor for the proclaimed success of microservices. This section will throw some light on service testing, debugging, and troubleshooting.

# Access token pattern

We talked about the contributions of the API gateway for attaining the intended success of the microservices architecture pattern. The API gateway is the first entry point for client services and it works thereafter on behalf of the client services. However, the challenge is how to do user identification, authentication, and authorization. That is, how to communicate the identity of user agents/requesting services to the requested services to kick-start the task as per the expressed intention.

The API gateway authenticates the request and passes an access token (for example, JSON Web Token, `https://jwt.io/`) that securely identifies the requestor in each request to the services. A service can include the access token in requests it makes to other services.

# Service component test pattern

Testing microservices and their instances is very important for service verification and validation. Writing exemplary test cases and leveraging automated testing tools comes in handy in checking whether services function as intended. The end-to-end testing of applications that in turn involve many distributed and decentralized microservices is not an easy affair indeed. The solution approach is to use a proven test suite. Microservices pass the test in isolation but testing microservices-based applications present a few challenges.

# Log aggregation pattern

Each instance of any microservice writes information about what it is doing to a log file in a standardized format. The log file typically contains errors, warnings, information, and debug messages. The challenge is to understand the application behavior and to troubleshoot the application using the individual logs. The way forward is to use a centralized logging service that innately aggregates all the logs being produced by each service instance. There are automated tools for log analytics. In general, log analytics prewarn if there is any substantial deviation in the functioning of both software and hardware components. Administrators and users separately visit the log store and search for any useful information out of the logs to ponder about the next course of action.

# Application metrics pattern

This is another way prescribed to understand and articulate application behavior. All along, we have been bombarded with a number of software design and evaluation metrics. Finalizing all the right and relevant metrics for microservices is a good starting point in order to reach the goal of getting to know application behavior. The recommended solution is to have a centralized metrics service that gathers and stocks the decision-enabling statistics of each of the service operations. Microservices can push their metrics information to the metrics service. On the other side, the metrics service can pull metrics from the microservice. Metrics services are emerging as an important ingredient in the MSA world.

# Audit logging pattern

The auditability of services is very essential. This helps in understanding the behavior of users as well as applications. Keeping an audit of all the user interactions is going to be helpful in setting up and sustaining the microservices environment. The auditing code has to be intertwined with the business logic.

# Distributed tracing pattern

The currently available techniques and tools for software testing and troubleshooting are being found obsolete and incompetent, especially for microservice-based applications. As we move from the monolithic era to the promising microservices era, there is a need for a bunch of versatile tools for checking services in isolation as well as microservice-centric applications in totality. As individual services cannot give the big picture, the new-generation testing and debugging tools have to have the distinct capability to do the same at the application level. That is, the tools must present the complete picture of application performance along with how the application delivers its functionality.

Therefore, this pattern recommends the leverage of a distributed tracing tool, which can track every request and capture the associated data as it scans through multiple microservices. The tool then aggregates the collected details to give an integrated and 360-degree view of the application behavior and performance. The solution approach is to instrument each microservice with code that assigns each external request a unique ID. The code enables to pass the ID to all the services involved in handling the request, to include the ID in all the log messages, and finally to record the value-adding information such as start and end times. This pattern enables developers to see how an individual request is being handled by searching across aggregated logs.

# Exception tracking pattern

Microservices and their various instances are made to run on multiple BM servers, VMs, and even inside Docker containers. Errors may occur when services handle requests from other services. Typically, services throw an exception with an error message and a stack trace. The need here is to de-duplicate the exceptions, record, and investigate them consciously to understand and resolve the issue. The approach is to report all exceptions to a centralized exception tracking service. Developers and debugging professionals can view exceptions and ensure their resolution in time.

# Health check API pattern

The health check has been an important part of the IT industry. All kinds of software and hardware systems are being regularly checked for their health. It is the same with microservices. Services are running, but sometimes, they are unable to handle service requests due to various reasons. In these circumstances, the service monitoring system has to generate an alert and send it to the operational team to act upon in real time. The load balancer also understands any failed service instances and accordingly routes requests to the live services in order to guarantee business continuity. The service registry also has to take note of the failing instances so that any client service is given the access details of functioning services. The solution mechanism is to have a health check API endpoint for each of the services to perform various health check-ups.

# Microservices composition patterns

The composition activity is being achieved through two ways: orchestration and choreography. The composition task goes beyond service composition. That is, process, UI, and data composition is also very much important for service engineering. Service mesh is a new buzzword in the industry and there are platforms, practices, and patterns for creating service meshes in order to envision hitherto unknown service compositions that are business and process-aware.

## Server-side page fragment composition pattern

There are customer-facing applications such as B2C e-commerce web applications and corporate portals. These are being designed and developed by using multiple services (purpose-specific and agnostic). There are proven mechanisms such as business capability, technology superiority, cross-cutting concerns, domain-centricity, **quality of service** (**QoS**), and so on to partition the original application into many microservices or to build microservices from the ground up. One aspect here is some UI screens/pages services have to display data from multiple services. UI designers sketch the overall look whereas web application developers focus on different HTML fragments that implement the particular region of the web page. The UI team is responsible for developing the page templates that build pages by performing server-side aggregation of the service-specific HTML fragments.

## Client-side UI composition pattern

The challenge, as articulated previously, is to implement a UI screen or page that displays data aggregated from multiple services. The web developers construct client-side UI components that ultimately implement the region of the web page. A UI team is responsible for implementing the page skeletons that build pages/screens by composing multiple, service-specific UI components.

## Messaging-based microservices composition pattern

Some communication between services is a requirement, even when they're isolated. Since applications consist of several microservices, the microservices will need to function together as an application in some way. Changes in the state of a given service may be of interest to other microservices. Data from one microservice may be needed by another microservice. There are many reasons for services to communicate. Good architectures manage communications by making the microservice API the only entry point for accessing its services.

Microservices APIs can be either synchronous or asynchronous. Synchronous patterns can be problematic because of network latencies and intermittent connectivity. Hence, asynchronous, non-blocking messaging is on the rise because it lets microservices continue processing without waiting for each other. These messages form a basis of the loose coupling between microservices. Asynchronous messaging requires a small compromise in consistency—it is an eventually consistent model. The loose coupling and performance gained, as a result, makes this a good trade-off.

An asynchronous, message-based, event-driven system honors the need for isolation between microservices by making the required communications between them non-intrusive. Microservices can produce events without needing to be aware of which services are consuming these events and how the events are being handled. For microservices development teams, an event-driven architecture allows each team to focus on their own problem domain.

Microservices generally comprise the full technology stack including the UI, the middle-tier application, and the last tier of data persistence. Composition patterns are being used in every tier and layer separately based on the business needs. An integrated view is one such requirement. Similarly, data stores need to be logically integrated in order to retrieve data to give a consolidated view. Finally, there are certain situations and scenarios wherein multiple discrete and atomic services ought to be integrated and orchestrated to create powerful composites. Thus, the involvement of composition patterns is growing great and grandeur in shaping up and propping up the era of microservices.

# Resilient and reliable microservices patterns

Instead of replicating the application, one or more services, which are the part of the application, can be scaled out independently. That is the power of microservices. The scalability feature is insisted for tackling extra user and data loads. Microservice instances can easily fit into Docker containers. Creating additional containers is quite easy and fast and hence, for achieving real-time scalability, microservices embedded inside containers are turning out to be the appropriate approach. In this section, we are going to discuss the various patterns for readying reliable, resilient, elastic, and available microservices-centric applications.

# Circuit breaker pattern

Microservices-based application design has wrought in a subtle and smart change in the way software applications are being designed, deployed, and delivered. Applications now become a dynamic collection of services that rely on each other to perform various tasks. Highly complicated and sophisticated applications are bound to involve a large number of interdependent microservices. More dependencies mean more complications and complexities. This pattern acquires prominence because it contributes immensely for avoiding cascading service failure. The idea of the pattern is to continuously monitor the application's microservices and the traffic flowing among them in order to prevent failures. When failures do happen, this pattern comes handy in minimizing the impact of those failures on the application. This pattern also attempts to prevent failure in the first place. For some types of error conditions such as running out of memory, it is possible to recognize that failure is imminent and to take appropriate measures to prevent it.

This is typically accomplished by the service signaling that it is becoming unhealthy and the circuit breaker then gives the service a chance to recover by throttling back the number of requests or rerouting them completely. Once the service gets recovered, the circuit breaker slowly ramps up requests to the service so as not to immediately overwhelm it and risk it becoming unhealthy again.

For microservices, the circuit breaker pattern guarantees the bottom-up resilience. If this pattern is implemented correctly, it can help in avoiding cascading failures by ensuring continuity of service even when services are unavailable. Precisely speaking, it is possible to build MSA applications that use this pattern to gracefully degrade functionality when a method call fails.

# Shared caching layer pattern

All the instances of any microservice at any point in time have the same data requirements, so it makes a lot of sense to have and share a caching layer across these instances. This practice is often not followed when each instance has its own internal *cache* in its memory for storing session state. This sort of arrangement fragments data across different instances that should be treated as a whole. Sharing a caching layer eliminates the operational complexity that results from this otherwise fragmented data tier, but it places requirements on the shared caching layer.

The application layer has a single view of user data and it is accessible through any instance. When using a shared cache, updates to data are available to all microservice instances. If the data layer is not shared, then each service would have a myopic view of the data and the architecture would have to be set up so that any given user is always routed to the same instance. Thus, having a shared caching layer gives an integrated and uniform view of data. A shared caching layer provides an isolation layer to the backing store(s). Changes to the backing store can be done in just one place, and these changes benefit all the microservice instances.

As indicated previously, adding additional instances instantaneously gives cloud-native applications an effective and efficient way of scaling the application logic and improving performance. For the overall system to benefit from this, the data layer also has to get this capability. The application performance and scalability can be significantly eroded if the data layer is a bottleneck. The introduction of a shared cache and its real-time scalability comes in handy in ensuring the application performance. The data latency is very low also. The scalability of the cache layer can be achieved through data distribution and replication.

# High availability microservices pattern

Scaling out microservices by adding their instances ensures the service availability and resilience. If a microservice instance goes down, then another instance of the same microservice can simply come forward to replace the failed one so that the business continuity is being ensured through such kinds of technological solutions. Microservices instances can be added or removed at will depending on the evolving capacity needs. By running every instance in a different container/virtual machine/bare metal server, an added degree of availability can be assured. Fault tolerance is another attribute in the cloud era and this is accomplished simply by running each instance on a different server within the cloud center or on a geographically distributed cloud server. The shared data cache should provide a similar degree of fault tolerance from server failures or site outages.

High availability and fault-tolerance requirements are essential for services to be beneficial for enterprise-grade business applications. Microservices in association with Docker containers can fulfil the need for horizontal scalability by automatically adding additional instances of microservices in the case of an emergency and urgency. That is, the formation of service clusters and meshes is the key differentiator for the digital world. Google tinkers with millions of containers every day in order to keep up its business obligations to the consumers, customers, and clients. Server failures are proactively identified and resolved in order to ensure the business continuity. Reliability and resilience of microservices go a long way in their adoption and adaption.

If a server running a microservice fails, the system automatically re-routes work to an alternate instance of the microservice, spins up a new instance to restore capacity, and provides access to the same data from the new instance. This recovery scenario has several implications for how the data layer is set up for accommodating various types of failures.

# Concurrent requests for data pattern

Running multiple application instances will have a solid impact on the shared caching layer because there will be a rise in the number of concurrent requests to avail data. Therefore, the shared caching layer also needs to be strengthened by adding instances on a need basis. That is, the cache layer also has to have the elasticity capability to meet the additional requests.

# Event store pattern

A key component of the solution is an event store. The event store system is immutable, sequential, and serves as the destination for the event streams from each service. Consumers of these events can then subscribe to and read the events of interest. The event store essentially serves as an event source for each consumer. Consumers maintain their own logic related to the filters that will be applied to determine whether an event is of interest. Each consumer also maintains their own pointer/offset into the event store to serially process the events.

Events can be generated either from the application layer or directly from the data layer. Generating events from the application layer provides visibility into and control over the flow of events, but this comes at the cost of having to manage and maintain the flow of events across all the producers and consumers. Having the events emanating from the data layer frees the application layer, and developers, from having to essentially build major pieces of an event-driven system within the application.

# Event streams and the unified event log pattern

A unified event log is the collection point/storehouse for all events (state changes, threshold break-ins or any noteworthy deviations, deficiencies, disturbances, and so on) that occurred in any participating microservice. Each participating service can also opt to retain a local log of its own state changes. However, collecting and stocking all kinds of event logs in a single and unified event store is capable of opening up a host of fresh possibilities and opportunities. The complete and 360-degree view of all the events presented in the unified event log can be used to play back selected events and create a projection of the information in any way desired. A variety of data analytics can be done on the event data in real time in order to extract actionable insights. The microservices' performance/throughput, scalability, availability, auditability, security, operational status, and so on can be easily deduced from the event store. The predictive and preventive maintenance of microservices can also be achieved through such a centralized and consolidated event log data.

A unified log can have demanding requirements for performance and scalability given a large number of microservices that can potentially source event streams. Apache Kafka's design for speed, scale, durability, and massive concurrency, together with its model allowing only immutable records to be written to it, makes it an increasingly popular choice as a unified log. Kafka maintains message feeds in distributed and replicated partitions.

Due to the continuous explosion of multifaceted, networked, and embedded devices, the number of events getting generated and captured is growing rapidly. The need is undoubted to have a highly scalable messaging platform that is able to receive a very high number of events emanating from different and distributed sources. We all know that the Apache Kafka messaging platform has the inherent ability to receive millions of events per second. The events are then partitioned so that both batch and real-time processing requirements can be met. Since service architecture patterns call for smart endpoints and dumb pipes, Kafka will do just enough for most application and system integration use cases.

## Asynchronous command calls pattern

Composing services' atomic calls into complex flows often require proper orchestration over asynchronous actions. These are usually local integration use cases, connecting related microservices that must exchange messages with a delivery guarantee. The messaging layer in this use case has substantially different needs from an event firehose since its messages are point-to-point (queues instead of topics). This usually requires a delivery guarantee and most are short-lived (albeit still asynchronous) and conversational. It's a traditional broker-centric use case, reliably connecting endpoints through asynchronous communication. The communication flows through atomic messages exchanged between parties, instead of a constant stream of events potentially handled by multiple processes.

In summary, the highly distributed nature of microservices-based applications introduces several lingering questions about how the data layer should be handled. Microservices facilitate complete isolation and autonomy. The dependency-related issues simply disappear here. But how multiple microservices can be found, connected, and aggregated to produce composite services is a challenge in a truly distributed environment. The performance and security queries pop up in a distributed environment, leveraging powerful and pioneering design practices, patterns, and processes to produce next-generation modernized applications. An in-memory caching layer brings fast response times for both read and write access to data needs:

- Asynchronous updates and event-driven architecture protect the autonomy between teams and allow for high-velocity software development
- The elasticity and scalability of a service's architecture are inextricably tied to the elasticity and scalability of the data layer
- Legacy systems can be modernized and carried forward into the world of microservices with the help of a caching isolation layer

This is the age of digital transformation. Everything in and around us is systematically getting digitized to enable every kind of physical, mechanical, electrical, and electronic system to join in the mainstream computing. The digital economy and era are staring at us. We need competent information technologies, agile development platforms, practices, and patterns. Microservices architecture (MSA) is an offshoot of the fully matured and stabilized SOA paradigm and is emerging as the way forward for developing, deploying, and delivering digital services and applications. This chapter is specially crafted and drafted for discussing the prominent and dominant patterns for risk-free adoption and acceleration of the promising MSA paradigm. Patterns are recognized as one indispensable ingredient for any paradigm to be conveniently and confidently used. Readers will be trustfully inspired to formulate fresh patterns to make MSA penetrative, participative, and pervasive.

# Summary

In this chapter, we got a brief about microservice architecture patterns and we also learned about the uniqueness of the fast emerging and evolving MSA and the associated architectural patterns. We also covered the architectural and design patterns being associated with the raging MSA.

Bibliography and additional resources for this chapter:


- `http://microservices.io/patterns/microservices.html</agt;`
- `https://dzone.com/articles/microservice-design-patterns`
- `https://azure.microsoft.com/en-us/blog/design-patterns-for-microservices/`
- `https://www.sumologic.com/blog/devops/top-patterns-building-successful-microservices-architecture/`
- `https://mapr.com/blog/event-driven-microservices-patterns/`
- `https://content.pivotal.io/blog/messaging-patterns-for-event-driven-microservices`
- `http://soapatterns.org/design_patterns/microservice_deployment`
- `http://blog.christianposta.com/`
- `https://blogs.oracle.com/developers/getting-started-with-microservices-part-three`

# 10
# Patterns for Containerized and Reliable Applications

The Docker-enabled containerization paradigm is on the right track to becoming an impactful and insightful technology with a number of crucial advancements being brought in by a growing array of third-party products and tool vendors. Especially, the future belongs to containerized cloud environments with the ready availability of proven container development, deployment, networking, and composition technologies and tools. The Docker-enabled containers in association with orchestration, governance, monitoring, measurement, and management platforms such as Kubernetes, Mesos, and so on, are to contribute immensely to setting up and sustaining next-generation containerized cloud environments that are very famous for delivering enterprise-class, microservices-based, event-driven, service-oriented, cloud-hosted, knowledge-filled, insights-attached, AI-enabled, people-centric, carrier-grade, production-ready, and infrastructure-aware applications. Besides containers, the concepts of microservices and microservices-centric applications acquire special significance. The basic requirement for building reliable applications lies with the faster realization of resilient microservices, which are being positioned as the standard and optimized building-block and deployment unit for the next-generation applications. This chapter focuses on the following topics:

- The containerization patterns
- Resilient microservices patterns
- Reliable applications patterns

# Introduction

Undeniably, Docker is the most popular and powerful technology these days in the **information technology** (**IT**) sector. There are two principal trends in the Docker landscape. Firstly, the open-source Docker platform is being continuously equipped with more right and relevant features and functionalities in order to make it the most exemplary IT platform, not only for software developers, but also for on-premises as well as off-premises IT operational teams. The second trend is the unprecedented adoption of the Docker-inspired containerization technology by various IT service and solution providers across the globe in order to bring forth a growing array of premium offerings to their venerable consumers and clients. The enhanced simplicity in developing fresh software applications, the automated and accelerated deployment of Docker containers, and the extreme maneuverability of Docker containers are being widely touted as the key differentiators for its unprecedented success.

We would like to shed more light on Docker and show why it is being touted as the next best thing for the impending digital, idea, API, knowledge and insightful economy.

# The key drivers for containerization

The first and foremost driver for Docker-enabled containerization is to competently and completely overcome the widely expressed limitations of the virtualization paradigm. Actually, we have been working on the proven virtualization techniques and tools for quite a long time now in order to realize the much-demanded software portability. That is, with the goal of decimating the inhibiting dependency between software and hardware, there have been several initiatives that incidentally include the matured and stabilized virtualization paradigm. Virtualization is a kind of beneficial abstraction, which is accomplished through the incorporation of an additional layer of indirection between hardware resources and software components. Through this freshly introduced abstraction layer (hypervisor or **virtual machine monitor** (**VMM**)), any kind of software application can run on any underlying hardware without any hitch or hurdle. In short, the software portability is being achieved through this middleware layer. However, the much-published portability target is not fully met even by the virtualization technique. The hypervisor software and different data encapsulation formats from different vendors come in the way of ensuring the much-needed application portability. Furthermore, the distribution, version, edition, and patching differences of operating systems and application workloads hinder the smooth portability of workloads across systems and locations.

Similarly, there are various other drawbacks being attached with the virtualization paradigm. In data centers and server farms, the virtualization technique is typically used for creating multiple VMs out of physical machines and each VM has its own **operating system** (**OS**). Through this solid and sound isolation enacted through automated tools and controlled resource-sharing, multiple and heterogeneous applications are being accommodated in a physical machine. That is, the hardware-assisted virtualization enables disparate applications to be run simultaneously on a single physical server. With the virtualization paradigm, various kinds of IT infrastructures (server machines, storage appliances, and networking solutions) become open, programmable, remotely monitorable, manageable, and maintainable. However, because of the verbosity and bloatedness (every VM carries its own operating system), VM provisioning typically takes a few minutes. This is a big setback for real-time and on-demand scalability.

The other widely expressed drawback that is being closely associated with virtualization is that the performance of virtualized systems also goes down due to the excessive usage of precious and expensive IT resources (processing, memory, storage, network bandwidth, and so on). The execution time of virtual machines is on the higher side because of multiple layers ranging from a guest OS, a hypervisor, and the underlying hardware.

Finally, the compute virtualization has flourished, whereas the other closely associated network and storage virtualization concepts are just taking off. Precisely speaking, building distributed applications and fulfilling varying business expectations mandate for the faster and flexible provisioning, high availability, reliability, scalability, and maneuverability of all the participating IT resources. Compute, storage, and networking components need to work together in accomplishing the varying IT and business needs. With more virtualized elements and entities in an IT environment, the operational complexity is bound to grow rapidly.

Move over to the world of containerization; all the preceding barriers get resolved in a single stroke. That is, the evolving concept of application containerization coolly and confidently contributes to the unprecedented success of the software portability goal. A container generally contains an application/service/process. Along with the primary application, all of its relevant libraries, binaries, files, and other dependencies are stuffed and squeezed together to be packaged and presented as a comprehensive yet compact container. The application containers can be readily shipped, run, and managed in any local as well as remote environments. Containers are exceptionally lightweight, highly portable, rapidly deployable, extensible, horizontally scalable, and so on. Furthermore, many industry leaders have come together to form a kind of consortium to embark on a decisive and deft journey towards the systematic production, packaging, and delivery of industry-strength and standardized containers.

This conscious and collective move makes Docker deeply penetrative and pervasive. The open-source community is simultaneously spearheading the containerization conundrum through an assortment of concerted activities for simplifying and streamlining the containerization concept. The containerization life cycle steps are being automated through a variety of third-party tools.

The Docker ecosystem also grows fast in order to bring in as much automation as possible in the IT landscape. Container clustering and orchestration are gaining a lot of attention, thereby geographically distributed containers and their clusters can be readily linked up to produce bigger and better process-aware and composite containers. The new concept of containerization assists with distributed computing. Containers enable the formation of federated cloud environments in order to accomplish specialized business targets. Cloud service providers and enterprise IT environments are all set to embrace this unique compartmentalization technology in order to escalate the resource utilization and to take the much-insisted infrastructure optimization to the next level. On the performance side, there are sufficient tests showcasing Docker containers achieving the bare metal server performance. In short, the IT agility through the DevOps aspect is being guaranteed through the smart leverage of the Docker-enabled containerization and this, in turn, leads to business agility, adaptivity, and affordability.

# Design patterns for Docker containers

The Docker-enabled containerization is fast emerging and evolving. With the complexity of the container lifecycle management escalating, the need for enabling patterns is being felt. The concerned professionals and pundits are working in unison to formulate and firm up various container-specific patterns. In the days ahead, we will come across many more patterns. Whatever is widely articulated and accepted is concisely presented in this section and in the forthcoming sections.

With the unprecedented proliferation of the Docker-enabled containers in cloud environments (public, private, and fog/edge), Docker enthusiasts, evangelists, and experts consciously bring forth a bevy of enabling patterns. The readers can find them in this section. Let us start with container building patterns. Building Docker images and containers is constrained with a number of challenges and concerns. The Docker patterns need to reach a level of stability.

# Container building patterns

This section describes a few common ways to build Docker images. As per Alex Collins (`https://alexecollins.com/developing-with-docker-building-patterns/`), there are several choices: `scratch + binary`, `language stack`, and `distribution+ package manager`. The `scratch + binary - scratch` is the most basic base image and it does not contain any files or programs at all. We must build a *standalone binary application* to use this. Here is an example. Firstly, we will build a standalone binary application using Docker. The steps are as follows:

1. Create an empty directory and then create a `main.go` application:

```
package main
import "fmt"
// this is a comment
func main() {
    fmt.Println("Hello World")
}
```

2. Compile the application:

```
docker run --rm -ti -v $(pwd):/go/src/myapp google/golang go
build myapp
```

3. Create a Dockerfile for the application:

```
FROM scratchADD myapp /CMD ["myapp"]
```

4. Finally, build and run the image:

```
docker build -t myapp:1 .docker run --rm -ti myapp:1
```

This outputs `Hello World` in the terminal.

This is suitable for applications that can be packaged as standalone binaries. As there is no language runtime, larger applications are bound to consume more disk space.

Docker provides a number of pre-built base images for the runtime for common languages. Here is an example as follows:

1. Create a new empty directory and detail the `Main.java` application:

   ```
   public class Main {  public static void main(String[] args) {
   System.out.println("Hello World");   }}
   ```

2. Now, compile this application using the **Java Development Kit** (**JDK**):

   ```
   docker run --rm -ti -v $(pwd):/myapp -w /myapp java:8-jdk javac
   Main.java
   ```

3. Create the following Dockerfile with the **Java Runtime Environment** (**JRE**):

   ```
   FROM java:8-jreADD Main.class /CMD ["java", "-cp", "/", "Main"]
   ```

4. Finally, build and run this Docker image:

   ```
   docker build -t myapp:1 .docker run --rm -it myapp:1
   ```

It is faster to deploy this application once the base image is downloaded, and if the same base image is used for many other applications, then the additional layer needed is very small.

To build an image that is not on a supported language stack, it is necessary to roll your own image starting with a distribution, and then it is all about using a package manager to add the mandated dependencies. Linux always contains a package manager.

This comment installs the JRE:

```
FROM ubuntu:15.10 RUN apt-get update && apt-get install --no-install-
recommends -y openjdk-8-jre ADD Main.class / CMD ["java", "-cp", "/",
"Main"]
```

Now, build and run this base image:

```
docker build -t myapp:1 .docker run --rm -it myapp:1
```

The advantage is that we can build an application and it is possible to put multiple applications into a single image (using `systemd`).

# Docker image building patterns

As we all know, Docker containers are a fantastic way to optimally and organically encapsulate complex build processes. Typically, any software package requires a host of dependencies. As indicated in `Chapter 9`, *Microservices Architecture Patterns*, every microservice is being developed and delivered as a Docker image. Each microservice has its own code repository (GitHub) and its own CI build job. Microservices can be coded using any programming language. Let us focus on the Java language here. If a service is built and run using a compiled language (Java, Go, and so on), then the build environment can be separated from the runtime environment. A Java service's `Dockerfile.build` is from the `openjdk-7-jdk` directory and its Dockerfile is from the `openjdk-7-jre` directory which is substantially smaller than JDK.

For the Java programming language, it requires additional tooling and processes before its microservices become executable. However, the JDK are not required when a compiled program is running. Another reason is that the JDK is a bigger package when compared with the **Java Runtime Environment** (**JRE**). Furthermore, it seems farsighted to develop and reuse a repeatable process and a uniform environment for deploying microservices. It is therefore paramount to package the Java tools and packages into containers. This setup allows the building of Java-based microservices on any machine, including a CI server, without any specific environmental requirements such as JDK version, profiling and testing tools, OS, Maven, environment variables, and so on.

Resultantly, for every service, there are two Dockerfiles: one for service runtime and the second is packed with the required tools to build the service. First, it is all about crafting the `Dockerfile.build` file, which can speed up the Maven build. Now, it is straightforward to compile and run the microservice on any machine (local or remote). This segregated approach goes a long way in simplifying the **continuous integration** (**CI**) process.

The recipe is as follows:

1. **Build file**: Have one Dockerfile with all the tools and packages required to build any service. Name it `Dockerfile.build`.
2. **Run file**: Have another Dockerfile with all the packages required to run the service. Keep both files along with the service code.
3. Build a new builder image, create a container from it, and extract build artifacts using volumes or the `docker cp` command.
4. Build the service image.

Thus, segregating the building process from the runtime process stands well for the intended success of the containerization paradigm. One is to perform a build and another is to ship the results of the first build without the penalty of the build-chain and tooling in the first image. Terra Nullius has posted the relevant details at `http://blog.terranillius.com/post/docker_builder_pattern/`. The builder pattern describes the setup that developers have to follow for building a container. It generally involves two Docker images:

- A *build* image with all the build tools installed, capable of creating production-ready application files
- A *service* image capable of running the application

The basic idea behind the builder pattern is simple: create additional Docker images with the required tools (compilers, linkers, and testing tools), and use these images to produce lean, secure, and production-ready Docker images.

# Multi-stage image building pattern

The latest Docker release facilitates the creation of a single Dockerfile that can build multiple helper images with compilers, tools, and tests, and use files from images to produce the *final* Docker image, as vividly illustrated in the following section.

The Docker platform can build Docker images by reading the instructions from a Dockerfile. A Dockerfile is a text file that contains a list of all the commands needed to build a new Docker image. The syntax and core principle of a Dockerfile is pretty simple and straightforward as follows:

```
1 Dockerfile -> 1 Docker Image
```

That is, every Dockerfile creates a Docker image. This principle works just fine for basic use cases, but for creating advanced, secure, and lean Docker images, a single Dockerfile is just not enough.

Multi-stage builds are a new feature incorporated in the latest Docker version, and this is interesting for anyone who has struggled to optimize Dockerfiles while keeping them easy to read and maintain. One of the biggest challenges when building Docker images is keeping the image size down. Each instruction in the Dockerfile adds a layer to the image. The software engineer has to clean up any artifacts that are not needed before moving on to the next layer. To write a really efficient Dockerfile, he traditionally needs to employ the shell tricks and other logic to keep the layers as lean and light as possible and to ensure that each layer has the artifacts it needs from the previous layer and nothing else.

It is always common to have one Dockerfile for development and a slimmed-down version of the Dockerfile for production. Maintaining two Dockerfiles is not ideal. With multi-stage builds, he can use multiple `FROM` statements in his Dockerfile. Each `FROM` instruction can use a different base, and each of them begins a new stage of the build. He can selectively copy artifacts from one stage to another, leaving behind everything he doesn't want in the final image. The end result is the same tiny production image as before, with a significant reduction in complexity.

# The pattern for file sharing between containers

Docker is a popular containerization tool used to package and provide software applications with a filesystem that contains everything they need to run. Docker containers are ephemeral in the sense that they can run for as long as it takes for the command issued in the container to complete. There are occasions wherein applications need access to data, to share data to, or do data persistence after a container is deleted. Typically, Docker images are not suitable for databases; user-generated content for a website and log files that applications have to access to do the required processing. The much-needed persistent access to data is provided with Docker volumes. At some point, the production-ready application files need to be copied from the build container to the host machine. There are two ways of accomplishing that:

- Using `docker cp`
- Using `bind-mount volumes`

Matthias Noback (`https://matthiasnoback.nl/2017/04/docker-build-patterns/`) has supplied the description for both along with an easy-to-understand example.

# Using bind-mount volumes

It is not good to have the compilation step as a part of the build process of the container. The overwhelming expectation is that Docker images need to be highly reusable. If the source code is modified, then it is necessary to rebuild the build image, but it is desired to *run the same build image* again.

Therefore, the compilation step has to be moved to the ENTRYPOINT (`https://docs.docker.com/engine/reference/builder/#entrypoint`) or CMD instruction.
The source/files shouldn't be part of the build context and instead, mounted as a bind-mount volume inside the running build container.

The advantages are many here. Every time one runs the build container, it will compile the files in the `/project/source/` and produce a new executable in the `/project/target/`. Since `/project` is a bind-mount volume, the executable file is automatically available on the host machine in `target/`. There is no need to explicitly copy it from the container. Once the application files are on the host machine, it will be easy to copy them to the service image, since that can be done using the regular `COPY` instruction.

# Pipes and filters pattern

An application is required to perform a variety of tasks of varying complexity on the information that it receives. A monolithic module could do this, but there are several inflexibilities. Suppose an application receives and processes data from two sources. The data from each source is processed by a separate module that performs a series of tasks to transform this data, before passing the result to the business logic of the application. The processing tasks performed by each module or the deployment requirements for each task could change. Some tasks might be compute-intensive and could benefit from running on powerful hardware, while others might not require such expensive resources. Also, additional processing might be required in the future, or the order in which the tasks are performed by the processing could change.

The viable solution is to break down the processing required for each data stream into a set of separate components (or filters), each performing a single task. By standardizing the format of the data that each component receives and sends, these filters can be combined together into a pipeline. This helps to avoid duplicating code and makes it easy to remove, replace, or integrate additional components if the processing requirements change.

The time it takes to process a single request depends on the speed of the slowest filter in the pipeline. One or more filters could be a bottleneck, especially if a large number of requests appear in a stream from a particular data source. A key advantage of the pipeline structure is that it provides opportunities for running parallel instances of slow filters, enabling the system to spread the load and improve throughput.

The filters that make up a pipeline can run on different machines, enabling them to be scaled independently and take advantage of the elasticity that many cloud environments provide. A filter that is computationally intensive can run on high-performance hardware, while other less demanding filters can be hosted on less expensive commodity hardware.

If the input and output of a filter are structured as a stream, it is possible to perform the processing for each filter in parallel. The first filter in the pipeline can start its work and output its results, which are passed directly on to the next filter in the sequence before the first filter has completed its work. If a filter fails or the machine it's running on is no longer available, the pipeline can reschedule the work that the filter was performing and direct this work to another instance of the component.

By using the proven pipes and filters pattern in conjunction with the compensating transaction pattern, there is an alternative approach to implement the complex distributed transactions. A distributed transaction can be broken down into separate and compensable tasks, each of which can be implemented by using a filter that also implements the compensating transaction pattern. The filters in a pipeline can be implemented as separate hosted tasks running close to the data that they maintain, thus there emerge newer possibilities.

For the container world, the preceding pattern is beneficial. That is, for taking the generated files out of a container, streaming the file to `stdout` leveraging the preceding *pipes and filters* pattern is being made out as an interesting workaround. This streaming has many advantages too:

- The data doesn't have to end up in a file anymore as it can stay in memory. This offers faster access to the data.
- Using `stdout` allows sending the output directly to some other process using the pipe operator (`|`). Other processes may modify the output, then do the same thing, or store the final result in a file.
- The exact location of files becomes irrelevant. There is no coupling through the filesystem if we only use `stdin` and `stdout`. The build container would not have to put its files in `/target`, and the build script would not have to look in `/target`, they just pass along data.

# Containerized applications - Autopilot pattern

Deploying containerized applications and connecting them together is a definite challenge because typically, cloud-native applications are made up of hundreds of microservices. Microservice architectures provide organizations with a tool to manage the burgeoning complexity of the development process, and application containers provide a new means to manage the dependencies to accelerate the deployment of those microservices. But deploying and connecting those services together is still a challenge.

Operationalizing microservices-based applications brings forth several challenges. Developers have to embed several things inside for simplified deployment and delivery. Autopilot applications are a powerful design pattern for solving these problems. The autopilot pattern automates in the code the repetitive and boring operational tasks of an application, including start-up, shutdown, scaling, and recovery from anticipated failure conditions for reliability, ease of use, and improved productivity. By embedding the distinct responsibility and the operational tasks into the application, the workload on operational team members is bound to come down.

The autopilot pattern is for both developers and operators. It is for operators that want to bring sanity to their lives and for developers who want to make their applications easy to use. It is primarily for microservices applications and multi-tiered applications. Most importantly, it is designed to live and grow with our applications at all stages of development and operations.

The autopilot pattern automates the life cycle of each component of the application. There can be multiple components in any application. Web and application server, DB server, in-memory cache, reverse proxy, and so on, are the most prominent components for any application. Each of these components can be containerized and each container contributing for the application has its own life cycle. Most autopilot pattern implementations embrace single-purpose or single-service containers. The autopilot pattern does require developers and operators to think about how the application is operated at critical points in the life cycle of each component. The author of this unique pattern has provided some valid questions at `http://autopilotpattern.io/`, and those questions come in handy while designing the autopilot pattern.

There are some applications emerging with at least some of this logic built in. Traefik is a proxy server with automatic discovery of its backends using Consul or other service catalogs. Traefik does not self-register in those service catalogs so that it can be used by other applications. ContainerPilot, a helper written in Golang that lives inside the container, can help with this.

ContainerPilot provides microservices architectures with application orchestration, dependency management, health checks, error handling, lifecycle management, and linear and non-linear scaling of stateful services. Furthermore, it provides a private init system designed to live inside the container. It acts as a process supervisor, reaps zombies, runs health checks, registers the app in the service catalog, watches the service catalog for changes, and runs your user-specified code at events in the life cycle of the container to make it all work correctly. ContainerPilot uses Consul to coordinate global state among the application containers.

Using a small configuration file, ContainerPilot can trigger events inside the container to automate operations on these events, including preStart (formerly onStart), health, onChange, preStop, and postStop.

Here is a sample scenario (readers can find the details at `http://autopilotpattern.io/example`). The author of this example has started with two services, sales, and customers. Nginx acts as a reverse proxy. Requests for `/customers/ go` to customer's, and `/sales/` to sales. The sales service needs to get some data from the customer's service to serve its requests, and vice versa. There are a few crucial problems here. The configuration is static. This prevents adding new instances and makes it harder to work with a failed instance. Configuring this stack via configuration management tools means packaging new dependencies with this application, but configuring statically means redeploying most of the containers every time a new instance gets added. There is a need for a mechanism to have the applications self-assemble and self-manage the everyday tasks, and hence there is a surging popularity for the autopilot pattern.

Engaging autopilot! The author of this autopilot design pattern has come out with the appropriate Dockerfile for the customer's service. It's a small Node.js application that listens on port `4000`. He uses Consul for service discovery and each service will send TTL heartbeats to Consul. All nodes know about all other nodes, and hence there is no need to use an external proxy or load balancer for communicating between the nodes. The diagram vividly illustrates everything.

However, there is a need to make each of the services aware of Consul. For that, the author uses ContainerPilot. The source code and other implementation details are given at `https://github.com/autopilotpattern/workshop`.

A re-usable Nginx base image got implemented according to the autopilot pattern for automatic discovery and configuration. The goal is to create a Nginx image that can be reused across environments without having to rebuild the entire image. The configuration of Nginx is entirely through ContainerPilot jobs and watch handlers, which update the Nginx configuration on disk through consul-template. The relevant details are supplied at `https://github.com/autopilotpattern/nginx`. Similarly, there are autopilot implementations for other popular applications such as WordPress. Bringing a bevy of automation into various microservices-based software applications is gaining a lot of momentum.

As indicated previously, a number of manual tasks are getting automated at different layers and levels, especially some of the crucial automation requirements are increasingly implemented at the application level. With the faster maturity and stability of the Docker platform, Docker containers are spreading their wings fast and wide. With the widespread availability of container management software solutions, microservices-based applications are gaining a lot of market and mind shares. Furthermore, there are a few service mesh frameworks, and hence the days of resilient microservices and reliable applications are not too far away. A growing bunch of automation capabilities is being attached to these applications, and this advancement enables the applications to exhibit adaptive behavior. Now, the autopilot pattern plays a key role in adding additional automation features and facilities.

# Containers - persistent storage patterns

Typically, the container space originates with application containers that are not for permanently storing data. That is, when a container collapses, the data stored or buffered in the container gets lost. However, the aspect of data persistence is insisted for several reasons, including the realization of stateful applications, and hence fresh mechanisms are being worked out in order to safely and securely persist data in containers. Therefore, for persisting data, additional container types, such as data or volume containers were introduced.

# The context for persistent storages

There is a concern widely expressed that containers are great for stateless applications, but are not so good for stateful applications that persist data. Thus, persistent storage patterns are acquiring special significance in the container world. A brief description about stateless and stateful applications is given as follows paragraph.

A random number generator is stateless because we get a different value from it every time we run it. We could easily Dockerize it and if the instance fails, we can have it running in another host instantaneously to continue the service without any break and lag. The instance's behavior remains the same in the new host as well. However, that is not the case with our bank accounts. If the bank account application has to be re-provisioned on a new server, it has to have the original data from the first server instance.

Here is a stateful data categorization. Typically, configuration data, including keys and other secrets, is often written to disk in various files. This data is easy to recover when provisioning instances. User generated content includes text, video, or bank transactions. There are dynamic configuration details. The suitable example is of those services *A* and *B* connecting with one another. Connecting an application/service to its backend database system is another prominent example. Typically, applications/services treat this discovery and connectivity as configuration data along with other configuration details. In order for an application to be scalable and resilient, it is necessary to update this configuration information while the application is running. That is, as we add or remove instances of a service, we have to update all the other service instances that connect to the service. Otherwise, the intended performance increment would not happen. Other pertinent configuration details can include performance-tuning parameters. These configuration details can be stocked in the application repository in order to facilitate the application/service versioning and easier tracking. The other option for configuration information is leveraging the dynamic storage so they can be changed without re-building and re-deploying the application. It is also possible to do automatic replication of repository contents to the configuration store using a tool such as `git2consul`. The best practice is to keep configuration data and templates in a consistent distributed key/value data store.

# The persistent storage options

Containers are meant to be ephemeral, and so scale pretty well for stateless applications. Stateful containers, however, need to be treated differently. For stateful applications, a persistent storage mechanism has to be there for the container idea to be right and relevant. Containers can be developed and dismantled without the data persistence. The data resides within the container. If there is any change, then the data gets lost. For some situations, this data loss is not a big issue. For certain scenarios, the data loss is not accepted; the data persistence feature has to be there. The solution approach prescribed by Docker is given in the following section.

It is possible to store data within the writable layer of a container, but there are a few downsides:

- The data won't persist when that container is no longer running, and it can be difficult to get the data out of the container if another process needs it.
- A container's writable layer is tightly coupled to the host machine where the container is running. Moving the data somewhere else is a difficult affair.
- Writing into a container's writable layer requires a storage driver to manage the filesystem. The storage driver provides a union filesystem, using the Linux kernel. This extra abstraction reduces performance as compared to using *data volumes*, which write directly to the host filesystem.

Docker offers three different ways to mount data into a container from the Docker host: *volumes*, *bind mounts*, or *tmpfs mounts*. Volumes are almost always the right choice. Volumes are the preferred mechanism for persisting data generated by and used by Docker containers. While bind mounts are dependent on the directory structure of the host machine, volumes are completely managed by Docker. Volumes have several advantages over bind mounts:

- Volumes are easier to back up or migrate than bind mounts
- Volumes are easy to manage by using Docker CLI commands or the Docker API
- Volumes work on both Linux and Windows containers
- Volumes can be more safely shared among multiple containers
- Volume drivers allow storing volumes on remote hosts or cloud providers, to encrypt the contents of volumes, or to add other functionality
- A new volume's contents can be pre-populated by a container

Volumes are often a better choice than persisting data in a container's writable layer, because using a volume does not increase the size of containers using it, and the volume's contents exist outside the life cycle of a given container.

If a container generates non-persistent state data, then consider using a tmpfs mount to avoid storing the data anywhere permanently, and to increase the container's performance by avoiding writing into the container's writable layer.

All the three options are discussed as follows:

- **Volumes** are stored in a part of the host filesystem that is *managed by Docker* (`/var/lib/docker/volumes/` on Linux). Non-Docker processes cannot modify this part of the filesystem.
- **Bind mounts** may be stored *anywhere* on the host system. They may even be important system files or directories. Non-Docker processes on the Docker host or a Docker container can modify them at any time.
- **The tmpfs mounts** are stored in the host system's memory only and are never written to the host system's filesystem.

Let's discuss more about them.

# Volumes

We can create a volume explicitly using the `docker volume create` command, or Docker can create a volume during container or service creation. When we create a volume, it is stored in a directory on the Docker host. When we mount the volume into a container, this is the directory that is mounted on the container. This is similar to the way that bind mounts work, except that volumes are managed by Docker and are isolated from the core functionality of the host machine.

A given volume can be mounted into multiple containers simultaneously. When no running container is using a volume, the volume is still available to Docker and is not removed automatically. You can remove unused volumes using `docker volume prune`. Volumes also support the use of *volume drivers*, which allow the storing of data on remote hosts, cloud providers, and so on.

## Bind mounts

When we use a bind mount, a file or directory on the *host machine* is mounted on a container. The file or directory is referenced by its full path on the host machine. The file or directory does not need to exist on the Docker host already and it can be created on demand. Bind mounts are very performant, but they rely on the host machine's filesystem having a specific directory structure available. It is not possible to use Docker CLI commands to directly manage bind mounts.

## The tmpfs mounts

A tmpfs mount is not persisted on disk either on the Docker host or within a container. It can be used by a container during the lifetime of the container, to store non-persistent state or sensitive information. For instance, internally, swarm services use tmpfs mounts to mount secrets into a service's containers.

# Docker compose configuration pattern

We are increasingly hearing, reading, and even experiencing multi-container applications. That is, composite applications are being achieved through multi-container composition. The composition technique acquires special significance because of two key trends. Firstly, the powerful concept of microservices is gradually changing the IT industry. That is, large monolithic services are slowly giving way to swarms of small and autonomous microservices. Different and distributed microservices are being found, checked and chained together to create and run business-class, production-ready, process-aware, mission-critical, enterprise-grade, composite applications. The second is that the Docker-enabled containerization changes not only the architecture of services but also the structure of environments used to create them. Now, software gets methodically containerized, stocked, and distributed and developers gain the full freedom to choose the preferred applications. Resultantly, even complex environments such as **continuous integration** (**CI**) servers with database backend systems and analytical infrastructure can be instantiated within seconds. In short, software development, deployment, and delivery become easier and faster.

Docker Compose is a tool for defining and running complex applications with Docker. With Compose, it is possible to define a multi-container application in a single file, and then spin the application up in a single command that does everything that needs to be done to get it running. Using Compose is basically a three-step process:

1. Define your application's environment with a Dockerfile so it can be reproduced anywhere
2. Define the services that make up the application in `docker-compose.yml` so they can be run together in an isolated environment
3. Lastly, run `docker-compose up` and compose will start and run the entire application

We can pass in environment variables via Docker Compose in order to realize a container image once and reuse it on any environment (development, staging, and production). With this approach, it is possible to develop compose-centric containers that require a piece of configuration management for handling pre-start events based on the values of the environment variables. The author of this pattern has detailed the source code at `https://github.com/jay-johnson/docker-schema-prototyping-with-mysql`.

The author has built this project for rapid-prototyping a database schema using a MySQL Docker container that deploys its own ORM schema file and populates the initial records on startup. By setting a couple of environment variables, it is possible to provide our own Docker container with a usable MySQL instance, browser-ready phpMyAdmin server, and our database, including the tables, initialized exactly how we want. Interested readers are requested to visit the preceding page to get finer details on this unique pattern.

# Docker container anti-patterns

We have discussed most of the available container-specific patterns in the previous section. Many exponents and evangelists of Docker-enabled containerization have brought in a few anti-patterns based on their vast experience in developing, deploying, and delivering containerized services and applications. This section is exclusively allocated for conveying the anti-patterns discovered and disseminated by Docker practitioners.

Container creation and deployment are becoming easier and faster with the ready availability of both open-source and commercial-grade tools. DevOps team members ought to learn some of the techniques and tips in order to avoid mistakes when migrating to Docker.

# Installing an OS inside a Docker container

There is rarely a good reason to host an entire OS inside a container using Docker. There are platforms for generating and running system containers. The Docker platform is specially crafted and fine-tuned for producing application containers. That is, applications and their runtime dependencies are being stuffed together, packaged, and transmitted to their destinations.

# Go for optimized Docker images

When building container images, we should include only the services that are absolutely essential for the application the container will host. Anything extra wastes resources and widens the potential attack vector that could ultimately lead to security problems. For example, it is not good to run an SSH server inside the container because we can use the Docker *exec* call to interact with the containerized application. The related suggestions here are to create a new directory and include the Dockerfile and other relevant files in that directory. Also consider using `.dockerignore` to remove any logs, source code, and so on before creating the image. Furthermore, make it a habit to remove any downloaded artifacts after they are unzipped.

It is not correct to use different images or even different tags in development, testing, staging, and production environments. The image that is the *source of truth* should be created once and pushed to a repository. That image should be used for different environments going forward. Any system integration testing should be done on the image that will be pushed into production.

The containers produced by the Docker image should be as ephemeral as possible. By *ephemeral*, it is meant that it can be stopped and destroyed and a new one can be built and put in place with an absolute minimum of setup and configuration.

The best practice is to not keep critical data inside containers. There are two prime reasons for this. When containers collapse inadvertently or deliberately, the data inside them gets lost immediately. The second reason is that the security situation of containers is not as good as virtual machines, and hence storing confidential, critical, customer, and corporate information, inside containers is not a way forward. For persisting data, there are mechanisms to be used. The popular ELK stack could be used to store and process logs. If managed volumes are used during the early testing process, then it is recommended to remove them using the `-v` switch with the `docker rm` command.

Also, do not store any security credentials in the Dockerfile. They are in clear text and this makes them completely vulnerable. Do not forget to use `-e` to specify passwords as runtime environment variables. Alternatively, `--env-file` can be used to read environment variables from a file. Also, go for CMD or ENTRYPOINT to specify a script, and this script will pull the credentials from a third party and then configure the application.

# Storing container images only inside a container registry

A container registry is designed solely for the purpose of hosting container images. It is not good to use the registry as a general-purpose repository for hosting other types of data.

# Hosting only one service inside a container

In the microservices world, applications are being partitioned into a dynamic collection of interactive, single-purpose, autonomous, API-driven, easily manageable, and composable services. Containers emerge as the best-in-class runtime environment for microservices. Thus, it is logical to have one service inside a container. Thus, for running an application, multiple containers need to be leveraged for running many services. For example, one container would install and use MySQL, WordPress, possibly even phpMyAdmin, nginx, and an SSH daemon. Also, multiple instances of a service can be hosted in different containers. The redundancy capability being achieved through containers goes a long way in ensuring the business continuity through fault-tolerance, high availability, horizontal scalability, independent deployment, and so on. Now, with the emergence of powerful container orchestration platforms, distributed and multiple containers can be linked up to come out with composite applications. An advantage of containerization is the ability to quickly re-build images in the case of a security issue, for example, and roll out a whole new set of containers quickly. And because containers are single-concern, there is no need to redeploy the cloud infrastructure every time. Similarly, multiple Docker images can be built from a base image. Furthermore, containers can be also converted to new images.

We can use the CMD and ENTRYPOINT commands while formulating a Dockerfile. Often, CMD will use a script that will perform some configurations of the image and then start the container. It is better to avoid starting multiple processes using that script. This will make managing containers, collecting logs, and updating each individual process hard. That is, we need to follow the *separation of concerns* pattern when creating Docker images. Breaking up an application into multiple containers and managing them separately is the way forward.

# Latest doesn't mean best

It is incredibly tempting when writing a Dockerfile to grab the latest version of every dependency. The *golden rule* though is to create containers with known and stable versions of the system and dependencies that we know our software will work on.

# Docker containers with SSH

A related and equally unfortunate practice is to bake an SSH daemon into an image. Having an SSH daemon inside a container may lead to undocumented, untraceable changes to the container infrastructure, but Docker containers are being touted as the immutable infrastructure.

There are a few use cases for SSHing into a container:

- Update the OS, services, or dependencies
- Git pull or update any application in some other fashion
- Check logs
- Backup some files
- Restart a service

Instead of using SSH, it is recommended to use the following mechanisms:

- Make the change in the container Dockerfile, rebuild the image, and deploy the container.
- Use an environment variable or configuration file accessible via volume sharing to make the change and possibly restart the container.
- As indicated before, use `docker exec`. The `docker exec` command starts a new command in a running container, and hence has to be the last resort.

# IP addresses of a container

Each container get assigned with an IP address. In a containerized environment, multiple containers have to interact with one another in order to achieve business goals. Also, containers are terminated often and fresh containers are being created. Thus, relying upon IP addresses of containers for initiating container communication is beset with real challenges. The preferred approach is to create services. This will provide a logical name that can be referred to independent of the growing and shrinking number of containers. And it also provides a basic load balancing.

Also, do not use `-p` to publish all the exposed ports. This facilitates in running multiple containers and publishing their exposed ports. But this comes with a price. That is, all the ports will be published, resulting in a security risk. Instead, use `-p` to publish specific ports.

# Root user

This is a security-mitigation tip. Don't run containers as a root user. The host and the container share the same kernel. If the container is compromised, a root user can do more damage to the underlying hosts. Instead, create a group and a user in it. Use the user instruction to switch to that user. Each user creates a new layer in the image. Also, avoid switching the user back and forth to reduce the number of layers.

# Dependency between containers

Often, applications rely upon containers to be started in a certain order. For example, a database container must be up before an application can connect to it. The application should be resilient to such changes as the containers may be terminated or started at any time. In this case, have the application container wait for the database connection to succeed before proceeding further. Do not use *wait-for* scripts in a Dockerfile for the containers to start up in a specific order.

In conclusion, containers are the new and powerful unit of development, deployment, and execution. Business applications, IT platforms, databases, and middleware are formally containerized and stocked in publically available and accessible image repositories so that software developers can pick up and leverage them for their software-building requirements. The system portability is a key advantage. The easier and faster maneuverability, testability, and composability of container images are being touted as the most promising and potential advantages of containerization. The inevitability of distributed computing is greatly simplified by the concept of containerization. Multiple containers across clusters can be easily linked to realizing smart and sophisticated applications.

# Patterns for highly reliable applications

The IT systems are indispensable for business automation. The widely articulated challenge for our IT and business applications is to showcase high reliability. Systems ought to be responsive, resilient, elastic, and secure in order to intrinsically demonstrate the required dependability. Systems are increasingly multimodal and multimedia. Systems have to capture, understand, and exhibit the appropriate behavior. Also, systems have to respond all the time under any circumstance. Also, with the dawn of big data, distributed computing is all set to the mainstream compute model. In this section, we will discuss the prominent patterns for constructing reliable systems for professional as well as personal requirements. The promising approaches include:

- Reactive and cognitive programming techniques
- Resilient microservices
- Containerized cloud environments

In a distributed system, failures are bound to happen because of multiple moving parts and the sickening dependencies between the participating systems' modules. Hardware can fail, the application may go down, and the network can have transient failures. Rarely, an entire service or region may experience a disruption. Clouds are emerging as the one-stop IT solution.

**Resiliency** is the ability of a system to withstand and tolerate faults in order to function continuously. Even if it fails, it has the wherewithal to bounce back to the original state. Precisely speaking, it is all about not avoiding failures but how quickly it can recover from the failures to serve without any breakdown and slowdown. Also, a fault in a component of a system should not cascade into other components in order to bring down the whole system. There are resiliency strategies, patterns, best practices, approaches, and techniques.

**High availability** (**HA**) is the ability of the application to continue running in a healthy state, without significant downtime. That is, the application continues to be responsive to users' requests.

**Disaster recovery** (**DR**) is the ability to recover from rare but major incidents: non-transient, wide-scale failures, such as service disruption that affects an entire region. Disaster recovery includes data backup and archiving, and may include manual intervention, such as restoring a database from backup.

Resiliency must be designed into the system, and here is a general model to follow:

1. **Define** the application availability requirements based on business needs.
2. **Design** the application architecture for resiliency. Start with an architecture that follows proven practices and architectural decisions, and then identify the possible failure points in that architecture. Take care of the dependencies. Also, choose the best-in-class architectural patterns and styles that intrinsically support resiliency.
3. **Develop** the application using the appropriate design patterns and incorporate strategies to detect and recover from failures.
4. **Build and test** the implementation by simulating faults and triggering forced failovers and debug the identified issues to the fullest.
5. **Decide** the infrastructure capacity accordingly and **provision** them.
6. **Deploy** the application into production using a reliable and repeatable process.
7. **Monitor** the application to detect failures. The monitoring activity helps to gauge the health of the application. The health check comes in handy in providing instantaneous responses.
8. **Respond** if there are incidents that require any kind of manual interventions.

# Resiliency implementation strategies

As the resiliency requirement is insisted, IT departments of various business enterprises are exploring various ways and means in order to build and release resilient application services. At different levels (infrastructure, platform, database, middleware, network, and application), the virtue of resiliency is being mandated so that the whole system and environment become resilient.

In this section, we will dig deeper and describe how the elusive target of resiliency is being endeavored and enunciated to see the reality. There are a few noteworthy failures. The key ones are include as follows:

- **Retry transient failures**: Transient failures can occur due to many causes, deficiencies, and disturbances. Often, a temporary failure can be resolved simply by retrying the request. However, each retry adds to the total latency. Also, too many failed requests can cause a bottleneck as pending requests accumulate in the queue. These blocked requests might hold critical system resources such as memory, threads, database connections, and so on. A sellable workaround here is to increase the delay between each retry attempt and limit the total number of failed requests.
- **Load balance across instances**: This is a common thing happening in IT environments. A **load balancer** (**LB**) instance in front of an application facilitates adding more application instances in order to improve resiliency.
- **Replicating data**: It has been a standard approach for handling non-transient failures in a database and filesystem. The data storage technologies innately provide built-in replication. However, to fulfill the high-availability requirement, replicas are being made and put up in geographically distributed locations. So, if one region goes down, the other region can take care of the business continuity. However, this significantly increases the latency when replicating the data across the regions. Typically, considering the long distance between regions, the data replication happens in an asynchronous fashion. In this case, we can not expect real-time and strong consistency. Instead, we need to settle for eventual consistency. Corporates have to tolerate for potential data loss if a replica fails.
- **Degrade gracefully**: If a service fails and there is no failover path, the application may be able to degrade gracefully while still providing an acceptable user experience.
- **Throttle high-volume users**: Sometimes, a small number of users create excessive load. This can have a bad impact on other users. The application might throttle the high-volume users for a certain period of time. Throttling does not imply the users are acting maliciously. The throttling starts if the number of requests exceeds the threshold.

# The testing approaches for resiliency

Testers have to test how the end-to-end workload performs under failure conditions that only occur intermittently, there are two types as follows:

- **Fault injection testing**: This is one way of testing the resiliency of the system during failures, either by triggering actual failures or by simulating them.
- **Load testing**: There are open source as well as commercial-grade load generation tools, and through those tools load testing of the application is being insisted. Load testing is crucial for identifying failures that only happen under loads such as the backend database being overwhelmed or service throttling. Test for peak load, using production data or synthetic data that is as close to production data as possible. The goal is to see how the application behaves under real-world conditions.

# The resilient deployment approaches

Software deployment is an important facet for establishing and sustaining resiliency. After applications are deployed in production-grade servers, the software updates also can be a source for errors. Any incomplete and bad update results in system breakdown. There are a few proven deployment and update methods in order to avoid any kind of downtime. The proper checks have to be in place before deployment and subsequent updates. Deployment typically includes provisioning of various server, network, and storage resources, deploying the curated and refined application code, and applying the required and right configuration settings. An update may involve all three or a subset of the three tasks. It is therefore recommended to have a tool-assisted, automated, and idempotent process in place. There are two major concepts related to resilient deployment:

- **Infrastructure as code** is the practice of using code to provision and configure infrastructure. Infrastructure as code may use a declarative approach or an imperative approach, or a combination of both.

- **Immutable infrastructure** complies with the principle that the infrastructure should not be disturbed or modified after it has gone to production.

# The deployment patterns

**Blue-green deployment** is a technique where an update is deployed into a production environment separate from the live application. After the deployment gets validated, then switch the traffic routing to the updated version.

In the case of **canary releases**, instead of switching all traffic to the updated version, we can roll out the update to a small percentage of users, by routing a portion of the traffic to the new deployment. If there is a problem, back off and revert to the old deployment. Otherwise, route more of the traffic to the new version, until it gets 100% of the traffic.

Whatever approach is preferred, it is mandatory to make sure that we can roll back to the last-known good deployment, in case the new version is not functioning as per the expectation. Also, if errors occur, the application logs must indicate which version caused the error.

# Monitoring and diagnostics

Continuous and tools-assisted monitoring of applications is crucial for achieving resiliency. If something drags, lags, or fails, the operational team has to be informed immediately along with all the right and relevant details to consider and proceed with a correct course of action. As we all agree, monitoring a large-scale distributed system poses a greater challenge. With the overwhelming acceptance of the *divide and conquer* technique, the number of moving parts of any enterprise-scale application has grown steadily and sharply. Today, as a part of the compartmentalization, we have virtualization and containerization concepts widely accepted and adopted. The number of VMs in any IT environment is growing. Furthermore, due to the lightweight nature, the number of containers being leveraged to run any mission-critical application has escalated rapidly and remarkably. In short, monitoring bare metal servers, VMs, and containers precisely is definitely a challenge for operational teams. Also, every kind of software and hardware generates a lot of log files resulting in massive operational data. It has become common to subject all sorts of operational data to extract actionable insights. Not only are the IT systems distributed, but they are also extremely dynamic. The monitoring, measuring, and management complexities of tomorrow's data centers and server farms are consistently on the climb.

Monitoring is not the same as failure detection. For example, our application might detect a transient error and retry, resulting in no downtime. But it should also log the retry operation so that we can monitor the error rate, in order to get an overall picture of application health.

The resiliency strategy is essential to ensure the service resiliency of IT systems and business applications. As enterprises increasingly embrace the cloud model, the cloud service providers are focusing on enhancing the resiliency capability of their cloud servers, storage, and networks. Application developers are also learning the tricks and techniques fast in order to bring forth resilient applications. With the combination of resilient infrastructures, platforms, and applications, the days of the resilient IT, which is mandatory towards agile, dynamic, productive, and adaptive businesses, is not too far away.

# Resiliency realization patterns

Patterns are always a popular and peerless mechanism for unearthing and articulating competent solutions for a variety of recurring problems. We will look at a host of promising and proven design patterns for accomplishing the most important goal of resiliency.

## Circuit breaker pattern

The circuit breaker pattern can prevent an application from repeatedly trying an operation that is likely to fail. The circuit breaker wraps the calls to a service. It can handle faults that might take a variable amount of time to recover from when connecting to a remote service or resource. This can improve the stability and resiliency of an application.

**The problem description**—Remote connectivity is common in a distributed application. Due to a host of transient faults such as slow network speed, timeouts, the service unavailability, or the huge load on the service, calls to remote application services can fail. These faults, being transient, typically correct themselves after a short period of time. The retry pattern strategy suggests that a robust cloud application can handle these transient faults easily in order to meet up the service requests.

However, there can also be situations wherein the faults are due to bigger issues. The severity levels vary from temporary connectivity loss to the complete failure of the service due to various reasons and causes. Here, it is illogical to continuously retry to establish the broken connectivity. Instead, the application has to understand and accept the situation to handle the failure in a graceful manner.

Suppose the requested service is very busy, then there is a possibility for the whole system to break down.

Generally, an operation that invokes a service is configured to implement a timeout and to reply with a failure message if the service fails to respond within the indicated time period. However, this strategy could cause many concurrent requests to the same operation to be blocked until the timeout period expires. These blocked requests might hold critical system resources such as memory, threads, database connections, and so on. Finally, the resources could become exhausted, causing failure of other associated and even unrelated system components. The idea is to facilitate the operation to fail immediately and only to attempt to invoke the service again if it is likely to succeed. The point here is to set up a timeout intelligently because a shorter timeout might help to resolve this problem but the shorter timeout may cause the operation to fail most of the time.

**The solution approach**—The solution is the proven circuit breaker pattern, which can prevent an application from repeatedly trying to execute an operation that's likely to fail. This allows it to continue without waiting for the fault to be fixed or wasting CPU cycles while it determines that the fault is long lasting. The circuit breaker pattern also enables an application to detect whether the fault has been resolved. If the problem appears to have been fixed, the application can try to invoke the operation.

The retry pattern enables an application to retry an operation in the expectation that it will succeed. On the other hand, the circuit breaker pattern prevents an application from performing an operation that is likely to fail. An application can combine these two patterns by using the retry pattern to invoke an operation through a circuit breaker. However, the retry logic should be highly sensitive to any exceptions returned by the circuit breaker and abandon retry attempts if the circuit breaker indicates that a fault is not transient. Also, a circuit breaker acts as a proxy for operations that might fail. The proxy should monitor the number of recent failures that have occurred, and use this information to decide whether to allow the operation to proceed, or simply return an exception immediately. The proxy can be implemented as a state machine with the following states:

- **Closed**: This is the original state of the circuit breaker. Therefore, the circuit breaker sends requests to the service and a counter continuously tracks the number of recent failures. If the failure count goes above the threshold level within a given time period, then the circuit breaker switches to the *open* state.
- **Open**: In this state, the circuit breaker opens up and immediately fails all requests without calling the service. The application instead has to make use of a mitigation path such as reading data from a replica database or simply returning an error to the user. When the circuit breaker switches to the open state, it starts a timer. When the timer expires, the circuit breaker switches to the half-open state.

- **Half-open**: In this state, the circuit breaker lets a limited number of requests go through to the service. If they succeed, the service is assumed to be recovered and the circuit breaker switches back to the original closed state. Otherwise, it reverts to the open state. The half-open state prevents a recovering service from suddenly being inundated with a series of service requests.

The circuit breaker pattern ensures the system's stability while the system slowly yet steadily recovers from a failure and minimizes the impact on the system's performance. It can help to maintain the response time of the system by quickly rejecting a request for an operation that is likely to fail rather than waiting for the operation to time out. If the circuit breaker raises an event each time, it changes the state. This information can be used to monitor the health of the part of the system protected by the circuit breaker or to alert an administrator when a circuit breaker trips to the open state.

The pattern is highly customizable and can be adapted according to the type of the possible failure. For example, it is possible to use an increasing timeout timer to a circuit breaker. We can place the circuit breaker in the open state for a few seconds initially and if the failure hasn't yet been resolved, then increase the timeout to a few minutes, and so on. In some cases, rather than the open state returning a failure and raising an exception, it could be useful to return a default value that is meaningful to the application.

In summary, this pattern is used to prevent an application from trying to invoke a remote service or access a shared resource if this operation is highly likely to fail. This pattern is not:

- For handling access to local private resources in an application, such as an in-memory data structure
- As a substitute for handling exceptions in the business logic of your applications

The circuit breaker pattern is becoming very common with microservices, emerging as the most optimized way of partitioning massive applications and presenting applications as an organized collection of microservices.

# Bulkhead pattern

**The problem description**—cloud applications typically comprise multiple and inter-linked services. A service can run on different and distributed services as service instances. There can be multiple requests from multiple consumers for each of those service instances. When the consumer sends a request to a service that is misconfigured or not responding, the resources used by the client's request may not be freed in a timely manner.

As requests to the service continue incessantly, those resources may soon be exhausted. The resources occupied include the database connection. The ultimate result is that any request to other services of the cloud application gets impacted. Eventually, the cloud application may not be available to the consumer. This is the case with other consumers too. In short, a large number of requests originating from one client may exhaust available resources in the service. This is the cascading effect and this pattern comes in handy in surmounting this issue.

**The solution approach**—the solution is to smartly partition service instances into different groups, based on consumer load and availability requirements. This design helps to isolate failures, and allows sustaining service functionality for some consumers, even during a failure. A consumer can also partition resources, to ensure that resources used to call one service don't affect the resources used to call another service. For example, choosing different connection pools for different services is a workable option. Thus, the collapse of one connection pool does not stop other connections.

The benefits of this pattern include the following:

- This isolates service consumers and services from cascading failures. This isolation firmly prevents an entire solution from going down.
- The instance-level isolation helps to retain the other instances of the services. Thus, the service availability is guaranteed and similarly, other services of the application continue to deliver their assigned functionality.
- This helps to identify the demands of consuming applications and accordingly allows deploying services that offer a different **Quality of Service** (**QoS**). That is, a high-priority consumer pool can be configured to use high-priority services.

In summary, any sort of failures in one subsystem can sometimes cascade to other components resulting in the system breakdown. To avoid this, we need to partition a system into a few isolated groups, so that any failure in one partition does not percolate to others. Containerization in conjunction with polyglot microservices is an overwhelming option for having partitioned and problem-free systems.

# Compensating transaction pattern

This is a transaction that undoes the effects of another completed transaction. In a distributed system, it can be very difficult to achieve strong transactional consistency. Compensating transactions are a way to achieve consistency by using a series of smaller and individual transactions that can be undone at each step.

**The problem description**—a typical business operation consists of a series of separate steps. While these steps are being performed, the overall view of the system state might be inconsistent, but when the operation has completed and all of the steps have been executed, the system should become consistent again. A challenge in the eventual consistency model is how to handle a step that has failed. In this case, it might be necessary to undo all of the work completed by the previous steps in the operation. However, the data can't simply be rolled back because other concurrent instances of the application might have changed it. Even in cases where the data hasn't been changed by a concurrent instance, undoing a step might not simply be a matter of restoring the original state. This mandates the application of various business-specific rules. If an operation that implements eventual consistency spans several heterogeneous data stores, undoing the steps in the operation will require visiting each data store in turn. The work performed in every data store must be undone reliably to prevent the system from remaining inconsistent.

In a **service-oriented architecture** (**SOA**) environment, an operation could invoke an action in a service and cause a change in the state held by that service. To undo the operation, this state change must also be undone. This can involve invoking the service again and perform another action that reverses the effects of the first.

**The solution approach**—the solution is to implement a compensating transaction. The steps in a compensating transaction must undo the effects of the steps in the original operation. A compensating transaction might not be able to simply replace the current state with the state the system was in at the start of the operation because this approach could overwrite changes made by other concurrent instances of an application. Instead, it must be an intelligent process that takes into account any work done by concurrent instances. This process will usually be application specific, driven by the nature of the work performed by the original operation.

A common approach is to use a workflow to implement an eventually consistent operation that requires compensation. As the original operation proceeds, the system records information about each step and how the work performed by that step can be undone. If the operation fails at any point, the workflow rewinds back through the steps it has completed and performs the work that reverses each step.

It is recommended to use this pattern only for operations that must be undone if they fail. If possible, design solutions to avoid the complexity of requiring compensating transactions.

## Health endpoint monitoring pattern

**The problem description**—applications and their services need to be continuously monitored to gain a firm grip on their availability and performance levels and patterns. Monitoring services running in off-premises, on-demand, and online environments are quite difficult compared to any on-premises services. There are many factors that affect cloud-hosted applications, such as network latency, the performance and availability of the underlying compute and storage systems, and the network bandwidth between them. The service can fail entirely or partially due to any of these factors. Therefore, we must verify at regular intervals that the service is performing correctly.

**The solution approach**—we need to do health monitoring by sending requests to an endpoint on the application. The application should perform the necessary checks and return an indication of its status. A health-monitoring check typically combines two factors:

- The assigned checks performed by the application or service in response to the request to the health verification endpoint
- The analysis of the results by the health-monitoring tool that performs the health verification check.

There are several parameters and conditions being checked by a health-monitoring tool in order to completely and concisely understand the state of the application.

It is also useful to run these checks from different on-premises or hosted locations to measure and compare response times. As customers are geographically distributed, the checks have to be initiated and implemented from those locations that are close to customers.

Another point is to expose at least one endpoint for the core services that the application uses and another for lower priority services. This allows different levels of importance to be assigned to each monitoring result. Also, it is good to consider exposing more endpoints such as one for each core service for additional monitoring granularity. Increasingly, health-verification checks are being done on the database, storage, and other critical services. The uptime and response time decide the quality of applications.

This pattern is extremely useful for checking the health condition of websites, web and mobile applications, and cloud-hosted applications.

## Leader election pattern

**The problem description**—a typical cloud application has many tasks working in a coordinated manner. These tasks could all be instances running the same code and requiring access to the same resources, or they might be working together in parallel to perform the individual parts of a complex calculation. The task instances might run separately for much of the time, but it might also be necessary to coordinate the actions of each instance to ensure that they don't conflict, cause contention for shared resources, or accidentally interfere with the work that other task instances are performing.

For example, cloud systems guarantee scalability through scale-up or scale-out. In the case of scale-out (horizontal scaling), there can be multiple instances of the same task/service. Each instance serves different users. If these instances write to a shared resource, then it is necessary to coordinate their actions to prevent each instance from overwriting the changes made by the others. Similarly, if the tasks are performing individual elements of a complex calculation in parallel, the results need to be duly aggregated to give the final answer. The task instances are all peers, so there isn't a natural leader that can act as the coordinator or aggregator.

**The solution approach**—a single task instance should be elected to act as the leader, and this instance should coordinate the actions of the other subordinate task instances. If all of the task instances are running the same code, they are each capable of acting as the leader. Therefore, the election process must be managed carefully to prevent two or more instances taking over the leader role at the same time. The system must provide a robust mechanism for selecting the leader. This method has to cope with events such as network outages or process failures. In many solutions, the subordinate task instances monitor the leader through some type of heartbeat method or by polling. If the designated leader terminates unexpectedly, or a network failure makes the leader unavailable to the subordinate task instances, it's necessary for them to elect a new leader. This is like choosing a cluster head in a sensor mesh.

This pattern performs best when the tasks in a distributed application, such as a cloud-hosted solution, need careful coordination and there is no natural leader. It is prudent to avoid making the leader a bottleneck in the system. The purpose of the leader is to coordinate the work of the subordinate tasks, and it doesn't necessarily have to participate in this work itself—although it should be able to do so if the task isn't elected as the leader.

## Queue-based load leveling pattern

Applications may experience sudden spikes in traffic, which can bombard backend systems. If a backend service cannot respond to requests quickly enough, it may cause requests to queue (back up), or it can cause the service to throttle the application. To avoid this, we can use a queue as a buffer. When there is a new work item, instead of calling the backend service immediately, the application queues a work item to run asynchronously. The queue acts as a buffer that smooths out peaks in the load.

**The problem description**—for arriving at competent and composite applications that are business-centric and process-aware, cloud applications ought to interact with one another. The services can be locally available or accessible remotely. Various enthusiastic software developers bring modern applications and provide them for worldwide subscribers for a small fee, or sometimes for free. Similarly, there are **independent software vendors** (**ISVs**) contracting with hosted service providers to run their software to be found and bound. That is, various cloud services have to connect and collaborate with many others in order to be right and relevant to their consumers. In this intertwined environment, if a service is subjected to intermittent heavy loads, it can potentially cause performance or reliability issues. The predictability of the number of service users at a particular time is also a tough affair. Thus, static capacity planning is out of the discussion. *Dynamism* is the new buzzword in the IT landscape.

As indicated previously, an application can be segmented into multiple services. Each service can be run in different containers as separate instances. That is, multiple instances of a service can be run in an IT environment. In the service world, everything is API-enabled in order to be found and leveraged by other services. A service can be used by many tasks concurrently. A service could be part of the same application as the tasks that use it or it could be provided by a third-party service provider. For example, the service can be a resource service, such as a cache or a storage service.

A service might experience peaks in demand that cause it to overload and be unable to respond to requests in a timely manner. Flooding a service with a large number of concurrent requests can also result in the service failing if it's unable to handle the contention these requests cause.

**The solution approach**—it is suggested to refactor the solution and introduce a queue between the task and the service. The task and the service run asynchronously. The task posts a message containing the data required by the service to a queue. The queue acts as a buffer, storing the message until it is retrieved by the service. The service retrieves the messages from the queue and processes them. Requests from a number of tasks, which can be generated at a highly variable rate, can be passed to the service through the same message queue.

This pattern provides the following benefits:

- It can help to maximize availability of applications because delays arising in services will not have an immediate and direct impact on the application, which can continue to post messages to the queue even when the service is not available or is not currently processing messages
- It can help to maximize scalability because both the number of queues and the number of services can be varied to meet demand
- It can help to control costs because the number of service instances deployed only has to be adequate to meet the average load rather than the peak load

# Retry pattern

**Problem description**—we have discussed a bit about this pattern previously. Applications are distributed in the sense that the application components are being expressed and exposed as a service and delivered from different IT environments (private, public, and edge clouds). Typically, the IT spans across embedded, enterprise, and cloud domains. With the fast-growing device ecosystem, the connectivity has grown to various devices at the ground level. That is the reason that we very often hear, read, and even experience **cyber-physical system** (**CPS**). Also, the enterprise-scale applications (both legacy and modern) are accordingly modernized and moved to cloud environments to reap the distinct benefits of the cloud idea. However, certain applications, due to some specific reasons, are being kept in enterprise servers/private clouds. With embedded and networked devices joining in the mainstream computing, edge/fog devices are being enabled to form kind of ad hoc clouds to facilitate real-time data capture, storage, processing, and decision-making. The point to be noted here is that application services ought to connect to other services in the vicinity and remotely hold services over different networks. Faults can occur, stampeding the application calls. As articulated previously, there are temporary faults impacting the service connectivity, interaction, and execution. However, these faults are typically self-correcting and if the action that triggered a fault is repeated after a suitable delay, the connectivity and accessibility may go through.

**The solution approach**—in cloud environments, transient faults are common and an application should be designed to handle them elegantly and transparently. This minimizes the effects faults can have on the business tasks the application is duly performing. If an application detects a failure when it tries to send a request to a remote service, it can handle the failure using the following strategies:

- **Cancellation**: If the fault indicates that the failure is not temporary (that is, persists for more time), or is likely to be unsuccessful if repeated, the application should cancel the operation and report an exception.
- **Retry**: If the specific fault reported is unusual or rare, it might have been caused by some unusual circumstances such as a network packet getting corrupted while it was being transmitted. In this case, the application can try again as the subsequent request may attain the required success.
- **Retry after delay**: If the fault is caused by one of the more commonplace connectivity or busy failures, then the application has to wait for some time and try again.

The application should wrap all attempts to access a remote service in code that implements a retry policy matching one of the strategies listed previously. Requests sent to different services can be subjected to different policies. Some vendors provide libraries that implement retry policies, where the application can specify the maximum number of retries, the time between retry attempts, and other parameters. An application should log the details of faults and failing operations. This information is useful to operators. If a service is frequently unavailable or busy, it's often because the service has exhausted its resources. We can reduce the frequency of these faults by scaling out the service. For example, if a database service is continually overloaded, it might be beneficial to partition the database and spread the load across multiple servers.

In conclusion, having understood the strategic significance that the resiliency, robustness, and reliability of next-generation IT systems are to fulfil the various business and people needs with all the QoS and **Quality of Experience** (**QoE**) traits and tenets enshrined and etched, IT industry professionals, academic professors, and researchers are investing their talents, treasures, and time to unearth scores of easy-to-understand and useful techniques, tips, and tricks to simplify and streamline software and infrastructure engineering tasks. I ask the readers to visit `https://docs.microsoft.com/en-us/azure/architecture/patterns/category/resiliency` for further reading.

# Summary

Both legacy and modern applications are remedied to be a collection of interactive microservices. Microservices can be hosted and run inside containers. There can be multiple instances for each microservice. Each container can run a microservice instance. Thus, in a typical IT environment, there can be hundreds of physical machines (also called **bare metal servers**). Each physical machine, in turn, is capable of running hundreds of containers. Thus, there will be tens of thousands of containers. The management and operational complexities are therefore bound to escalate. This pattern comes handy in successfully running microservice-hosted containers. There are technologies, such as Istio and Linkerd, for ensuring the resiliency of microservices. This resiliency ultimately ensures the application's reliability. Together with software-defined cloud infrastructures, reliable applications ensure the reliability of cloud environments for hosting and delivering next-generation business workloads.

The forthcoming chapters will discuss the various software-defined cloud application design and deployment patterns.

# 11

# Software-Defined Clouds - the Architecture and Design Patterns

The cloud paradigm is on the fast track. There are a number of game-changing advancements in the cloud space, and hence the adoption rate of the cloud concept is consistently on the rise. Legacy applications are being accordingly modified and migrated to cloud environments (private, public, and hybrid). There is a bevy of enabling tools for cloud migration, integration, orchestration, brokerage, deployment, delivery, and management propping up the strategically relevant cloud journey. There are integrated processes, best practices, key guidelines, evaluation metrics, highly synchronized platforms, and so on to make the cloud idea penetrative, participative, and pervasive. Furthermore, there is a growing family of architectural and design patterns for producing optimized cloud environments and applications. This chapter is specially prepared for throwing sufficient light on the patterns emerging and evolving in the cloud landscape. How those patterns are being used in order to simplify and streamline the cloud adoption will be articulated in this chapter.

# Reflecting the cloud journey

With the evolutionary and revolutionary traits of cloud computing, there is a major awareness on the charter of data center optimization and transformation. The acts of simplification and standardization for achieving IT industrialization are garnering a lot of attention these days. The various IT resources, such as memory, disk storage, processing power, and I/O consumption are critically and cognitively monitored, measured, and managed towards their utmost utilization. The pooling and sharing of IT solutions and services are being given paramount importance towards the strategic IT optimization. Also, having a dynamic pool of computing, storage, and network resources enable IT service providers, as well as enterprise IT teams to meet any kinds of spikes and emergencies in resource needs for their customers and users.

The mesmerizing cloud paradigm has, therefore, become the mainstream concept in IT today. And its primary and ancillary technologies are simply flourishing due to the overwhelming acceptance and adoption of cloud theory. The cloudification movement has blossomed these days and most of the IT infrastructures and platforms, along with business applications, are being methodically remedied to be cloud-ready in order to reap all the originally envisaged benefits of the cloud idea. The new buzzword of **Cloud Enablement** has caught up fast and there are collaborative and concerted initiatives to unearth techniques, best practices, patterns, metrics, products and other enablers to understand the cloud fitment and to modernize IT assets and software applications to be cloud-oriented for the ensuing era of knowledge.

Even with all the unprecedented advancements in the cloud landscape, there are a plenty of futuristic and fulsome opportunities and possibilities for IT professors and professionals to take the cloud idea to the next level in its long journey. Therefore, the concept of **software-defined cloud environments** (**SDCEs**) is gaining a lot of accreditation these days. Product vendors, cloud service providers, system integrators, and other principal stakeholders are keen to have such advanced and acclaimed environments for their clients, customers, and consumers. The right and relevant technologies for the realization and sustenance of software-defined cloud environments are fast maturing and stabilizing, and hence the days of SDCEs are not too far away.

In conclusion, the various technological evolutions and revolutions are remarkably enhancing the quality of human lives across the world. Carefully choosing and smartly leveraging the fully matured and stabilized technological solutions and services towards the much-anticipated and acclaimed digital transformation is necessary for a safe, smarter, and sustainable planet.

# Traditional application architecture versus cloud application architecture

As articulated previously, we are heading towards SDCEs that comprise **software-defined compute** (SDC), **software-defined storage** (SDS), and **software-defined networking** (SDN). The virtualization and containerization enable software-defined clouds towards workload-aware and elastic infrastructures. The maneuverability or programmability, consumability, accessibility, sustainability, and simplicity of software defined clouds are greater compared to the inflexible infrastructures. There are new patterns (architecture and design) being introduced for cloud infrastructures and applications. The emergence of the cloud idea has brought in telling impacts on the application architectures. In this section, we will discuss how cloud application architectures differ from the legacy application architectures.

## The traditional application architecture

Most of the traditional applications were built using the matured three-tier application architecture patterns (presentation tier, middle tier, and data tier). Each tier runs on a dedicated server and is statically configured with the hostnames and IP addresses of the servers of the other tiers it depends on. These applications have very little knowledge of the infrastructure they run on. If the infrastructure changes or fails, these applications also fail. Therefore, these applications are mandated to be hosted on highly reliable and resilient networks and servers. When the load (user and/or data) gets increased, these applications could not automatically scale up or scale out. Scaling is instead done manually through the purchase and installation of additional server machines. This is a time-consuming process, aggravating the complexity. Load balancers are being put up in front of web and application servers in order to bring in the much-needed auto-scaling. However, with the conventional application architecture, the real scalability could not be achieved.

# The cloud architecture

As articulated previously, the concept of virtualization has brought in a programmable infrastructure. That is, the scalability of applications is being achieved through the inherent elasticity of infrastructural components. The resource utilization with the conscious adoption of virtualized infrastructures has gone up significantly. The virtualization idea has penetrated into every infrastructural module these days creating waves of innovations, disruption, transformations, and optimizations for IT environments. That is not only server virtualization, but also network virtualization, storage virtualization, service virtualization, database virtualization, and so on, are being systematically realized in order to bring the originally envisaged virtual, open, flexible, and adaptive IT infrastructures that are intrinsically ready to anticipate and act upon business changes and challenges. The smart usage of cloud technologies, tools, and tips are resulting in business-aware IT infrastructures. The tool ecosystem is steadily growing in order to automate tasks, such as resource provisioning, software deployment, infrastructure monitoring, measurement and management, orchestration, security, governance, and so on.

The cloud management layer also provides user interfaces for developers and architects to programmatically design and build the infrastructure they need to run their applications. The cloud APIs provided by the cloud management layer also allows applications to take control of the infrastructure they run on. The cloud applications can dynamically scale up or scale down, deploying or removing application components on the infrastructure. The game-changing concept of virtualization and containerization has made it possible to have programmable infrastructures. That is, hardware modules are being expressed as services to be found, used, and even composed. The hardware programming is becoming real these days with the cloud movement. Such a scenario is enabling the days of flexible and maneuverable infrastructures that guarantee workload-awareness, productivity, and high utilization.

# The cloud application architecture

As indicated previously, the traditional applications need to be accordingly modernized in order to reap the cloud benefits. The scalability and other requirements of modern applications need to be inscribed within the application. There are certain programming languages and architectural patterns in order to attach **non-functional requirements** (**NFRs**) into applications. The traditional applications typically use a single database to store all the application information. This database provides the information stored in it to various application clients (users as well as other application components) on a need basis. However, with the data explosion, the conventional databases could be scaled up.

The scale-out (horizontal scalability) of SQL databases is beset with a lot of challenges. However, due to the massiveness of cloud infrastructures, cloud databases have to be designed and developed using new database types, such as NoSQL, NewSQL, in-memory, and in-database databases for data storage and analytics. The object storage is very popular in the cloud era. Every cloud service provider is betting and banking on cloud storage to meet the fast-rising storage needs. Apart from databases, there are enterprise-grade data warehouses and data lakes. Data storage options are on the rise. Cache storage is one such which is garnering a lot of support. Furthermore, there are distributed filesystems, such as HDFS for big data storage and analytics. There are database abstractions on filesystems in order to provide several possibilities for developers, database administers, and businesses. Besides, there are backup and archival options for data in order to ensure data and **disaster recovery** (**DR**). The following diagram vividly illustrates where and how cloud application architecture deviates and differs from traditional applications. With multi-channel, device, media, and modal clients, cloud applications are being methodically advanced:

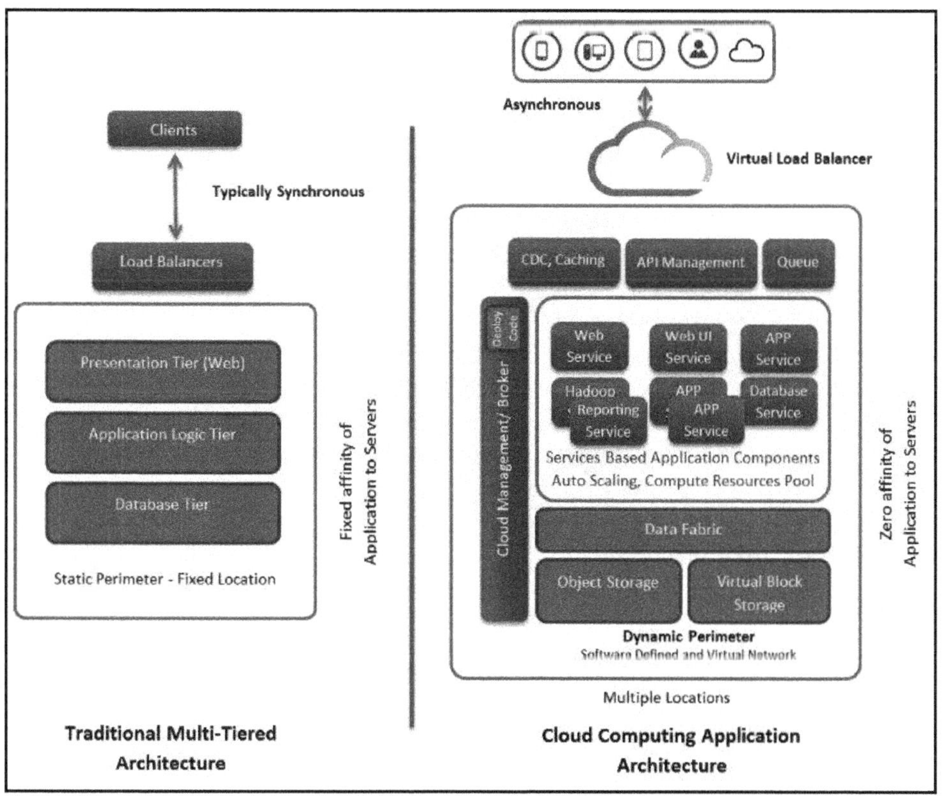

Cloud applications are distinctively different. Increasingly, applications are service-oriented with the faster maturity and stability of service-oriented applications. In the recent past, there have been further refinements and optimizations in order to tackle newer requirements. Polyglot programming is picking up. That is, there are several programming and script languages to bring forth cloud applications as a dynamic collection of microservices. In addition, there is a myriad of database management systems. Each database type is appropriate for certain application needs. Thus, the flexibility of linking multiple technologies, tools, and techniques for bringing forth cloud applications is being facilitated by the most popular **microservices architecture** (**MSA**). With the widespread adoption of containers (Docker) as the highly optimized application holder and runtime environment, there is a sharp convergence of multiple technologies in order to enable agile and accelerated software engineering, deployment, delivery, and management. Multi-container and multi-host cloud applications spearheaded and shepherded by the containerization movement is the talk of the town.

In short, with the cloud embarkation, the widely deliberated **quality of service** (**QoS**) and **quality of experience** (**QoE**) factors and facets of next-generation applications are being accurately accomplished. The cloud infrastructures are being astutely tweaked in order to tackle brewing challenges at the infrastructure level. Another prominent design requirement is to design cloud applications to handle the latency issue. That is, fault tolerance is one such important factor for cloud applications, platforms, and infrastructures. The cascading effect of failures and bugs needs to be arrested in the budding stage itself. As clouds are being built on commodity servers, the failure rate is quite high. Besides, there can be network congestion/outages, resource conflicts, request contentions, and IOPS challenges for storage systems. Furthermore, there can be hardware and software failures. Cloud environments are becoming hugely complicated, and hence viable complexity mitigation and moderation techniques need to be in place. Systems have to come out gracefully from any kind of constricting and cascading issues and limitations. A popular design pattern to address latency and failure is the request/response queue, where requests and responses are stored in queues. Also, cloud and application interfaces have to be highly intuitive, informative, and instructive. The user experience has to be maintained even if cloud resources and assets are not responsive.

# Cloud integration patterns

There are a number of noteworthy advancements happening in the field of cloud computing. Patterns are of much use for the complicated and growing subject of cloud computing. Patterns are being unearthed with the aim of simplifying the deeper understanding and adoption of the cloud paradigm. A number of prospective areas, such as **Infrastructure as a Service (IaaS)**, **Platform as a Service (PaaS)**, **Software as a Service (SaaS)**, **Business Process as a Service (BPaaS)**, and so on, in the cloud space are being revisited to bring forth fresh and competent patterns. There are special patterns being readied for cloud application development. There are cloud integration platforms (**Integration Platform as a Service (IPaaS)**) for enabling a kind of seamless and spontaneous integration among different and distributed cloud applications and data sources. Therefore, integration-specific patterns are being formed and articulated.

These days, the cloud concept has matured and stabilized beautifully in order to give hundreds of novel services for business houses and individuals. On the data services side, we have a **Database as a Service (DBaaS)**, **Data Warehouse as a Service (DWaaS)**, **Data Lake as a Service (DLaaS)**, and so on. Newer databases have emerged in order to tackle a different set of requirements. We all hear, read, and even experience NoSQL and NewSQL databases. Then there are in-memory databases and **in-memory data grids (IMDGs)**. Data analytics happens within the database itself, and hence we read about in-database analytics. Similarly, the cloud environments are being prescribed as the best-in-class for various other application domains. All kinds of operational, transactional, and analytical applications are being hosted, managed, and delivered through cloud infrastructures and platforms. Then there are new-generation web, mobile, gaming, wearable, embedded, enterprise, IoT, and blockchain applications getting developed, deployed, and delivered through cloud infrastructures and instances. Everything is being expressed and exposed as a service, and undoubtedly, clouds are the elegant, enabling, and execution environments. In the recent past, we have heard more about cloud orchestration, configuration, deployment, migration, governance, and brokerage services. **DevOps** is another buzzword in the cloud landscape. With such a legion of cloud services, there is a need expressed widely by many and a collective call to create beneficial cloud-centric patterns for fulfilling various IT and business capabilities.

# Tier/Layer-based decomposition

The complex functionality of this application is divided into multiple discrete, easily manageable, and loosely-coupled components. Each component is ordained to do one task well. This partition or componentization of application functionality results in a logical decomposition of the original application. These logically separated components run in multiple tiers of a server cluster, and this kind of segmentation is done at the infrastructure level.

# Process-based decomposition

The next is process-based decomposition. Enterprise-grade and complicated applications are typically process-centric. Herein, we can bring in process-based decomposition. Each process internally comprises many tasks that need to be performed in a certain sequence. Each task is done separately and aggregated in the desired order to get the application functionality. There are plenty of automated tools for enabling such decomposition, automation, and finally, orchestration.

# Pipes-and-filters-based decomposition

The third decomposition type is pipes-and-filters-based decomposition, that focuses on the data-centric processing of an application. Each filter provides a certain function that is performed on input data and produces output data after processing. Multiple filters are interconnected with pipes, that is, through messaging.

These layering and decomposition patterns aptly decompose the application into logical layers, enabling independent deployment and horizontal scalability. The layering of application and cloud infrastructures is being touted as the most vital need for developing, deploying, and delivering next-generation distributed applications.

# Service messaging pattern

**Messages as the unifying mechanism**: Messages are the most unifying factor among disparate and distributed cloud services. The goals of cloud service integration get accomplished through message passing. The following section lists and details the various service message patterns. Service messages can be authenticated, routed, enriched, filtered, secured, and composed in order to fulfill the expectations of federated clouds. Cloud intermediation and remediation can be performed through smart messaging. Path-breaking and hitherto unknown services can be built and deployed through the innovative usage of service messages.

How do different distributed and decentralized cloud services find, bind, access, and collaborate with one another in a loosely coupled as well as decoupled manner?

| | |
|---|---|
| **Problem** | Services can be run on one virtual machine or in different virtual machines within a cloud environment. Services can even be run on geographically distributed clouds. There are public, private, and hybrid clouds and there are a few communication protocols. The conventional protocols induce a possibility of tight coupling between services. These, in turn, impose certain restrictions on service reusability, testability, and modifiability. |
| **Solution** | Going forward, loose coupling and decoupling are the viable and valuable solution approaches. As even loose coupling has some constraints, decoupling among services is being touted as the most promising solution, and messaging is the way forward for establishing decoupled communication, which in turn eliminates the drawbacks of traditional communication methods |
| **Impacts** | Messaging technology brings a few QoS concerns, such as reliable delivery, security, performance, and transactions. |

**Problem**: Different applications usually use different languages, data formats, and technology platforms. When one application (component) needs to exchange information with another one, the format of the target application has to be respected. Sending messages directly to the target application results in a tight coupling of sender and receiver since format changes directly affect both implementations. Also, direct sending tightly couples the applications regarding the addresses by which they can be reached.

Cloud applications and services communicate using a variety of protocols. **Remote procedure call** (**RPC**), **remote method invocation** (**RMI**), **Windows Communication Framework** (**WCF**), and service protocols (SOAP and REST over HTTP) are some of the leading mechanisms for cloud resources to connect and collaborate purposefully. However, all these lead to a kind of tight coupling, which in turn becomes a hitch or hurdle for services to seamlessly and spontaneously cooperate to achieve bigger and better things. The urgent requirements are therefore loose coupling and decoupling. How can cloud application services communicate remotely through messages while being loosely coupled regarding their location and message format? Another brewing requirement is to enable complete decoupling among services.

**Solution**: The context is that distributed applications or their service components exchange information using messaging. Messaging comes as a viable alternative communication scheme that does not rely on persistent connections. Instead, messages are being transmitted as independent units of communication routed through the underlying infrastructure. That is, simply connect applications through an intermediary; the message-oriented middleware hides the complexity of addressing and availability of communication partners as well as supports transformation of different message formats.

Communication partners can now communicate through messages without the need to know the message format used by the communication partner or the address by which it can be reached. The message-oriented middleware provides message channels (also referred to as **queues**). Messages can be written to these queues or read from them. Additionally, the message-oriented middleware contains components that route messages between channels to intended receivers, as well as handle message format transformation.

The messaging framework must have the following capabilities:

- Guaranteeing the delivery of each message or guaranteeing a notification of failed deliveries
- Securing message contents beyond the transport
- Managing state and context data across a service activity
- Transmitting messages efficiently as part of real-time interactions
- Coordinating cross-service transactions

Without these types of extensions in place, the availability, reliability, and reusability of services will impose limitations that can undermine the strategic goals associated with cloud-hosted services.

## Messaging metadata pattern

| | |
|---|---|
| **Problem** | Services generally work in a stateless fashion. That is, they do not store any state data in order to facilitate the next course of action. As the message is the intermediary in order to empower different and distributed services to interact together towards accomplishing business transactions and operations, they need to have or carry all the state data (metadata). |
| **Solution** | The content encapsulated within the message envelope, therefore, has to be supplemented with activity-specific metadata that can be interpreted and processed separately at runtime. |
| **Impacts** | The interpretation and processing of messaging metadata adds to runtime performance overhead and increases service activity design complexity. |

**Problem**: In the traditional method, the state and context data about the current service interaction are placed in the memory. However, in a service environment, services are being designed, developed, and deployed as stateless resources to be highly reusable. Therefore, the messages that are being transmitted among services are being mandated to carry the right and relevant data to initiate the correct actions sequentially to accomplish the business process tasks.

**Solution**: As messages carry the state data, business rules, and even processing instructions, services can be designed in a very generic manner. The service complexity will come down, the reusability level will go up, modifiability will be easier, enrichment will be quicker, and so on.

Though the overall memory consumption is reduced by avoiding a persistent binary connection, the performance demands are increased by the requirement for services to interpret and process metadata at runtime. Agnostic services especially can impose more runtime cycles, as they may need to be outfitted with highly generic routines capable of interpreting and processing different types of messaging headers so as to participate effectively in multiple composition activities. Due to the prevalence and range of technology standards that intrinsically support and are based on messaging metadata, a wide variety of sophisticated message exchanges can be designed. This can lead to overly creative and complex message paths that may be difficult to govern and evolve.

# Service agent pattern

How can event capturing and processing logic be separated and governed independently?

| | |
|---|---|
| **Problem** | Service composition (orchestration and choreography) can become large and inefficient, especially when required to invoke granular capabilities across multiple services. |
| **Solution** | Event-driven service composition is emerging as an important factor for crafting composite services. Event-driven logic can be easily deferred to event-driven programs that don't require explicit invocation, thereby reducing the size and performance strain of service composition. |
| **Impacts** | The complexity of composition logic increases when it is distributed across services, and event-driven agents and reliance on service agents can further tie inventory architecture to proprietary vendor technology. |

**Problem**: Decomposition and composition are the highly successful methods for simplifying and streamlining software engineering. In a service environment, applications are built by assembling a variety of services. In software engineering, the application to be realized is to start with a series of business processes (simple and compound) and each process, in turn, gets implemented by leveraging a number of services (process elements). That is, applications are decomposed into a collection of interoperable and interactive services and services are smartly composed to form next-generation applications.

Service composition logic consists of a series of service invocations, and each invocation enlists a service to carry out a segment of the overall parent business process logic. Larger business processes can be enormously complex, especially when having to incorporate numerous *what if* conditions through compensation and exception handling subprocesses. Therefore, service composition can grow correspondingly large. Furthermore, each service invocation comes with a performance hit resulting from having to explicitly invoke and communicate with the service itself. The performance of larger compositions can suffer from the collective overhead of having to invoke multiple services to automate a single task.

**Solution**: *Separation of concerns* has been an interesting technique in software engineering. Service logic that is triggered by a predictable event can be isolated into a separate program specially designed for automatic invocation upon the occurrence of the event. This reduces the amount of composition logic that needs to reside within services and further decreases the number of service invocations required for a given composition.

Event-driven agents provide yet another layer of abstraction to which multiple service compositions can form dependencies. Although the perceived size of the composition may be reduced, the actual complexity of the composition itself does not decrease. Composition logic is simply more decentralized as it now also encompasses service agents that automatically perform portions of the overall task.

# Intermediate routing pattern

How can dynamic runtime factors affect the path of a message?:

| | |
|---|---|
| **Problem** | The larger and more complex a service composition is, the more difficult it is to anticipate and design for all possible runtime scenarios in advance, especially with asynchronous and messaging-based communication. |
| **Solution** | Message paths can be dynamically determined through the use of intermediary routing logic. |
| **Impacts** | Dynamically determining a message path adds layers of processing logic and correspondingly can increase performance overhead. Also, the use of multiple routing logic can result in overly complex service activities. |

**Problem**: A service composition can be viewed as a chain of point-to-point data exchanges between composition participants. Collectively, these exchanges end up automating a parent business process. The message routing logic (the decision logic that determines how messages are passed from one service to another) can be embedded within the logic of each service in a composition. This allows for the successful execution of predetermined message paths. However, there may be unforeseen factors that are not accounted for in the embedded routing logic, which can lead to unanticipated system failures. For example:

- The destination service a message is being transmitted to is temporarily (or even permanently) unavailable
- The embedded routing logic contains a *catch-all* condition to handle exceptions, but the resulting message destination is still incorrect
- The originally planned message path cannot be carried out, resulting in a rejection of the message from the service's previous consumer

Alternatively, there may simply be functional requirements that are dynamic in nature and for which services cannot be designed in advance.

**Solution**: Generic and multi-purpose routing logic can be abstracted so that it exists as a separate part of the architecture in support of multiple services and service compositions. Most commonly, this is achieved through the use of event-driven service agents that transparently intercept messages and dynamically determine their paths.

This pattern is usually applied as a specialized implementation of a service agent. Routing-centric agents required to perform dynamic routing are often provided by messaging middleware and are fundamental components of **enterprise service bus** (**ESB**) products. These types of out-of-the-box agents can be configured to carry out a range of routing functions. However, the creation of custom routing agents is also possible and not uncommon, especially in environments that need to support complex service compositions with special requirements.

# State messaging pattern

How can services remain stateless while contributing to stateful interactions?:

| | |
|---|---|
| **Problem** | When services are required to maintain state information in memory between message exchanges with consumers, their scalability can be compromised, and they can become a performance bottleneck on the surrounding infrastructure. |
| **Solution** | Instead of retaining the state data in memory, its storage is temporarily delegated to messages. |
| **Impacts** | This pattern may not be suitable for all forms of state data and should the message be lost, any state information they carried may be lost as well. |

**Problem**: Services are sometimes required to be involved in runtime activities that span multiple message exchanges. In these cases, a service may need to retain state information until the overarching task is completed. This is especially common with services that act as composition controllers. By default, services are often designed to keep this state data in memory so that it is easily accessible and essentially remains alive for as long as the service instance is active. However, this design approach can lead to serious scalability problems and further runs contrary to the service statelessness design principle.

**Solution**: Instead of the service maintaining state data in memory, it moves the data to the message. During a conversational interaction, the service retrieves the latest state data from the next input message.

There are two common approaches for applying this pattern, both of which affect how the service consumer relates to the state data. The consumer retains a copy of the latest state data in memory and only the service benefits from delegating the state data to the message. This approach is suitable for when this pattern is implemented using WS-Addressing, due to the one-way conversational nature of **endpoint references** (**EPRs**).

Both the consumer and the service use messages to temporarily offload state data. This two-way interaction with state data may be appropriate when both consumer and service are actual services within a larger composition. This technique can be achieved using custom message headers.

When following the two-way model with custom headers, messages that are lost due to runtime failure or exception conditions will further lose the state data, thereby placing the overarching task in jeopardy. It is also important to consider the security implications of state data placed on the messaging layer. For services that handle sensitive or private data, the corresponding state information should either be suitably encrypted and/or digitally signed, and it is not uncommon for the consumer to not gain access to protected state data.

Furthermore, because this pattern requires that state data be stored within messages that are passed back and forth with every request and response, it is important to consider the size of this information and the implications on bandwidth and runtime latency. As with other patterns that require new infrastructure extensions, establishing inventory-wide support for state messaging will introduce cost and effort due to the necessary infrastructure upgrades.

# Service callback pattern

How can a service sync up asynchronously with its consumers?:

| | |
|---|---|
| **Problem** | When a service needs to respond to a consumer request for the issuance of multiple messages or when service message processing requires a large amount of time, it is often not possible to communicate synchronously. |
| **Solution** | A service can require that consumers communicate with it asynchronously and provide a callback address to which the service can send response messages. |
| **Impacts** | Asynchronous communication can introduce reliability concerns and can further require that surrounding infrastructure be upgraded to fully support the necessary callback correlation. |

**Problem**: When service logic requires that a consumer request is responded to with multiple messages, a standard request-response messaging exchange is not appropriate. Similarly, when a given consumer request requires that the service perform prolonged processing before being able to respond, synchronous communication is not possible without jeopardizing scalability and reliability of the service and its surrounding architecture.

**Solution**: Services are designed in such a manner that consumers provide them with a callback address at which they can be contacted by the service at some point after the service receives the initial consumer request message. Consumers are furthermore asked to supply correlation details that allow the service to send an identifier within future messages so that consumers can associate them with the original task.

# Service instance routing

How can consumers contact and interact with service instances without the need for proprietary processing logic?:

| | |
|---|---|
| **Problem** | When required to repeatedly access a specific stateful service instance, consumers must rely on the custom logic that more tightly couples them to the service. |
| **Solution** | The service provides an instance identifier along with its destination information in a standardized format that shields the consumer from having to resort to custom logic. |
| **Impacts** | This pattern can introduce the need for significant infrastructure upgrades, and when misused can further lead to overly stateful messaging activities that can violate the service statelessness principle. |

**Problem**: There are cases where a consumer sends multiple messages to a service and the messages need to be processed within the same runtime context. Such services are intentionally designed to remain stateful so that they can carry out conversational or session-centric message exchanges. However, service contracts generally do not provide a standardized means of representing or targeting instances of services. Therefore, consumer and service designers need to resort to passing proprietary instance identifiers as part of the regular message data, which results in the need for proprietary instance processing logic.

**Solution**: The underlying infrastructure is extended to support the processing of message metadata that enables a service instance identifier to be placed into a reference to the overall destination of the service. This reference (also referred to as an **endpoint reference**) is managed by the messaging infrastructure so that messages issued by the consumer are automatically routed to the destination represented by the reference. As a result, the processing of instance IDs does not negatively affect consumer-to-service coupling because consumers are not required to contain proprietary service instance processing logic. Because the instance IDs are part of a reference that is managed by the infrastructure, they are opaque to consumers. This means that consumers do not need to be aware of whether they are sending messages to a service or one of its instances because this is the responsibility of the routing logic within the messaging infrastructure.

# Asynchronous queuing pattern

How can a service and its consumers accommodate isolated failures and avoid unnecessarily locking resources?:

| | |
|---|---|
| **Problem** | When a service capability requires that consumers interact with it synchronously, it can inhibit performance and compromise reliability. |
| **Solution** | A service can exchange messages with its consumers through an intermediary buffer, allowing services and consumers to process messages independently by remaining temporally decoupled. |
| **Impacts** | There may be no acknowledgment of successful message delivery, and atomic transactions may not be possible. |

**Problem**: Synchronous communication requires an immediate response to each request, and therefore forces two-way data exchange for every service interaction. When services need to carry out synchronous communication, both service and service consumer must be available and ready to complete the data exchange. This can introduce reliability issues when either the service cannot guarantee its availability to receive the request message or the service consumer cannot guarantee its availability to receive the response to its request. Because of its sequential nature, synchronous message exchanges can further impose processing overhead, as the service consumer needs to wait until it receives a response from its original request before proceeding to its next action. Prolonged responses can introduce latency by temporarily locking both consumer and service.

Another problem forced synchronous communication can cause is an overload of services required to facilitate a great deal of concurrent access. Because services are expected to process requests as soon as they are received, usage thresholds can be more easily reached, thereby exposing the service to multi-consumer latency or overall failure.

**Solution**: A queue is introduced as an intermediary buffer that receives request messages and then forwards them on behalf of the service consumers. If the target service is unavailable, the queue acts as temporary storage and retains the message. It then periodically attempts retransmission. Similarly, if there is a response, it can be issued through the same queue that will forward it back to the service consumer when the consumer is available. While either service or consumer is processing message contents, the other can deactivate itself (or move on to other processing) in order to minimize memory consumption.

# Reliable messaging pattern

How do we enable and ensure services to interact reliably in an unreliable environment?:

| | |
|---|---|
| **Problem** | Messages need to reach the right services and should not be tampered within their path. That is, unreliable communication protocols and service environments are said to be the main barriers for service reliability. |
| **Solution** | An intermediate reliability mechanism has to be in place in order to guarantee that messages reach the right services and their integrity and confidentiality are being maintained appropriately. Also, this middleware has to guarantee message delivery. |
| **Impacts** | Using a reliability framework adds processing overhead that can affect service activity performance. It also increases composition design complexity and may not be compatible with atomic service transactions. |

**Problem**: When services are designed to activate and act through messages, there is a natural tendency for the loss of quality of service due to the stateless nature of underlying messaging protocols, such as HTTP. The binary communication protocols maintain a persistent connection until the data transmission between a sender and receiver is completed. However, with message exchanges, the runtime platform may not be able to provide feedback to the sender as to whether or not the message was successfully delivered to the target service endpoint. With more services and more network links, the complexity of service composition grows accordingly.

If the middleware infrastructure being employed is not able to guarantee reliable message delivery, then risks erupt. How can messages be exchanged while guaranteeing that messages are not lost in the case of system or communication failures? Reliability agents further manage the confirmation of successful and failed message deliveries through positive (ACK) and negative (NACK) acknowledgment notifications. Messages may be transmitted and acknowledged individually, or they may be bundled into message sequences that are acknowledged in groups (and may also have sequence-related delivery rules).

When messages are exchanged in distributed systems, errors can occur during the transmission of messages over communication links or during the processing of messages in system components. Under these conditions, it should be guaranteed that no messages are lost and that messages can be eventually recovered after a system failure.

**Solution:** The underlying infrastructure is fitted with a reliability framework that tracks and temporarily persists message transmissions and issues positive and negative acknowledgments to communicate successful and failed transmissions to message senders. Message exchange during communication partners is performed under transactional context, guaranteeing ACID behavior. In the cloud, there are several messaging systems that can be accessed as a service, such as Amazon SQS or the queue service part of Windows Azure Storage.

As articulated previously, cloud integration patterns are very vital for cloud-based distributed application development, deployment, and delivery. There are specialized adapters, connectors, drivers, and other plugins to simplify and streamline cloud integration requirements. The integration patterns are crucial for the success of the cloud paradigm.

# Cloud design patterns

This section will discuss various cloud application design patterns that are highly useful for building reliable, scalable, and secure applications in the cloud. Readers can find deeper and decisive details of the patterns on the Microsoft website: `https://docs.microsoft.com/en-us/azure/architecture/patterns/`.

# Cache-aside pattern

The gist of this pattern is to load data on demand into a cache from a data store. This pattern can improve performance and also helps to maintain consistency between data held in the cache and the data in the data store. Applications use a cache to optimize repeated access to information held in a data store. However, it is usually impractical to expect that cached data will always be completely consistent with the data in the data store.

There are many commercial caching systems providing read-through and write-through/write-behind operations. In these systems, an application retrieves data by referencing the cache. If the data is not available in the cache, it is transparently retrieved from the distant data store and added to the cache. Any modifications to data held in the cache are automatically written back to the data store as well. For caches that do not provide this functionality, it is the responsibility of the applications that use the cache to maintain the data in the cache. An application can emulate the functionality of read-through caching by implementing the cache-aside strategy. This strategy effectively loads data into the cache on demand.

Cloud application performance is often questioned by many. Hence, there is a bevy of performance enhancement techniques and tips being unearthed and promoted. This pattern is one such breakthrough solution technique in order to supply all the right and relevant information for application designers to substantially increase cloud performance.

The usage scenarios include:

- A cache doesn't provide native read-through and write-through operations
- Resource demand is unpredictable

# Circuit breaker pattern

We all know that distributed computing is the way forward for new-generation businesses. Connectivity to remote services and resources is a core requirement in distributed computing environments. Remote connectivity has the habit of failure. That is, an application is trying to get connected with a remote service or data source and is not able to get access due to some transient fault, such as slow network connection, timeouts, the resources being overloaded, temporarily unavailable, and so on. These faults typically correct themselves after a short period of time, and a robust cloud application should be prepared to overcome these by using a well-drawn strategy, such as that described by the retry pattern.

However, there may also be situations where faults occur out of unexpected events that are quite tough to anticipate. Furthermore, those faults may take a longer time to get rectified. These faults can range in severity, from a partial loss of connectivity to the complete failure of a service. In these situations, it may be pointless for an application to continually retry performing an operation that is unlikely to succeed, and instead, the application should quickly accept that the operation has failed and handle the failure accordingly.

The circuit breaker pattern can prevent an application repeatedly trying to execute an operation that is likely to fail, allowing it to continue without waiting for the fault to be rectified or wasting CPU cycles while it determines that the fault is long lasting. The circuit breaker pattern also enables an application to detect whether the fault has been resolved. If the problem appears to have been rectified, the application can attempt to invoke the operation.

The circuit breaker pattern is different from the retry pattern. The retry pattern enables an application to retry an operation with the expectation that it will succeed, but the circuit breaker pattern prevents an application from performing an operation that is likely to fail. An application may combine these two patterns by using the retry pattern to invoke an operation through a circuit breaker. However, the retry logic should be sensitive to any exceptions returned by the circuit breaker and abandon retry attempts if the circuit breaker indicates that a fault is not transient.

A circuit breaker acts as a proxy for operations that may fail. The proxy should monitor the number of recent failures that have occurred, and then use this information to decide whether to allow the operation to proceed, or simply return an exception immediately.

# Compensating transaction pattern

We all know that any business and financial transaction has to strictly fulfill the ACID properties. Steadily, transactional applications are being deployed in cloud environments. Now, in the big data era, distributed computing is becoming the mainstream computing model. NoSQL databases are very prominent and dominant these days in order to do justice to big data. Increasingly, there is an assortment of segregated yet connected data sources as well as stores to perform high-performance data access, processing, and retrieval. In this case, strong transactional consistency is not being maintained. Rather, the application should go for eventual consistency. While these steps are being performed, the overall view of the system state may be inconsistent, but when the operation has completed and all of the steps have been executed, the system should become consistent again.

A significant challenge in the eventual consistency model is how to handle a step that has failed irrecoverably. In this case, it may be necessary to undo all of the work completed by the previous steps in the operation. However, the data cannot simply be rolled back because other concurrent instances of the application may have since changed it. Even in cases where the data has not been changed by a concurrent instance, undoing a step might not simply be a matter of restoring the original state. It may be necessary to apply various business-specific rules.

Compensation has been the typical response when a transaction fails. This pattern is mainly to undo the work performed by a series of steps, which together define an eventually consistent operation if one or more of the steps fail. A compensating transaction might not be able to simply replace the current state with the state the system was in at the start of the operation because this approach could overwrite changes made by other concurrent instances of an application. Rather, it must be an intelligent process that takes into account any work done by concurrent instances. This process will usually be application-specific, driven by the nature of the work performed by the original operation.

A common approach to implementing an eventually consistent operation that requires compensation is to use a workflow. As the original operation proceeds, the system records information about each step and how the work performed by that step can be undone. If the operation fails at any point, the workflow rewinds back through the steps it has completed and performs the work that reverses each step.

# Competing consumers pattern

With the surging popularity of web-scale applications, there can be a large number of requests from different parts of the world for those applications. The user and data loads are generally unpredictable. The task/operation complexity is also unpredictable. Because of heavy loads, cloud applications find it difficult to process every request and deliver the reply within the stipulated timeline. One option is to add new server instances. There are some practical difficulties in clustered and load-balanced environments too. However, these consumers must be coordinated to ensure that each message is only delivered to a single consumer. The workload also needs to be load balanced across consumers to prevent an instance from becoming a bottleneck.

An overwhelming solution approach here is to use a messaging system (message queue or broker) in between any requesting applications/users and the processing applications. A **message-oriented middleware** (**MOM**) is a way forward for meeting a large number of concurrent consumers. This middleware approach supports asynchronous communication and processing, thereby the massive number of requests can be answered quickly.

A message queue/broker/bus is used to establish the communication channel between the application and the instances of the consumer service. The application posts requests in the form of messages to the queue and the consumer service instances receive messages from the queue and process them. This approach enables the same pool of consumer service instances to handle messages from any instance of the application. The following figure illustrates this architecture:

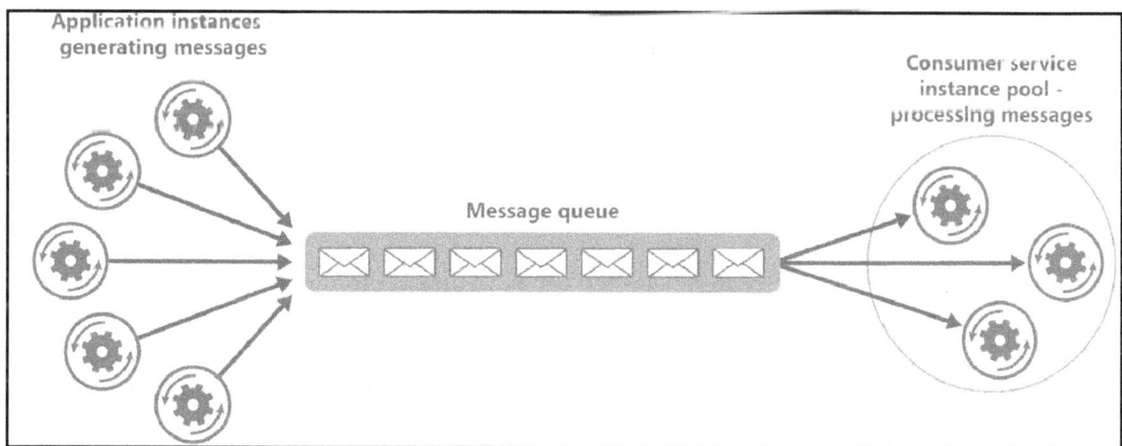


This pattern enables multiple concurrent consumers to process messages received on the same messaging channel. This pattern enables a system to process multiple messages concurrently to optimize throughput, to improve scalability and availability, and to balance the workload.

# Compute resource consolidation pattern

There are several architectural patterns, such as MVC, **service-oriented architecture** (**SOA**), **event-driven architecture** (**EDA**), **resource-oriented architecture** (**ROA**), **microservices architecture** (**MSA**), and so on, recommending the application partitioning for various benefits. However, there are occasions wherein consolidating multiple tasks or operations into a single computational unit brings forth a number of advantages.

A common approach is to look for tasks that have a similar profile concerning their scalability, lifetime, and processing requirements. Grouping these items together allows them to scale as a unit. The elasticity provided by many cloud environments enables additional instances of a computational unit to be started and stopped according to the workload. This pattern can increase compute resource utilization, and reduce the costs and management overhead associated with performing compute processing in cloud-hosted applications.

# Command and query responsibility segregation (CQRS) pattern

In traditional database management systems, both commands (updates to the data) and queries (requests for data) are executed against the same set of entities in a single data repository. These entities may be a subset of the rows in one or more tables in an RDBMS. Typically, in these systems, all **create**, **read**, **update**, and **delete** (**CRUD**) operations are applied to the same representation of the entity. Traditional CRUD designs work well when there is only limited business logic applied to the data operations. There are a few serious issues being associated with the CRUD approach, as follows:

- There may be a mismatch between the read and write representations of the data, such as additional columns or properties that must be updated correctly even though they are not required as a part of an operation
- It risks encountering data contention in a collaborative domain (where multiple actors operate in parallel on the same set of data) when records are locked in the data store, or update conflicts caused by concurrent updates when optimistic locking is used

This pattern segregates operations that read data from operations that update data by using separate interfaces. This pattern can maximize performance, scalability, and security, support evolution of the system over time through higher flexibility, and prevent update commands from causing merge conflicts at the domain level.

**The event sourcing pattern and the CQRS pattern**: CQRS-based systems use separate read and write data models. Each model is tailored to relevant tasks and often located in physically separate stores. When used with event sourcing, the store of events is the write model, and this is the authoritative source of information. The read model of a CQRS-based system provides materialized views of the data as highly denormalized views. These views are tailored to the interfaces and display requirements of the application and this helps to maximize both display and query performance.

Using the stream of events as the write store, rather than the actual data at a point in time, avoids update conflicts on a single aggregate and maximizes performance and scalability. The events can be used to asynchronously generate materialized views of the data that are used to populate the read store.

# Event sourcing pattern

Most applications work with data, and the overwhelming approach is for the application to maintain the current state of the data by updating it as users work with the data. For example, in the CRUD model, a data process reads data from the store, makes some modifications to it, and updates the current state of the data with the new values. The problem with this approach is that performing update operations directly against a data store may degrade performance and responsiveness. The scalability aspect may also be affected. In a collaborative environment, there are many concurrent users, and hence there is a high possibility for data update conflicts because the update operations take place on a single item of data.

The events are persisted in an event store that acts as the source of truth about the current state of the data. The event store typically publishes these events so that consumers can be notified and can handle them if needed. Consumers could, for example, initiate tasks that apply the operations in the events to other systems. The point to be noted here is that application code that generates the events is decoupled from the systems that subscribe to the events.

The solution is to use an append-only store to record the full series of events that describe actions taken on data in a domain, rather than storing just the current state so that the store can be used to materialize the domain objects. This pattern can simplify tasks in complex domains by avoiding the requirement to synchronize the data model and the business domain. This pattern improves performance, scalability, and responsiveness. Furthermore, it provides consistency for transactional data and maintains full audit trails and history that may enable compensating actions.

# External configuration store pattern

The majority of application runtime environments include configuration information that is held in files deployed with the application, located within the application folders. In some cases, it is possible to edit these files to change the behavior of the application after it has been deployed. However, in many cases, changes to the configuration require the application to be redeployed, resulting in unacceptable downtime and additional administrative overhead.

Local configuration files also limit the configuration to a single application, whereas, in some scenarios, it would be useful to share configuration settings across multiple applications. Managing changes to local configurations across multiple running instances of the application is another challenge. The approach is to store the configuration information in external storage. This moves configuration information out of the application deployment package to a centralized location. This pattern can provide opportunities for easier management and control of configuration data, and for sharing configuration data across applications and application instances.

# Federated identity pattern

There are many applications hosted by different cloud service providers. Predominantly, there are email and social networking applications. These applications are being subscribed to and used by many people from different parts of the world. Typically, users need to memorize and use different credentials for accessing each of these customer-centric, collaborative, and cloud applications. Managing multiple credentials is a tough assignment. The solution is to implement an authentication mechanism that can use the proven concept of federated identity. This is accomplished by separating the aspect of user authentication from the application logic code and delegating the authentication requirement to a trusted and third-party identity service provider. The trusted identity providers can authenticate users on behalf of application service providers. The identity service providers have, for example, a Microsoft, Google, Yahoo!, or Facebook account. This identity pattern can simplify development, minimize the requirement for user administration, and improve the user experience of the application.

# Gatekeeper pattern

Cloud applications need to be protected from malicious users. Also, some cloud applications are provided by multiple cloud service providers. Users are therefore in a position to choose one service provider according to his or her terms. Cloud broker is a new software product enabling users to zero down the appropriate cloud service providers. Thus, a kind of gatekeeper software solution is needed to act as a broker between application clients and application services, validate and sanitize requests, and pass requests and data between them. This can provide an additional layer of security, and limit the attack surface of the system.

This pattern minimizes the risk of clients gaining access to sensitive information and services. This gateway solution contributes as a façade or a dedicated task that interacts with clients and then hands off the request perhaps through a decoupled interface to the hosts or tasks that'll handle the request.

# Application health monitoring pattern

Cloud applications ought to fulfill the various service and operational expectations that are formally contracted through an SLA agreement. Hence, it is pertinent to have a competent health monitoring system to precisely and minutely monitor the functioning and health of cloud applications, database systems, middleware solutions, and so on. The health check is, therefore, an important factor in ensuring the agreed quality parameters. The monitoring is not an easy thing to do. Cloud environments are hugely complicated due to the massive scale, such as increasingly software-defined, federated, and shared. The way forward here is to put a health monitoring system in place in order to send requests to an endpoint on the application so as to capture the right and relevant data to act upon with clarity and confidence.

# Leader election pattern

Cloud applications are extremely complicated yet sophisticated. Multiple instances of cloud applications can run in a cloud environment. Similarly, different components of an application can run on clouds. The tasks might be working together in parallel to perform the individual parts of a complex calculation.

The task instances might run separately for much of the time, but it might also be necessary to coordinate the actions of each instance to ensure that they don't create any sort of conflict, cause contention for shared resources, or accidentally interfere with the work that other task instances are performing. So, there is a need for adept coordinator software; each action has to be coordinated.

A single task instance should be elected to act as the leader, and this instance should coordinate the actions of the other subordinate task instances. If all of the task instances are running the same code, then one instance can act as the leader. However, the election of the leader has to be done smartly. There has to be a robust mechanism in place for leader selection. This selection method has to cope with the events, such as network outages or process failures. In many solutions, the subordinate task instances monitor the leader through some type of heartbeat method, or by polling. If the designated leader terminates unexpectedly, or a network failure makes the leader unavailable to the subordinate task instances, it is necessary for them to elect a new leader.

# Materialized views pattern

When storing data, developers and database administrators are more concerned about how the data is stored. They are least bothered about how the data will be read. The chosen data storage format is usually closely related to the format of the data, requirements for managing data size and data integrity, and the kind of store in use. For example, when using a NoSQL document store, the data is often represented as a series of aggregates, each containing all of the information for that entity. However, this can have a negative effect on queries. When a query only needs a subset of the data from some entities, such as a summary of orders for several customers without all of the order details, it must extract all of the data for the relevant entities in order to obtain the required details.

To support efficient querying, a common solution is to generate, in advance, a view that materializes the data in a format suited to the required results set. The materialized view pattern describes generating prepopulated views of data in environments where the source data isn't in a suitable format for querying, where generating a suitable query is difficult, or where query performance is poor due to the nature of the data or the data store.

These materialized views, which only contain data required by a query, allow applications to quickly obtain the information they need. In addition to joining tables or combining data entities, materialized views can include the current values of calculated columns or data items, the results of combining values or executing transformations on the data items, and values specified as part of the query. A materialized view can even be optimized for just a single query. This pattern can help support efficient querying and data extraction, and improve application performance.

# Pipes and filters pattern

An application is mandated to perform a variety of tasks of varying complexity on the information that it receives, processes, and presents. Traditionally, a monolithic application is produced to perform this duty. However, the monolithic architecture and approach are bound to fail in due course due to various reasons (modifiability, replaceability, reusability, substitutability, simplicity, accessibility, sustainability, scalability, and so on). Therefore, the proven and potential technique of *divide and conquer* has become a preferred approach in the field of software engineering. **Aspect-oriented programming** (**AOP**) is a popular method. There are other decomposition approaches.

Furthermore, some of the tasks that the monolithic modules perform are functionally very similar, but the modules have been designed separately. Some tasks might be compute intensive and could benefit from running on powerful hardware, while others might not require such expensive resources. Also, additional processing might be required in the future, or the order in which the tasks are performed by the processing could change.

Considering all these limitations, the recommended approach is to break down the processing required for each stream of tasks into a set of separate components (filters), and each component (filter) is assigned to perform a single task. By standardizing the format of the data that each component receives and sends, these filters can be combined together into a pipeline. This helps to avoid duplicating code and makes it easy to remove, replace, or integrate additional components if the processing requirements change. This unique pattern can substantially improve performance, scalability, and reusability by allowing task elements that perform the processing to be deployed and scaled independently.

# Priority queue pattern

Applications can delegate specific tasks to other services to perform them, such as some background processing or the integration with third-party or external applications or services. Employing middleware solutions to perform those intermediary jobs has been a widely followed activity. The message queue is a prominent one in enterprise and cloud environments to realize tasks, such as intermediation, enrichment, filtering and funneling, and so on. Here, the order of the requests is not important. That is, giving a kind of priority for a particular task is being insisted in certain scenarios. These requests should be processed earlier than lower priority requests that were sent previously by the application.

A queue is usually a **first-in, first-out** (**FIFO**) structure, and consumers typically receive messages in the same order that they were posted to the queue. However, some message queues support priority messaging. The application posting a message can assign a priority and the messages in the queue are automatically reordered so that those with a higher priority will be received before those with a lower priority. This pattern is useful in applications that offer different service-level guarantees to individual clients.

# Queue-based load leveling pattern

Cloud applications may sometimes be subjected to heavy loads (user and data). Applications are being designed and developed accordingly and are made to run on clustered environments in order to meet sudden or seasonal spikes. When applications are under heavy loads, the application performance may go down. Especially, some crucial tasks that are the part of the application may come under heavy bombardment.

The viable approach is to refactor the application and introduce a queue between the task and the service. The idea here is that the task and the service run asynchronously. The task posts a message containing the data required by the service to a queue. The queue acts as a buffer, storing the message until it's retrieved by the service. The service retrieves the messages from the queue and processes them. Requests from a number of tasks, which can be generated at a highly variable rate, can be passed to the service through the same message queue. This pattern can help to minimize the impact of peaks in demand on availability and responsiveness for both the task and the service.

# Retry pattern

Applications are spread across multiple clouds, across continents, countries, counties, and cities. Not only public clouds are being leveraged as the application deployment, delivery, and management platform, but also mission-critical, high-performance, and secure applications and data stores are being deployed and delivered through private clouds. Some enterprises continue with traditional IT environments. Applications literally have to connect, access and use nearby, as well as remotely held, applications or databases often as a part of successfully fulfilling any brewing business process requirements. But applications connecting and collaborating with other applications in the vicinity or in off-premise environments are not that straightforward.

There can be transient faults in the way of accessing other applications. The network connectivity, the failure of the requested applications due to overload, the temporary unavailability of the application, and so on, are being touted as the challenges for applications talking to one another over any network.

Applications ought to be designed in such a way that they try again to connect and proceed with their task-fulfillment. If the application request fails, the application can wait and make another attempt. If necessary, this process can be repeated with increasing delays between retry attempts, until some maximum number of requests has been attempted. The delay can be increased incrementally or exponentially, depending on the type of failure and the probability that it'll be corrected during this time.

# Runtime reconfiguration pattern

Traditionally, a static configuration has been the way for any application. If there is a need to make changes in the configuration, then the application has to be shut down and restarted after incorporating the configuration changes. Now in the web world, the downtime is not liked. Therefore, there is a need for a workable technique to achieve runtime configuration. That is, while the application is still running and delivering its service, the required configuration has to be brought in. The application has to immediately consider the changes and act on that. Similarly, the application has to convey the configuration changes to all its components.

The success of this pattern squarely depends on the features available in the application runtime environment. Typically, the application code will respond to one or more events that are raised by the hosting infrastructure when it detects a change to the application configuration. This is usually the result of uploading a new configuration file, or in response to changes in the configuration through the administration portal or by accessing an API.

The source code that handles the configuration change events can examine the changes and apply them to the components of the application. These components have to detect and react to the changes. The components should use the new values so that the intended application behavior can be achieved. This helps to maintain availability and minimize downtime.

# Scheduler agent supervisor pattern

Enterprise-class applications are slated to do many tasks in sequence or in parallel. Each task is performed by a microservice architecture that can comfortably run inside Docker containers. Some tasks may have to connect and collaborate with remote application services or third-party services. As stated previously, the remote connectivity is beset with a number of challenges because there are other components contributing to the remote connectivity and access. Now, complex applications are being simplified through process flows comprising control as well as data flows. That means an application has to orchestrate all the steps/services in order to ensure its capability for consumers. In the distributed computing arena, all services have to play their unique role and deliver value to their application. If anyone fails to transact, then the retry pattern can be leveraged. If that also fails to take off, then the entire operation has to be canceled.

The solution is to use the scheduler agent supervisor pattern that skillfully orchestrates all the right and relevant steps to finish the expected job. This orchestration software solution manages all the participating and contributing steps in a resilient and rewarding fashion in distributed work environments. The scheduler, which is the principal component of the scheduler agent supervisor, arranges for the steps that make up the task to be executed and orchestrates their operation. These steps can be combined into a pipeline or workflow. The scheduler is responsible for ensuring that the steps in this workflow are performed in the right order. The self-recovery of services is being termed as one of the paramount properties of new-generation software services.

# Sharding pattern

In the big data world, data stores need to store a humongous amount of data. Due to the extraordinary growth of data collection, storage, processing, and analysis, there arise several operational and management challenges including storage space. Furthermore, interactive querying and data retrieval are also difficult.

Data is becoming big data that in turn promises big insights. Batch and real-time processing of big data are also mandated by business houses. The new normal is poly-structured data. Thus, massive amounts of multi-structured data structurally and operationally challenge the traditional SQL database management systems. That is, in the new world order, NoSQL and NewSQL databases are very popular. The prime reason for this new trend is the faster maturity and stability of sharding, which is unambiguously partitioning big databases into smaller and manageable databases. These segregated databases are being run in different and distributed commoditized server machines. The sharding intrinsically supports horizontal scalability (scale out), whereas the SQL databases support the scale up (vertical scalability). The runtime incorporation of schema changes is also being supported by NoSQL databases.

This pattern has the following benefits:

- The database system can scale out by adding further shards running on additional storage nodes
- A system can use off-the-shelf hardware rather than specialized and expensive computers for each storage node
- You can reduce contention and improve performance by balancing the workload across shards
- In the cloud, shards can be located physically close to the users that'll access the data

# Throttling pattern

The load on a cloud application typically varies over time based on the number of active users or the types of activities they are performing. There can be more users during business hours. During festivities, more users will come to electronic commerce and e-business applications. There might also be sudden and unanticipated bursts in activity. If the processing requirements of the system exceed the capacity of the resources that are available, it will suffer from poor performance and can even fail. If the system has to meet an agreed level of service, such kinds of failures could be unacceptable.

There are several strategies and workarounds for tackling this important challenge. A viable solution is to use resources only up to a limit and then throttle them when the assigned limit is reached. An alternative strategy to auto-scaling is to allow applications to use resources only up to a limit, and then throttle them when this limit is reached.

The system should monitor how it's using resources so that, when usage exceeds the threshold, it can throttle requests from one or more users. This will enable the system to continue functioning and meet any **service level agreements** (**SLAs**) that are in place.

# Workload distribution pattern

IT resources and business workloads are sometimes subjected to heavy usage. When the number of users goes up sharply, the problems, such as performance degradation, reduced availability, reliability, and so on, can arise and choke the system. There are a few interesting solutions being recommended for overcoming these issues. Horizontal scalability and the leverage of load balancers in front of web, application, and database servers are being widely and wisely implemented in order to fulfill the agreed SLAs between the providers and the users. Workload instances need to be distributed to tackle heavy user loads.

# Cloud workload scheduler pattern

The cloud workload scheduler automates, monitors, and controls the workload throughout the cloud infrastructure. This automation usually manages hundreds of thousands of workloads per day from a single point of control. The cloud scheduler could also be an orchestration engine automatically scheduling workloads. The scheduler must be provided, the security level required by the workload.

There are fresh design patterns for accelerating cloud application design. While the cloud idea is progressing fast and is seeing a surging popularity, there can be additional design patterns. We will come across exclusive and elegant patterns for cloud brokerage services and orchestration capabilities. There will be focuses on unearthing competent solutions and patterns for deeper and decisive automation of cloud activities. **Self-service** is another buzzword being given extreme importance so that clouds become business-friendly and business-aware. Serverless computing is another pragmatic and popular topic of deeper study and research in the cloud arena. Docker-enabled containerization is the mainstream topic of deliberations and discourses, and in the near future, we will hear more about containerized cloud infrastructures, platforms, and application workloads. Highly beneficial design patterns will emerge and empower next-generation cloud applications.

# Cloud reliability and resilience patterns

The reliability or dependability of cloud applications has to be ensured through technologically sound solutions. Cloud infrastructures too have to be accordingly empowered to be reliable. The second aspect is cloud resilience. As business workloads and IT platforms are being increasingly modernized and moved to cloud environments, the need for cloud resilience has gone up drastically. Viable mechanisms are being worked by cloud professionals in order to boost the confidence of people on the cloud paradigm. Having competent patterns for those recurring requirements and common problems is one sure way for tackling the QoS and QoE factors. This section is dedicated to illustrating prominent cloud reliability and resilience patterns.

# Resource pooling pattern

For scalability purposes, IT resources have to be pooled in order to provide additional resources on a need basis. The auto-scaling capability can be realized when the appropriate resources are pooled. The challenge here is that of manually establishing and maintaining the level of required synchronicity across a collection of shared resources. Any kind of variance or disparity among shared IT resources potentially can lead to inconsistency and sometimes result in risky operations. The solution is to get identical IT resources and pool them to be leveraged when necessary. The key resources include **bare metal** (**BM**) servers, **virtual machines** (**VMs**), and containers. Furthermore, the fine-grained resources include memory, storage, processing cores, I/O, and so on. There are several monitoring, measurement, and management tools in place for resource provisioning, replication, and utilization.

# Resource reservation pattern

Capacity planning is an important factor in realizing highly optimized IT infrastructures and resources for meeting the various tricky demands of applications. If not properly done, then there is a possibility of getting into the issue of resource constraints. When more cloud consumers try to access a shared IT resource, which does not have the capacity to fulfill the consumers' processing needs, then this condition of resource constraint creeps in. The result may be performance degradation or even the request may not be fulfilled at all. Depending on how IT resources are designed for shared usage and depending on their available levels of capacity, concurrent access can lead to a runtime exception condition called **resource constraint**.

A resource constraint is a condition that occurs when two or more cloud consumers have been allocated to share an IT resource that does not have the capacity to accommodate the entire processing requirements of the cloud consumers. As a result, one or more of the consumers will encounter a sort of degraded performance or be rejected altogether.

The solution is primarily dynamic capacity planning and to have an IT resource reservation system in order to protect cloud service consumers. This reservation system guarantees a minimum amount of IT resources for each cloud consumer.

# Hypervisor clustering pattern

Any kind of IT infrastructures and resources can go down at any point in time. It is good practice to expect failure of IT systems in order to design IT systems in a better-informed fashion. Now hypervisors, alternatively touted as **virtual machine monitors** (**VMMs**), represent an additional abstraction in order to emulate underlying hardware. The issue is that hypervisors too are liable failure. When hypervisors fail, then all the virtual machines on them are bound to fail. Thus, it becomes critical for the high-availability of hypervisors.

A high-availability hypervisor cluster is created to establish a group of hypervisors that span physical servers. As a result, if a given physical server or hypervisor becomes unavailable, hosted virtual servers can be moved to another physical server or hypervisor.

# Redundant storage pattern

Cloud storage is gaining a lot of attention these days because of the enhanced flexibility and extreme affordability. There are block storage, object storage, file storage, and so on. Storage devices are also subject to failure and disruption due to a variety of causes including network connectivity issues, storage controller failures, general hardware failure, and security breaches. When a cloud storage system gets compromised, the result will be unprecedented. A secondary cloud storage device is incorporated into a system that synchronizes its data with the data in the primary cloud storage device. When the primary device fails, a storage service gateway diverts requests to the secondary device automatically to fulfill the **business continuity** (**BC**) requirements.

This pattern fundamentally relies on the resource replication mechanism to keep the primary cloud storage device synchronized with secondary cloud storage devices. Cloud service providers may put secondary storage appliances in a geographically different location for ensuring data and disaster recovery.

# Dynamic failure detection and recovery pattern

Cloud environments comprise a large number of IT infrastructures in a consolidated and centralized fashion in order to fulfill the variable IT needs of worldwide consumers. Cloud environments ensure self-service capability. The major portions of the IT infrastructures are virtualized, shared, and commoditized servers, storage appliances, and networking solutions. The failure rate is quite high and hence failure detection proactively is turning out to be a key requirement for successfully running cloud environments.

A resilient watchdog system has to be established to monitor, measure, and respond to a wider range of predefined failure scenarios. This system is further able to notify and escalate certain failure conditions that it cannot automatically solve itself.

# Redundant physical connection for virtual servers pattern

A virtual server is connected to an external network through a virtual switch uplink port. If the uplink fails (due to cable disconnection, port failure, or any other accidents and incidents), the virtual server becomes isolated and disconnects from the external network. One or more redundant uplink connections are established and positioned in standby mode. A redundant uplink connection is available to take over as the active uplink connection whenever the primary uplink connection becomes unavailable or experiences failure conditions.

Cloud environments promise to have some unique capabilities, such as infrastructure elasticity and application scalability. These enhance cloud availability. There are techniques and patterns being experimented in order to guarantee cloud reliability/dependability. Furthermore, resiliency is being given the sufficient thrust by cloud professors so that the goals of reliability and resiliency out of cloud assets can be met quite easily and quickly.

# Cloud security patterns

As widely accepted and articulated, the issue of cloud security has been the principal barrier for individuals, institutions, and innovators towards readily and confidently leveraging the cloud environments; especially the public clouds for hosting and delivering their enterprise-grade, business-critical, and high-performance applications and databases (customer, corporate, and confidential). In this section, we will discuss some of the prominent cloud security patterns in order to empower cloud security architects, consultants, and evangelists with all the right details.

# Cryptographic key management system pattern

Cryptography is the unique approach to ensuring data security. Encryption and decryption are the two major components of this mathematical theory. Keys are generated and stored securely and are used fluently for securing data while in transit, rest, and being used by software applications. The worry here is how to safely and securely keep the keys generated. If the keys are somehow lost, then the encrypted data cannot be decrypted. Therefore, the industry recommends having a **cryptographic key management system** (**CKMS**), which consists of policies, procedures, components, and devices that are used to protect, manage, and distribute cryptographic keys and certain specific information, called **metadata**. A CKMS includes all devices or subsystems that can access an unencrypted key or its metadata. Encrypted keys and their cryptographically protected metadata can be handled by computers and transmitted through communication systems and stored in media that are not considered to be part of a CKMS.

# Virtual private network (VPN) pattern

In the connected world, the internet is the cheap, open, flexible and public communication infrastructure. The **virtual private network** (**VPN**) is a network that uses a public telecommunication infrastructure, such as the internet, to provide consumers with secure connections to their organization's network. The VPN ensures privacy through security procedures and tunneling protocols, including the **layer two tunneling protocol** (**L2TP**). Data is encrypted at the sending end for transmission and decrypted at the receiving end, as shown in the following figure:

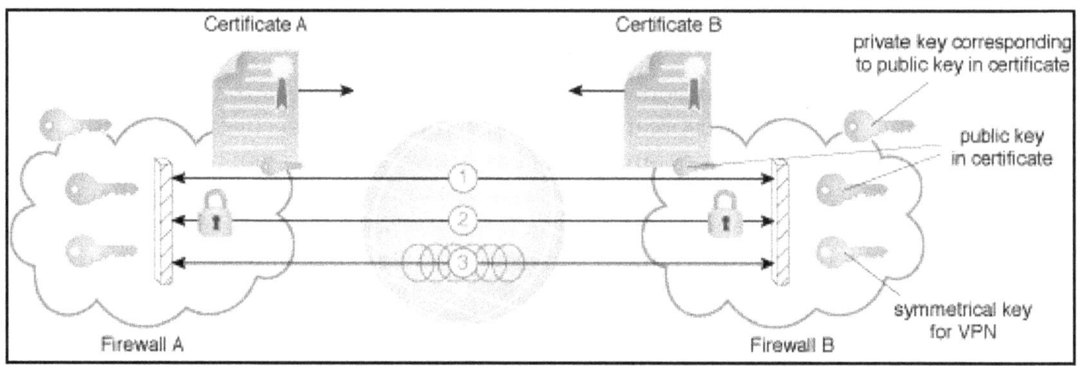


The figure shows two firewalls establishing a VPN between two clouds. They first exchange each other's certificates and use asymmetric encryption to securely exchange keying material to establish efficient symmetric key encryption. IPsec is a framework of open standards for private communications over public networks. It is a network layer security control that is used to create the VPN.

# Cloud authentication gateway pattern

Cloud consumers are compelled to support multiple authentications, communication, and session protocols in order to access and use various cloud services. An authentication service authenticates cloud consumers to access cloud services. The authentication service uses the diverse protocols required by cloud service providers for authenticating cloud consumers.

An **authentication gateway service** (**AGS**) can be established as a reverse proxy frontend between the cloud consumer and the cloud resource. This AGS intercepts and terminates the consumer's encrypted network connection and authenticates the cloud consumer. Furthermore, it authenticates itself and the consumer to the cloud provider and then proxies all communication between the two.

# In-transit cloud data encryption pattern

Data security is an important component for the continued growth of the cloud concept. With data analytics gaining widespread significance, the need for secure data capture, transmission, exchange, persistence, and usage has grown greatly. Data transmission networks, data management systems, data analytics platforms, data storage appliances, filesystems, and so on, are the prominent ingredients for the next-generation knowledge era. Encryption is the primary mechanism for securing data interchanged between data sources and servers.

# Cloud storage device masking pattern

As illustrated previously, data security is essential for boosting the confidence of cloud consumers on cloud-based enterprise applications and databases. Authorized data access is the foremost thing for ensuring utmost data security. Data stored in a shared cloud environment can be vulnerable to many security risks, threats, vulnerabilities, and holes. An LUN masking mechanism can enforce defined policies at the physical storage array in order to prevent unauthorized cloud consumers from accessing a specific cloud storage device in a shared cloud environment.

# Cloud storage data at rest encryption pattern

Data stored in a cloud environment requires security against access to the physical hard disks forming the cloud storage device. The solution is to leverage any encryption mechanism supported by the physical storage arrays to automatically encrypt data stored on the disks and decrypt data leaving the disks.

# Endpoint threat detection and response pattern

Endpoint security refers to the protection of an organization's network when accessed through remote devices, such as smartphones, tablets, and laptops. **Endpoint threat detection and response** (**ETDR**) focuses on the endpoint as opposed to the network. It is recommended to leverage integrated security tools in order to understand the security holes of edge devices in order to strengthen the cloud networks and servers.

# Threat intelligence processing pattern

The act of analytics is becoming pervasive these days. Operational, behavioral, security, log, and performance data of IT environments are consciously collected and subjected to a variety of investigations. Deeper and decisive analytics on security-related data emits a lot of useful information for security analysts, architects, and advisors. The extracted insights come in handy in proactively putting appropriate security mechanisms in place in order to ward off any kind of security attacks and exploitations.

A threat intelligence system can be put in place to receive and process external intelligence feeds as well as to gain intelligence gained from analyzing attacks internally. The details received and collected can be fed into security-enablement systems, such as security information and **event management systems** (SIEMs), **network forensics monitors** (NFM), **endpoint threat detection and response systems** (ETDRs), **intrusion detection and protections systems** (IDPSs), and so on. Also, those sensitive details can be shared across cloud security operational teams to enable them to ponder and proceed with the best course of action.

# Cloud denial of service (DoS) protection pattern

Cloud DoS attacks are multifaceted and prevent consumers of cloud services from accessing their cloud resources. A cloud DoS protection service has to be incorporated into the security architecture to shield the cloud provider from DoS attacks. A network DoS protection service updates the **domain name service** (**DNS**) to route all cloud provider traffic through the protection service, which filters attack traffic and routes only legitimate traffic to the cloud provider. Alternately, the cloud provider can route traffic to a DoS protection service when experiencing an attack, or create its own DoS protection service. Considering the insistence for unbreakable and impenetrable cloud security solutions, fresh cloud security patterns are being unearthed by security experts and researchers. In the future, there will be a few more security-related patterns.

# Summary

Patterns have been the principal enabling tools for strategic and simplified design and engineering of all kinds of business and social systems. The IT domain too has embraced the proven and potential concept of patterns in order to overcome the inherent limitations of IT systems and services engineering. This chapter is specially prepared for describing the various architectural and design patterns being unearthed and articulated by various cloud computing professionals. The readers can find the right amount of detail for each of the patterns. With the cloud paradigm on the fast track, there is a need for detailing various and recently articulated cloud patterns and their correct details. This chapter comes in handy for interested IT people in understanding cloud-related patterns.

# Bibliography

The cloud patterns registry: `http://cloudpatterns.org/`

Cloud design patterns by Microsoft: `https://docs.microsoft.com/en-us/azure/architecture/patterns/`

Cloud computing patterns: `http://www.cloudcomputingpatterns.org/`

Cloud design patterns by Amazon Web Services: `http://en.clouddesignpattern.org/index.php/Main_Page`

Cloud architecture patterns: `http://shop.oreilly.com/product/0636920023777.do`

# 12
# Big Data Architecture and Design Patterns

Big data is the digital trace that gets generated in today's digital world when we use the internet and other digital technology. Whatever we do digitally leaves a massive volume of data. Interestingly, we can do far smarter analysis with those traces and so, therefore, make smarter decisions and much more. For example, when you log in to any website it shows an advertisement for a product that you searched or browsed earlier, even if it was on an entirely different website. So by showing the product that you are interested in, regardless of the specific product selling site, the results of big data analysis and a smart way of selling means that the end user might like the product and be more likely to buy it.

This chapter intends to introduce readers to the more common big data architectural patterns. Some brief details on the core parts of big data, its core principles, and characteristics are outlined, including analytics principles, big data workload patterns, and optimal decision-making patterns.

Please be aware that this chapter is a mere introduction to the patterns. Readers need to refer to other materials (references sections) that are available online and offline.

# The four V's of big data

Big data has many definitions and many different implementations across various sectors. However, there are four common elements of any big data definition, which are popularly referred to as the V's of big data. They are as follows:

- **Velocity**: This refers to the speed of data accumulation
- **Volume**: This refers to the scale of data or the phase that data storage grows
- **Variety**: This refers to the diversity of the data, such as structured, semi-structured, unstructured, and so on
- **Veracity**: This refers to collected data's accuracy and its reflection of facts

The latest addition to the V's group is **value**. This refers to our ability and needs to turn accumulated data into things of value. That is not just business value, but it can also be any significant added value for social, medical, and common causes.

# Big data analysis and technology concepts

Let's start with the technology prerequisites for big data analysis, and then we will cover the life cycle of big data analysis. The prerequisites are:

- Flexible architectures, that supports various data types and patterns
- Upstream use of analytics for data relevance optimization
- Advanced analytics and real-time visualization to accelerate actions and understandings
- Collaborative approaches for aligning stakeholders

## Data analysis life cycle

Big data analysis life cycle provides a step-by-step methodology for organizing the data activities and tasks related to data acquiring, processing, analyzing and repurposing. The following are the stages of data analysis life cycle with a brief overview of each of them.

- **Data discovery**: Learn the business domain, frame the business problems as analytics challenges, and strategize and formulate initial hypotheses to start learning data.

- **Data preparations**: Data **Extraction**, **Load**, and **Transform** (**ELT**) and data **Extraction**, **Transform**, and **Load** (**ETL**) should be used to become familiarized with the data.
- **Model planning**: Determine and formulate techniques, workflows, and best practices to follow. Learn about relationships between variables and choose the most suitable methods.
- **Model building**: Develop datasets for testing, training, and production deployments. Evaluate tools to run the models and suggests additional tools, workflows, and execution environments, if needed.
- **Communicate results**: Identify critical findings, quantify the business values of the current exercise, the success criteria, risks, and mitigations, and present them to stakeholders.
- **Operationalize**: Deliver proofs of concepts, final reports, and technical documents.

# Big data analysis and data science

Big data is the result of collecting and managing large amounts of diverse data; data mining is all about searching data for unrecognized patterns.

## Data analysis

Data analysis is about breaking the mined data and assessing the impact of those unrecognized methods. It may even create new patterns over time and help to develop working applications.

## Data science

Data science is the process of cleaning, mining, and analyzing the data to derive insights of value from it. Extract data insights through a combination of exploratory data analysis and modeling. Data science is the process of distilling insights from data to inform decisions.

Data science creates models that capture the underlying patterns of complex systems and helps those models to become working applications:

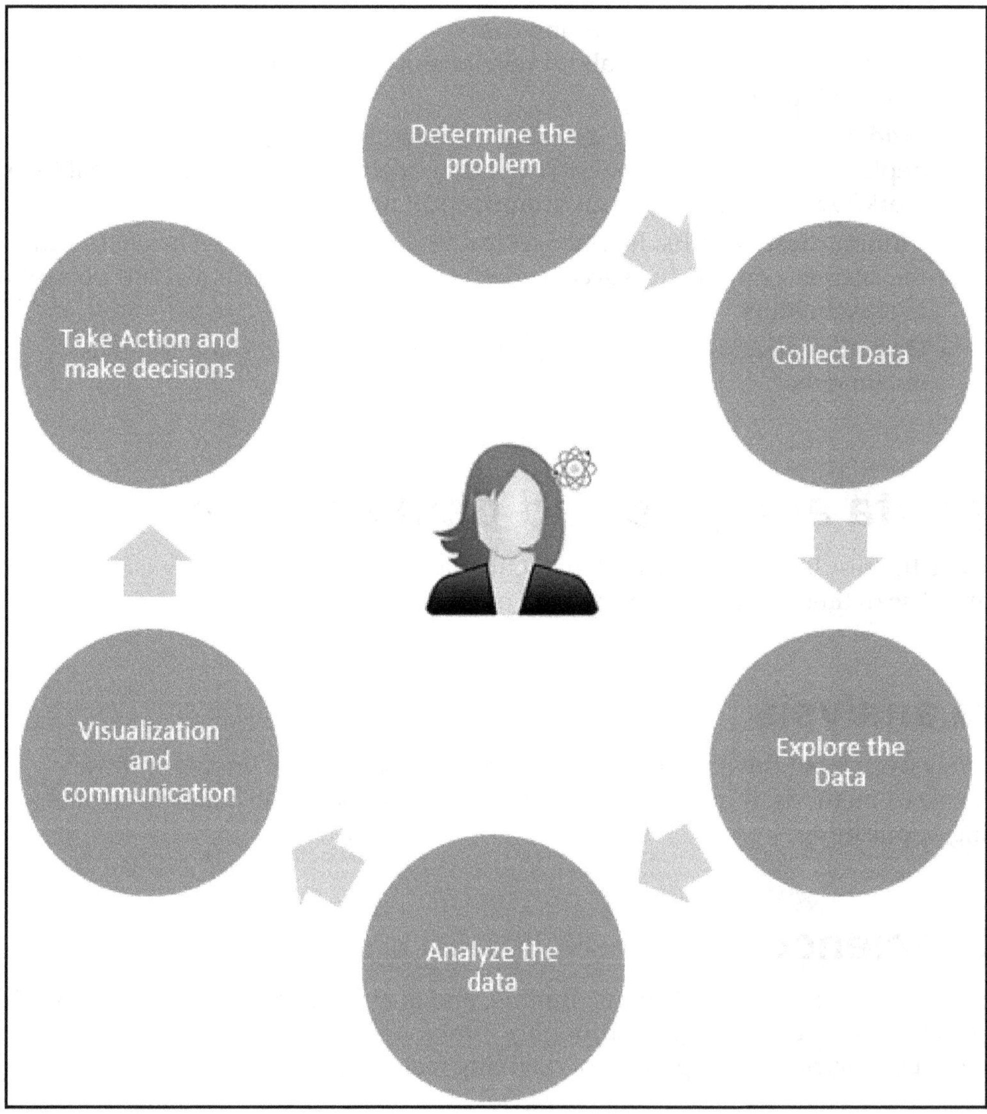


The preceding diagram intends to represent the data science process followed by a data scientist.

# Big data platform

Any software or hardware platform should support large datasets; otherwise, it is hard to support those large datasets with traditional database tools:

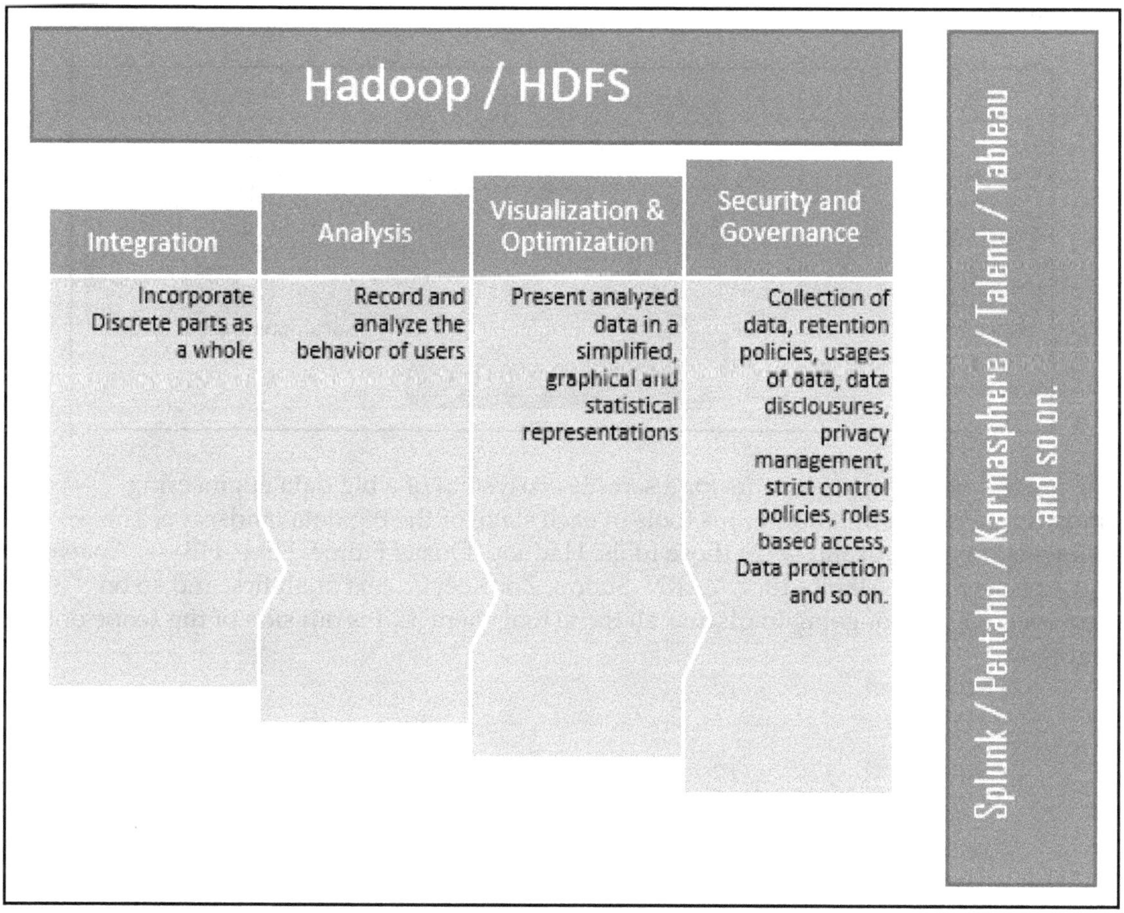

Hadoop / HDFS

Integration
Incorporate Discrete parts as a whole

Analysis
Record and analyze the behavior of users

Visualization & Optimization
Present analyzed data in a simplified, graphical and statistical representations

Security and Governance
Collection of data, retention policies, usages of data, data disclousures, privacy management, strict control policies, roles based access, Data protection and so on.

Splunk / Pentaho / Karmasphere / Talend / Tableau and so on.

The preceding diagram depicts a sample big data platform with supported sample tools, servers, hardware, and so on.

# Big data engineering

Big data engineering gets the most value out of the vast amount of disparate data, data staging, profiling, and data cleansing in any big data platform. Also, it represents optimal ways of migrating the data from back office systems to the front office to help data analysts and data scientists:

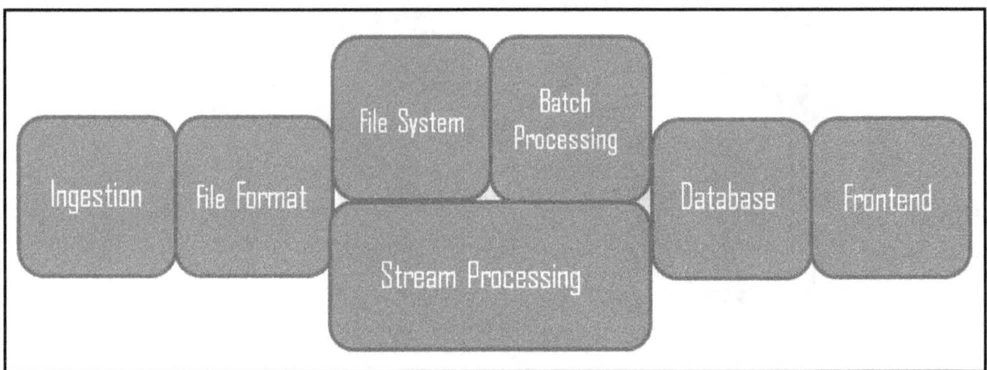


The preceding diagram accounts for a sample ecosystem of a big data engineering landscape. One can find numerous tools in each stage of the big data landscape. The following are some examples of those tools: Hadoop, Oozie, Flume, Hive, HBase, Apache Pig, Apache Spark, MapReduce, YARN, Sqoop, ZooKeeper, text analytics, and so on. However, we are not going to discuss all those tools here as it is out side of the scope of this chapter.

# Big data governance

Any big data enterprise would need to develop and enhance broader enterprise information governance by bringing rules or policies for optimization and privacy and also find avenues for monetizing (value) at the same time as ensuring regulatory compliance and facilitating prudent risk management:

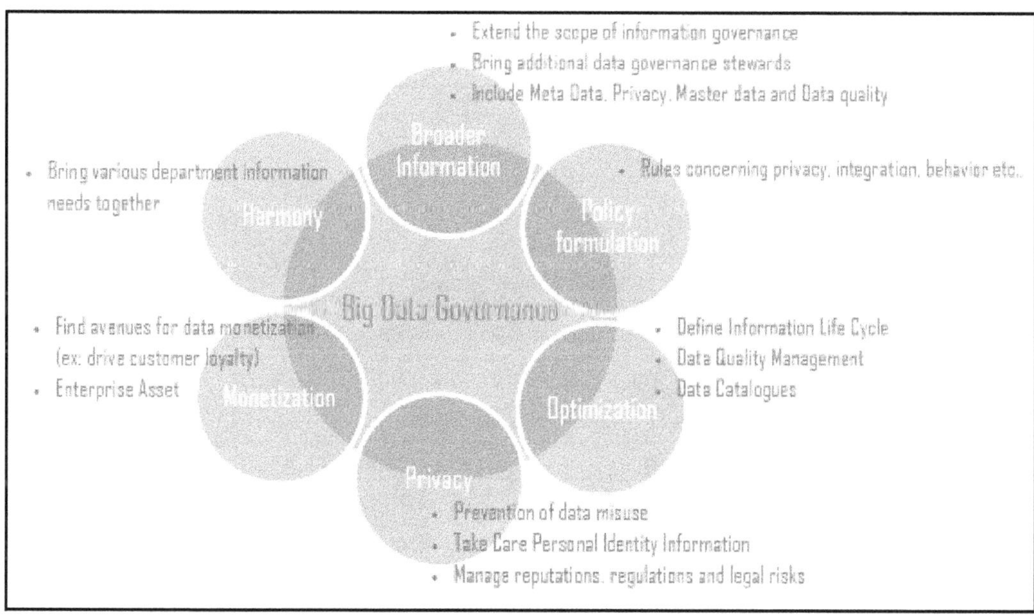

# Big data architecture landscape and layers

You should be able to extract valuable, meaningful information (**insights**) from the enormous volumes of data to improve an organization's decisions that involve various challenges, such as data regulations, faster decisions, interactions with customers, dealing with legacy systems, disparate data sources, and so on. So, to address all those challenges efficiently, researchers came up with a unified architecture consisting of layers at different levels:

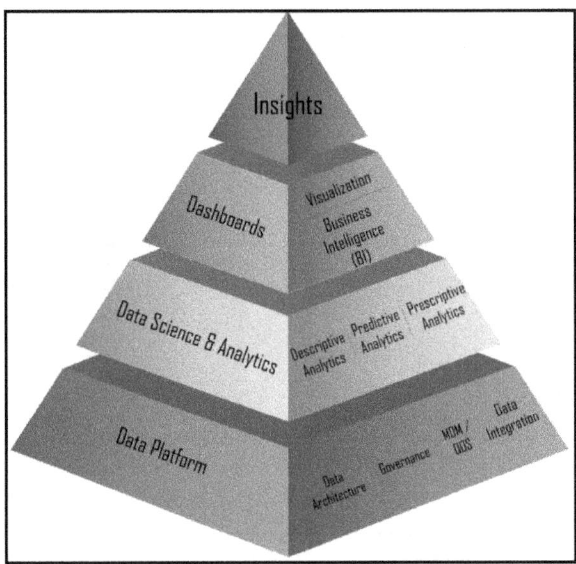


The preceding pyramid depicts the significant attributes of big data layers and the problems that are addressed in each layer. As we have mentioned earlier, big data is not a single technology or a framework solving just a set of use cases; it is a set of tools, processes, technologies, and a system infrastructure that helps businesses to make much smarter analysis and take smarter decisions based on the massive volume of data traces.

Unified big data architecture consists of various layers. It provides a way to organize different components to address problems and it represents unique functions:

- **Big data sources**: Data coming from several channels, such as handheld devices, software applications, sensors, legacy databases, and so on
- **Data messaging and storage**: Acquires data from the data sources, data compliance, and storage formatting

- **Data analysis**: Data model management, analytics engines, and access to data message stores
- **Data consumption**: Dashboards, insights, reporting, and so on

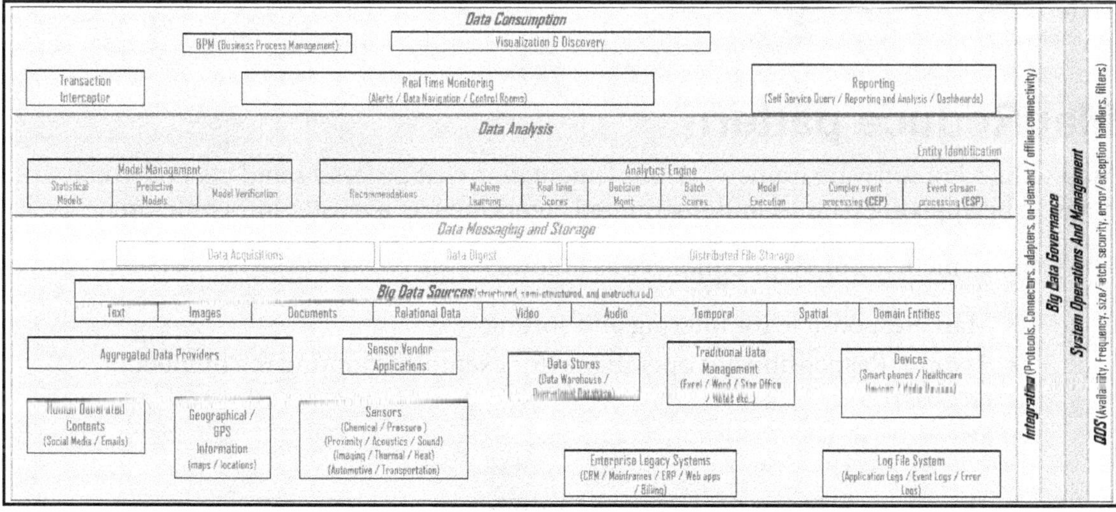


The preceding diagram depicts different levels and layers of the big data landscape. These layers perhaps may be considered as a summary of our earlier introductions of big data concepts and the realization of values in each layer.

Before we look at patterns, let's summarize the big data architecture principle as follows:

- Decoupled data bus
- Right tool usage for the job
- Data structure, latency, throughput, access patterns
- Lambda architecture
- Immutable logs, batch/speed/serving layer
- Cloud-based infrastructure
- System maintenance with low or no admin
- Cost-effective

# Big data architecture patterns

In this section, we will take you through big data design patterns, based on the following big data architectural patterns, and give a brief overview of the big data architectural patterns.

## MapReduce pattern

MapReduce is a software framework implementation that processes and generates big datasets by applying parallel and distributed algorithms on a cluster infrastructure.

The primary methods of MapReduce are as follows:

- **Map**: Responsible for filtering and sorting
- **Reduce**: Responsible for operations (for example, counting the number of records)

## Lambda architecture pattern

To address big data challenges (described earlier in this chapter), there needs to be a data processing architecture to handle massive quantities of data to process rapidly with batch processing and stream processing methods.

Some fundamental characteristics of the Lambda architecture are as follows:

- It is dependent on underlying data principles of append-only, immutable, and atomic
- It thrives on balancing latency, throughput, and fault-tolerance
- It correlates with the growth of big data and real-time analytics
- It helps to mitigate the latencies of MapReduce

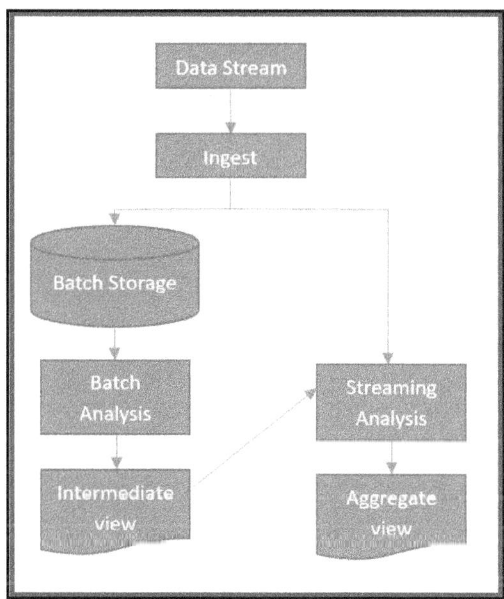


The preceding diagram depicts the Lambda architecture with three primary layers called the batch processing layer, the speed or real-time processing layer, and serving layers for responding to queries.

The three primary layers are explained here:

- **Batch layer**: This precomputes results, using a distributed processing system output to the read-only data store, and updates views by replacing the existing precomputed views. Data accuracy in the views is high with batch jobs (accuracy over latency).
- **Speed/Real-time layer**: This processes data streams in real time and the views are almost instantaneous, but maybe with less data accuracy (latency over accuracy). However, those views can be updated later by batch methods (accuracy over latency).
- **Serving layer**: This stores outputs from the batch and speed layers to respond to ad-hoc queries either by precomputed views or new views from the processed data.

# Data lake architecture pattern

In established enterprises, the most common business case is to make use of existing data infrastructure along with big data implementations. The data lake architecture pattern provides efficient ways to achieve reusing most of the data infrastructure and, at the same time, get the benefits of big data paradigm shifts.

Data lakes have the following essential characteristics to address:

- Manage abundant unprocessed data
- Retain data as long as possible
- Ability to manage the data transformation
- Support dynamic schema

The following diagram depicts a data lake pattern implementation. It is getting raw data into data storage from different data sources. Also, the received data needs to be retained as long as possible in the data warehouse. Conditioning is conducted only after a data source has been identified for immediate use in the mainline analytics:

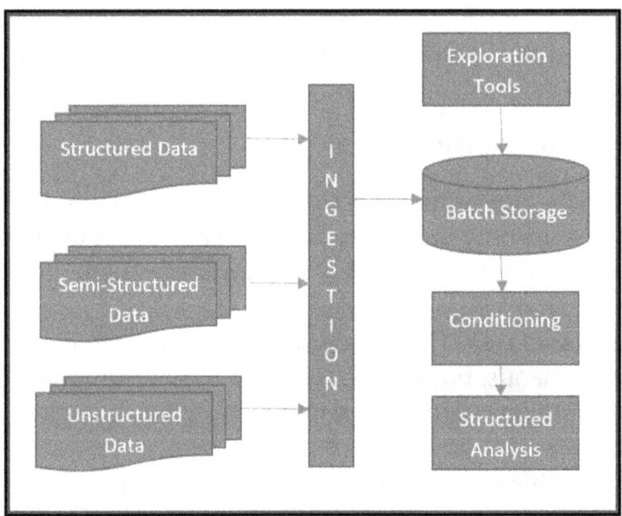


Data lakes provide a mechanism for capturing and exploring potentially useful data without incurring additional transactional systems storage costs, or any conditioning effort to bring data sources into those transactional systems.

Data lake implementation includes HDFS, AWS S3, distributed file systems, and so on. Microsoft, Amazon, EMC, Teradata, and Hortonworks are prominent vendors with data lake implementation among their products and they sell these technologies. Data lakes can also be a cloud **Infrastructure as a Service** (**IaaS**).

# Big data design patterns

This section covers most prominent big data design patterns by various data layers such as data sources and ingestion layer, data storage layer and data access layer.

## Data sources and ingestion layer

Enterprise big data systems face a variety of data sources with non-relevant information (noise) alongside relevant (signal) data. Noise ratio is very high compared to signals, and so filtering the noise from the pertinent information, handling high volumes, and the velocity of data is significant. This is the responsibility of the ingestion layer. The common challenges in the ingestion layers are as follows:

- Multiple data source load and prioritization
- Ingested data indexing and tagging
- Data validation and cleansing
- Data transformation and compression

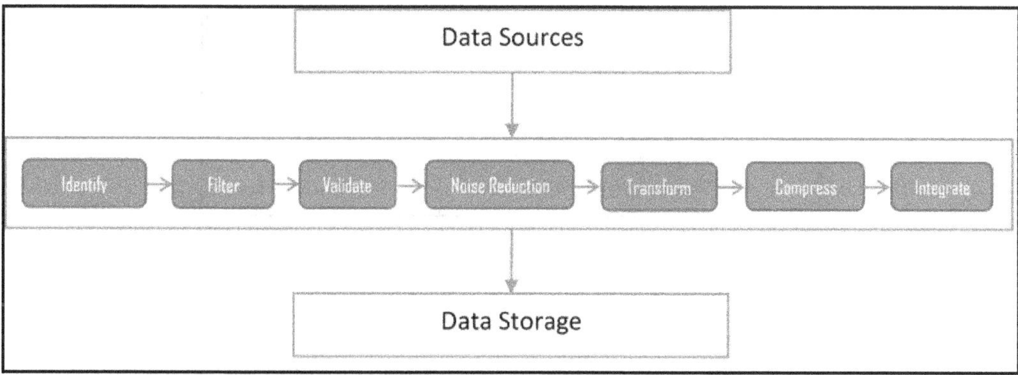


The preceding diagram depicts the building blocks of the ingestion layer and its various components. We need patterns to address the challenges of **data sources** to ingestion layer communication that takes care of performance, scalability, and availability requirements.

In this section, we will discuss the following ingestion and streaming patterns and how they help to address the challenges in ingestion layers. We will also touch upon some common workload patterns as well, including:

- Multisource extractor
- Multidestination
- Protocol converter
- **Just-in-time** (**JIT**) transformation
- Real-time streaming pattern

## Multisource extractor

An approach to ingesting multiple data types from multiple data sources efficiently is termed a *Multisource extractor*. Efficiency represents many factors, such as data velocity, data size, data frequency, and managing various data formats over an unreliable network, mixed network bandwidth, different technologies, and systems:

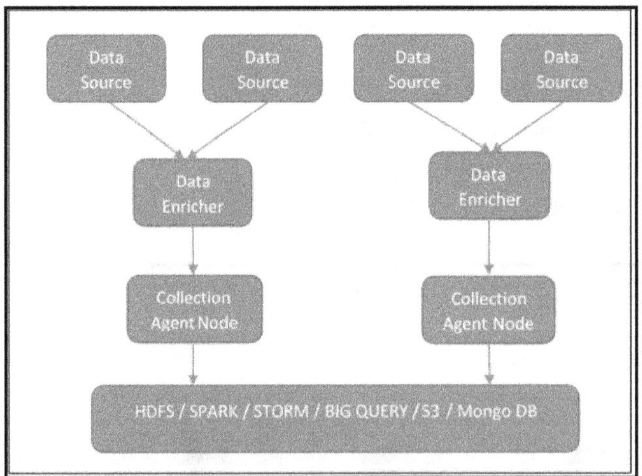


The multisource extractor system ensures high availability and distribution. It also confirms that the vast volume of data gets segregated into multiple batches across different nodes. The single node implementation is still helpful for lower volumes from a handful of clients, and of course, for a significant amount of data from multiple clients processed in batches. Partitioning into small volumes in clusters produces excellent results.

Data enrichers help to do initial data aggregation and data cleansing. Enrichers ensure file transfer reliability, validations, noise reduction, compression, and transformation from native formats to standard formats. Collection agent nodes represent intermediary cluster systems, which helps final data processing and data loading to the destination systems.

The following are the benefits of the multisource extractor:

- Provides reasonable speed for storing and consuming the data
- Better data prioritization and processing
- Drives improved business decisions
- Decoupled and independent from data production to data consumption
- Data semantics and detection of changed data
- Scaleable and fault tolerance system

The following are the impacts of the multisource extractor:

- Difficult or impossible to achieve near real-time data processing
- Need to maintain multiple copies in enrichers and collection agents, leading to data redundancy and mammoth data volume in each node
- High availability trade-off with high costs to manage system capacity growth
- Infrastructure and configuration complexity increases to maintain batch processing

# Multidestination pattern

In multisourcing, we saw the raw data ingestion to HDFS, but in most common cases the enterprise needs to ingest raw data not only to new HDFS systems but also to their existing traditional data storage, such as Informatica or other analytics platforms. In such cases, the additional number of data streams leads to many challenges, such as storage overflow, data errors (also known as data regret), an increase in time to transfer and process data, and so on.

The multidestination pattern is considered as a better approach to overcome all of the challenges mentioned previously. This pattern is very similar to multisourcing until it is ready to integrate with multiple destinations (refer to the following diagram). The router publishes the improved data and then broadcasts it to the subscriber destinations (already registered with a publishing agent on the router). Enrichers can act as publishers as well as subscribers:

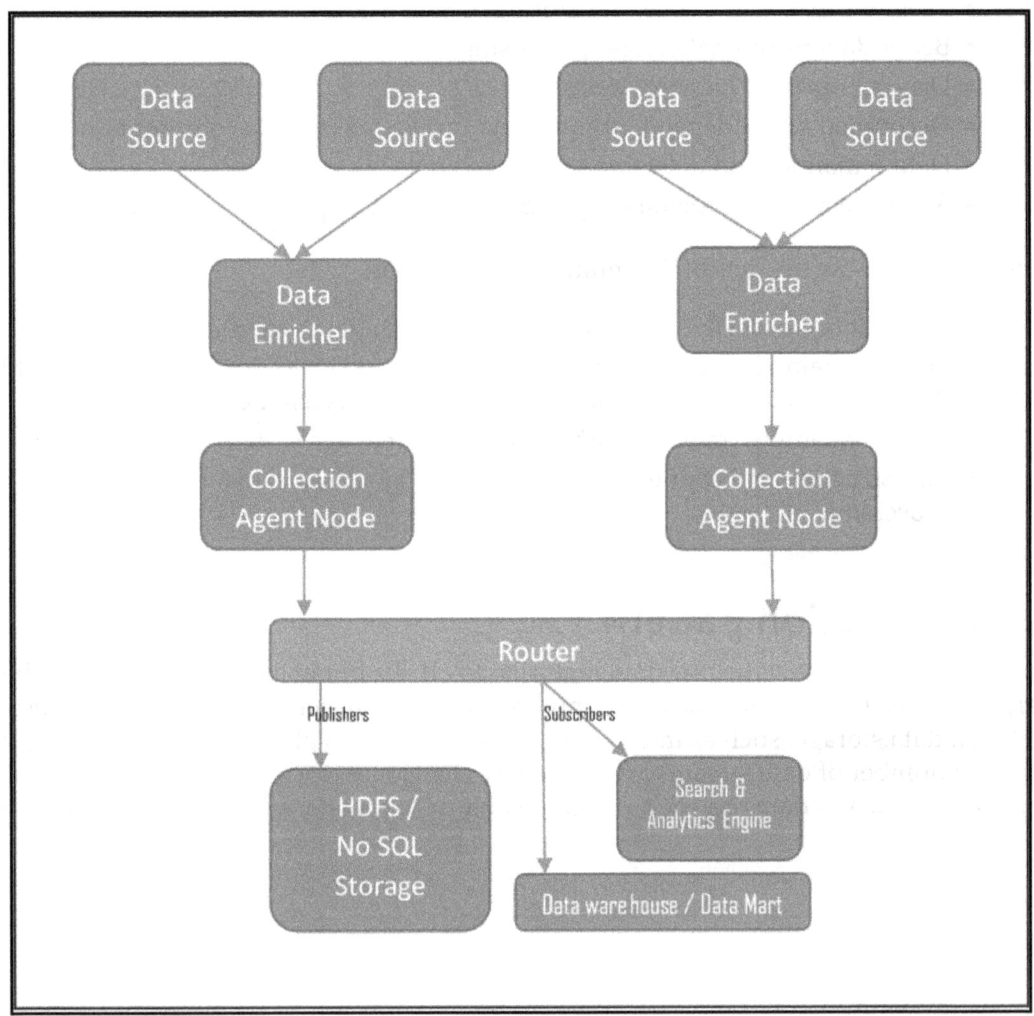

Deploying routers in the cluster environment is also recommended for high volumes and a large number of subscribers.

The following are the benefits of the multidestination pattern:

- Highly scalable, flexible, fast, resilient to data failure, and cost-effective
- Organization can start to ingest data into multiple data stores, including its existing RDBMS as well as NoSQL data stores
- Allows you to use simple query language, such as Hive and Pig, along with traditional analytics
- Provides the ability to partition the data for flexible access and decentralized processing
- Possibility of decentralized computation in the data nodes
- Due to replication on HDFS nodes, there are no data regrets
- Self-reliant data nodes can add more nodes without any delay

The following are the impacts of the multidestination pattern:

- Needs complex or additional infrastructure to manage distributed nodes
- Needs to manage distributed data in secured networks to ensure data security
- Needs enforcement, governance, and stringent practices to manage the integrity and consistency of data

## Protocol converter

This is a mediatory approach to provide an abstraction for the incoming data of various systems. The protocol converter pattern provides an efficient way to ingest a variety of unstructured data from multiple data sources and different protocols.

The message exchanger handles synchronous and asynchronous messages from various protocol and handlers as represented in the following diagram. It performs various mediator functions, such as file handling, web services message handling, stream handling, serialization, and so on:

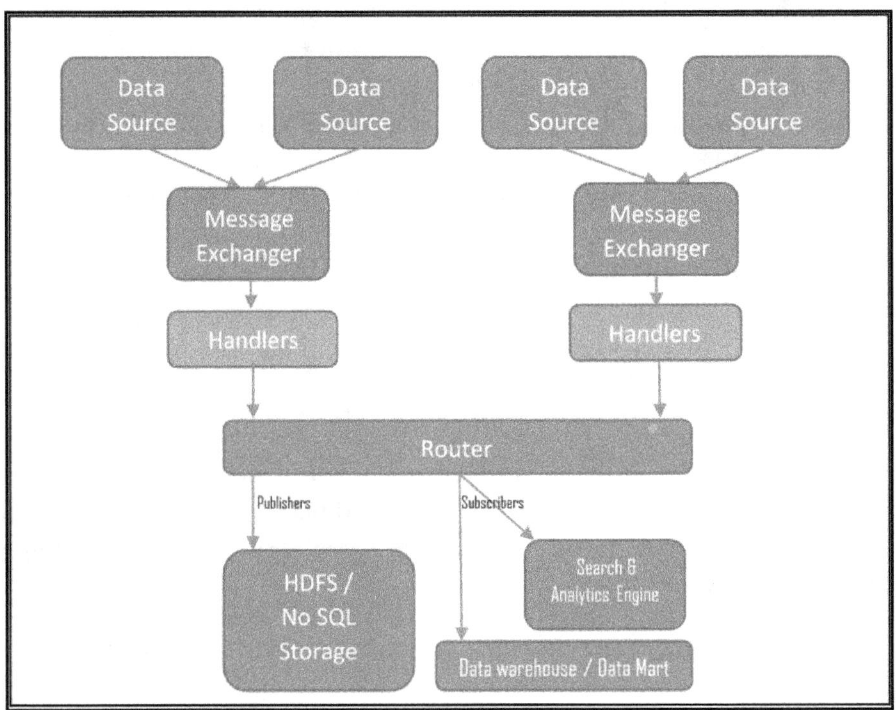


In the protocol converter pattern, the ingestion layer holds responsibilities such as identifying the various channels of incoming events, determining incoming data structures, providing mediated service for multiple protocols into suitable sinks, providing one standard way of representing incoming messages, providing handlers to manage various request types, and providing abstraction from the incoming protocol layers.

## Just-In-Time (JIT) transformation pattern

The JIT transformation pattern is the best fit in situations where raw data needs to be preloaded in the data stores before the transformation and processing can happen. In this kind of business case, this pattern runs independent preprocessing batch jobs that clean, validate, corelate, and transform, and then store the transformed information into the same data store (HDFS/NoSQL); that is, it can coexist with the raw data:

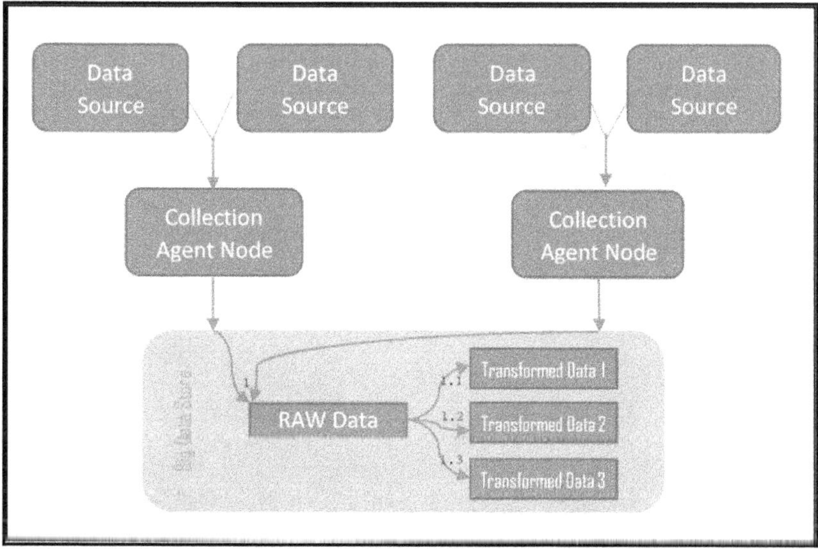


The preceding diagram depicts the datastore with raw data storage along with transformed datasets. Please note that the data enricher of the multi-data source pattern is absent in this pattern and more than one batch job can run in parallel to transform the data as required in the big data storage, such as HDFS, Mongo DB, and so on.

## Real-time streaming pattern

Most modern businesses need continuous and real-time processing of unstructured data for their enterprise big data applications.

Real-time streaming implementations need to have the following characteristics:

- Minimize latency by using large in-memory
- Event processors are atomic and independent of each other and so are easily scalable
- Provide API for parsing the real-time information
- Independent deployable script for any node and no centralized master node implementation

The real-time streaming pattern suggests introducing an optimum number of event processing nodes to consume different input data from the various data sources and introducing listeners to process the generated events (from event processing nodes) in the event processing engine:

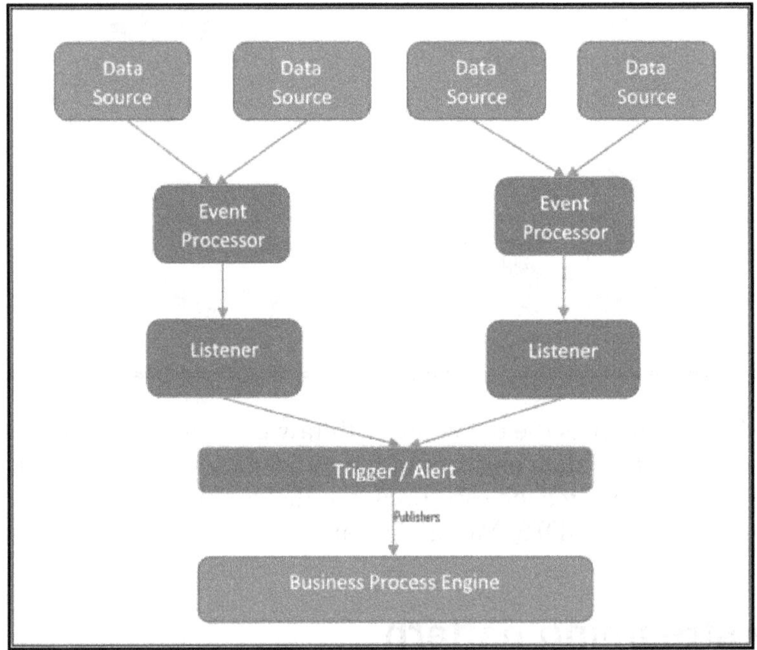


Event processing engines (event processors) have a sizeable in-memory capacity, and the event processors get triggered by a specific event. The trigger or alert is responsible for publishing the results of the in-memory big data analytics to the enterprise business process engines and, in turn, get redirected to various publishing channels (mobile, CIO dashboards, and so on).

# Big data workload patterns

Workload patterns help to address data workload challenges associated with different domains and business cases efficiently. The big data design pattern manifests itself in the solution construct, and so the workload challenges can be mapped with the right architectural constructs and thus service the workload.

The following diagram depicts a snapshot of the most common workload patterns and their associated architectural constructs:

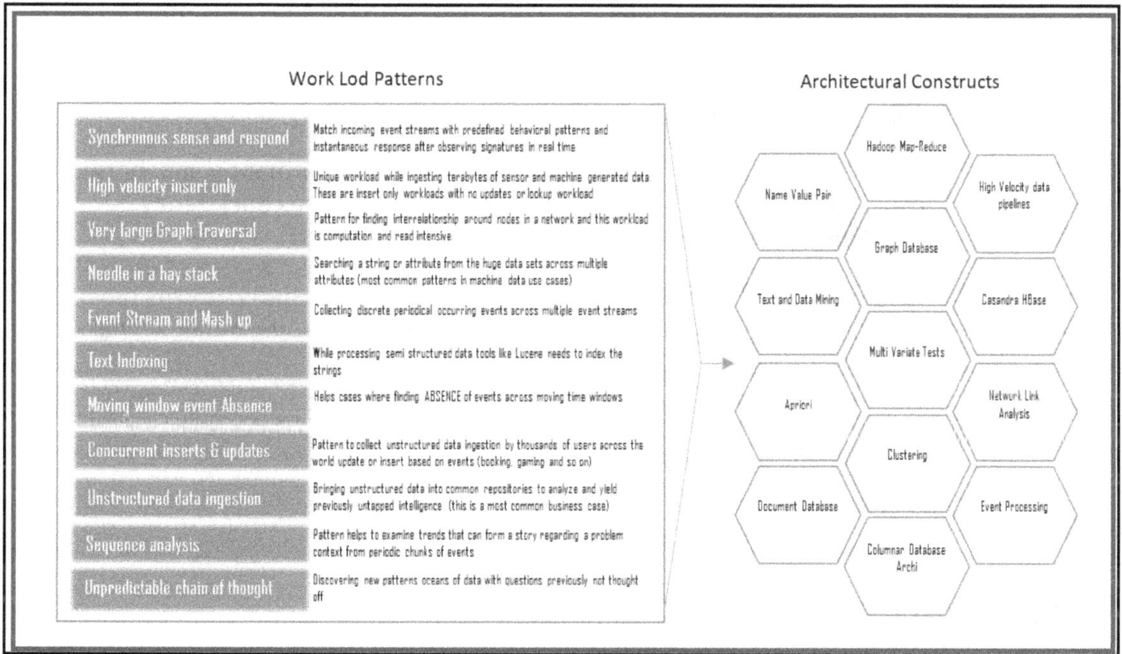


Workload design patterns help to simplify and decompose the business use cases into workloads. Then those workloads can be methodically mapped to the various building blocks of the big data solution architecture.

# Data storage layer

Data storage layer is responsible for acquiring all the data that are gathered from various data sources and it is also liable for converting (if needed) the collected data to a format that can be analyzed. The following sections discuss more on data storage layer patterns.

## ACID versus BASE versus CAP

Traditional RDBMS follows **atomicity, consistency, isolation, and durability** (**ACID**) to provide reliability for any user of the database. However, searching high volumes of big data and retrieving data from those volumes consumes an enormous amount of time if the storage enforces ACID rules. So, big data follows **basically available**, **soft state**, **eventually consistent** (**BASE**), a phenomenon for undertaking any search in big data space.

Database theory suggests that the NoSQL big database may predominantly satisfy two properties and relax standards on the third, and those properties are **consistency, availability, and partition tolerance** (**CAP**).

With the ACID, BASE, and CAP paradigms, the big data storage design patterns have gained momentum and purpose. We will look at those patterns in some detail in this section. The patterns are:

- Façade pattern
- NoSQL pattern
- Polyglot pattern

## Façade pattern

This pattern provides a way to use existing or **traditional existing data warehouses** along with big data storage (such as Hadoop). It can act as a façade for the enterprise data warehouses and business intelligence tools.

In the façade pattern, the data from the different data sources get aggregated into **HDFS** before any transformation, or even before loading to the **traditional existing data warehouses**:

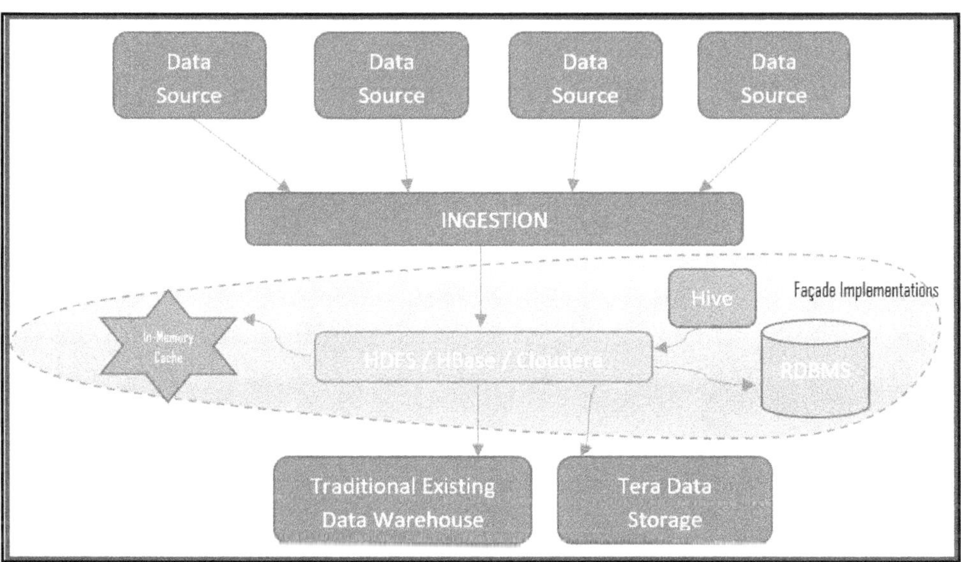


The façade pattern allows structured data storage even after being ingested to HDFS in the form of structured storage in an **RDBMS**, or in NoSQL databases, or in a memory cache. The façade pattern ensures reduced data size, as only the necessary data resides in the structured storage, as well as faster access from the storage.

# NoSQL pattern

This pattern entails getting NoSQL alternatives in place of traditional RDBMS to facilitate the rapid access and querying of big data. The NoSQL database stores data in a columnar, non-relational style. It can store data on local disks as well as in HDFS, as it is HDFS aware. Thus, data can be distributed across data nodes and fetched very quickly.

Let's look at four types of NoSQL databases in brief:

- **Column-oriented DBMS**: Simply called a columnar store or big table data store, it has a massive number of columns for each tuple. Each column has a column key. Column family qualifiers represent related columns so that the columns and the qualifiers are retrievable, as each column has a column key as well. These data stores are suitable for fast writes.

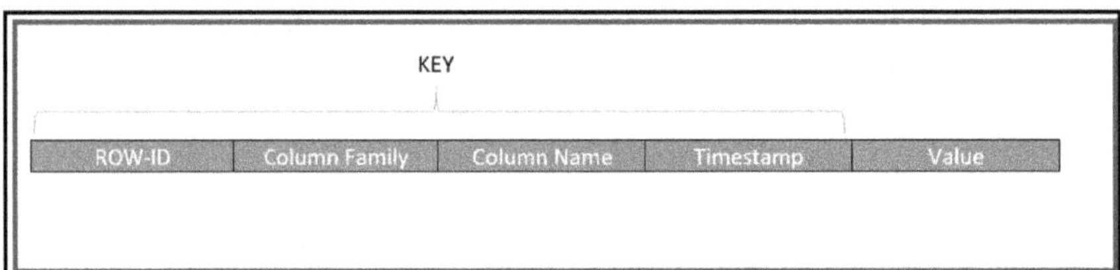


- **Key-value pair database**: A key-value database is a data store that, when presented with a simple string (key), returns an arbitrarily large data (value). The key is bound to the value until it gets a new value assigned into or from a database. The key-value data store does not need to have a query language. It provides a way to add and remove key-value pairs. A key-value store is a dictionary kind of data store, where it has a list of words and each word represents one or more definitions.
- **Graph database**: This is a representation of a system that contains a sequence of nodes and relationships that creates a graph when combined. A graph represents three data fields: nodes, relationships, and properties. Some types of graph store are referred to as triple stores because of their node-relationship-node structure. You may be familiar with applications that provide evaluations of similar or likely characteristics as part of the search (for example, a user bought this item also bought... is a good illustration of graph store implementations).

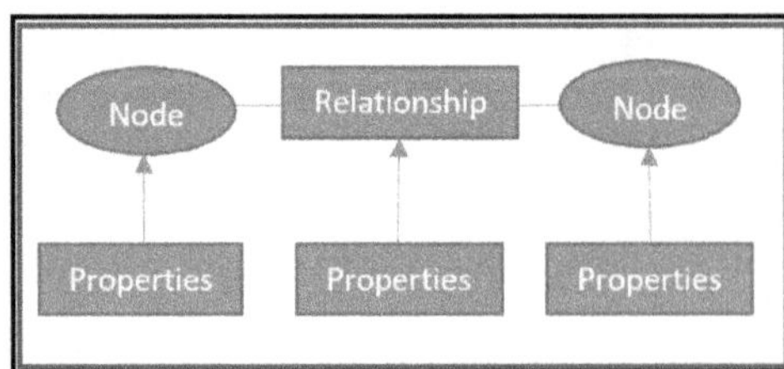

- **Document database**: We can represent a graph data store as a tree structure. Document trees have a single root element or sometimes even multiple root elements as well. Note that there is a sequence of branches, sub-branches, and values beneath the root element. Each branch can have an expression or relative path to determine the traversal path from the origin node (root) and to any given branch, sub-branch, or value. Each branch may have a value associated with that branch. Sometimes the existence of a branch of the tree has a specific meaning, and sometimes a branch must have a given value to be interpreted correctly.

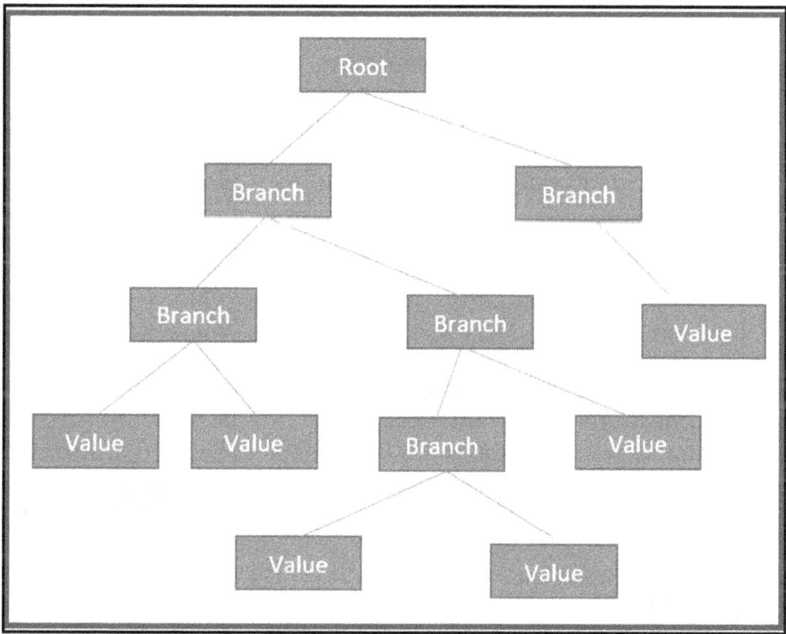

The following table summarizes some of the NoSQL use cases, providers, tools and scenarios that might need NoSQL pattern considerations. Most of this pattern implementation is already part of various vendor implementations, and they come as out-of-the-box implementations and as plug and play so that any enterprise can start leveraging the same quickly.

| **NoSQL DB to Use** | **Scenario** | **Vendor / Application / Tools** |
|---|---|---|
| Columnar database | Application that needs to fetch entire related columnar family based on a given string: for example, search engines | SAP HANA / IBM DB2 BLU / ExtremeDB / EXASOL / IBM Informix / MS SQL Server / MonetDB |
| Key Value Pair database | Needle in haystack applications (refer to the *Big data workload patterns* given in this section) | Redis / Oracle NoSQL DB / Linux DBM / Dynamo / Cassandra |
| Graph database | Recommendation engine: application that provides evaluation of *Similar to / Like*: for example, *User that bought this item also bought* | ArangoDB / Cayley / DataStax / Neo4j / Oracle Spatial and Graph / Apache Orient DB / Teradata Aster |
| Document database | Applications that evaluate churn management of social media data or non-enterprise data | Couch DB / Apache Elastic Search / Informix / Jackrabbit / Mongo DB / Apache SOLR |

## Polyglot pattern

Traditional (RDBMS) and multiple storage types (files, CMS, and so on) coexist with big data types (NoSQL/HDFS) to solve business problems.

Most modern business cases need the coexistence of legacy databases. At the same time, they would need to adopt the latest big data techniques as well. Replacing the entire system is not viable and is also impractical. The polyglot pattern provides an efficient way to combine and use multiple types of storage mechanisms, such as Hadoop, and RDBMS. Big data appliances coexist in a storage solution:

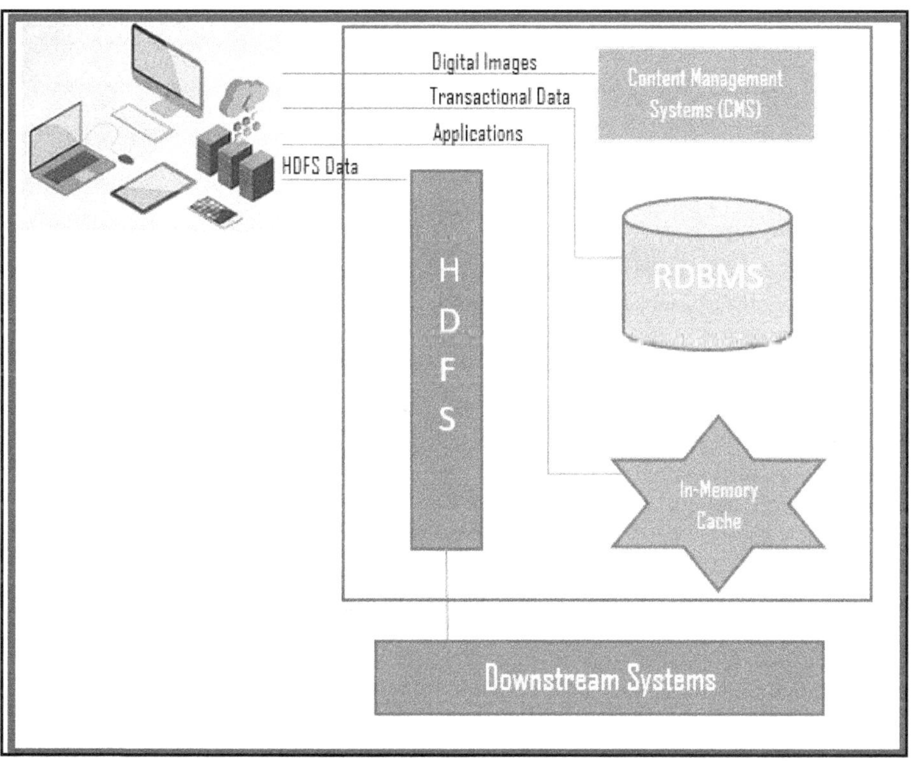


The preceding diagram represents the polyglot pattern way of storing data in different storage types, such as RDBMS, key-value stores, NoSQL database, CMS systems, and so on. Unlike the traditional way of storing all the information in one single data source, polyglot facilitates any data coming from all applications across multiple sources (RDBMS, CMS, Hadoop, and so on) into different storage mechanisms, such as in-memory, RDBMS, HDFS, CMS, and so on.

# Data access layer

Data access in traditional databases involves JDBC connections and HTTP access for documents. However, in big data, the data access with conventional method does take too much time to fetch even with cache implementations, as the volume of the data is so high.

So we need a mechanism to fetch the data efficiently and quickly, with a reduced development life cycle, lower maintenance cost, and so on.

Data access patterns mainly focus on accessing big data resources of two primary types:

- End-to-end user-driven API (access through simple queries)
- Developer API (access provision through API methods)

In this section, we will discuss the following data access patterns that held efficient data access, improved performance, reduced development life cycles, and low maintenance costs for broader data access:

- Connector pattern
- Lightweight stateless pattern
- Service locator pattern
- Near real-time pattern
- Stage transform pattern

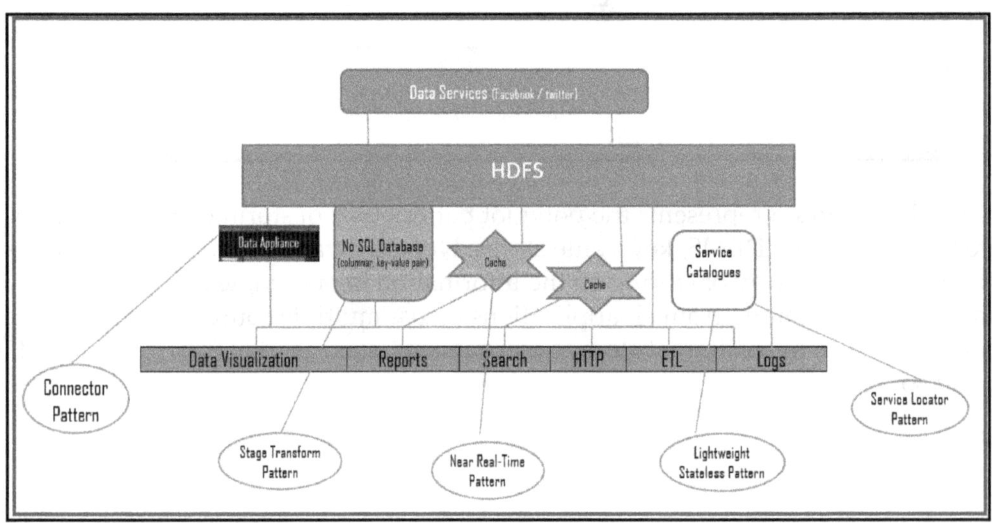

The preceding diagram represents the big data architecture layouts where the big data access patterns help data access. We discuss the whole of that mechanism in detail in the following sections.

## Connector pattern

The developer API approach entails fast data transfer and data access services through APIs. It creates optimized data sets for efficient loading and analysis. Some of the big data appliances abstract data in NoSQL DBs even though the underlying data is in HDFS, or a custom implementation of a filesystem so that the data access is very efficient and fast.

The connector pattern entails providing developer API and SQL like query language to access the data and so gain significantly reduced development time. As we saw in the earlier diagram, big data appliances come with connector pattern implementation. The big data appliance itself is a complete big data ecosystem and supports virtualization, redundancy, **replication using protocols** (**RAID**), and some appliances host NoSQL databases as well.

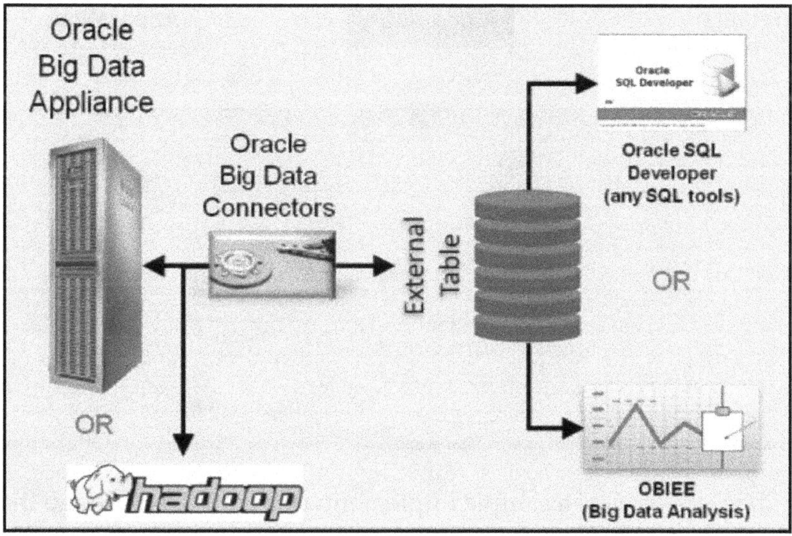

The preceding diagram shows a sample connector implementation for Oracle big data appliances. The data connector can connect to Hadoop and the big data appliance as well. It is an example of a custom implementations that we described earlier to facilitate faster data access with less development time.

## Lightweight stateless pattern

This pattern entails providing data access through web services, and so it is independent of platform or language implementations. The data is fetched through restful HTTP calls, making this pattern the most sought after in cloud deployments. WebHDFS and HttpFS are examples of lightweight stateless pattern implementation for HDFS HTTP access. It uses the HTTP REST protocol. The HDFS system exposes the REST API (web services) for consumers who analyze big data. This pattern reduces the cost of ownership (pay-as-you-go) for the enterprise, as the implementations can be part of an **integration Platform as a Service** (**iPaaS**):

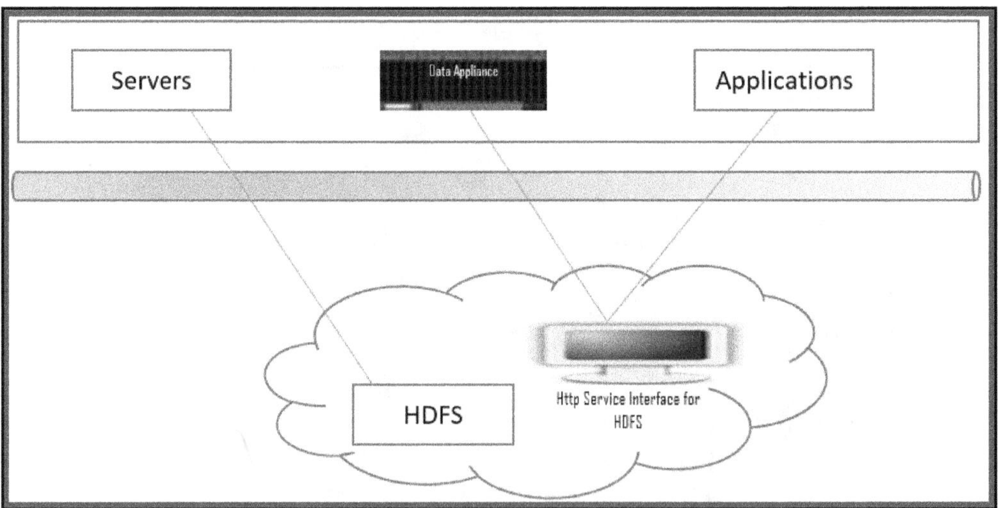


The preceding diagram depicts a sample implementation for HDFS storage that exposes HTTP access through the HTTP web interface.

## Service locator pattern

In a big data storage landscape, there are different types of data format (polyglot persistence), and if one needs to select and analyze a specific storage type from the list of stored data, then the service locator pattern comes in handy. It provides the flexibility to manipulate, filter, select, and co-relate services from the service catalog when storage access is with a SaaS model:

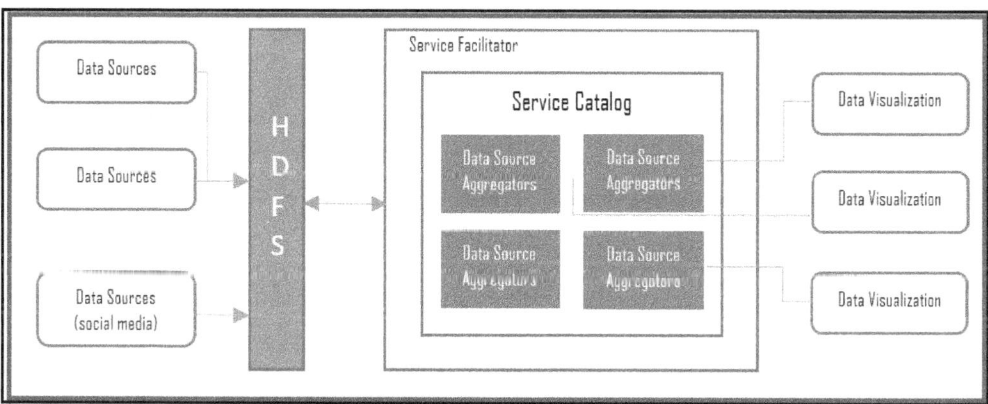


The preceding diagram shows a sample implementation of a service locator pattern. Observed data from various sources get aggregated and exposed through a service catalog and is available for visualization, or perhaps for further analysis. Service aggregators can aggregate services within or outside of enterprises. Different visualization tools can mix and match these services to show enterprise data alongside social media which is a different format than the other data source formats.

## Near real-time pattern

For any enterprise to implement real-time data access or near real-time data access, the key challenges to be addressed are:

- **Rapid determination of data**: Ensure rapid determination of data and make swift decisions (within a few seconds, not in minutes) before the data becomes meaningless
- **Rapid analysis**: Ability to analyze the data in real time and spot anomalies and relate them to business events, provide visualization, and generate alerts at the moment that the data arrived

Some examples of systems that would need real-time data analysis are:

- Radar systems
- Customer services applications
- ATMs
- Social media platforms
- Intrusion detection systems

Storm and in-memory applications such as Oracle Coherence, Hazelcast IMDG, SAP HANA, TIBCO, Software AG (Terracotta), VMware, and Pivotal GemFire XD are some of the in-memory computing vendor/technology platforms that can implement near real-time data access pattern applications:

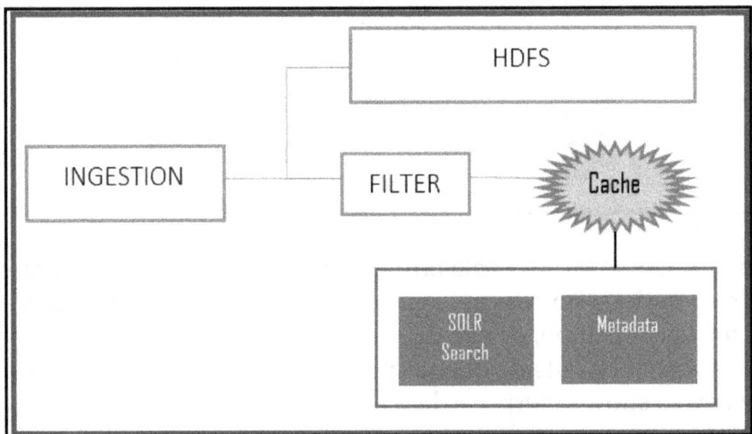


As shown in the preceding diagram, with multi-cache implementation at the ingestion phase, and with filtered, sorted data in multiple storage destinations (here one of the destinations is a cache), one can achieve near real-time access. The cache can be of a NoSQL database, or it can be any in-memory implementations tool, as mentioned earlier. The preceding diagram depicts a typical implementation of a log search with SOLR as a search engine.

## Stage transform pattern

In the big data world, a massive volume of data can get into the data store. However, all of the data is not required or meaningful in every business case. The stage transform pattern provides a mechanism for reducing the data scanned and fetches only relevant data.

HDFS has raw data and business-specific data in a NoSQL database that can provide application-oriented structures and fetch only the relevant data in the required format:

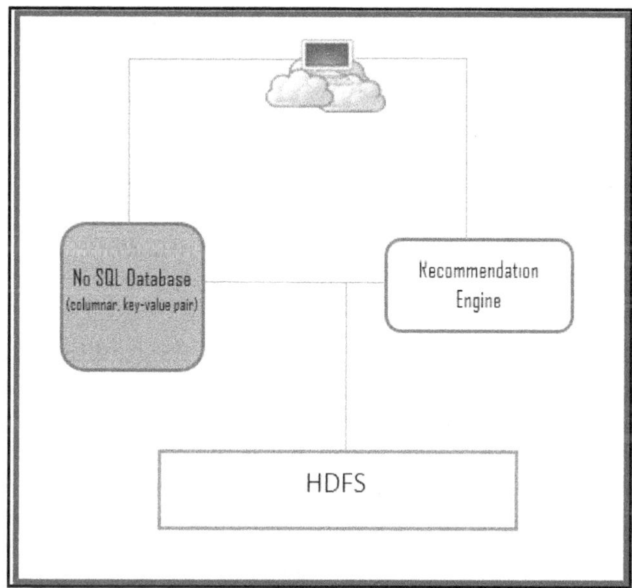


Combining the stage transform pattern and the NoSQL pattern is the recommended approach in cases where a reduced data scan is the primary requirement. The preceding diagram depicts one such case for a recommendation engine where we need a significant reduction in the amount of data scanned for an improved customer experience.

The implementation of the virtualization of data from HDFS to a NoSQL database, integrated with a big data appliance, is a highly recommended mechanism for rapid or accelerated data fetch. We have already seen that in the near real-time implementation shown earlier in this section.

## Rapid data analysis pattern

For faster data processing and access, the enterprise can choose any of the following tools in its data landscape. Each implementation has its own merits and purpose; we suggest reading each implementation in detail from the references that we have provided and choose the best for your enterprise needs:

- Apache Hadoop
- Bash Reduce
- Disco (Nokia Research)
- Apache Spark
- Graph Lab
- Apache Storm
- Google Big Query

## Data discovery and analysis layer

Data discovery and analysis in big data is different from the traditional analysis of structured RDBMS data from limited sets. Big data analysis needs a more sophisticated mechanism, as it involves natural language processing, unstructured texts, videos and images, RFID data, and so on. This section touches upon some data discovery and analysis patterns and mentions the tools that are supporting these patterns. Readers are encouraged to read other referenced materials to get a more profound understanding of each pattern:

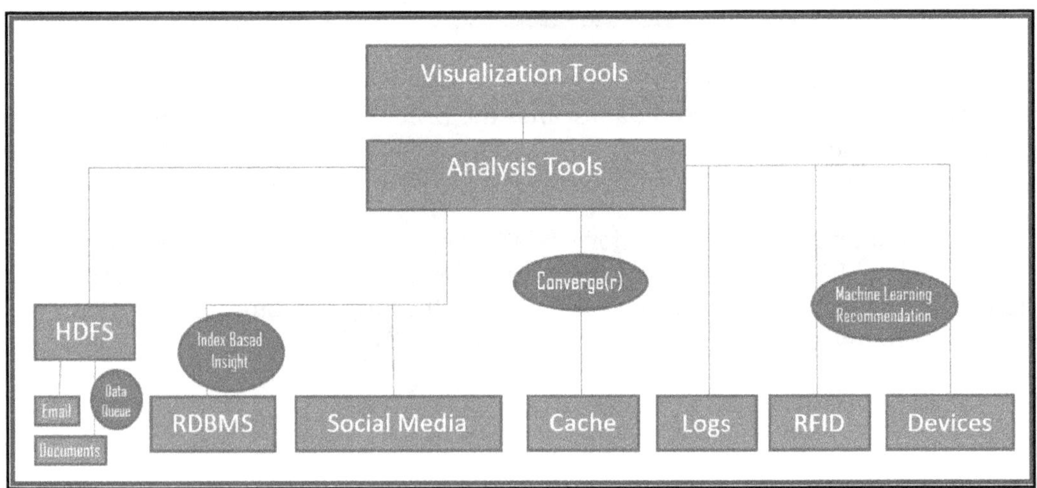

## Data queuing pattern

It is a most common situation that a system needs to handle spikes while analyzing data. This pattern introduces a workflow or process to queue additional chunks of data and then route them to available nodes:

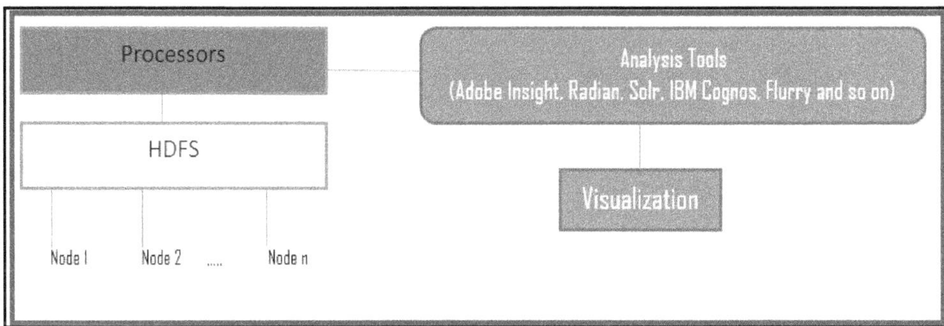


The preceding diagram depicts a sample implementation of a data queue and processors for additional workflows and routes to available nodes (of multiple nodes).

Using cloud IaaS is the best option to handle the spikes dynamically and yield better cost savings. It spins additional virtual machines as needed, with more when there is a spike, and fewer when traffic is slow or average).

## Index-based insight pattern

This pattern defines indexes (keys) based on the inputs from the users who interact with customers. Iteratively, finding a range of indexes is the mechanism suggested by the index-based insight pattern. It sets the analysis mechanism or pattern to index a variable and to provide insight into common behaviors such as parents buying toys, and all children aged above 13 in a neighborhood. This pattern helps to find a crucial efficient lookup for rapid scanning but keeps related columns together.

## Machine learning pattern

This pattern helps to find a pattern of data inputs generated from heterogeneous devices, such as RFID devices, energy meters, signal devices, weather-related devices, and so on.

Understanding data generated by automated systems, or devices without manual intervention, is a challenging task, and one needs to rely on algorithms and statistical methods. Fortunately, there are excellent algorithms that help to analyze this data, and some of the conventional algorithms are as follows:

- Naïve Bayes classifier algorithm
- K Means clustering algorithm
- Support vector machine algorithm
- Apriori algorithm
- Linear regression
- Hypothesis testing
- Clustering
- ANOVA
- Logistic regression
- Neural networks / artificial neural networks
- Random forests
- Decision trees
- Nearest neighbors
- Principal component analysis
- Conjoint analysis
- Ensemble methods

We can use one or more combinations of these algorithms as needed. Readers are encouraged to refer to other materials to get an insight into each algorithm, as covering them is not in the scope of this section.

## Converge(r) pattern

In most business cases, as we have seen earlier, enterprises need to deal with traditional (structured) data and at the same time make use of big data to get enterprise-wide insights. The converge(r) pattern provides an efficient way to merge unstructured data with structured data and get insights and make decisions.

In some business cases, enterprises may need to understand the sentiments (views and opinions) of their product from social media. The converge(r) pattern, combining external data formats with internal enterprise data formats, is one of the best options. This pattern entails combining those views and opinions from social media with internal data analysis to get combined data insights.

The data convergence needs to happen before the enterprise data is analyzed. So we can use the façade pattern (refer to the *Data storage layer* section in this chapter), and also use machine learning patterns to use the grouped data from the social media (for impacts, revenues, brand images, churn rates, and so on).

Tools such as DrivenData, TianChi, Crowd Analytics, InfoChimps, Kaggle, and TopCoder provide out-of-the-box converge(r) implementation, and we can use those tools along with ETL tools for data transformation, cleansing, and enrichment, and get insights by combining the data.

## Data visualization layer

Data visualization's primary responsibility is to provide more insights from the massive volume of data by using visual representations, such as statistical reports, charts, and so on. Visualization of insights is the most visible portion to the stakeholders and sponsors; it is the most impactful part of the whole big data paradigm.

As visualization is most impactful and considering the vastness of the visualization, this section aims to provide only a brief introduction to a few of the common visualization patterns. However, we encourage readers to explore the exclusive visualization materials that we have provided in the reference sections.

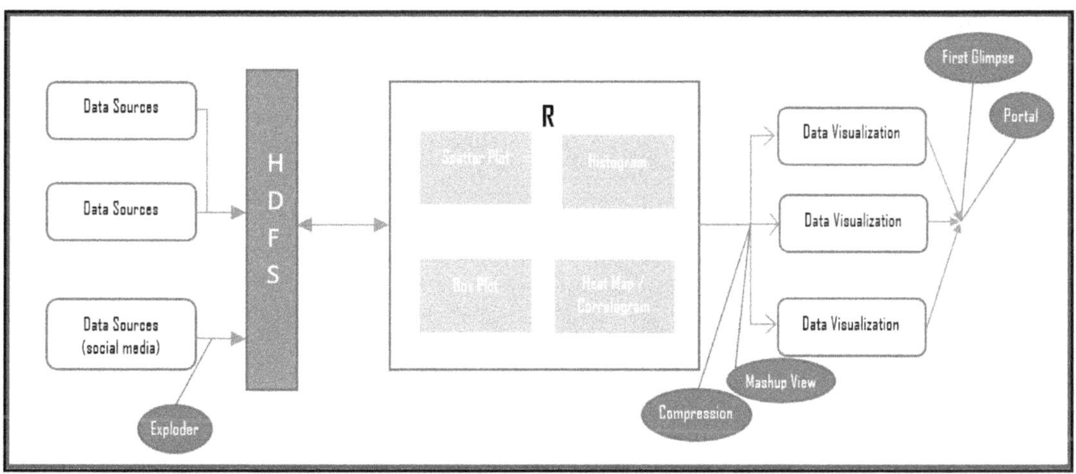

The preceding diagram depicts data visualization patterns in a sample big data landscape. Visualization patterns need to support high-level views and also granular level details as visual representations. Moreover, visualization patterns can be used in conjunction with data access patterns to leverage the rapid access of data and its presentation.

## First glimpse pattern

As the name suggests, this is an approach that provides primary or minimalistic visualization data and pulls detailed information only on demand.

This pattern entails fetching only the most critical and essential data (which may be decided by machine learning patterns, rankings, scores, and so on) as a first glimpse and fetches drill-down data on demand. An example could be a search application displaying search results as only one page (the first page) and providing more data when the user needs it on subsequent pages.

## Portal pattern

With most common cases where the enterprise already has reporting applications and intends to reuse the same for the visualization of big data, then this pattern entails enhancing the web application (portal) with scripting frameworks to enhance the legacy visualization, thus saving the enterprise the cost of having a new visualization tool.

The following lists some of the scripting frameworks one may want to include and enhance with enterprise portal and realize the portal pattern:

- D3.js
- Chart.js
- HighChart.js
- ChartList.js
- Raphel
- Processing.js
- Pixi.js
- Webix
- AnyChart
- Flot
- Pykcharts
- Cytoscape.js

# Mashup view pattern

Mashup view creates an aggregated mashup view from heterogeneous data stores such as Hadoop, cache, and RDBMS, thereby reducing the analysis time by aggregating the results of the queries.

It helps to achieve higher performance for the queries by storing an aggregated mashups view in the HIVE layer, similar to the traditional data warehouse. The updates to the data warehouse are made as offline batch jobs:

| Some mashup view supported (vendor) tools | Some data integration mashup tools |
|---|---|
| • IBM Netezza<br>• Cassandra<br>• Vertica, Cloudera Impala<br>• Hortonworks Stinger | • Damia<br>• Yahoo Pipes<br>• MS Popfly<br>• **Google Mashup Editor** (GME)<br>• Exhibit<br>• Apatar<br>• MashMaker |

Table 12.2: Mashup view supported tools and data integration tools

Some drawbacks with mashups that you may need to be aware of are text/data mismatch, object identifiers, schema mismatches, abstract level mismatches, and lower data quality or accuracy (due to data integration from independent sources).

# Compression pattern

Compression is one of the data reduction methods of big data analysis, as reduced data size is computationally less expensive.

The compression pattern provides a mechanism in situations where the enterprise needs to access data without aggregation or mashups. The compression pattern can help with faster data access from data storage by having standardized formats (with the need to transform to a standardized format regardless of data sources). The advantage of having formats is to ensure data correctness and consistency.

The most popular compression data analysis platform is R, and one can explore in-memory compression with ReRams as well.

## Exploder pattern

This is a pattern to help data analysts to look at different datasets, finding a relation between different datasets, and also providing different perspectives. The exploder pattern is a useful pattern in cases where an enterprise need various views (visuals) for the data and there are no restrictions with the same kind of visual patterns.

It also allows one to drill down from one view to a different chart type or visualization pattern with a click.

# Summary

Although the development field of data analytics is not new, it has become more critical than ever as it experiences prodigious quantities of data generated by businesses, sensors, applications, and so on. Once the generated data gets stored, it can give extraordinary insights and helps not only business enterprises but also government and non-government enterprises, social communities, the economy, and much more.

In current technology trends, big data has been involved in many evolutions, from just buzzwords to crunching data from machine learning algorithms. With the exponential explosion of high velocity, high volume, high variety, and the veracity of data sources and streams (the four V's), big data has become the inevitable representative of the architectures, tools, and technologies that handle enterprises increasingly demanding requirements.

In this chapter, we have gone through a brief introduction of the four V's of big data, data analysis technology, and concepts. We also touched upon the big data life cycle and how it helps different stakeholders to achieve and realize their data insights. A brief section covered big data landscapes, and the data layers, as well as most of the architectural patterns associated with big data, involving data pipelines: that is an ordered combination of data acquisition, integration, ingestion, fast processing, storage, rapid access, and analytics stages.

The most crucial theme of this book is architectural patterns, and this chapter reflects it in its big data architecture, and design patterns section, in a sequence of architecture patterns, such as MapReduce, Lambda, and data lake. Then we have covered most common big data (application) design patterns by layers: that is patterns in various big data architectural layers, such as data sources and the ingestion layer, the data storage layer, the data access layer, the data discovery and analysis layer, and the data visualization layer.

Covering big data architectural patterns in one chapter has been very challenging for us, and we have tried our best by providing samples of big data concepts and the most common patterns that help data architects and other data technology stakeholders. We hope this chapter provides them with a head start on their big data journey. As mentioned in many places across this chapter, we strongly encourage readers to refer to the citations section should they need to get exclusive patterns and details of implementations.

# References

Citations and reference materials:


- **Big data**: *Application Architecture Q&A, A Problem-Solution Approach* by Nitin Sawant and Himanshu Shah (Apress 2013)
- **Big data governance**: *An Emerging Imperative* by Sunil Soares, (MC Press, October 2012)


Other sources:


- `http://assured-cloud-computing.illinois.edu/files/2015/02/Cristina_Abad.pdf`
- `http://bigr.io/architecture/`
- `http://blog.flutura.com//2012/08/11-core-big-data-workload-design.html`
- `http://ercoppa.github.io/HadoopInternals/HadoopArchitectureOverview.html`
- `http://insightdatascience.com`
- `http://www.bcs.org/upload/pdf/enterprise-architecture-patterns-201016.pdf`
- `http://www.bigdatapatterns.org/design_patterns/automated_dataset_execution`
- `http://www.bigdatapatterns.org/overview`
- `http://www.bigdatascienceschool.com/selfstudy`
- `http://www.infoworld.com/article/2616959/big-data/7-top-tools-for-taming-big-data.html`
- `http://www.pentaho.com/sites/default/files/uploads/resources/forrester_patterns_in_big_data.pdf`
- `http://www.refcodes.org/resources/Big%20data%20processing%20the%20lean%20way%20-%20a%20case%20study%20-%20v1.7.pdf`

- http://www.yottastor.com/design-principles-big-data
- https://arxiv.org/ftp/arxiv/papers/1201/1201.4479.pdf
- https://bigdatawg.nist.gov/_uploadfiles/M0060_v1_8912129783.pdf
- https://blogs.msmvps.com/abu/2010/10/16/data-architecture-patterns-design-patterns-and-solution-patterns/
- https://conferences.oreilly.com/strata/big-data-conference-ca-2015/public/schedule/detail/38774
- https://conferences.oreilly.com/strata/strataeu2014/public/schedule/detail/37305
- https://hackernoon.com/ingestion-and-processing-of-data-for-big-data-and-iot-solutions-659431e37b52
- https://iwringer.wordpress.com/2015/08/03/patterns-for-streaming-realtime-analytics/
- https://link.springer.com/book/10.1007%2F978-1-4302-6293-0
- https://static1.squarespace.com/static/55007c24e4b001deff386756/t/564a2b7de4b0c1a8406915fb/1447701373291/Maniyam%2C+Sujee.pdf
- https://vision.cloudera.com/the-six-principles-of-modern-data-architecture/
- https://www.datameer.com/wp-content/uploads/pdf/white_paper/Data-Preparation-Modern-BI-Common-Design-Patterns.pdf
- https://www.dezyre.com/article/types-of-analytics-descriptive-predictive-prescriptive-analytics/209
- https://www.ibm.com/developerworks/library/bd-archpatterns1/index.html
- https://www.import.io/post/best-big-data-tools-use/
- https://www.linkedin.com/pulse/top-10-guiding-principles-big-data-architecture-ram-narasimhan
- https://www.researchgate.net/publication/296634867_Device_Data_Ingestion_for_Industrial_Big_Data_Platforms_with_a_Case_Study
- https://www.slideshare.net/AmazonWebServices/big-data-architectural-patterns-and-best-practices
- https://www.slideshare.net/AsterData/sas-ny-big-analytics-conference
- https://www.slideshare.net/cscyphers/big-data-platforms-an-overview
- https://www.slideshare.net/ZachGemignani/7-design-principles-44395597

# Index

## A

# C

# D

# F



# G

# M

# N

# T

## U



## V



## W



## X



## Z

www.ingramcontent.com/pod-product-compliance
Lightning Source LLC
Chambersburg PA
CBHW060644060326
40690CB00020B/4511

* 9 7 8 1 7 8 7 2 8 7 4 9 5 *